LONGMAN LINGUISTICS LIBRARY

HISTORICAL LINGUISTICS

General editors
R. H. Robins, University of London
Martin Harris, University of Manchester
Geoffrey Horrocks
University of Cambridge

A Short History of Linguistics
Third Edition
R. H. ROBINS

Structural Aspects of Language Change
JAMES M. ANDERSON

Text and Context
Explorations in the Semantics and Pragmatics of Discourse
TEUN A. VAN DIJK

Introduction to Text Linguistics
ROBERT-ALAIN DE BEAUGRANDE
AND WOLFGANG ULRICH DRESSLER

Spoken Discourse
A Model for Analysis
WILLIS EDMONDSON

Psycholinguistics
Language, Mind, and World
DANNY D. STEINBERG

Dialectology
W. N. FRANCIS

Principles of Pragmatics
GEOFFREY N. LEECH

Generative Grammar
GEOFFREY HORROCKS

Norms of Language
Theoretical and Practical Aspects
RENATE BARTSCH

The English Verb
Second Edition
F. R. PALMER

A History of American English
J. L. DILLARD

Pidgin and Creole Languages
SUZANNE ROMAINE

General Linguistics
An Introductory Survey
Fourth Edition
R. H. ROBINS

A History of English Phonology
CHARLES JONES

Generative and Non-linear Phonology
JACQUES DURAND

Modality and the English Modals
Second Edition
F. R. PALMER

Linguistics and Semiotics
YISHAI TOBIN

Multilingualism in the British Isles I: the Older Mother Tongues and Europe
EDITED BY SAFDER ALLADINA
AND VIV EDWARDS

Multilingualism in the British Isles II: Africa, Asia and the Middle East
EDITED BY SAFDER ALLADINA
AND VIV EDWARDS

Dialects of English
Studies in Grammatical Variation
EDITED BY PETER TRUDGILL AND
J. K. CHAMBERS

Introduction to Bilingualism
CHARLOTTE HOFFMANN

Verb and Noun Number in English
A functional explanation
WALLIS REID

English in Africa
JOSEF SCHMIED

Linguistic Theory
The Discourse of Fundamental Works
ROBERT DE BEAUGRANDE

Historical Linguistics:

Problems and Perspectives

edited by Charles Jones

LONGMAN

LONDON AND NEW YORK

Nils Danyer, Newcastle, 1995

Longman Group UK Limited,
Longman House, Burnt Mill,
Harlow, Essex CM20 2JE, England
and Associated Companies throughout the world

Published in the United States of America
by Longman Publishing, New York

First published 1993

British Library Cataloguing-in-Publication Data

A catalogue record for this book is
available from the British Library

Library of Congress Cataloging-in-Publication Data

Historical linguistics: problems and perspectives/edited by Charles Jones.
p.   cm. — (Longman linguistics library)
Includes bibliographical references and index.
ISBN 0–582–06086–9. — ISBN 0–582–06085–0 (pbk.)
1. Historical linguistics. I. Jones, Charles, 1939– .
II. Series.
P140.H585 1993
417'.7—dc20   92–8632
CIP

Typeset in 10/12 Times by 8M
Produced by Longman Singapore Publishers (Pte) Ltd.
Printed in Singapore

Contents

Notes on the Contributors

John Anderson is Professor of English Language at the University of Edinburgh. The author of many books and papers on syntactic and phonological themes, notably *On Case Grammar* (1977) and *Principles of Dependency Phonology* (with C. J. Ewan: 1987), he has made several major contributions to the theory of language change and is associated with the development of the model of Notional Grammar.

Raimo Anttila is Professor of Linguistics at the University of California, Los Angeles. He is the author of *Historical and Comparative Linguistics* (1989) and *Analogy* (1977) and is one of the foremost exponents of models for linguistic reconstruction and language change.

Bernard Comrie is Professor of Linguistics at the University of Southern California at Los Angeles. He is well known for his contributions to the study of linguistic typology as well as case representations in Slavic languages. He is the author of *Aspect* (1976), *The Russian Language since the Revolution* (with G. Stone, 1978) and *Language Universals and Linguistic Typology* (1989).

Patricia Donegan is Professor of Linguistics at the University of Hawaii at Manoa. With David Stampe, she was the developer of the Natural Phonology model and is the author of *On the Natural Phonology of Vowels* (1985) and (with D. Stampe) *The Study of Natural Phonology* (1979).

Nancy C. Dorian is Professor of Linguistics at Bryn Mawr College and an authority on language contact and language obsolescence. She has made an extensive study of the process of decline in East Sutherland Scottish Gaelic and is the author of *Language Death: The Life Cycle of a Scottish Gaelic Dialect* (1981) and the editor of *Investigating Obsolescence: Studies in Language Contraction and Death* (1989).

Roger Lass is Professor of Linguistics and Chairman of the Linguistics Department at the University of Cape Town. He has made a major contribution to the understanding of phonological change, especially in the history of English. His major books include *Old English Phonology* (with J. M. Anderson: 1975); *Phonology: An Introduction to Basic Concepts* (1984); *On Explaining Language Change* (1980).

Chinfa Lien is currently Associate Professor in the Institute of Linguistics of the National Tsinghua University in Taiwan. He has received several awards from the National Science Council of the Republic of China for research in Chinese historical linguistics, and has published extensively in this area.

David Lightfoot is Professor of Linguistics and Chairman of the Linguistics Department at the University of Maryland. He has produced some of the most innovative ideas relating to syntactic change, especially in the area of the development of auxiliary and modal verb types in English. In addition to a host of theoretical papers, he is the author of *The Principles of Diachronic Syntax* (1979) and *The Language Lottery* (1982), and *How to set parameters: Arguments from language change* (1991).

James Milroy is perhaps best known for his research into the sociolinguistic patterning of Modern English in Belfast. His work stresses the importance of the connection between sociolinguistic phenomena and ongoing and completed language change. The author of a great number of sociolinguistic papers, he has also written *Regional Accents of English: Belfast* (1981) and *Linguistic Variation and Change* (1992). He was, until recently, Chairman of the Department of Linguistics at the University of Sheffield.

John Ohala is Professor of Linguistics at the University of California at Berkeley. His contribution to our understanding of the physical nature of speech sounds and its relation to and importance for both phonological and phonetic mutation is widely recognized. In addition to an extensive number of scholarly papers, he is the editor of *Nasalfest* (1975) and *Experimental Phonology* (1986).

Wayne O'Neil is Professor of Linguistics and Head of the Department of Linguistics and Philosophy at MIT. The author of papers on historical phonology and morphology, he has made a special contribution in the area of Old English metrical phonology. He has recently undertaken studies of the variety of English spoken in Nicaragua and of adult second language acquisition. His most recent books are *Rule Generalization and Optionality in Language Change* (with S. J. Keyser, 1985) and *Linguistic Theory in Second Language Acquisition* (with S. Flynn, 1988).

Theo Vennemann is Professor of Theoretical and Germanic Linguistics at the University of Munich. He has written many papers on the causes of phonological change (especially within the framework of Natural Generative Phonology) and has drawn insightful conclusions on the nature of syntactic (especially word-order) mutation and the diffusion of processes under temporal change. He is the author of *Preference Laws for Syllable Structure and the Explanation of Sound Change* (1988) and the editor of *The New Sound of Indo-European* (1989).

William S-Y. Wang is Professor of Linguistics at the University of California at Berkeley and is the founder of its Phonology Laboratory. He is the editor of *Human Communication* (1966); *Language, Writing and the Computer* (1986); *The Lexicon in Phonological Change* (1977) and the author of *The Basis of Speech* (1989) and *Explorations in Language* (1991). He has also contributed many papers to international journals on psychology and linguistics. His studies of lexical diffusion hold a central place in recent historical linguistic research.

Editor's Preface

It is difficult to accept that it is almost twenty years since John Anderson and I inaugurated and organized the *First International Conference on Historical Linguistics* at the University of Edinburgh in 1973. The motivation behind the setting up of that conference was our desire to create a forum to assess the impact of the (then quite recent) upsurge of interest in the way in which syntactic, semantic and phonological theory might affect attitudes to and explanations for general language change through time. The interest in historical linguistic study since then has intensified and the usefulness and appropriateness of historical materials as test beds for a variety of theoretical linguistic stances substantiated.

It seemed to me that, for a variety of reasons, the time was ripe to sample the attitudes now current among some of the most eminent exponents in the field of language change, to gauge the extent to which synchronic theoretical models have been found useful or wanting as accounts of temporal language mutation; how the evidence of language change itself may have given rise to new hypotheses appropriate for synchronic materials and, above all, what progress had been made in producing general models to provide explanations for language change itself, the actuation of that change and its dissemination through and between language communities.

This collection of papers addresses many of the most important · issues currently under discussion by scholars of historical linguistics. On the one hand, we see the significance for theories of language (especially syntactic and morphological) change of some recent developments in generativist theoretical models and their associates, although there are also proposals accounting for such events set out in frameworks quite divorced from these. The collection also contains discussions concerning the validity and usefulness of linguistic reconstruction and whether this time-honoured exercise should be treated as merely an attempt at sophisticated etymology, the realization of a set of generalized formulaic 'heads', or an exercise capable of producing concrete guides to the actual phonetics of the reconstructed language. The recent decades have seen important advances in linguistic typology and the relationships and differences between this activity and historical reconstruction are examined in detail.

As one might expect, the argument continues over what constitutes actuation in language change in temporally disparate or in language contact situations. Writers in this collection discuss whether impulsion for innovation can be treated in principle at all; to what extent its source is teleological or systematic; the direct result of non-linguistic (especially social) features; a consequence of the constraints upon observability, parsability and general perception; or is best considered to be the reorganization of a postulated rule-governed, internalized knowledge system inherited or acquired by speakers. There is also an important discussion examining the extent to which the transmission of historical phonological change can be considered to operate in a lexically gradual manner.

This collection represents the ways in which some of today's foremost scholars of language change view their discipline and its future development; that they do so in as diverse a fashion as that witnessed in the *Proceedings of the First International Conference on Historical Linguistics* says something about the inherent complexity of the subject itself and perhaps serves to dampen still further that expectation of explanation so many of us felt would spring from what seemed to be the qualitatively different impetus to theories of language change provided by the 'new' theoretical models of the 1960s and 1970s.

CHARLES JONES
Department of English Language
University of Edinburgh

Acknowledgements

While any project for bringing together a set of papers by eminent scholars in a particular research area is one of those academic pursuits which at its inception provokes both enthusiasm and promise, its realization is always tortuous and inevitably delayed. While I hope that my enthusiasm for this venture is no less now than it was at the beginning, the completion of the collection was only possible thanks to the patience and understanding of contributors who have overlooked with equanimity the hiatus which materialized between the submission of their paper and its appearance in print. My thanks to all of them for their forbearance.

Chapter 1

Parameters of syntactic change: a notional view

John Anderson

Syntactic theory circumscribes syntactic variation and thus syntactic change: potential changes (ones that might be contemplated pre-theoretically) are, in the first place, either impossible, as infringing universals of syntax, or possible. Assessing the likelihood of possible changes, potentiality for recurrence, is apparently more complex, however. Many recurrent changes involve minimal incremental or decremental modification, such that the change involves a local increase or decrease in what is allowed within the syntax of a particular language, where locality is defined by syntactic theory. But it has been claimed that the histories of languages can also experience major restructurings. Such, for instance, would be involved in the innovation of a category 'modal' in the history of English, as proposed by Lightfoot (1974, 1979: ch. 3). Here I consider various changes in the syntax of English, some of them with quite widespread repercussions (and including the history of the 'modals'), which nevertheless can be related to local, minimal modifications to the syntax of English: I suggest that these are preferred, most likely.[1] I am concerned specifically with 'categorial' changes, with respect to which it might further be suggested that 'radical restructuring' is even impossible, excluded by syntactic theory; if such changes can be restricted to the minimal modifications outlined and exemplified below, then we can put firm bounds on the notion of possible change in categorization. The establishment of this depends on the adoption of a restrictive theory of syntax such as has been developed within notional grammar.

Notional grammar provides for each language a set of notionally defined categories out of which syntactic representations are built in accordance with particular parameter settings

PARAMETERS OF SYNTACTIC CHANGE

appropriate to that language. A hierarchy of categories is established by the inherent complexity of the representations they require: some categories are more basic and require fewer (notional) features. Consider, for instance, a notional theory whereby categories are identified in terms of the notional components, or features, P(redicative) and N(ominal), presence of P being associated with categories that are situation-defining, and of N with categories that are entity-defining. In these terms, (finite) verbs and (proper) names can be simply characterized, respectively, as {P}, i.e. as (categorially) predicative, and as {N}, nominal, and functors (adpositions) as { }, categorially unspecified; while other categories, such as adjectives, are identified by combinations of the two features, and are thereby more complex, less basic.

Combinations may be simple, symmetrical, or asymmetrical. Some basic possibilities, involving asymmetrical and symmetrical combination, are illustrated in (1):

(1) P   P;N   P:N   N;P   N
     finite verbs non-finites adjectives common nouns names

The feature on the left of the semi-colon preponderates over, or governs, that on the right, which is dependent; the colon indicates mutual dependency. With non-finite verbs P governs, preponderates over, N; with common, as opposed to proper, nouns, the preponderance is reversed; with adjectives, the two properties are mutually preponderant. Further, more complex categories can be provided for by second-order combinations, such as are illustrated in (2.a) and exemplified in (2b):

(2.a)   P;(P:N)   (P:N);P
         participles   deverbal adjectives

(2b.i)   Bruce is neglecting Sheila (*participle*)

(2b.ii)   Bruce is neglectful of Sheila (*deverbal adjective*)

In (2.a) the second-order representations are composed of the same elements, P, the 'finite verb property', and P:N, the 'adjectival property', but the preponderance, or direction of dependency, of 'finite-verb-ness' and 'adjectiveness' is reversed between the two. Participles are more verb-like than deverbal adjectives: see s. 3.2 below.

Elsewhere (notably Anderson 1988, 1989a, 1990, 1991b) I have discussed the notional definitions of the features and the motivations for attributing particular combinations to particular categories; the role of the representations in providing appropriately for cross-classification (in terms of shared features or combinations); markedness (in terms of relative inherent complexity); and hierarchization – e.g. degree of 'nouniness' – (in terms of the relative preponderance of a particular feature or combination). And there, too, I have illustrated how other syntactic properties (syntagms, linearity) are constructed on the basis of such notional characterizations for individual words. It has also been argued that the representation of phonological segments, most analogously of the categorial gesture, displays the same properties (cf. e.g. Anderson 1985a, 1986, 1987a; Anderson and Ewen 1987). Here, I am not concerned directly with these issues, though some of what follows will be relevant to them; rather, we shall be focusing on the role of such a conception of syntax in circumscribing possible syntactic change.

Such a notional theory of categories allows for languages to vary in the number of categorial distinctions made: these are recognized on the basis of the distributional and morphological characteristics of the language concerned, and identified on notional grounds. The minimal system seems to be {P} vs. {N} vs. { } (Anderson 1990).

Languages may also vary in the categories that are contrastive, given lexical status, associated with distinct lexical classes. Thus, many languages have distinct finite and non-finite verb classes, or one class that can be both and one that is only non-finite (with distinctive finites often being called 'auxiliaries'), while others allow all verbs to occur in both finite and non-finite positions and/or to show both finite and non-finite morphology. Not all the categories appropriate to the syntax of a language will be recognized as classes. Also, though a lexical class will contain as prototypical members items satisfying the notional requirements of the category, there are likely to be items which are distributionally appropriate but notionally less so. Thus, some nouns ('relational nouns'), such as *friend* in English, are perhaps as much situation-defining as entity-defining.

Unless otherwise constrained, the theory sets no upper limit on the set of possible categories. It may be possible to establish such a limit: e.g. second-order combinations of the character of (2) may instantiate the maximal complexity to be allowed to categorial representations. (Sub-categorial representations, distinguishing sub-classes whose distribution and/or morphological differentiation is a proper sub-part of that associated with the category as a whole, e.g. gender sub-classes of the noun, are not relevant to this question.) More importantly, however, at least from the point of view of our present concerns, the theory provides a restricted alphabet out of which any categorial representation must be constructed, and the representations themselves provide an inherent measure of complexity. The complexity measure imposes a hierarchy on representations, and on language systems. Systems can be ranked in terms of the complexity of the representations they invoke.

It is a natural property of such a hierarchy of systems that the set of representations invoked by any system be continuous and minimalist, at a contrastive level. We require that the presence in a system of a complex representation presupposes the independent presence in the same system of the components out of which it is constructed (e.g. adjectives presuppose verbs and names). Inter-language variation in categories invoked is not randomly distributed. Let us refer to this property of systems of categories as category continuity, roughly formulated as in (3):

(3) *Category continuity*
     With respect to a particular language system:
       a) a category {A,B} presupposes categories {A} and {B};
       b) combinations {A;B} and {A:B} presuppose combination {B;A}
     where A and B are variables over (possibly unitary) feature combinations, and "," is neutral among simple combination, asymmetrical combination and symmetrical (mutually dependent) combination.

Compare here the discussion by Anderson and Ewen (1987: s. 4.2) of the relationship between (categorial) phonological representations (structured in the same way as syntactic categories) and the 'structural laws' of Jakobson (1968). The naturalness of such a requirement at a lexical level follows from the assumption of contrastivity: that initial, lexically distinctive categorial representations are minimally distinct. Additional categorial distinctiveness (to allow for detailed distributional properties) may be attributed to a class by lexical redundancy or by the rules building syntactic structure, but these distinctions are non-contrastive – and they too are constrained by (3).

Such considerations circumscribe the ways in which categories can be innovated, the kind of category that can evolve, given the input system. Given also the universal hierarchical scheme of categories, constrained by (3), category change can be limited to three cases: (i) minimal incremental change; (ii) minimal decremental change; (iii) lexical realignment. (i) involves differentiation (over time) of a category by minimal addition in accordance with (3) – either of a new combination of already existing categorial components or of asymmetric combinations where only simple combination was present or of a symmetric combination on the basis of pre-existing asymmetricals. (ii) involves conflation of two categories along the same dimensions as invoked in (i). We can represent these possibilities, schematically, as in (4.a) and 4.b) respectively:

(4.a) {A} {B} → {A} {B} {A.B}
      {A.B} → {A;B} {B;A}
      {A;B} {B;A} → {A;B} {B;A} {A:B}

(4.b) {A} {B} {A.B} → {A} {B}
      {A;B} {B;A} → {A.B}
      {A;B} {B:A} {A:B} → {A;B} {B;A}

where "." indicates simple combination (no dependency), and (4.a) illustrates minimal system increments and (4.b) minimal decrements, as allowed by (3) above.

The third possibility for category change (iii, lexical realignment) involves a change in the relationship between categories and lexical classes: a categorial distinction may be given lexical recognition (it comes to be associated with distinct classes of lexical items) or it may lose such differentiation. If such developments are associated with a continuity condition like (3), then we can envisage as permissible the possibilities in (5):

(5.a) categories {A}   {B}   {A}   {B}

          $\cdot$ $\cdot$ →   :   :

      classes   {X} X_1 X_2

(5.b) categories {A}   {B}   {A}   {B}

          :   :   → $\cdot$ $\cdot$

      classes   X   Y   X,Y

with once again (minimal) differentiation (5.a) vs. conflation (5.b), and with the relationship between A and B (themselves possibly complex) being governed by (3). Where (before differentiation, and after conflation) a single class is associated with more than one distributional category, one categorial possibility will be provided for by redundancy; this is illustrated in section 1 below (see particularly (8)).

These various developments are also subject to the prototypicality requirement of the notional theory: the lexical classes involved must satisfy the requirement that they contain prototypical members notionally appropriate to the category they are associated with. Thus, the prototypical members of X_1 and X_2 in (5.a) must conform to the notional characteristics of A and B respectively; and category differentiation must likewise be notionally natural. I shall now attempt to illustrate from the history of English the legitimate developments allowed by (3).

1 Realignment: modals

Let us consider, yet again, the evolution of the English modals against the background of such a framework for category change. Much controversy surrounds the characterization of this evolution: controversy concerning the dating of changes, concerning the lexical items involved, concerning, above all, the nature of the changes themselves. Lightfoot (1974, 1979: ch. 3) saw the early Modern English innovation of a contrastive category associated with items that had previously been (irregular) verbs; Plank (1984), too, though critical of many aspects of the Lightfoot scenario (see also Warner 1983), espouses a categorial change of such a character; its nature is reinterpreted by Roberts 1985. Anderson (1976: ch. 2) argues that modals remain categorially verbs, distinguished as a sub-class thereof principally by their lack of a non-finite paradigm. Others (e.g. Goossens 1987; Brinton 1988: section 3.2) appear to take the view that modals are already categorially distinct (or somehow on the way to being so) in Old English, in (for Brinton) already belonging to a category AUX. (See too Denison 1988.) Much in this (briefly outlined) partial history of modal studies is obscured by uncertainty or disagreement – implicit and explicit – as to what constitutes categoriality, as well as by the interplay of two distinct, though related, developments, that associated with the modals as such and that involving auxiliarihood in general. Warner (1990) provides perhaps the most careful study of the categoriality of the modals. He suggests (p. 540) that 'what develops in Early Modern English (or slightly before) isn't so much a class of modals as a wider class of auxiliary, containing a group of modals'. This seems to me crucial to an understanding of the modals story.

As modals rather than auxiliaries – i.e. if we ignore their auxiliary rather than strictly modal properties – these items continue to manifest in Present-day English a sub-part of the distributional and morphological potential of verbs: they lack (in most varieties of English) potential for occurrence in non-finite positions and the associated morphology, and they lack the non-past third person singular inflexion of other verbs (including other auxiliaries), as illustrated in (6) for *may* (and exemplified more fully in Huddleston 1979, for example):

(6.a)   *Brenda will may leave

(6.b)   *Brenda is maying leave

(6.c)   *Brenda has might leave

(6.d)   *Brenda's maying leave came to his attention

(6.e)   *For Brenda to may leave surprise him

(6.f)   *Brenda mays leave

But as modals these items do not exhibit a distinctive (non-verbal) distribution; they are characterized by a subset of verbal properties. Since the early Modern English or late Medieval period the modals have constituted a relatively well-defined sub-class of verbs (including, for the moment, auxiliaries and main verbs); in this respect, the conclusion (noted above) reached by Anderson (1976) is appropriate.

Further, attempts to motivate the status of syntactic (sub-)class for modals at earlier periods are unconvincing (for detailed discussion see Anderson 1991a): either the distinctive properties invoked do not uniquely characterize modals (e.g. 'transparency' with respect to argument structure, which is a property of subject-raising verbs) or they are semantic (e.g. desemanticization, periphrastic status: Anderson 1989b). Uses of some of the prototypical modals have for some time shown the notional characteristics (including those just mentioned, notably the use of modals as subjunctive periphrases) that one might associate with a syntactic (sub-)class of modal. Anderson (1991a), for instance, points to the common *dicitur*, or commentative use of both *sceolde* and the subjunctive (cf. too the examples in Wülfing 1901: 31–2; Standop 1957: 101–2), as illustrated in (7):

(7.a)   Þæs Apollines dohtor sceolde beon gydene
         'The daughter of [that] Apollo was (allegedly) a goddess'

(7.b)   Þara he sæde þæt he syxa sum ofsloge
         'Of those he said that he and five others (allegedly) killed'
         syxtig on twam dagum
         'sixty in two days'

(the former from the Alfredian translation of Boethius, the latter from the Alfredian translation of Orosius). (Compare too, e.g. Mitchell's (1985: s. 1014) cautious discussion of *magan* as a subjunctive periphrasis, some of the 'uses' of *sceolde* discussed by

Visser (1973: ss. 1483–561), and Denison's (1988: s. 3.1) discussion of *wil*.) But while it might be plausible to attribute to *sceolde* (or *agan*) a periphrastic use, such that it exhibits a simple (semantic) opposition with respect to the 'simple form', a distinction which may be otherwise marked morphologically, this does not require that the governing element in the periphrasis (here *sceolde*) belong to a distinct (sub-)class: see section 3.6 below, where this is illustrated. It is not until the late-to-post-medieval period that the modals exhibit distributional coherence, and thus syntactic status.

With respect to the set of auxiliaries and main verbs as a whole, as I have indicated, the distributional and morphological characteristics of the modals warrant only sub-class status. But the post-medieval situation is more complex than this. The modals are excluded from non-finite positions; but main verbs are in turn excluded from finite position in the so-called NICE contexts, as illustrated by the familiar alternation of (8):

(8.a)   Jeremy trembled

(8.b)   Did Jeremy tremble

(cf. e.g. Huddleston 1976, 1979). Only non-modal auxiliaries (*be*, *have*, and perhaps *do*) show a comprehensive verbal distribution. Not much is explained by attributing the development of these restrictions to the innovation of the categories 'modal' and 'auxiliary', previously absent from the syntax of English: modals as such do not warrant categorial status, and the proposed innovation of a distinct category 'auxiliary' suggests an unwarranted discontinuity in the syntactic categories of English and their distribution. (I reject as incoherent the view (cf. Steele et al.: 1981) that Old English possessed a syntactic category AUX whose primary manifestation was morphological only.) Such innovations, moreover, are excluded by the restrictive notional theory of category change outlined above.

Old English verbs obey the lexical redundancy in (9):

(9) $\{P\} \rightarrow \& \{P;N\}$

i.e. those items categorized as finites are also non-finite. Old English verbs are contrastively $\{P\}$; (9) allows the class the full distributional range required by the syntax and morphology. In Old English, perhaps only *mot* and *sceal*, among verbs commonly used, are exceptions to (9). Whereas in Present-day English the class of modals as a whole (i.e. those verbs that lack a non-past third singular inflexion) is exceptional – if this redundancy were to be true of Present-day as well. But, as we have observed, the distribution of main verbs as finites is severely limited; only auxiliaries can occur as finite in certain environments. This suggests some kind of categorial differentiation at a lexical, contrastive level, specifically a realignment of these various items with respect to the categories finite and non-finite. Anderson (1990) proposes that whereas the categories {P} and {P;N} are still appropriate to Present-day English, their lexical alignments have indeed changed.

The association for Old English is simply as in (10.a):

(10.a)   {P}
             :
            verbs

(10.b)   {P}   {P} & {P;N}   {P;N}
             :   :   :
            verbs$_1$ verbs$_2$ verbs$_3$
          = modals   = auxiliaries   = main verbs
                        (non-modal)

with (9) allowing a non-finite potentiality for all verbs (with possible lexical exceptions); but in Present-day English we have rather (10.b), with lexical differentiation in terms of distinct categorial representations for subsets of the former class of verbs (cf. scenario (a) in (5) above). In Present-day English, modals are finite only; other auxiliaries are both finite and non-finite; main verbs are basically non-finite. There is not a simple division into auxiliary and main, such as one might attribute to Basque, for example (Saltarelli 1988: section 1.2.1). Modals in English are defective auxiliaries, in lacking non-finite forms. And main verbs, though basically non-finite (as, for the major system, in Basque), have a restricted potential for finiteness, limited to certain syntactic conditions. Concerning this, Anderson (1990) argues that main verbs may achieve finite status derivatively, in the course of building syntactic structure, specifically only when the rules of linearization permit a main verb to be amalgamated (realized simultaneously) with an empty governing finite verb otherwise realized (when non-adjacent) as *do*, as in (8.a) vs. (8.b). Main verbs may be syntactically {P} and {P;N}; but their capacity to function as {P}, as in (8.a), is syntactically determined, not lexically distinctive: they are finite only when the finite and non-finite verb positions can coincide, as they do in (8.a) but not (8.b).

If this is just, then the history of modals, and of the other auxiliaries in this respect, exhibits no category change – certainly not a major restructuring of the syntax – but rather a change in the alignment of lexical classes with categories that have remained constant throughout the history of English, a realignment that is minimal, in accordance with continuity: lexical classes are established by minimal extension of {P} and with respect to categories shared (via (8)) by the members of the classes at an earlier stage. And the realignments also seem to be notionally appropriate, with the class showing most preponderant P (the modals) having as prototypical members items (the epistemics) whose major role is situation-defining.

2 Conflation: infinitives

Let us now turn to an instance of category-conflation. In section 1, I characterized non-finites, following (1) above, as simply {P;N}. But (2) above introduced a distinctive representation for participles, namely {P;(P:N)}; and we can in like manner distinguish gerunds (vs. deverbal nouns) as {P;(N;P)} (vs. {(N;P);P} for deverbal nouns), with the verb property dominant over the nominal (cf. again (1) above and section 3.1 below, and see further Anderson 1988, 1989a). Finally, the infinitive, as most highly verbal, involves a combination of P with P;N; but since, in Present-day English, at least, it is not apparently to be distinguished from a category with a different proportion of these (cf. gerunds vs. deverbal nouns), the representation {P.(P;N)} will suffice. We can thus distinguish the three non-finite categories appropriate to Present-day English as in (11):

(11) P.(P;N)   P;(P:N)   P;(N;P)
      infinitives   *participles*   *gerunds*

with infinitives as the least marked non-finite. The hierarchization which emerges from these representations, with gerunds as most 'noun-like', accords with the semantic distinctions that have been attributed to, for instance, the infinitive/gerund distinction (cf. e.g. Bolinger 1968).

These representations are non-lexical, allowed for by lexical redundancy

(12) {P;N} → {P.(P;N)} & {P;(P:N)} & {P;(N;P)}

and the lexical representations for verbs in (10) can stand as such. However, verbs that take verbal arguments will be subcategorized for the particular kind of (verbal) argument they take, rather than as simply taking, say, S' or VP. Deverbal adjectives and deverbal nominals will be specified lexically as in (13):

(13) P.(P:N)   P.(N;P)
      deverbal As   *deverbal Ns*
      (neglectful)   (neglect)

specified redundantly as in (14.a) and (b), respectively:

(14.a) {P.(P:N)} → {(P:N);P}

(14.b) {P.(N;P)} → {(N;P);P}

as a consequence of (12), to preserve (derivative) distinctiveness, and in accordance with (3).

The Present-day English infinitive exhibits reduced verbality compared with finite forms. Typically, it does not represent a situation independently; it is an argument of another verb, a participant argument in (15):

(15.a) To please Ermintrude was his passion

(15.b) His passion was to please Ermintrude

or of an adjective or noun:

(16.a) He is eager to please Ermintrude

(16.b) his impulse to please Ermintrude

An infinitive may also be a circumstantial argument (an adjunct), particularly in expressions of purpose, like (17):

(17) Florence did it to please Ermintrude

Typically, too, the infinitive is (overtly) subjectless (as in the above examples), though the status of the pre-infinitival expressions in, e.g. (18):

(18.a) For Ermintrude to like Florence would be surprising

(18.b) No-one expects Ermintrude to like Florence

is controversial.

On the other hand, the infinitive, like other non-finites, as is again familiar, retains the (verbal) capacity to take an unmarked (bare) object. Consider:

(19.a) Pam suspects Bobby

(19.b) Pam seems to suspect Bobby

(19.c) Pam is suspicious of Bobby

(19.d) Pam's suspicions of Bobby

12 PARAMETERS OF SYNTACTIC CHANGE

Only items with preponderant P allow an unmarked object. Also, despite the *to*, infinitives do not combine non-zeugmatically with prepositional phrases, thus (20.a) is strange:

(20.a) *Andy is prone to lethargy and (to) fall asleep

(20.b) Andy worked both for pleasure and to fund his trip to Tahiti

but it may coordinate, as in (20.b), as a purpose circumstantial. The infinitive also rejects all the appurtenances of adjectival or nominal constructions (modification by *very*, articles, possessive inflexion, etc.).

However:

> the Anglo-Saxon had two infinitives: (1) the uninflected, or simple, infinitive in *-an* . . ., which in origin is the petrified nominative-accusative case of a neuter verbal noun; and (2) the inflected, or gerundial, or prepositional, infinitive, made up of the preposition *to* plus the dative case of a verbal noun ending in *-anne* (*-enne* . . .)
> (Callaway 1913: 2)

The uninflected infinitive is recessive, and is eventually superseded by the *to*-form which descends from *to* + inflected infinitive, except after modals and some other verbs. The picture in Old English is thus not clearcut. And things are further complicated by the fact that, for example, the uninflected infinitive can occur in syntactic situations which are otherwise unexpected, if it is coordinated with an inflected infinitive. But certain trends suggesting functional differentiation and thus categorial distinctiveness for the two infinitives emerge from a consideration of their attested distribution.

Neither infinitive occurs uncontroversially as subject in Old English (Bock 1931; Mitchell 1985: ss. 1537–9), but either may occur as (non-subjective) complement (participant argument) to the verb:

(21.a) Ða begann se wer dreorig wepan
        'Then began the man sad to-weep'

(21.b) . . . and begunnon ða to wyrcenne
        '. . . and they-began then to work'

(Mitchell 1985: s. 1549). Callaway (1913: 60–71) attempts a functional differentiation based on whether the governing verb otherwise takes an accusative object (uninflected infinitive) or a non-accusative (inflected infinitive) or both (either), though there is a number of exceptions to such a generalization. But this does at least perhaps suggest that the uninflected infinitive was more directly associated with the governing verb, and was, in fact, more verbal. And this is confirmed by the prevalence of the uninflected infinitive with the ancestors of the modals (except *agan* and *beon/wesan*), some of which had already established a periphrastic use (cf. section 1; and, again, Anderson 1991a). Verbal periphrases are in minimal (semantic) opposition with the 'simple form'. I shall argue in section 3.6 that, not unnaturally, given such a status for periphrases, the dependent element in a periphrasis is necessarily verbal (with preponderant P). If this is so, then the respective availability and non-availability of the uninflected and inflected infinitives as the dependent element in a modal periphrasis supports the positing of a categorial difference between the two infinitives involving a difference in the preponderance of P.

Whereas, too, the uninflected form (particularly in verse) is commonly used to mark purpose after verbs of motion (Mitchell 1985: ss. 1554, 2942):

(22) He eode eft sittan siððan mid his ðegnum
'He went then to-sit afterwards with his nobles'

otherwise (especially in prose) the inflected infinitive is much more common in expressions of purpose (Callaway 1913: 146). Contrariwise, while an uninflected infinitive accompanying a finite intransitive verb of rest or motion can frequently be interpreted as indicating 'simultaneity' (van der Gaaf 1934), as in (23.a):

(23.a) And þa þær com fleogan drihtnes ængel
'And then there came to-fly (the) angel of-the-lord'

(23.b) . . . and gæð secende þæt an þe him losode
'. . . and goes seeking the one that to-him got-lost'

– cf. the 'participial' construction in (b) – Mitchell (1985: ss. 967–8) remains 'unconvinced' that alleged instances of this involving the inflected infinitive do not involve purpose, and thus non-simultaneity. With examples like (22), on the other hand, it seems to me that the element of purpose is debatable. Again, the uninflected infinitive is preferred in the more 'integrated', more 'periphrasis'-like, construction.

So, too, the inflected infinitive is the natural choice for the so-called 'absolute' use (Callaway 1913: 169):

(24) Forðam unriht is to wide mannum gemæne
'Thus sin is too widely prevalent in men'

7 unlaga leof, 7, raðost is to cweðenne,
'and (the) unlawful dear, and, (it) is fastest to say',
Godes laga laðe 7 lara forsawene
'God's law hateful and (his) teachings despised'

(Mitchell 1985: s. 960).

With governing noun or adjective, rather than verb, the inflected infinitive is the norm, as illustrated in (25.a) and 25.b), respectively:

(25.a) He geceas him timan to acennenne on menniscnysse,
'He chose for-him the time to take on human-form,'
to ðrowigenne, . . .
'to suffer, . . .'

(25.b) Ðis fers is swiðe deoplic eow to understandenne
'This verse is very profound (for) you to understand'

(Mitchell 1985: s. 926). And, perhaps most strikingly, we find predominantly the inflected infinitive coordinated or apposed with *to* + noun phrase, as in (26.a), and even with other prepositional phrases (26.b):

(26.a) . . . hæfde opene eagan to forhæfednysse, to
'. . . he-had open eyes to temperance, for'
ælmesdagum to ðancigenne Gode
'alms-days to thank God'

(26.b) Ne lufode he woruldrice æhta for his neode ana,
'Not loved he worldly possessions for his pleasure alone',
ac to dælenne eallum wædliendum
'but to share it with all (the) poor'

(Mitchell 1985: s. 965 and 1158, respectively), though Mitchell (s. 2946) also draws our attention to coordinations involving the uninflected infinitive expressing purpose. Mitchell (1985: s. 965) notes further the alternation between (27.a) and (27.b):

(27.a) ða leafe . . . þære bodunge, 'the permission for preaching'

(27.b) leafe to bodianne, 'permission to preach'

in the translation of Gregory's Dialogue.

Morphologically and syntactically, the Old English inflected infinitive is clearly more nominal than the uninflected, though it is restricted to occurrence (as nominal) with *to* as a preposition. (The various functions of the two infinitives are conveniently tabulated in Mitchell 1985: s. 971.) Lightfoot (1979: s. 4.2) argues that the Middle English infinitive construction was a Noun Phrase (NP). Much of the evidence he adduces, as he himself in part admits, is inconclusive, and crucially it involves invented examples. One of the two most obviously nominal properties of the *to*-infinitive, its inflexion, is already non-contrastive in the Old English period. The Middle English infinitive does occur as the object of prepositions, as Lightfoot documents (1979: 192–3), which is evidence of some nominality, at least. Whatever the intervening history, the prepositional character of Present-day English infinitival *to* is much less apparent; and in purpose phrases it is frequently supported with *in order* . . .. There is indeed some controversy concerning its categorial status (cf. e.g. Pullum 1982, for one suggestive view). The nominality of the Present-day infinitive is much less apparent than that of the Old English inflected infinitive. But its potential for distribution as an argument is much wider than that typical of the Old English uninflected infinitive.

We can, in the light of this, perhaps differentiate between the two Old English infinitives, in terms of the theory of categories outlined here, as in (28):

(28)   P;(P;N)   (P;N);P
       uninflected   *inflected*

i.e. as parallel to the distinction in Present-day English between gerund and derived nominal. And the residual higher degree of nominality in Middle English of the inflected infinitive is reflected perhaps in its ability to be the object of a preposition. The Present-day form – {P.(P;N)} – is a conflation of these which retains a high proportion of P; on the basis of the metric suggested by Anderson (1990), we have:

(29)   A;B = 3.1
       A.B = 2:2
       P;N = 3P:1N
       P;(P;N) = 3P:1(3P:1N) = 12P:(3P:1N) = 15P:1N
       (P;N);P = 3(3P:1N):1P = (9P:3N):4P = 13P:3N
       P.(P;N) = 2P:2(3P:1N) = 8P:(6P:2N) = 14P:2N = 7P:1N

which simply spells out, in terms of the metric, the overall preponderances to be read off from the categorial notation. (Step 3 in (29) involves multiplying each side of the outer equation by four, and adjusting the inner values where necessary to add up to the outer value assigned to the combination.) The history of the English infinitives involves overall a minimal categorial decrement.

3   Differentiation: gerund and participles

In other verbal sub-systems English seems to have shown
minimal increments, but the dating of these is sometimes
contentious. I shall devote some (though not very precise)
attention to the question of dating. This is an issue of some
interest in its own right; indeed, one that warrants a much fuller
treatment than can be given here. But also, for our present
purposes (and developments thereof), it is only if the change
occurs in a historical (textually manifested) period that we can
hope to obtain direct evidence of the circumstances and staging
of the change – though the interpretation of this evidence is, of
course, not unproblematical, with respect to dating and otherwise
(cf. e.g. Warner 1983; Koopman 1990).

3.1   The gerund

A distinction in Present-day English between deverbal noun and
gerund is well motivated, as exemplified by (30):

(30.a)   John's desertion of Mary

(30.b)   John's deserting Mary

-ing, of course, marks not only the gerund, but also the present
participle (see below), as well as a large number of (particularly)
'factitive' deverbals, such as *dwelling*, *calling* (profession),
swelling, and so on (e.g. Marchand 1969: s. 4.48). These last are
clearly lexical, as is the deverbal noun in (30.a); its categorial
representation ($\{P.(N;P)\}$) is contrastive. And deverbal nouns
display the properties of lexicality (as discussed by Anderson
1984, for example): lexical idiosyncrasy ('derivational gaps' –
derived forms without bases (*dereliction*), bases with no derivative of a particular type) and semantic idiosyncrasy ('non-
compositionality' – *revolution*, in the sense of 'successful
uprising'), as well as derivational formations independent of the
base verb (*misgivings*).

By (14.b), the deverbal noun is redundantly (31.a):

(31.a)   (N;P);P

(31.b)   P;(N;P)

(again in response to (12)), distinguished from the non-lexical
gerund (b) by the relative preponderance of the verbal and
nominal categorial components. Its greater nominality is reflected,
for instance, in its failure to take an unmarked object, as in

(30.a), its capacity for adjectival rather than adverbial modification:

(32.a)   John's cruel/*cruelly desertion of Mary

(32.b)   John's *cruel/cruelly deserting Mary

its absence from verbal periphrases parallel to (33.a), and by its rejection of a preceding argument such as that in (33.b):

(33.a)   John's having deserted Mary

(33.b)   John deserting Mary

(see further Anderson 1988).

We can even distinguish for Present-day English an intermediate category, exemplified in (34):

(34)   John's deserting of Mary

– a so-called action nominal in *-ing*. It takes a prepositional object, is not associated with structures such as those in (33), and rejects adverbial modification, but is less happy with adjectival modification than the derived nominal:

(35)   John's ?*cruel/*cruelly deserting of Mary

It also shares with the derived nominal the variant in (36):

(36.a)   The desertion of Mary (by John)

(36.b)   *The deserting Mary (by John)

(36.c)   The deserting of Mary (by John)

but it is less happy with that in (37):

(37.a)   Tuesday's rejection of the offer

(37.b)   ?*Tuesday's rejecting of the offer

It is highly productive and is perhaps not lexical. This suggests that a derived representation involving mutual dependency – {P:(N;P)} – might be appropriate for action nominals.

No such differentiation is apparent in Old English. The deverbal noun in *-ung/-ing* is apparently productive, but shows lexical idiosyncrasies (cf. e.g. Kastovsky 1985: s. 3.2.10). It also seems to be less commonly used than the Present-day *-ing* form, though this impression, as others, may reflect the limitations of our corpus: *-ung* is much more frequent in certain styles, such as Ælfric's Homilies. It displays typical nominal inflexion (though with some idiosyncrasies – see Campbell 1959: s. 589 (8)), and nominal modification and 'external' syntax, as illustrated by the

following examples from Ælfric's Homily on the Parable of the
Vineyard:

(38.a) . . . his apostolas on mycelre twynunge wæron
        '. . . his apostles in much doubt were'

(38.b) . . . þæs ecan lifes teolunge
        '. . . the eternal life's work'

(38.c) . . . ealle ða geleaffullan gelaðunge
        '. . . all the faithful congregations'

Like the Present-day -*ing* form it can be 'factitive' rather than
'actional', as perhaps in (38.c) or with *wununge* in (39):

(39) . . .hi on Abrahames wununge buton pinungum
      '. . . they in Abraham's dwelling without torments'
      for heora godnysse wunedon
      'on account of their goodness dwelt'

Verbal subjects and objects typically appear as genitives:

(40) . . . toeacan þæs landes sceawunge
      '. . . besides for observing (of) the country'

(from a well-known passage in the Alfredian translation of
Orosius). See too Anderson 1985b, where is also documented the
alternation between the -*ung* form and other derived nouns (with
accompanying genitives of varied semantic role) in another well-
known passage from the translation of Bede's account of the life
of Cædmon.

The argument-structure (semantic roles) of the base verb is
preserved with -*ung* forms, and may be made overt:

(41) Ac biddað eow þingunge æt þyssum unscæððigum
      martyrum
      'But we-ask from-you intercession for these innocent
      martyrs'

(from Ælfric's Homily on the Holy Innocents). But this is also
true of other deverbal formations (-*ness*, etc.). And with them
and with -*ung* we lack the syntactic stigmata of verb-hood
associated with the modern gerund (Jack 1988: 17, 37–40).

There seems to be no motivation for attributing to Old English
a distinction between gerund and deverbal noun; a syntactic
category with preponderant verbality is a later development.
Callaway's (1929) Old English examples are unconvincing
(Mustanoja 1960: 568–9). Donner (1986) concludes that the gerund
is infrequent even in late Middle English; but Jack (1988) argues,

partly on the basis of Tajima's (1985) evidence, that, nevertheless, the category is established in the Middle English period. Its belated establishment is perhaps further evidenced by the comparatively late proliferation of the verb + gerund complement construction (*He anticipated returning late*, etc. – Visser 1973: ch. 12, section 1).

The *-ung* form in Old English can be characterized lexically as in (42):

(42)   P.(N;P)

as with the deverbal nominals of Present-day English; but there is no derivative contrast between a P-preponderant and a N;P preponderant category (and perhaps one where they are mutually dependent). The development to Present day English involves a minimal increment in the range of categories required by the syntax – or increments, if we are to allow for the action nominal of (34). Indeed, the role of this construction in the evolution of these changes is worthy of more extensive investigation (cf. e.g. Nehls 1974: s. 4). Jack (1988) argues that a major (but not the only) motivation for the development of the gerund is the restricted distribution as arguments of the infinitive(s), especially failure to be governed by prepositions (cf. here the brief discussion in section 2 above of the evolution of the modern infinitive). The gerund provides a category that is sufficiently nominal to occur in such positions.

3.2   Participles in Present-day English

The status of participles/deverbal adjectives in Old English is less clear, and is particularly problematical in the absence of informants – as emerges strikingly from Mitchell's (1985) discussions. In Present-day English it seems appropriate to distinguish categorially between participles and derived adjectives as in (2.i) above, namely as {P;(P:N)} vs. {(P:N);P}. The latter are lexically {P.(P:N)}, expanded by (14.a) to differentiate them from the participles, a non-contrastive possibility given by (12). We can differentiate syntactically between the two categories, even when there is identity of expression, as illustrated by (43):

(43.a)   Meryl is (*very) frightening Billy-Jo

(43.b)   Meryl is (very) frightening to Billy-Jo

wherein the participle in (43.a) takes an unmarked object and the derived adjective does not, but, unlike the participle, allows modification by *very*. Semantically, (43.a) is 'dynamic' (preserving the 'dynamism' of the 'simple' verb); (43.b) is 'static'. The form in (43.b) displays (adjectival) derivational properties not established with respect to the base verb – e.g. the possibility of *unfrightening* – even though *un-* can also occur in Present-day English as a verbal prefix (*undo*, etc.). Deverbal adjectives are clearly lexical, characterized by semantic idiosyncrasy (cf. e.g. *(very) stunning*) and by lexical idiosyncrasy (e.g. absence of a base – that for *uplifting*, for instance, is scarcely current). These latter properties are, however, particularly difficult to assess in the absence of informants, somewhat limiting our capacity to chronicle their history.

We need to distinguish between three participles in Present-day English; while all being categorizable as {P;(P:N)}, these have distinct secondary properties. The past participle in (44.a):

(44.a) Moriarty has eaten the cheese

(44.b) Moriarty is eating the cheese

is differentiated from the present participle in (44.b) by (whatever else) being associated with a (unspecified) past-time reference secondary to the time reference of the finite verb:

(45)   P;(P:N)   P;(P:N)
            :
        past

The derived adjectives in (46):

(46.a) His face is swollen

(46.b) His eyes are exciting

are differentiated in the same way, except, of course, that with the past derived adjective the tense reference is attached to a categorially subordinate element:

(47) (P:N);P   (P:N);P
            :
        past

and the temporal reference is intra-lexical, and thus less prominent in the overall interpretation. Accordingly, although the past-time reference of the past participle is normally indefinite (**His face has swollen last Tuesday*); this restriction is suppressed when the governing *have* is non-finite (so *His face must have swollen last Tuesday*); this is not the case with the adjective (**His face is/must be swollen last Tuesday*), whose past-time reference is less accessible syntactically.

The passive participle is characterized by offering up as subject of its governing verb not the argument highest on the subject-selection hierarchy but the next, as evidenced by the passive structures in (48):

(48.a) The ducklings are killed by the farmer

(48.b) This bed is slept in by hundreds

That is, the *be* associated with the passive participle is a raising verb whose victim is not the argument of the lower verb which would be the subject in the corresponding active but the next most accessible argument: the agents in (48) are ignored as raisees and instead the neutral (theme, absolutive) of (48.a) and the locative noun phrase of (48.b) are raised. The passive participle is not associated with a past-time reference, unlike the past participle, with which it is formally identical – and unlike the corresponding periphrasis in Latin (see section 3.5). We can perhaps then characterize the passive participle simply as (49):

(49)   P;(P:N)
         :
         pass(ive)

where pass, syntactically, is an instruction to project out the highest argument in the subject selection hierarchy, and, semantically, alters the unmarked topic slot. The corresponding derived adjectives, however, do have a past reference as well as the property of projecting out the subject-claimant, as illustrated by (50.a–c):

(50.a) Her face is (un-)washed

(50.b) She always leaves (un-)washed

(50.c) She keeps her face (un-)washed

(50.d) Her face is washed every night by her mother

Contrast the syntactic passive in (50.d). We might characterize such adjectives, for present purposes, as in (51):

(51) (P:N);P
         :
         past
         pass

But it seems likely that the derivational pattern with the adjectives simply reflects a general absence of reference to subjects in the lexicon (Anderson 1984, 1986): the derivational relations in (46.a), (46.b) and (50.a) are based on the semantic function neutral (theme), involving the so-called 'ergative' relation of Lyons (1968: 352). The passive is a syntactic extension of this pattern, adapted to a domain in which subject rather than neutral is (derivatively) pivotal. I do not pursue this here, however, nor the possibility that further, intermediate categories may have to be recognized (e.g. Granger 1983).

3.3 *Beon/Wesan* + Intransitive 'second participle'

As I have indicated, the status of the participle/deverbal adjective distinction in Old English is unclear, and possibly different in the different cases, at least as far as can be determined by the available evidence. There is perhaps least evidence for the development in Old English of a participle/derived adjective distinction in the case of the past participle/adjective (henceforth P/A) of intransitive verbs governed by *beon/wesan* 'be', an instance of what Mitchell (1985: s. 23) calls the 'second participle' (as distinct from the 'present participle'), given the formal identity in Old as well as Present-day English between the passive P/A and the past. I shall not be concerned here with the complex and possibly intractable question of what distinction if any might be associated with the use of forms of *beon* rather than *wesan*, or with the similar, but much less frequent construction with *weorþan* as governor (see Visser 1973: s. 1897; Mitchell 1985: ss. 734–9). Indeed, in what follows in section 3 I shall (given the appropriateness of the usual limitations apologia) focus on constructions with 'be' and 'have' as governor, while acknowledging that this renders our history only partial.

Mustanoja (1960: 499–503), for example, considers that the constructions we are concerned with in this and the following section may represent in both Old and Middle English 'perfect tenses' – i.e. in the terms used here, the governed form is a participle with past-time reference. Clearly, however, the adjectival construction was (also) current (as Mustanoja acknowledges), and has persisted. And there are examples of *beon/wesan* (and other verbs) + P/A which are difficult to interpret as non-adjectival (Mitchell 1985: s. 741): P/A forms with no attested base verb (*cellod* 'formed like a boat/keel'), though often this may reflect the limits of our corpus, rather; P/A forms coordinated with adjectives, as in (52.a):

(52.a) Næs his reaf horig ne tosigen
        'His apparel was neither dirty nor worn-out'

(52.b) 7 se swiþe gewundad wæs
        'and he very wounded was'

(52.c) cymeð him se deað unþinged
'comes to-him the death unexpected'

(where *-en* in (52.a) is the appropriate (strong) P/A ending); P/A forms with adjectival modification (52.b) or morphology (52.c) (from *The Seafarer*) (both with a weak P/A, ending in *-d*), in these cases of a transitive verb. Likewise, the idiosyncratic distribution of *beon/wesan* vs. *habban* + intransitive past P/A is suggestive of a lexical category: although some generalizations are discernible (*beon/wesan* was 'frequently used, especially, but by no means exclusively, with intransitive verbs relating to motion or change' – see Visser 1973: s. 1898), Visser's examples reveal much apparent exceptionality.

We can attribute to Old English a past deverbal adjective, one which in attributive and nominal function seems to display the full range of relevant adjectival morphology (*se foresprecena here* 'the aforementioned army', weak masculine nominative singular, etc.). But it is often unclear in constructions governed by *beon/wesan* how to draw a participle/adjective distinction, presumably parallel to that between the Present-day sentences in (53):

(53.a) His face is swollen

(53.b) His face has swollen

Characterizations of the distinction in terms like 'state' vs. 'the effect or result of an action' (Mustanoja 1960) are not very helpful, given that both possibilities involve, however they differ, a past action with present relevance. And attempts to associate the distinction with evidence of agreement or the lack of it have been unsuccessful (Mitchell 1985: s. 727). The example in (54) shows plural agreement with the nominative:

(54) Soðlice hi sind forðfarene, ðaðe . . .
'Truly they are passed on, those who . . .'

(Mitchell 1985: s. 737). But in the singular there is no indication of agreement or otherwise, as in the examples of (52).

It may well be that we have here a use of a category (past P/A of intransitives governed by *beon/wesan*) that only later splits. Later examples like Shakespeare's *The enemy is pass'd the marsh* or *My life is run his compass* and even earlier similar uses, such as (55.a), together with instances of a past P/A with an adjectival complement, as in (55.b–c):

(55.a) Now is kyng Richard passyd the see

(55.b) Mi vleschs is i flured & bicumen al neowe

(55.c) Al the wode was waxen grene

(Visser 1973: s. 1900), suggest the establishment of a verbal construction by the mid Middle English period. But the picture throughout is complicated not only by the possible (interpretational) indeterminacy of *beon/wesan* + 'second participle' between 'intransitive perfect' and passive with verbs that can be either intransitive or transitive (Mitchell 1985: s. 785) but also by the fact that even in Old English past intransitive P/As can be governed by *habban* instead of *beon/wesan*. The motivations for selection of one or the other require still further investigation, and whether and what kind of a semantic distinction might be involved; and I shall not pursue this here. Nor shall I discuss the alleged motivations for the preferences of individual verbs in Old English (cf. Mitchell 1985: s. 722) and later (e.g. Zimmermann 1973; Fridén 1948; Rydén and Brorström 1987), whereby the *have* forms come to be the general perfect marker. The development of a past participle category seems to be most directly associated with, or at least most apparent in, the development of the Old English *habban* + past P/A construction, to which we now turn. Once more, though, there are problems of dating.

3.4 *Habban* + 'second participle'
Mitchell sums up the problem of establishing the status of this construction as follows (1985: s. 724):

> we need, I think, have little hesitation in accepting the orthodox view that in the original form of the periphrasis the participle was inflected and adjectival. That it is verbal in MnE sentences like 'I have seen it again' is certain. Between the two there is, inevitably, a plethora of disputed examples.

In Present-day English perfect *have* is distinguished from *have* + a range of adjectival and verbal complements both positionally (cf. perfect *have* + participle (+ object/complement) vs. *have* + object + complement – as in (50.c) above), and by its strict adherence to the NICE requirements (cf. *Do you have it finished?*). (On the latter, see Visser 1973: ss. 2116–22.) Neither of these is criterial in Old English. Old English shows both pre-P/A and post-P/A objects. But while there seem to be plausible examples of the adjectival construction with object in pre-P/A position, as perhaps in (56.a) (Mitchell 1985: s. 725), many examples suggest a participal use, even with the order 'object + P/A', as in (56.b):

(56.a) Se læce . . . hæfð on his agnum nebbe opene wunde
unlacode
'The physician . . . has on his own nose open wounds
unhealed'

(56.b) . . . and hæfde ær his ðing þearfum gedælede
'. . . and he-had before his possessions with the needy
divided'

(ibid. s. 726). Here there seems to be no question of a current
'possessive' relation between subject and object, no motivation
for interpreting *gedæled* as an 'object predicative'.

The postulated source construction could be expected (for
reasons not pursued here – see, e.g. Anderson 1973a) to show
concord between the adjective and the object to which it is
predicative. Already in Old English the P/A in such a
construction is often and increasingly uninflected (though there
are again doubtful examples where the expected inflexion would
be null anyway – Mitchell 1985: s. 709). And the distinction
inflected/uninflected also does not seem to coincide with the
adjectival/participial division: the P/As in both (56.a) and (56.b),
for instance, are inflected. Neither position nor concord coincides
with the postulated categorial distinction.

But despite the absence of clear correlates of expression, a
participle/adjectival distinction appears to have been established
by the Old English period (as illustrated by (59) below and the
like). And this, no doubt, (together with the ambiguities of the
beon/wesan + 'second participle' construction) encouraged the
extension of the *habban* perfect to intransitives. Indeed, its
extension to verbs with non-accusative objects (rarely, if at all,
accompanied by concord), as in (57):

(57) Todæg ge habbað Gode gecwemed 7 eowere handa
gehalgode
'Today you have God+*dat* pleased and your hands made-
holy'

(Mitchell 1985: s. 709), here coordinated with a participle with
accusative object, strongly supports the postulation of a 'perfect'
with *habban* and a past participle. The conditions of use for the
Old English perfect were no doubt different from those for the
Present-day, as from the Latin, to go by Alfric's testimony (ibid.
s. 729), but it seems clear that in this case the participle/adjectival
split has already taken place by the Old English period.

With *habban* + P/A this involves, as Mitchell (ibid. s. 728)
points out, not merely, in terms of the present framework of

categories, a (minimal) differentiation of {P.(P:N)} as {P;(P:N)} vs. {(P:N);P}, but also the suppression of the pass feature of the participle. This is accompanied by a weakening of the 'stative/ possessive' character of the governing verb. Since this is a recurrent change (as witness, e.g. developments in Romance – cf. e.g. Meillet 1924; Kuryłowicz 1931; Benveniste 1968 – as well as elsewhere in Germanic), a principled explanation is called for. It may be that the development is simply in part a consequence of de-lexicalization: given my remarks at the end of section 3.2, what is involved is a move out of a domain to which subject-formation is irrelevant, and neutral (theme) is the pivotal relation, to one, the syntax, in which subject is derivatively pivotal. The preferred subject is agentive, in terms of the hierarchy for subject selection; and Ikegami (1986: 381) thus regards the 'dynamicization' of the construction as 'a result of bringing into a clearer focus the implied notion of the agent presumed to have been responsible for the state referred to by the past participle'. Further investigation of this scenario, and others, however, lies outside the scope of the present chapter. (On the complex of issues surrounding the development of 'possessive' and 'perfect' constructions, see further, e.g. van Ginneken 1939; Allen 1964; Lyons 1968: s. 846; Anderson 1973a.)

3.5 *Beon/wesan* + transitive 'second participle'

This bring us, in a way, to the construction in which the expected subject is discarded in favour of a hierarchically lower argument, the other construction involving the 'second participle', the passive. The Present-day English passive is distinguished from the corresponding deverbal adjective not only categorially (relative preponderance of P) but in terms of the absence (vs. the presence) of a past-time reference: recall (50.a–c) vs. (d), distinguished as (51) vs. (49).

Old English has a construction with *beon/wesan* or *weorþan* + the 'second participle' of transitive verbs. The *beon/wesan* vs. *weorþan* distinction has been much discussed, traditionally in terms of 'state' (*beon/wesan*) vs. 'action' (*weorþan*) – cf. e.g. Frary 1929. But Mitchell has shown that this simple equation is untenable (1985: ss. 786–801); see too Kilpiö 1989: ch. 2. Jost (1909) associates *beon* with 'abstract' (generic) sentences, with 'concrete' use being limited to iterative, durative or future 'states', while *wesan* is associated with arguments which have specific reference. Again, such a simple equation is difficult to maintain (Kilpiö 1989: s. 2.8). I do not pursue this; but I would be cautious in rejecting totally hypotheses which at least account for certain clusterings in the uses of the different auxiliaries (cf. e.g. the range of these summarized in Kilpiö 1989: s. 2.7).

What is of particular interest in the present context, however, is Mitchell's claim that 'it is clear that *beon/wesan* could express an action as well as a state' (s. 796). This can be illustrated by (58) and many other examples:

(58) Æfter þæm Sempronius Craccus se consul
'After that Sempronius Craccus the consul'
for eft mid fierde
'went then with an army'
angean Hannibal, 7 gefliemde wearð,
'against Hannibal, and was put to flight,'
7 his here wæs micel wæl geslagen
'and his army was with great slaughter struck down'

(Mitchell 1985: s. 795). Though we cannot equate (syntactic) passive with 'action' and adjective with 'state' (some passives, for instance, are formed with 'statal' verbs: *Berlin is/was divided by the Wall*), 'dynamism'-preserving examples such as (58) suggest the existence of a syntactic passive, governed by *beon/wesan* and with, e.g. *geslagen* in (58) as participial (rather than adjectival). And this is confirmed by examples with expressed agents:

(59) Þær beoð þa sawla forgytene
'There are the souls forgotten'
fram eallum þam hi
'by all those (that) they/them'
ær cuðon on eorþan
'formerly knew on earth'

(Mitchell 1985: s. 815). Ikegami (1986: s. 3.1) once again (cf. s. 3.4 above) explicitly associates the 'dynamicization' of the governing verb with expression of agentivity:

> If we assume that the shift was triggered off by asking for the agent who did the act which resulted in the state in question . . . and this brought about the dynamicization of the past participle, which then affected the main verb *be*, we have an exactly parallel process to the one we posited . . . in our account of the perfect form.

Moreover, as in Present-day English, the participle usually does not introduce a past-time reference. Thus, in his Grammar Ælfric equates the Old English non-past construction of *beon/ wesan* + 'second participle' with the Latin synthetic present passive: *amor a te = ic eom gelufod fram ðe* (Mitchell 1985: s. 768).

Clearly, too, the adjectival construction is also current, and persists, as exemplified in (53) above. Already in Old English, however, occurrence vs. non-occurrence of concord on the P/A again does not serve to distinguish the two constructions (ibid. ss. 757–65), nor do sequential considerations (ibid. s. 767). Concerning the former, indeed, Mitchell observes that: 'In general . . . it can be said that throughout the OE period the participle agrees with its referent as far as the inflexional system allows, except when it is feminine singular' (ibid. s. 760). (Again, see too Kilpiö 1989: ch. 5.) But this should not prevent us from positing a distinction in Old English between (49) and (51), syntactic passive vs. 'passive' deverbal adjective. Whatever split may have occurred predates Old English.

However, the non-past of *beon/wesan* + 'second participle' is used sufficiently frequently in Old English to gloss the Latin periphrastic perfect passive (rather than the present), and the past to gloss the pluperfect, as in (60):

(60) Nu is ðonne sio æxs aset on ðane wyrttruman ðæs treowes
'Now has-been then the axe applied to the root of the tree'
Latin: Iam securis ad radicem arboris posita est

to suggest an intermediate construction, a syntactic passive which retains the past specification on the participle, as the closest approximation to (one sense of) the Latin perfect passive (itself ambiguous between 'pure perfect' and 'historic perfect'). (For discussion see Mitchell 1985: ss. 769–76; Kilpiö 1989: s. 2.1.2.) Thus, Old English may have shown a three-way distinction:

(61)   P;(P:N)   P;(P:N)   (P:N);P
       :   :   :
       pass   pass   pass
                    past   past

Visser (1973: ss. 1908–13), for example, distinguishes between a 'dynamic' passive, a 'statal' passive and a deverbal adjective, corresponding to the distinctions made in (61); but the nature of the difference between the last two remains unclear. Even if once independent, the verbal past passive (characterized by the second representation in (61)) is now recessive, its domain being occupied by *have been* + past participle. On this development see, e.g. Jespersen 1932: 102, who points, for instance, to the replacement of the Authorised Version *Blessed are those which are persecuted for righteousnesse sake* by recent translations of the Greek perfect participle such as *Happy are those that have been persecuted* .... This change would again involve a minimal decrement: in this case, loss of a form class distinguished by a secondary category, past. However, the distinction between the second and third category, in particular, requires further investigation, as well as in relation to the '*be*-perfect' discussed in section 3.3 above.

3.6 *Beon/wesan* + 'present participle'

In Present-day English we can distinguish, as illustrated by (2) and (43) above, between a non-past non-passive ('present') participle and a corresponding derived adjective, even where the morphological expression is non-distinctive (suffixation of *-ing*). Indeed, this same suffix marks gerunds and some derived nouns. Old English displays a distinctive non-past, non-passive, non-gerundive morphology: suffixation by *-ende*, though *-end* may also mark deverbal agentives. The forms so suffixed are commonly referred to as 'present participles' (cf. e.g. Campbell 1959; Mitchell 1985), without specific commitment as to their (verbal/adjectival) syntactic status. Mitchell (1985: s. 694) is (characteristically) pessimistic concerning the possibility of deciding 'whether the participle is adjectival, appositive, or an agent noun, or whether it combines with *beon/wesan* in a truly verbal periphrasis'. It is never made clear what is meant by 'a truly verbal periphrasis', but the problem is one that confronts the matching of any theory of categories with the Old English, and Present-day English, phenomena.

Nickel (1966) has associated the development of the 'expanded form' − i.e., in terms of the present system of categories, the evolution of a construction involving a participle, with the blending of three distinct constructions: *beon/wesan* + predicative adjective; *beon/wesan* + complement + 'appositive' derived adjective (*He wæs on temple lærende his discipulas*, 'He was in the temple teaching his disciples'); and *beon/wesan* + agent noun (*He wæs ehtend cristenra monna*, 'He was (a) persecutor of Christian men'). Nickel (1967) also offers a number of suggestive arguments supportive of the role of this last type in the evolution: he notes, for example the ambiguity of constructions like *Hie wæron ehtende Cristenra monna*, 'They were persecuting Christian men (*genitive*)'/'They were persecutors of Christian men', given that *ehtan* takes a genitive complement and that *-ende* is ambiguous between P/A and plural noun. Ikegami (1986: s. 3.2) sees the development of the 'expanded form' (whatever the model) as related to the 'dynamicization' of *be* and *have* mentioned above (in ibid.: ss. 3.4, 3.5). However, it is not clear that 'dynamicization' as such is anything more than a consequence of the establishment of a categorial status for participles (more verbal than deverbal adjectives).

Whatever the models and the motivation for the 'expanded form' might have been, it is often unclear in Old English what apparent examples of *beon/wesan* + present P/A can be regarded as 'verbal' (participial) constructions. The adjectival character of many examples is apparent. Consider, for example, the adjectival constructions of (62.a–b), as well as adverbial formations such as (62.c):

(62.a) forðon ðe hi sind rihtwise and behreosigende
        'because they are righteous and repenting'

(62.b) Ac nu manna gitsung is swa birnende swa þæt fyr on
        'But now men's avarice is as burning as the fire in'
        þære helle seo is on þam munte þe Atna hatte, . . .
        'the hell that is on the mountain that is-called Etna,
        . . .'

(62.c) Ða lioð þe ic wrecca geo lustbærlice song
        'The song that I (as) an exile once joyfully sang'
        ic sceal nu heofiende singan
        'I must now lamentingly sing'

and adjectival compounds such as (63):

(63)   Ne monn ne geseah þa git yfelwillende menn
        'Nor had then yet been seen evil-wishing men'

(all but (62.a) from the Alfredian Boethius; (62.a) is an Ælfrician example cited in Mitchell 1976: 480). Present P/As, like adjectives, could also occur in 'nominal function', as illustrated by *wædliendum* in example (26.b) above.

Compare now the sentence which immediately follows that excerpted in (62.b):

(64)   Se munt bið simle swefle birnende, ond
        'The mountain is continuously with sulphur burning, and'
        ealla þa neahstowa þærymbutan forbærnð
        'all the neighbourhood thereabouts it-burns-up'

Is *birnende* participial or adjectival, or has the distinction not yet been innovated? There is no doubt here a category intermediate between verb and adjective, of a character succinctly described by Sweet (1898: s. 2204) as follows:

They were no doubt originally formed on the analogy of the combination of the verb 'be' with adjectives, so that such a paraphrase as *hie wæron blissiende* 'they were rejoicing' was felt to be intermediate between *hie blissodon* 'they rejoiced' and *hie wæron bliþe* 'they were glad'.

But were there two such categories (derived adjective vs. participle)? It is, for instance, not enough, as proof of 'verbalness', to be able to associate with some examples of *beon/wesan* + non-past non-passive P/A expression of 'limited duration' (even if this were to be a necessary property of the (Present-day) participial construction). An adjectival construction can also refer to a temporally limited state, partly depending on the semantic character of the base and the nature of the arguments (as in Present-day, *That party was exciting*).

The Present-day English *be* + non-past non-passive participle construction is semantically a contrastive periphrasis, commonly labelled 'progressive', 'expanded', etc. (cf. again Anderson 1989b). As such it is in minimal (semantic) opposition with the 'simple form': they occupy mutually exclusive notional domains; neither can be used if the sense associated with the other is intended; they are mutually exclusive in a strict sense. In this respect the 'progressive' differs from locutions like *be in the habit of*, which merely insists on one possibility within the domain appropriate to the 'simple form'. Contrast the distinction between (a) and (b) and that between (b) and (c) in (65):

(65.a) Kevin was visiting his mother

(65.b) Kevin visited his mother

(65.c) Kevin was in the habit of visiting his mother

Even if the situational conditions are made similar:

(66.a) Kevin was always visiting his mother

(66.b) Kevin always visited his mother

the contrast between (66.a) and (66.b) remains.

Periphrastic status does not entail that the governor have a distinctive categorial status, say as an 'auxiliary'. Above (in section 1), I rejected the evidence that Old English *sceolde* was a subjunctive periphrasis as being an indication that (some of) the ancestors of the Present-day modals were auxiliary in Old English (and cf. again Anderson, 1991a). The appropriateness of this is illustrated by the behaviour of Present-day *get*, which though apparently constituting with the passive participle an alternative passive periphrasis:

(67) Kevin got caught (by the Drugs Squad)

is not an auxiliary, in so far as it lacks the NICE properties, as
for example (in (68):

(68) Did Kevin get caught (by the Drugs Squad)?

(cf. (7) above). However, the governed element, at least, in a
verbal periphrasis must be verbal (have predominant P). Thus
the P/A form dependent on *get* is participial; like the participle
with the *be* passive periphrasis – and unlike the corresponding
derived adjective – it lacks a past-time reference.

Does Old English *beon/wesan* + the P/A in *-ende* ever
constitute a periphrasis, so that the *-ende* form must be
participial? There are instances where it might be tempting to
conclude this, given translational equivalence. But many others
might occasion doubt. It is not merely that the conditions for the
use of this construction in Old English are clearly rather different
from those appropriate to the 'progressive', allowing, for
instance, unexpected (from the Present-day point of view)
coordinations:

(69) . . . he eac swylce swa smylte deað middangeard
      '. . . he also with such a so gentle death this-world'
      wæs forlætende, ond to his gesihðe becwom
      'was departing, and to his vision came'

(from the translation of Bede's account of the death of Cædmon).
But also, in this and many other examples, it is not clear that
semantically the *-ende* construction and the simple form constitute a
simple opposition: cf. Mitchell (1985: s. 686), who cites (70):

(70) Europe hio onginð . . . of Danai þære ie,
      'Europe she starts off . . . from the river Don'
      seo is irnende of norþdæle,
      'which is running from (the) north part,'
      of Riffeng þæm beorgum,
      'from the Riphaei mountains,'
      þa syndon neh þam garsecge
      'which are near the sea'
      þe man hateð Sarmondisc;
      'that is called Sarmatian'
      and se ea Danai irnð þonan suðryhte . . .
      'and the river Don runs thence southwards . . .'

which alternates 'simple form', *beon/wesan* + adjective and
beon/wesan + 'present participle' (cf. too Mitchell 1976: 484–5).

Both 'simple form' and *beon/wesan* + 'present participle' can be used for 'extended duration':

(71.a) And [he] symle syððan Drihtne folgode
'And he ever afterwards the Lord followed'

(71.b) Ge beoð mine frynd, gif ge wyrcende beoð ða ðing
'You are my friend, if you carrying-out are the things'
ðe ic bebiode eow to gehealdenne
'that I instruct you to observe'

(Mitchell 1985: ss. 687–8), unsurprising if *-ende* is adjectival. *-Ende* also tends to be attached to intransitive verbs, particularly verbs of state (*wunian*) or process (*faran*) (ibid.: s. 691), perhaps again suggesting a restricted derivational process rather than a periphrasis.

On the other hand, we do find transitives so used, and, unlike adjectives, they continue as *-ende* forms to govern the accusative (where appropriate), as in (71.b). Mitchell (ibid.: s. 978) argues that the conclusion, on this basis, that the *-ende* forms in (71.b) and (72) are participial ('purely verbal'):

(72) Efne ðaða se apostol þas lare sprecende wæs
'From that very time the apostle these teachings uttering was'

is precluded by 'examples in which the appositive participle takes a direct object', such as (73):

(73) He wæs on temple lærende his discipulas
'He was in (the) temple teaching his disciples'

(ibid.: s. 699). But if (72) involves a participle (i.e. a verb form, in the framework employed here), so too can (73); both participles and adjectives can be 'appositive'. We should not confuse syntactic categories, like adjective and participle, with what is not in itself categorial, such as 'appositive'-ness.

And even if we agree that examples like that in (70) 'suggest that the two forms were sometimes at any rate mere stylistic variants' (ibid.: s. 686), this does not preclude a periphrastic status for the one; indeed, quite the contrary. A periphrasis may involve a null opposition ('neutralization'), as is illustrated by 'periphrastic *do*' in later English, with distribution relative to the 'simple form' determined stylistically or by derived syntactic factors, such as the NICE properties of Present-day English (Anderson 1989b).

Perhaps we can say, at most, however, that we have in Old

English the beginning of a participial construction – and hope that we can in some way make more precise what this might mean (in terms, say, of stylistic, syntactic or other limitations). Certainly, we have at some point in the history of English a split of the character of (74):

(74)
$$P.(P:NP) \rightarrow \begin{cases} P;(P:N) \\ (P:N);P \end{cases}$$

i.e. an incremental change of the kind allowed for by the theory of categories outlined here, constrained by (3). It is likely that this had already occurred in Old English: the attribution of only {P.(P:N)} to Old English (despite examples like (72)) would be perhaps as much a measure of the limits of our (or my) ability to reconstruct with sufficient differentiation (particularly in relation to specific examples) as of anything else, but it does at least mark what that limit might be (cf. Anderson 1987b on the limits of phonological reconstruction in Gothic). Hopefully, others will be able to move the mark to a more illuminating position.

It is clear too that (despite Mossé 1938: s. 175 – 'le fait essentiel pour nous, c'est que le participe en -ing continue, sans interruption, le participe en -end du vieil-anglais') the development of the -ing participle did not involve a simple morphological replacement of the -ende form. Throughout the Middle English period, when the -ende participle continued to allow bare objects, the ancestor of the -ing participle, as befits a nominal, typically takes an of-complement: Visser's (1973: s. 1869) *He was writing of a letter* type, illustrated by (75):

(75)   . . . thanne thei ben not scorninge of God but worshipyng

(from Wyclif). (On these developments, see more generally Visser 1973: ch. 12, s. 3.2.) That is, in a sense, the 'present participle' has been innovated twice, from different sources: -ende is de-adjectival, -ing is de-gerundial, or ultimately de-nominal. The evolution of the modern participle involves a reinterpretation of part of the distribution of the gerund. Perhaps we can envisage the following developments for the -ing form:

(76)
$$P.(N;P) \rightarrow \begin{cases} P;(N;P) \rightarrow \begin{cases} P;(N;P) \\ P;(P:N) \end{cases} \\ (N;P);P \end{cases}$$

i.e. from verbal noun to verbal noun and gerund (cf. section 3.1 above), and then to verbal noun and gerund and participle, each development involving a minimal differentiation. The latter change produces a category already present in the system, realized as *-ende*, etc., which earlier realization is eventually lost in Standard English. This does not, of course, say anything about the mechanisms of the change from *-ende* to *-ing*, perhaps involving phonological reduction and partial identification of the descendants of *-ende* and *-ung* (cf. e.g. Nickel 1967: 266; Nehls 1974: s. 4.1) and input (notional and structural) from the *a*-Verb-*ing* construction: Visser's (1973: ss. 1865–71) *He is on hunting* and *He was a writing of a letter* types (cf. too Nehls 1974: s. 4.2):

(77) He's a-birding, sweet John

(Shakespeare *Merry Wives of Windsor*, IV, 2, 7). Indeed, the argument of Anderson (1973b) suggests that much more should be made, here and in general, of the relationship between preposition + abstract noun constructions and P/A constructions. But the categorial history seems clear in outline.

ss. 1–3 above are intended to illustrate the kinds of categorial change that are compatible with a restrictive notional theory of categories constrained by the continuity assumption. My hypothesis is that categorial changes are limited to the minimal increments, decrements and realignments described as legitimate therein. The hypothesis is intended to hold whether a particular change is 'indigenous' or 'imported'; and I have thus in the above eschewed the difficult debates over the role of 'Latin influence' and the like (cf. e.g. Fischer 1990: ch. 4). The postulation of minimality in change, however, introduces, even perhaps, rather, explains, the difficulties in dating the changes: in the absence of native-speaker judgements, the tools available for us to discriminate appropriately are over-crude. As indicated, I hope others can bring some refinement. But I also hope at least to have established the appropriateness of description in terms of minimal modifications to the system of categories, even where a particular change is apparently pre-textual.

I have said almost nothing about other kinds of syntactic change. In terms of the framework deployed here, these fall into two groups (if we exclude inter-component changes (morphologization)): (i) changes involving secondary categories, i.e. (sub-)categories determined by features such as past and pass introduced above; and (ii) changes involving derived syntactic properties, such as syntagmaticity and linearity. Specification of the former awaits the development of a theory of secondary categories, their interrelations and their relationships with the primary categories we have been concerned with here. By their very nature, however, as secondary categories not distinguishing word classes, these are unlikely in themselves to prove the locus of major changes, whatever their role in promoting particular categorial changes.

Categorial change might then be limited to the minimal modifications allowed by the framework outlined initially. But what of other changes: can they be bounded, or at least hierarchized in terms of likelihood for recurrence? The answers which might come from investigation of this depend in part on the relative independence of other syntactic properties from categoriality.

Among the properties included in (ii), since syntagmaticity (construction-formation), for instance, is determined by the valency and the value of individual items, there is apparently no scope for independent change in this domain. For instance, in Present-day English a modal will be specified as {P}; redundantly, such an item is subcategorized as requiring an infinitive, {P.(P;N)}, as argument; any verb, main or auxiliary (except modals) is given such a value by (12) above; a construction is formed when valency is satisfied by value, with the element exercising valency as head, the other as dependent – but also, by virtue of its own valency, potentially head of a further construction, as illustrated by the pattern of dependencies and associations in (78):

(78)
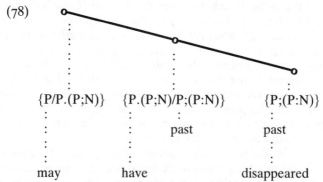

where "/X" specifies valency (that for *disappear* is ignored here), with the value for *disappear* again being supplied by (12). There is no scope for independent syntactic change in the constructions.

However, in certain circumstances, second-order constructions may be erected. Anderson (1986, 1991b), for instance, argues that in Present-day English sentence and verb phrase are both verb-headed constructions differentiated as second-order vs. first and by the direction of modification, as in, say, (79):

(79)

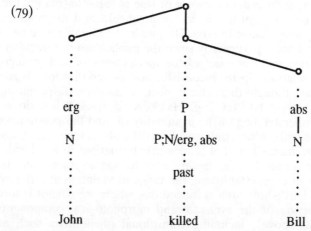

where, for convenience, second-order dependencies at both the syntactic and the lexical levels are indicated with a vertical; the valency of *kill* is satisfied jointly by *John* (erg(ative), agent) and *Bill* (abs(olutive), neutral, theme); and a second-order construction has been erected including as dependents just the subject and the verb. Erg and abs are secondary categories associated with the null class, { }, which is elsewhere realized as an adposition; here, as with the finite and non-finite categories realized as *killed*, governor and dependent are realized simultaneously.

The positing of second-order constructions raises the possibility that languages might vary in whether or not such a second-order construction is erected; whether, in this case, a language makes a distinction between sentence and verb phrase. And, indeed, DeArmond (1984) has argued that English has innovated a (phrasal) category verb phrase, i.e. a distinction between a first- and second-order phrase governed by the verb. Whatever the strength of these arguments, it is clear, however, that the erection of a second-order phrase in such instances may depend on the word-order type of the language – or of some of the sentence types therein (Anderson 1991b). That is, we might suggest in this case too, after all, that construction erection – the existence of particular phrasal categories – is not an independent variable, and thus not subject to independent change.

Basic word order, however, is partly independent of the valencies and values of individual items. Within a so-called consistent language (sub-)system, modifiers occur consistently on the same side of their head in different construction types. But even among such systems, choice of side is variable (parametric, if you like) – centripetal vs. centrifugal; and a language apparently may change in type. Despite a considerable volume of work in this area, particularly since the publication of Greenberg (1963), a restrictive account of the mechanisms of such change, and their relationship to 'inconsistencies' of serialization, is still unavailable, though there have been a number of promising developments of late (cf. e.g. Hawkins 1990). Still less do we have an understanding of the availability of, and the possibilities for change with, what Anderson (1991b) calls 'ectopic' modifications ('movements'), and of (and with) alternations in word order pattern in general. (Cf. again, e.g. Koopman 1990, on the difficulties of even establishing the range of variation at different periods.) This whole area is indeed one where we cannot ignore the interaction of the syntactic and morphological components (laid aside above), including transitional phenomena such as cliticization (cf. e.g. van Kemenade 1987). To quote Mitchell in another context (1985: s. 766 – but essentially passim): 'There is room for more work here'. But that work, too, will be dependent on the articulation of a restrictive theory of syntactic categories.

Note and Acknowledgements

1. Where the sources of examples of Old English are not to be identified via reference to Mitchell (1985), they are drawn from the passages of the works specified at the appropriate points in the discussion which are printed in *Sweet's Anglo-Saxon Reader*, edited by Dorothy Whitelock (Oxford: Oxford University Press, 1967), specifically the copy belonging to Isobel Williams, to whom I offer much thanks for this and (together with Herr Buchenmatth) other hospitalities of the Frey/Williams establishment. Thanks too, as ever, to Fran Colman for comments on a previous version.

References

ALLEN, W. S. (1964) 'Transitivity and possession', *Language* 40: 337–43.
ANDERSON, J. M. (1973a) 'Maximi Planudis in memoriam.' In KIEFER, F. and RUWET, N. (eds) *Generative Grammar in Europe*. Dordrecht: Reidel, pp. 20–47.
ANDERSON, J. M. (1973b) *An Essay Concerning Aspect*. The Hague: Mouton.
ANDERSON, J. M. (1976) *On Serialisation in English Syntax*, Ludwigsburg: Ludwigsburg Studies in Language and Linguistics, Vol. 1.

ANDERSON, J. M. (1984) *Case Grammar and the Lexicon*. Ulster: University of Ulster, Occasional papers.

ANDERSON, J. M. (1985a) 'Structural analogy and dependency phonology', *Acta Linguistica Hafniensia* 19: 5–44.

ANDERSON, J. M. (1985b) 'The case system of Old English: a case for non-modularity', *Studia Linguistica* 39: 1–22.

ANDERSON, J. M. (1986) 'Structural analogy and case grammar', *Lingua* 70: 79–129.

ANDERSON, J. M. (1987a) 'The tradition of structural analogy.' In STEELE, R. and THREADGOLD, T. (eds) *Language Topics: Essays in Honour of Michael Halliday*. Amsterdam: Benjamins, pp. 33–43.

ANDERSON, J. M. (1987b) 'Gothic obstruents: the limits of reconstruction'. In RAMAT, A. GIACALONE, CARRUBA, O. and BERNINI, G. (eds) *Papers from the 7th International Conference of Historical Linguistics*, Amsterdam: Benjamins, pp. 1–11.

ANDERSON, J. M. (1988) 'The localist basis for syntactic categories.' In KAKOURIOTIS, A. (ed.) *2nd Symposium on English and Greek: Description and/or Comparison of the Two Languages*. Thessaloniki, 1989: School of English, Aristotle University of Thessaloniki, pp. 7–32.

ANDERSON, J. M. (1989a) 'Reflections on notional grammar.' In ARNOLD, D. G., ATKINSON, M., DURAND, J., GROVER, C. and SADLER, L. (eds) *Essays on Grammatical Theory and Universal Grammar*. Oxford: Oxford University Press, pp. 13–36.

ANDERSON, J. M. (1989b) 'Periphrases and paradigms.' In ODENSTEDT, B. and PERSSON, G. (eds) *Instead of Flowers: Papers in Honour of Mats Rydén*. Stockholm: Almqvist & Wiksell, pp. 1–10.

ANDERSON, J. M. (1990) 'On the status of auxiliaries in notional grammar', *Journal of Linguistics* 26: 341–62.

ANDERSON, J. M. (1991a) *Should*. In KASTOVSKY, D. (ed.) *Historical English Syntax*. Berlin: Mouton de Gruyter, pp. 11–30.

ANDERSON, J. M. (1991b) 'Notional grammar and the redundancy of syntax', *Studies in Language*, 17: 301–33.

ANDERSON, J. M. and EWEN, C. J. (1987) *Principles of Dependency Phonology*. Cambridge: Cambridge University Press.

BENVENISTE, E. (1968) 'Mutations of linguistic categories.' In LEHMANN, W. P. and MALKIEL, Y. (eds) *Directions in Historical Linguistics*. Austin: University of Texas Press, pp. 83–94.

BOCK, H. (1931) 'Studien zum präpositionalen Infinitiv und Akkusativ mit dem *to*-Infinitiv', *Anglia* 55: 114–249.

BOLINGER. D. L. (1968) 'Entailment and the meaning of structures', *Glossa* 2: 119–27.

BRINTON, L. (1988) *The Development of English Aspectual Systems*. Cambridge: Cambridge University Press.

CALLAWAY, M. (1913) *The Infinitive in Anglo-Saxon*. Washington, DC: Carnegie Institution of Washington.

CALLAWAY, M. (1929) 'Concerning the origin of the gerund in English.' In MALONE, K. and RUUD, M. B. (eds) *Studies in English Philology in*

Honor of Frederick Klaeber. Minneapolis: Minnesota University Press, pp. 52–49.

CAMPBELL, A. (1959) *Old English Grammar*. Oxford: Oxford University Press.

DEARMOND, R. C. (1984) 'On the development of the verb phrase node in English syntax.' In BLAKE, N. F. and JONES, C. (eds) *English Historical Linguistics: Studies in Development*, pp. 205–26. Centre for English Cultural Tradition and Language, Conference Papers, Series 3, University of Sheffield.

DENISON, D. (1988) 'Auxiliary + impersonal in Old English', *Folia Linguistica Historica* 9: 139–66.

DONNER, M. (1986) 'The gerund in Middle English', *English Studies* 67: 390–400.

FISCHER, O. (1990) *Syntactic Change and Causation: Developments in Infinitival Constructions in English*, Vol. 2, Amsterdam Studies in Generative Grammar, Amsterdam.

FRARY, L. G. (1929) *Studies in the Syntax of the Old English Passive, with special reference to the Use of Wesan and Weorðan. Language Dissertation 5*. Baltimore, University of Pennsylvania.

FRIDÉN, G. (1948) *Studies on the Tenses of the English Verb from Chaucer to Shakespeare with Special Reference to the Late Sixteenth Century*. Cambridge, MA: Harvard University Press.

VAN DER GAAF, W. (1934) 'The connexion between verbs of rest (*lie, sit* and *stand*) and another verb, viewed historically', *English Studies* 16: 81–99.

VAN GINNEKEN, J. (1939) 'Avoir et être (du point de vue de la linguistique générale)'. In *Mélanges de Linguistique Offerts à Charles Bally*. Geneva: Georg H. Champion, pp. 83–92.

GOOSSENS, L. (1987) 'The auxiliarisation of the English modals: A Functional Grammar view.' In HARRIS, M. and RAMAT, P. (eds) *Historical Development of Auxiliaries*. Berlin: Mouton de Gruyter, pp. 111–43.

GRANGER, S. (1983) *The* Be + Past Participle *Construction in Spoken English, with Special Reference to the Passive*. Amsterdam: North-Holland.

GREENBERG, J. (1963) 'Some universals of grammar with particular reference to the order of meaningful elements.' In GREENBERG, J. (ed.) *Universals of Language*. Cambridge, MA: MIT Press, pp. 73–113.

HAWKINS, J. A. (1990) 'Seeking motives for change in typological variation.' In CROFT, W., DENNING, K. and KEMMER, S. (eds) *Studies in Typology and Diachrony*. Amsterdam: Benjamins, pp. 95–128.

HUDDLESTON, R. D. (1976) 'Some theoretical issues in the description of the English verb', *Lingua* 40: 331–83.

HUDDLESTON, R. D. (1979) 'Criteria for auxiliaries and modals.' In GREENBAUM, S., LEECH, G. and SVARTVIK, J. (eds) *Studies in English Linguistics*. London: Longman, pp. 65–78.

IKEGAMI, Y. (1986) 'The drift toward agentivity and the development of the perfective use of *have* + pp. in English.' In KASTOVSKY, D. and SZWEDEK, A. (eds) *Linguistics across Historical and Geographical*

Boundaries, I: Linguistic Theory and Historical Linguistics. Berlin: Mouton de Gruyter, pp. 381–6.

JACK, G. B. (1988) 'The origins of the English gerund', *NOWELE* 12: 15–75.

JAKOBSON, R. (1968) *Child Language, Aphasia and Phonological Universals*. The Hague: Mouton.

JESPERSEN, O. (1932) *A Modern English Grammar on Historical Principles*, Vol. IV. London: Allen & Unwin.

JOST, K. (1909) ' "Beon" und "Wesan": Eine syntaktische Untersuchung', *Anglistische Forschungen* 26: 1–141.

KASTOVSKY, D. (1985) 'Deverbal nouns in Old and Modern English: from stem-formation to word-formation.' In FISIAK, J. (ed.) *Historical Semantics – Historical Word-Formation*. Berlin: Mouton de Gruyter, pp. 221–61.

VAN KEMENADE, A. (1987) *Syntactic Case and Morphological Case in the History of English*. Dordrecht: Foris.

KILPIÖ, M. (1989) *Passive Constructions in Old English Translations from Latin, with special reference to the OE Bede and the* Pastoral Care. Vol. XLIX. Mémoires de la Société Néophilologique de Helsinki. Helsinki: Société Néophilologique.

KOOPMAN, W. F. (1990) *Word Order in Old English, with Special Reference to the Verb Phrase*, Vol. I, Amsterdam Studies in Generative Grammar, Amsterdam.

KURYŁOWICZ, J. (1931) 'Les temps composés du roman', *Prace Filologiczne* 15: 448–53.

LIGHTFOOT, D. W. (1974) 'The diachronic analysis of English modals.' In ANDERSON, J. and JONES, C. (eds) *Historical Linguistics* Vol. I. Amsterdam: North-Holland, pp. 219–50.

LIGHTFOOT, D. W. (1979) *Principles of Diachronic Syntax*. Cambridge: Cambridge University Press.

LYONS, J. (1968) *Introduction to Theoretical Linguistics*. Cambridge: Cambridge University Press.

MARCHAND, H. (1969) *The Categories and Types of Present-day English Word-Formation*, 2nd edn. München: Beck.

MEILLET, A. (1924) 'Le développement du verbe *avoir*.' In *Antidoron: Festschrift J. Wackernagel*. Göttingen: Vandenhoeck & Ruprecht, pp. 9–13.

MITCHELL, B. (1976) 'Some problems involving Old English periphrases with *beon/wesan* and the present participle', *Neuphilologische Mitteilungen* 77: 478–91.

MITCHELL, B. (1985) *Old English Syntax*, 2 vols. Oxford: Oxford University Press.

MOSSÉ, F. (1938) *Histoire de la Forme Périphrastique être et Participe Présent*, 2 vols. Paris: Klincksieck.

MUSTANOJA, T. (1960) *A Middle English Syntax, I*. Vol. XXXIX. Mémoires de la Société Néophilologique de Helsinki. Helsinki: Société Néophilologique.

NEHLS, D. (1974) *Synchron-diachrone Untersuchungen zur Expanded Form im Englischen*. München: Hueber.

NICKEL, G. (1966) *Die expanded Form im Altenglischen*. Neumünster: Karl Wachholtz.

NICKEL, G. (1967) 'An example of a syntactic blend in English.' *Indogermanische Forschungen* 72: 261–74.

PLANK, F. (1984) 'The modals story retold', *Studies in Language* 8: 305–64.

PULLUM, G. K. (1982) 'Syncategorematicity and the English infinitival *to*', *Glossa* 16: 181–215.

ROBERTS, I. G. (1985) 'Agreement parameters and the development of English modal auxiliaries', *Natural Language and Linguistic Theory* 3: 21–58.

RYDÉN, M. and BRORSTRÖM, S. (1987) *The* Have/Be *Variation with Intransitives in English*. Vol. LXX. Stockholm: Stockholm Studies in English.

SALTARELLI, M. (1988) *Basque*. London: Croom Helm.

STANDOP, E. (1957) *Syntax und Semantik der Modalen Hilfsverben im Altenglischen 'magan', 'motan', 'sculan', 'willan'*. Bochum-Langendreer: H. Boppinghaus.

STEELE, S. and AKMAJIAN, A. (1981) *An Encyclopedia of AUX: A Study of Cross-Linguistic Equivalence*. Cambridge, MA: MIT Press.

SWEET, H. (1898) *A New English Grammar, II: Syntax*. Oxford: Oxford University Press.

TAJIMA, M. (1985) *The Syntactic Development of the Gerund in Middle English*. Tokyo: Nan'un-Do.

VISSER, F. T. (1969) *An Historical Syntax of the English Language, Vol. III, No. 1*. Leiden: E. J. Brill.

VISSER, F. T. (1973) *An Historical Syntax of the English Language, Vol. III, No. 2*. Leiden: E. J. Brill.

WARNER, A. (1978) *Complementation in Middle English and the Methodology of Historical Syntax: A Study of the Wyclifite Sermons*. London: Croom Helm.

WARNER, A. (1983) 'Review of Lightfoot 1979', *Journal of Linguistics*, 19: 187–209.

WARNER, A. (1990) 'Reworking the history of English auxiliaries.' In ADAMSON, S. (ed.) *Papers from the Fifth International Conference on English Historical Linguistics*. Amsterdam: Benjamins, pp. 537–58.

WÜLFING, J. E. (1894–1901) *Die Syntax in den Werken Alfreds des Großen*, 2 vols. Bonn: Hanstein.

ZIMMERMANN, R. (1973) 'Structural change in the English auxiliary system: on the replacement of *be* by *have*', *Folia Linguistica* 6: 107–17.

Chapter 2

Change and metatheory at the beginning of the 1990s: the primacy of history

Raimo Anttila

Looking back we can characterize the past three decades in the following way, as far as historical linguistics goes.[1] The 1960s had really nothing to say about historical linguistics, although the period is extremely interesting from the point of view of the sociology of knowledge.[2] Of course, all kinds of claims were made. Earlier work was ridiculed or decreed inoperative. The previous emphasis on sound change and analogy was said to be a bad mistake – instead, both were combined under rule manipulations. Such a model was then extended to syntax, where it fared extremely badly (and traditional work on historical syntax was totally ignored). Semantic change was hardly touched upon at all (it had been handled earlier under analogy and the tropes). The position went so far that it was even suggested that the causation of change is a change in the rules of grammar, which then reflects into the real world and causes changes therein.[3] The position was openly innatist, and the fact that innatism is directly hostile to history was no deterrent, since history on paper 'worked' quite well (as a parlor game among the initiated).[4] All kinds of isms were summoned up in defence of innatism and the 'theory' in general, particularly rationalism, which was supposed to do away with empiricism.[5] This was total propaganda and arbitrary analysis, since transformational theory was/is a direct continuation of behaviourism (Itkonen 1978).[6]

The 1970s witnessed a sharp about-face: transformational-generative grammarians started returning to traditional concepts. But this did not happen openly; it was rather a 'usurpation' of ideas, since the earlier transformational terminology was kept, or new terms were created on the basis of it. A great progressive step was announced – analogy was now allowed to return, but under the terms of paradigm constraints and the like (see Anttila 1977), and morphology was called back from exile. Thus a 'psychological', or cognitive, aspect was restored.

Also in the 1970s, sociolinguistics started making inroads (although not into the dominating theory) by pointing out that language change happens in a social context whose factors guide the change, which is also true of history as we know it (even if in school one might concentrate on dominant individuals). Flanking support for sociolinguistics came from an incredibly lively activity in pidgin and creole studies, which of course had to draw in history as real history.[7]

Since also the return to holistic or gestalt traditions became noticeable in the 1970s (but, as in the case of analogy, hardly any credit went to the tradition), we can say that potentially the traditional lines were restored, and these have been 'developing' till today. But most importantly, already in the late 1960s, Henning Andersen and Michael Shapiro started applying Peircean semeiotic to language (under Jakobson's impetus), and by the mid-1970s the line was nicely off the ground (e.g. Andersen 1973, Shapiro 1976). It is this sector that is perhaps central today, although credit to it is rarely given.[8] Metatheoretically one must add the status of history: ever since Collingwood (1946) there has been a growing hermeneutic line, which, even if still in the minority in the Anglo-Saxon lands, became noticeable in the 1970s (e.g. von Wright 1971, Martin 1977). And finally, issues concerning norms and action theory peaked.[9]

These seven or so lines of inquiry did not of course all combine in most cases, with at best two or so joining forces for the benefit of historical linguistics at a time, but they were actively stirring, and it is on this basis that the 1980s were rather rich, even if no actual novelty is visible (except in sociolinguistics and in the application of semiotics to change in the 1970s), contrary to the frequent claims, but increased activity does bring a certain urgency with it (as it did within transformational-generative grammar). Iconicity and abduction were central, and the combination of abduction and analogy (Anttila 1977) became common.[10] The latter combination surfaced in artificial intelligence and problem-solving (e.g. Thagard 1988, Helman 1988), and metaphor received a new lease under the auspices of cognitive linguistics (scores and scores of works on the topic will not be listed) and also in artificial intelligence (Helman 1988). This, and requirements of sociohistorical linguistics (Romaine 1982), brought back the old philology, although typically again, this fact is hardly ever spelled out. In all these areas, the philological aspect becomes particularly strong because of the necessity of treating contexts. Here further belong experience and previous knowledge, so central in semeiotic (collateral experience; see e.g. Anttila 1989c; Shapiro 1991: 17, 24–25, 44, 47, 112, Savan 1988: 70; Pape 1989: § 7; and other Peircean explications). In addition to strong interest in the universals of language (which, like innatism, are not particularly interesting for *history*, certain statistical advantages notwithstanding) also a rich literature on the languages of the world, with thus all kinds of context issues, manifested itself.

Ever since the 'Chomskyan (social) revolution' linguists have remained openly hostile to the history of linguistics, and thus it has been easy for the newcomers to reinvent the wheel under more fashionable terminology. Often the wheel had quite an irregular rim. The strategies for progress were/are not new – Gellner had explicated them in his analysis of Oxford language philosophy (1968: 212; cf. Anttila 1977: 1–2):

a general recipe for a successful revolution. The recipe runs: take a viable system (social, of beliefs, or philosophical, etc. consisting of elements, a, b, c, etc.). Abolish or invert a, b, c, eliminating traces of them and of their past presence. Of course the New System, consisting of not-a, not-b, etc., will be highly revolutionary, novel, etc., and give you the réclame of a great innovator, revolutionary, etc.

However, the trouble so far is that not-a, not-b, etc., may form a system which is not merely revolutionary, but also absurd. No matter. If you have followed the recipe correctly and eliminated traces and memories of a, b, c, etc. (at least from your mind), you can now gradually reintroduce them, and slowly finish again with the original system a, b, c, etc. You now have both a viable system and the aura of a just innovator and revolutionary.

In its earlier stages, it was claimed to be revolutionary; more recently, the stress has been on continuity with the past. Novel ideas had to be claimed to justify the introduction of such novel practices: continuity is now claimed mainly in order to avoid the drawing up of balance sheets of how much the revolution had achieved. If it is merely a continuation, it is at least no worse than philosophies which preceded it, it is claimed, and there is no call for abrogating it if it has failed – as it has – to deliver the promised goods.

This is an exact description of what happened in transformational-generative historical linguistics (in the 1970s), but it is not too far off from what happened with philology, gestalt laws, analogy, and metaphor in cognitive linguistics (in the 1980s). Peter Maher has used the metaphor from St Peter at Antioch who required that converts to Christianity had to go through the synagogue.

Transformational-generative grammar is the linguistic synagogue in America. Skulls thus capped show.

The question is, what is the central aspect in historical language research *now*. It seems that one can rather confidently say that it is perception, representation, and action.[11] But there is no unified line – rather, there are individual scholars who are often unaware that there is a wider common theory. This is why a few words must be said about metatheory, since it determines the nature of explanation that is proper for language change. Also this is a topic that has aroused incredible resistance and ire.

Against the Chomskyan claim that linguistics is a natural science like physics and chemistry, strong (demolishing) proof has been presented to the contrary (e.g. Itkonen 1978, 1983: 294, Keller 1990: 159, 176; cf. Shapiro 1991: 4). But as Gellner said: 'No matter'. It is of course rather embarrassing that the so-called 'theoretical linguists' do not even come close to theory. Even if we would ignore the historical aspect, the fact is that linguistics belongs to the hermeneutic (human, historical, moral, etc.) sciences (Itkonen 1978), but once history and action is brought in the matter becomes of course doubly so (Itkonen 1983; Anttila 1988a). This means that the mode of explanation we need in historical linguistics is historical, genetic, teleological, and rational explanation, or pattern explanation (Diesing 1972). Or to phrase it in more general terms of better-known modes of inference: the explanation must be abductive, inductive, and/or practical.[12] The three have been around since Aristotle, so no novelty is necessary, and note that abduction and induction (and analogy) join forces as *ampliative inference*; this is where novelty in fact belongs. The proper hermeneutic maxim has been that meaning is where history is, or that mental activity is the product of history. In this sense history is the proper frame of mentalism (and meaning), not closed synchronic systems. It is in fact rational explanation that is crucial for the human sciences (Itkonen 1983: 92–107, Shapiro 1991: 7, 23), and it of course absorbs practical inference (or syllogism) in a necessary way (Itkonen 1983: 100–1; von Wright 1971; Zattini 1988; cf. Anttila 1989a: 404, 1992), as well as abduction, which characteristically is a 'reasoned' attempt at explanation. Most ('historical') linguists strive after deduction as in the natural sciences, which means that they are doomed to come out empty-handed (for results in 'science', even if not for career gain, since the wrong method has secured university positions at least).[13]

Itkonen's full-time efforts during the past two decades to prove linguistics a hermeneutic discipline, with the necessity of it

imposing corresponding modes of explanation, have not been
adequately appreciated, although there are others who have
supported the line of argument (e.g. I myself since about 1974).
With the current emphasis on and fashionableness of 'cognitive
science' and 'artificial intelligence' the matter has been brought to
a head. Itkonen pointed out that '[t]he validity of synthetic
models just proves the invalidity of the positivist philosophy of
science', and that 'the Chomskyan universal grammar is nothing
but synchronic syntax (mainly of English) masquerading as
psychology' (1983: 298). 'Now that global linguistic behavior has
become an object of systematic study, the computational
paradigm has no rival, as far as explicitness is concerned. The
only rational alternative to accepting the computational paradigm
is to reject the very idea of algorithmic or nomic rationality and
to espouse the more impressionistic mode of description consonant with non-nomic rationality' (ibid.). Itkonen finds that the self-
image of the practitioners of artificial intelligence is generally
wrong, since they think they are doing natural science. The
reasons for this are eloquently given by Bruner. He shows that
the goals of the original revolution in cognitive science were
abandoned with a turn to information processing and computa-
tion, which gave a new reductionism (1990: 6). But this
reductionism easily took in the behaviourists (and I would add,
with Itkonen, transformational-generative grammarians). A
'computational philosophy of science', however, can have the
right ingredients: Thagard expressly points out that for learning,
performance, and the acquisition of knowledge we need non-
deductive inferences (1988: 12, 13, 35, 36), the Tarskian approach is
of no help (68), '[m]eaning is not fixed by definitions, since there
rarely are any' [cf. Coates 1987: 320] – we need 'various inductive,
hierarchical, nondefinitional ways with other concepts. That is
how meaning emerges' (70, 72). The efficacy of the falsifiability
principle is to be doubted (ibid.: 139–55, 162), and in short '[t]he
scientific method is not based on the strict logical procedures that
the positivists and Popper advocated' (171).[14] Thagard discussed
the contrast between science and what he calls pseudoscience
(1988: 163–73). The latter includes all kinds of hocus pocus, magic,
etc. But the methods of humanities are not pseudoscientific, since
they do not aspire to be scientific. They are rather non-scientific
(ibid.: 167). Whatever the connotations now are, this term here
means 'hermeneutic'. Thagard classifies applied ventures as 'non-
scientific'. 'A[rtificial] I[ntelligence] becomes more empirical
when it is allied with cognitive psychology. . . . In this
collaboration with psychology, which I take to be the central

activity of cognitive science, AI blends into psychology and inherits its characterization as a young science' (ibid.: 172). But '[w]hat of nonapplied, nonpsychological AI? . . . AI is a very young field with evolving methods and standards whose relation to those of mature empirical sciences such as physics remains to be explored' (ibid.). I think Itkonen's explorations have in fact snuffed out this dream of becoming natural science.

Bruner's (1990) effort to restore the original thrust of the cognitive revolution now becomes extremely important. This is a poignant and succinct plea for hermeneutics. Bruner speaks expressly against positivists (1990: 6, 31, 44, 55, 61–2) and for human intentionality and agency (9, 41, 42, 77), history (35, 59), and culture (23, 106). For almost two decades I have been pointing out synonyms for hermeneutics, the chief one among them being interpretation. This is now Bruner's term (1990: 19, 47, 60, 61, 95, 107, 137, 138, 148) and I hope that it finally drives the issues home for linguists also.[15] The hermeneutic content comes out in his defence of a 'folk psychology', which would be better expressed as 'folk human science' (67), and further (118):

> A cultural psychology is an interpretive psychology, in much the sense
> that history and anthropology and linguistics are interpretive
> disciplines. But that does not mean that it need be unprincipled or
> without methods, even hard-nosed ones. It seeks out the rules that
> human beings bring to bear in creating meanings in cultural contexts.
> These contexts are always *contexts of practice*: it is always necessary to
> ask what people are *doing* or *trying* to do in that context. This is not a
> subtle point, that meaning grows out of use, but in spite of its being
> frequently sloganized, its implications are often unsuspected.

All to the point. The whole book is an eloquent expression of the notions, and Bruner's references are incredibly recent, mainly from the last years of the 1980s. 'Theoretical' linguists do not put linguistics in this context, and they are wrong.

The linguists' stance against hermeneutics is curious in that it is a truism that language does not change unless it is used in a situated context. Thus all system-internal approaches to change must be disqualified as the total solution. These two requirements translate directly into a full semiotic situation. And indeed, any realignment in the sign relations defines change, and one cannot even talk about change unless one understands the sign. Furthermore, an adequate semiotics gives a viable theory of cognition at the same time. Still, the dominating theory does not give any attention to the sign, rather, the 'theoreticians' are rather proud in proclaiming that they do not even understand

Saussure's notions of it. Hermeneutics translates directly into interpretation as we saw above, which in its turn is practically identical to semiotics (of which language takes the lion's share), and semiotics is a strong argument against positivism.[16] But still 'No matter' to linguists. This is extremely embarrassing. Of the nine sub-types of sign (see any Peircean exposition, e.g. Savan and Short as listed, or Shapiro 1983: 64, Anttila 1989a: x–xi, or Anttila and Embleton 1989: 155–7, Pape 1989: 498–512) linguists occasionally take to the type-token distinction (covering the last two in the stretch of qualisign-sinsign-legisign). But it is not appreciated that this kind of 'pulsation' within the sign is a dynamic cause of change. The sign's relation to the dynamic object, the main impetus in the sign, has had partial success. This is the icon-index-symbol continuum, and its success resides in the acceptance of iconicity as a force of change. Of the relations of the sign to its interpretant (rhema-dicisign-argument) the last two have again received some attention, in syntax and reasoning respectively, i.e. dicisigns as sentences with truth value and the argument through deduction.[17] Since truth-value semantics and deduction hardly have a chance in change it is no wonder that historical linguistics has profited nil, all kinds of fanfares to the contrary notwithstanding. All linguistic signs are symbols, and most change takes place around or in them, and thus the symbol needs theoretical attention in any treatment of change. We have to do with rhematic symbols without truth value. These are the familiar concepts, so differently funnelled into the lexicon in different languages. This funnelling in acquisition and learning is an important source of change (see the downward arrow in Shapiro's diagram of semiosis, 1976: 25; Anttila 1991: 11). What is even more conducive to change is the multiplicity of interpretants, up to twelve of them (Shapiro 1991: 24–39; Savan 1988: 48–72, Short 1981a: 209–19, 1982: 286, 288–9; Pape 1989: 337–42, or any exposition of Peirce's signs). Meaning is concatenation of interpretants (signs) toward habit (belief, action). This is the other 'weak spot' (which produces change), since it depends on the actant when s/he stops interpretation and takes to action (see the upward arrow in Shapiro's diagram). These 'weak spots' in the semiotic (hermeneutic) circle (spiral) are of course its glory, since it makes the system flexible for new use not predetermined. As for the interpretants, I just want to mention two here, the final and the dynamic ones. The former is, in Peirce's words, the 'effect the sign would produce upon any mind which circumstances should permit it to work out its full effect' (see Shapiro 1991: 44), and the latter is the 'direct effect actually produced by a sign upon an interpreter of it' (ibid.).[18]

By now the 'leaking aspects' of semiosis have been listed three times, from different angles. The funnelling of reality and experience into concepts starts with the perceptual component and ends with concepts, and representation. This is of course of thorough, crucial cognitive import for any living creature (life is where legisigns are; Short 1982: 298). The chain of interpretants leading to habit provides the background and propulsion for action. Now we can add the syllogisms characteristic in these sectors: abduction works with the 'downward chute' from perception to concepts (to follow Shapiro's diagram) and the practical syllogism is the ladder in the 'upward flue' from evaluation to habit. Both syllogisms 'leak' (and thus produce change),[19] but in between we have induction, which guides the drawing of representative samples on which action is based (cf. Savan 1980, a most important work). This also leaks, or at least does not guarantee certainty (Russell: the tragic problem of induction), and contributes to change. The fallibility of abduction is proverbial. Of course, normally in historical linguistics abduction and induction were not kept distinctly apart.

But more has come out in the hints above. The type-token (general law/replica) relation, the rhema (concept) as possibility (without truth value), and the final-dynamic distinction in the interpretant (all this could be referred to with the 'pulsation' of the sign, as above) is the indeterminacy in the functioning of the sign. Both the general (legisign/type, final interpretant) and the possible (rhema/concept) aspects of sign are not actual. Both flanks need embodiment in some indexical (actual) substance (= 'here and now'). The actual is the domain where history plays itself out. To quote from Short (1984: 30–1 quoting Peirce from 1893 and 1905) who discusses the growth of symbols or concepts in a very perspicacious and perspicuous way:

> Symbols grow. They come into being out of other signs, particularly icons, or from mixed signs partaking of the nature of icons and symbols. We think only in signs. These mental signs are of mixed nature; the symbol-parts of them are called concepts. If a man makes a new symbol, it is by thoughts involving concepts. So it is only out of symbols that a new symbol can grow. *Omne symbolum de symbolo*. A symbol, once in being, spreads among the peoples. In use and experience, its meaning grows. Such words as *force*, *law*, *wealth*, *marriage*, bear us very different meanings from those they bore to our barbarous ancestors.

Note particularly the importance of experience (which would

combine both the *Umgebung* and the *Umwelt*, lived experience), and Peirce's politeness in making our ancestors barbarous, not us (or our colleagues at least) who more often than not do not understand such basic things. Short goes on (ibid., from Peirce's MS 290.58–63):

> a symbol may, in its capacity as such, produce effects in the material universe. Indeed, without doing so a symbol could not function as such.

> [A symbol] may have rudimentary life, so that it can have a history, and gradually undergo a great change of meaning, while preserving a certain self-identity.

> Being able to produce external effects by virtue of its signification, it may by one branch of its signification act upon another branch of its signification; and there we have the first step toward self-control.

> the mind should be considered as belonging, as it certainly does, under the genus of symbols;

> Now a symbol cannot be adequate to the performance of all its functions without being associated with at least seven other kinds of signs.

We, as linguists, should know the rudimentary life and history of symbols as etymology (which is happily getting more attention again; cf. also Shapiro 1991: 92). (Some of the seven other kinds of sign have been mentioned above and will be further handled below.) Short proceeds by discussing Aristotle's notion that if the interpretation rules of a symbol change, there is no change at all (1984: 31–2). This may be the reason why change tends to be bracketed out even in linguistics, but such growth under accrual of new interpretation rules is change. Short adds to the 'life and history' issue (ibid: 35):

> [I]f a concept is a mere type of symbol defined by an interpretation rule, then there need be no symbols actually in use of that type. And in that case we cannot speak of the concept's having a history at all, since history entails changes and changes take place only with reference to the actual. In themselves, concepts, like meanings or interpretation rules, cannot change. But Peirce held that no law is real except in governing actual events. Concepts are real, then, only when they are types to which symbols actually replicated belong. Concepts so understood can still be considered in themselves, but their reality consists in the influence they actually have. The fact of belonging to that type determines how the replica will be interpreted. The fact that there are replicas of that type accounts for there being further

replications of the same type, as one person learns words from another and as concepts developed in one culture become translated into the language of another culture. And the fact that the concept, through replications of its symbols, becomes predicated of actual individuals means that we can learn more about the things of which that concept is or seems to be true, thus making those discoveries which lead to additions to or refinements of it. In these ways, their being real – their actually being expressed in the replication of symbols – is essential to concepts having a history. But it does not follow that any one formation rule is the principle of a concept's identity throughout the process of its development and communication.

Replication has brought us to the realm of the index (see Goudge 1965), which (Savan 1988: 37)

in its strict sense indicates only the active existence of some object. In order to identify the nature and description of the object, iconic sinsigns are essential. The rolling gait of the man walking in front of me is an index that something or other acted upon this man to produce this peculiar gait. But to identify that action as the heaving rolling motion of a sailing vessel requires iconic sinsigns as well as the knowledge of certain laws and regularities – of certain legisigns, then. So too, in our . . . problem with . . . Friday's footprint in the sand, we must say that these are sinsigns which act both indexically and iconically. They indicate both the existence of some producing agent, and through their shape and size they provide a likeness – hence an icon – of the producing agent.

The point about the centrality of the index and the indexical sword in history (or change) – but of course with its iconic and symbolic blades – is so important that I want to cite another synopsis (Short 1988: 86–8):

[T]he role of the icons and the indices in the original development and subsequent growth in meaning of a symbol is deducible from the fact that symbols are meant to serve a purpose. The realm of existence, of struggle, of action and reaction, is the arena in which purposes are pursued, in which means to their fulfilment are tested, and in which they themselves are found to be satisfactory or not. Indices are our only access to existence, and iconic sinsigns are the first step in any grasp and appreciation of the effects of action. Apart from their replication in actual circumstances, or apart from the subsequent interpretation of those replicas, there would be no real use and no test of any symbol. The use need not be narrowly utilitarian nor, indeed, practical in any but the broadest sense. Their application may serve no further purpose than to test symbols in their capacity as embodiments of knowledge. But without test, without trial, without struggle, there is no use of symbols and there are no symbols. The existence of symbols consists in purpose, and there is no purpose where it is not pursued.

In brief: it is the purposiveness of language and the inherent indefiniteness of purpose that accounts for the intrinsic dynamism of language.

We have reached another aspect that has fared rather badly among linguists, namely that the symbol is essentially a purpose and clearly future-oriented (Short 1981a: 199, Shapiro 1991: 28, 117). This of course makes history the primary ingredient in language, although it goes against the maxim taken to be Saussure's. This would be the place to go further into icons and indexes as change generators, but before doing so one must wrap up the purpose issue, since it agrees more directly with the theoretical side of hermeneutics (already mentioned).

Jakobson brought this idea of purpose and future in the symbol to linguists (cf. Anttila 1989a: 18) in America, and Coseriu did the same in Europe by showing that final causes are proper in matters of language (see now Coseriu 1979 and 1980; cf. Anttila 1989a: 401–2). (The social success of generative grammar eclipsed both pleas.) To study the potential future in the signs we study it paradoxically as the past, in its relation towards the future which we know as past. I have paraphrased Coseriu's position as follows (Anttila 1989a: 402) (which, of course, is not an adequate summary of all of his output):

That is, the chronological cut under study, C, has as its future B, which from our vantage point, A, is already past. In genetic explanation . . . the earlier state of affairs (B) does not explain causally ('from behind') the existing state (A), but from the point of view of future ('from in front'): the later point (B, A) in fact establishes the possibilities of the earlier state (C, B). In a strict synchronic mode one would not know about real possibilities at all, because they have to be realized by speakers in history . . . . A synchronic explanation is in fact impossible, because for any explanation one has to refer to something else . . . . In this way descriptive linguistics explains speech, not language. The moment one wants to account for why a language is the way it is, one has to resort to genetic explanation, as in history in general. We do not reduce forces to causes but we observe facts in their finalistic development. The question in human activity is 'for what purpose', that is, not 'Why did Brutus murder Caesar?', but 'For what purpose would I have murdered Caesar?' Answering questions of 'for what purpose?' we explain the earlier state of affairs by a later one, gaining deeper understanding of the facts. The important point is that the state of affairs is explained by its evolution with more exact understanding. The possibility is manifested and the openness of the system vindicated. Change is now just creation, use of language; history is an integral part of the object, not an addition to description. In natural objects we can separate being/existence from becoming to a reasonable degree, but not in cultural objects, or cultural activity where becoming is the very essence of existence. Language use is (re)interpreted tradition. In short, only historical linguistics does justice to our real experience with language and the essence of language. This does of course not deny synchrony. A synchronic-structural treatment of a given language state is the only reasonable one for description, although the description of a culture object belongs to a phase in its becoming. There is no contradiction between description and history. As Hermann Paul said, linguistics is really historical linguistics.

Add to the above (from further up) rational explanation, the practical syllogism, and final interpretants, and we see that there is no way out of the primacy of history and final causation, or in other words, teleological explanation. Final causation, like semiotic causation, is logical causation. What now follows in my exposition is enormously indebted to the work of Thomas Short and Michael Shapiro.[20]

There is incredible opposition to teleological explanation in linguistics, which means that most linguists deny the very essence of language. Teleology does not entail some mysterious pull of the future ('backwards causation'), but rather belongs to a doctrine of the potency of present possibilities, as we have now seen in the very nature of the symbol as essentially a purpose with an embryonic reality endowed with the power of growth (Shapiro 1991: 29, 119). Short shows that someone's purpose is the ideal type, which he wills to actualize (1981b: 369). Further, no final cause is actual, but directs actualizations. When the sign system is used the symbols tend to make themselves more and more definite. All sign types exist solely in order to be used as tokens (Short 1982: 292):

> For legisigns only exist *in order* to be used – that is, to signify through replication – and that presupposes the existence of creatures prone to interpret those replicas according to the rules associated with the legisigns replicated. Conversely, the interpretation of something as the replica of a legisign presupposes that it was produced *in order* to be interpreted *as* a replica of that legisign.
>
> Other signs may be used to signify, as a piece of cloth may be used as

a sample of its color, but, normally, they do not exist in order to be so used, and their significance does not depend upon the fact that they are so used.
It follows that the creation and replication of legisigns is goal-directed. In no other case is sign-production necessarily teleological, even though sign-interpretation always is.

When we talk about *use as*, we of course are talking about a goal (Shapiro 1991: 27). Thus the creation and replication of types (i.e. speech acts) is goal-directed (cf. also Shapiro 191: 31). Note the important fact that sign-production is goal-directed only for types/symbols, whereas sign-interpretation is that for all signs (one strives to retrieve the meaning intended or otherwise produced). As far as *language* goes, both sign-action and sign-interpretation are purely teleological. The symbol does of course also incorporate habits (of interpretation and action). But habits, as laws and types (= generals), do not consist in any particular acts that happen to instantiate them. They operate in agreement with final causation: specific manifestations of habits are the results of a certain type that would tend to occur even if the circumstances of their occurrence varied. Habits as intellectual entities manifest rationality and are hence subject to final causes and govern acts by making them conform to and manifest the general pattern (cf. Short 1981b: 370).
Final and efficient causation are hierarchically ordered, and both need each other. The latter is 'that kind of causation whereby the parts compose the whole', while the former is 'that kind of causation whereby the whole calls out its parts' (Shapiro 1991: 16, 29, from Peirce 1.220; Short 1981b: 370). Both directions obey teleological forces. Note that a notion like that of a natural class comes under final causation, because its members owe their existence as members of the class to a common final cause, the defining idea of the class (Shapiro 1991: 29; Short 1981b: 373). That functioning structures can change is due to the fact that efficient causation is subject to evolution, and this evolution is again teleological: the conformity of particular efficient causes to laws of efficient causation is itself an example of final causation (Short 1981b: 377; Shapiro 1991: 19, 29). Or, in other words, the relation of law, as a cause, to the action of force, as its effect, is final (or ideal) causation, not efficient causation. Typically again, primary hermeneutic ingredients lie behind (and even explain) the apparent positivistic notions. It should really not be that surprising that semeiotic is crucially dependent on final causation (Shapiro 1991: 21), because all

meaning is dependent on tautology or isotopy (cf. Anttila 1991: 35–8), held together by efficient causation under the laws of final causation (Short 1981b: 379)

> [whose] strength is that in itself the idea is not at all mysterious or exciting. To apply it to this or that phenomenon – i.e., to an apparent tendency toward results of a certain general type – we need only find a relevant tautology – i.e., a tautology that would explain why the apparent tendency observed is not merely coincidental but is, under the given conditions, a real tendency. The importance of this almost humdrum idea is in its application, e.g., in the theory of biological evolution, in statistical mechanics, and, if Peirce is right, in the cosmic evolution of efficient causation.

Need anything more be said? But as has become obvious, this is an area where overkill must be risked in order to bring historical linguistics into its proper course (Shapiro 1991: 23–4):

> Given that it is a particular kind of goal-directedness that defines the nature of the sign (i.e., for each sign there must be at least a potential goal of interpretation), the basic concept of Peirce's theory of signs is not sign but semeiosis, specifically in its aspect of sign-interpretation. From this it follows that sign-interpretation – semeiosis – is teleological. Note that since teleology necessarily involves change, change is eo ipso built into the very ontology of signs that are triadically produced. Also – and of particular importance to our main topic – all triadic action, being teleological for Peirce, necessarily involves the influence of final causes.

and (32):

> I would like to argue that what is most important in Peirce's sign theory is (1) that all semeiosis is teleological and (2) that the entelechy of a sign is its interpretant. From this it follows, I believe, that as far as linguistic meaning is concerned, change itself is an ontological component of meaning.

and further, the very final words of his book (119):

> *Language and its development are always teleological, because teleology is of their very essence.*

There is a distinction between *acting for* a purpose (goal-intention) and *existing for* a purpose (goal-direction) (Short 1981b: 374–5, Shapiro 1991: 16–18, 19, 39). The latter case includes organs or artefacts that have been selected to fulfil a function; that is, the existence of the organ is teleologically explained. This is true of biological units like the heart or grammatical structures like phonological rules or syntactic structures. This latter case is known as teleology of function, the former as teleology of purpose (Andersen 1973). The important point is that functional analysis belongs within teleology, that is, function is also essentially a historical concept, contrary to what is usually stated or believed. So is selection, a key concept in sign behaviour and even in linguistic analysis; it can only be understood under final causation (because it is an aspect of sign types: a selection from an inventory).

Social forces show clearly teleology of purpose. Speakers choose to modify their language to assimilate it to other people's norms. The idea of group membership is adopted first, and it then calls out an effect in pronunciation.[21] Similarly, avoidance of homophony is opted for by speakers because they want to be understood without noticeable complications. Homophony can be avoided, e.g. by grammatical conditioning of sound change or by lexical replacement (Itkonen 1983: 201–20, Anttila 1989a: 406–8). But this already involves teleology of function, because parts get selected for an efficient result; it is inherent in all human semiosis (Shapiro 1991: 45).

The difference in status between a pattern in the making and a pattern once established is particularly pronounced in language structure. This applies not only to change and its stable result but also to language acquisition (ibid.: 17). The child learning its native language has as its goal the acquisition of the patterns that make that language. While the goal is still unreached, the process is subordinated to teleological considerations: final causes call out for parts of the whole. The process is obviously gradual. Once the patterns have been learned, however, their fulfilment in adult speech changes character: the structure switches to efficient causes, the parts compose the whole.[22] The syllogism used in all learning (and thus in all change) is the abductive one, from the vantage point of perception under the human hermeneutic imperative. The result cannot be adduced or conjectured unless its content is already present in the premises. The syllogism 'leaks downward', from the goals and beliefs, i.e., through purposes toward goals. Similarly, the practical syllogism also leaks from the premises to the conclusion. In both cases the entailment is conducive to novelty and change.[23] Rationality is being governed by final causes (Peirce, 2.66 in Shapiro 1991: 7, 23; Itkonen 1983: §§ 3–4; Anttila 1989a: 405–6).

We can now draw a startling balance for many a would-be or

has-been 'theoretical' linguist: language and its development are always teleological. A purpose or other final cause is also the essence of mental phenomena, and it is mind that makes meaning. Change is the *telos* of language. This comes out admirably in Shapiro's conclusion (1991: 114–19; cf. also Pape 1989: § 8). More particularly it is the establishment of a pattern, namely a diagram (ibid.: 116), and there is no telos beyond diagrammatization (118): 'The formula "one form, one meaning" can now be restated in more direct semeiotic terms to read: "one diagram, one (set of) logical interpretant(s)".' I had lifted this 'formula' out of the linguistic tradition as an antidote to rule manipulations (Anttila [1972] 1989a, 1977). It has fared rather well and it has been widely quoted (with or without reference to the earlier treatments) under the current lionizing of iconicity, but Shapiro adds theoretical precision and depth to it. Shapiro's final words in his chapter 4 'Symbols, Growth, and Continuity' are again characteristically pithy: '*The link between truth and entelechy is, of course, history*' (113).

It is time now to go back to the question of the iconic sinsign and the diagrams that have cropped up above. Iconicity has been used by two groups for the explanation of language change. Let me just call them here Peirceans and 'Naturalists' (cf. Anttila and Embleton 1989: 158 fn. 1). Although iconicity is the cornerstone of the sign, we have seen enough statements that alone it is not enough, and in fact Itkonen, Andersen, and Shapiro (1991: 12–13, 123 fns. 13, 17) have criticized the Naturalists for their rather arbitrary or at least limited or deficient use of the notion of iconicity. What is imperative now is to provide the indexical anchorings for understanding change. The good news is that this has been done in basic outline in Anttila (1989a: xiv–xv) and in Anttila and Embleton (1989). The bad news is that I cannot repeat it *all* here.

For simplicity, let me rephrase the iconic sinsign as the iconic index, as I have done before. Change depends crucially on it. This is general in evolution. Units adapt to their environments by indexical stretching to produce an icon of the environment (cf. the Savan quotation above). Such an iconic index tends to become independent from the environment (symbolic) (Peirce, in Anttila 1989a: xiii–xv, 37–40, 407; Haley 1988: 85, 144, 148, 155), particularly if the environment is lost.[24] The forces are quite obvious in the development of writing systems, e.g. in the rebus principle. Note that even in 'picture' writing it is crucial to abstract a feature to write, i.e. prescind an aspect to draw. The foundation is thus the choice of an index, which has to be rendered iconically (iconic pull).[25] The rebus principle also shows that the sign spreads through analogy, i.e. diagrammaticity, giving thus an iconic push to the change, and it is no wonder that diagrammaticity is the central force in change (traditional analogy was right; Anttila 1989a: 180).

Allophonic variation is an index of the conditioning environment, and when this environment is lost, we get a split (independence, symbolicity). Pronunciation as a group marker is likewise an index, exactly like animal cries, and when one tries to produce it iconically one often improves on it (and produces hyper-correct change). The index here is already symbolic, e.g. meaning 'Southerner' and the like; as a final cause it calls forth efficient shapes and creates change. That morphological change and syntactic change are largely purely diagrammatic (analogy) needs hardly be mentioned (cf. Shapiro 1991: 35–8, 71), but I will return to their indexical aspects below. The curious thing is that classification of change by its results was so strongly criticized within transformational-generative grammar, but it has been the standard within historical syntax, and acceptable and theoretically elevated. As for semantic change, metonymy is clearly indexical, but so is metaphor as we will see below through Haley's exposition. Analogy as a momentum here is quite standard and obvious. But to prove the necessity of the concept of the iconic index, really drastic limiting cases had to be looked at, and these were found in rhyming slang and avoidance vocabulary (Anttila and Embleton 1989). It became apparent that such lexical changes could be explicated in a fundamental way through the iconic index: in the first case rhyme is of course iconic to the 'home base', as it were, but its raison d'être is to be the index to the home base. After conventionalization the index can be dropped, and a symbol ('synonym') results, e.g. *table mate* → *China plate* → *China* 'table mate'.[26] In taboo and avoidance vocabulary similarity to a word taken to be an index of a culturally proscribed form leads to loss, or rather replacement. Whether this replacement is through synonyms, borrowing, or tropes, in all cases it is through diagrams (Anttila 1989a: 179–81).

Analogy can be called an indexical icon (Anttila and Embleton 1989: 165; Anttila 1991: 44), because the crucial choice of the indexical basis must be established first, that is, the bases of analogy in traditional parlance. It was the lack of understanding of this that led to the impasse in generative theory, as well as the fact that its adherents required identity, and did not understand similarity (cf. Haley 1988: 148). Although analogy mixes induction and abduction, no harm is done, because in historical explanation we need just that. This is also the situation in the computational paradigm in which problem solving must be tied with induction (Thagard 1988: xi, 15, 19, 26, 70, and particularly his diagram: 28, which shows that in his system induction feeds into abduction), abduction (52–60), analogy (22, 24, 92–5), or analogical abduction (60–2).[27] What all this means is that analogy is crucial in any science, it improves explanations within theories and supports hypotheses already discovered (92, 94–5). Since analogy goes from individual to individual (Aristotle, Thagard 1988: 95, Melis 1989: 89) it is particularly handy in any real or historical context. It also supplies a frame for holistic thinking (Melis 1989: 89), or is in fact holistic and analytic at the same time (Haley 1988: 6). We know this from the Greeks who used a paradigm (example) as the index for analogy (proportion) toward the solution (cf. Wildgen 1987: 146, Anttila 1991: 44–5). Analogy can be taken as an inference that leads to a solution of a problem mixing thus abduction, induction, and the practical syllogism, i.e., perception and experiential context as premises (necessary conditions) lead to interpretation as conclusion (cf. Melis 1989: 96). Time and again it comes out that analogy is an agent of closure: 'Analogiebildung ist eine Möglichkeit der Vervollständigung unvollständiger Information' (ibid.: 89). This is to be expected, since this is how interpretants determine the symbol.[28] For modern formal linguists analogy was an anathema (is it still, or does the computational example now change the situation?), because only its strictest forms are formalizable, otherwise man is necessary (Melis 1989: 98–9, Coates 1987: 321, 319, 336), in that we need key words even in the computer programs (Melis 1989: 104). These of course bring in human knowledge about things through their interpretants. Also Thagard's program PI (= process of induction) requires background knowledge stored in concepts, and uses a goal-directed component (1988: 29), and schemas over propositions (ibid.: 31), concepts over rules (38–9, Coates 1987: 320, 337). No wonder formalists are unhappy. As for metatheory and for treating change, they are also wrong. To put the issue into a nutshell in this context: traditional analogy, as manifested and known in historical linguistics, was and is right (cf. the 'proportional' schemas in Thagard 1988: 93, and Melis 1989: 90).[29]

I have saved Haley's (1988) work on the indexical icons for last, not only because he deals with metaphor, the highest level of meaning, but also because it is semiotically most sophisticated, a real paragon of creative scholarship. Although Haley modestly emphasizes that he deals with synchronic structure only, his work bears directly on change, because, as we have seen, meaning is change.[30] This is the semiotic position (of Shapiro's) which he adopts. I will just refer to a small part which is relevant in this context. Haley points out that there is a powerful interactive index in metaphor (Haley 1988: 14):

> This indexical component of metaphor is . . . its clash of dissimilars
> . . . . Like a red flag, another Peircean example of the Index, the
> semantic shock of a novel metaphor is what brings it into the
> foreground of perception. Or we might say that the figural tension of
> the metaphor is the indexical 'smoke' which 'points' (the first function
> of any index) to the metaphorical 'fire'.

This kind of an index forces something to be an icon, 'meaningful metaphorical tension is that kind of index which *contains* an icon, as a photograph reliably "points" to the object represented by its iconic image' (ibid.: 15). Such indexical interaction (ibid.: 53) is crucial throughout. Haley's book culminates in a convincing map of semantic distance that causes this indexical tension, and the situation is much more intricate than, for example, in sound change (ibid.: 111–12):

> the metaphorical index points to an icon which it contains, the
> different kinds of tension shape the icon – or our perception of the
> icon – in various ways, thereby coloring or changing our evolving view
> of the icon and its object, as well as of the similarity condition they
> share. Second, the various kinds and degrees of indexical tension
> interact among themselves, frequently producing a gradual 'build-up'
> of semantic indexation, thereby facilitating the nonpoet reader's
> interpretive progress toward higher levels of linguistic, existential, and
> conceptual possibility (in the icon) which lie just beyond those same
> levels of *im*possibility in the index.

Such an index shapes its object and becomes 'something of an icon in itself' (ibid.: 135; cf. 98), which is also true of assimilation in sound change, it would seem. '[W]hat identifies something as a candidate for interpretation as metaphor is species opposition, for it is this that provokes the search for a figural icon, its object, and their similarity. If this search is successful, the utterance is confirmed as metaphor' (ibid.: 100). '[I]t is the metaphorical index that is forever forcing us to understand and appreciate the proliferation of semantic species' (ibid.: 151). Throughout his book Haley shows that when the iconic content approaches diagrammaticity or analogy the index is also enhanced, suggesting more imaginative possibilities (ibid.: 161; cf. also 22, 33, 56, 78, 84, 143), in fact he 'believe[s] diagrammatic thought must have been the breakthrough which crystallized the differentiation of semantic levels in language and consciousness' (ibid.: 153).[31]

The inductive attention-arousing indexical gap in the diagram is of course 'the initial problem' on which perception and abduction feed (major premise: 'The surprising fact, C, is observed', from Peirce; e.g. Anttila 1989a: 404, Kapitan 1989). Treating English place names Coates (1987: 330) 'suggests that the parameter of relatedness is distance apart, literally the distance on the ground – or the sea – between them' and uses this to explain analogical reformations. The distance can come from a mental map, of course, but 'nearness is the spatial expression of, and is prototypical for, the relation of similarity' (ibid.: 337). This is another convincing case of the index working itself into a kind of icon along the lines Haley suggests for the metaphor. Spotting such tension or a gap is of course an invitation to solve the problem, i.e. it is an imperative to action, and such action propels change, in fact and by definition, whether we want definitions or not. This indexical tension is a facet of the larger well-known component of 'strangeness' (the *átopon*) in hermeneutics, which also lurks in dissonance and coherence theories of meaning (cf. e.g. Itkonen 1983: 205–6, Anttila 1989a: 405–7, 409–11). This is also how the little girl Emily, as reported by Bruner (1990: 89), tried to make sense of her life. In addition to being profoundly sensitive to goals, young children are born to solve problems (ibid.: 78):

> A second requirement is early readiness to mark the unusual and to leave the usual unmarked – to concentrate attention and information processing on the offbeat. Young children, indeed, are so easily captivated by the unusual that those of us who conduct research with infants come to count on it. . . . Infants reliably perk up in the presence of the unusual: they look more fixedly, stop sucking, show cardiac deceleration, and so on.

The evolutionary background for hermeneutic attention is thus available, and the same has been noted for primates, too.

A few words must be said about action theory, which has been here in the background behind the practical syllogism and rational explanation. Action of course is directly implied by semiosis. This is not 'pseudoscience', but the very heart of historical explanation. After all, von Wright comes from the analytic tradition, and I have not seen valid arguments against Itkonen's application of the concepts in linguistics. As one would expect, the semiotic emphasis strongly supports it (Zattini 1988), and so does cultural anthropology (Bruner 1990). Such an expectation derives of course from the fact that in all these cases we have to make do with human (interpretative) sciences. Virtual identity between hermeneutic philosophy, linguistics, anthropology, and semiotics supports exactly the primacy of history in human affairs. But there is now further support for action theory within linguistics in Rudi Keller's work and in that of his colleagues (to list here only 1990, and, in English: Keller 1985, Nerlich 1989a, and his contribution in Nerlich 1989b). It seems that there is no influence in it from the traditions mentioned. Keller draws a stricter line between intended action and planned action, and this necessitates a division on the finalistic side. The normal dichotomy that natural phenomena are caused, and cultural ones are intentionally produced, has to be fine-tuned by splitting the man-made (finalistic) part in two: (1) results of intended human action (artefacts) and (2) unintended consequences of human action. Such consequences are caused by human action, and represent thus a kind of causality. These are 'phenomena of the third kind', an example being, e.g. a footpath across a lawn, or a normal traffic jam. The actors do not intend to create such a thing – it results from different people following the same or similar maxims of ease or taking shortcuts, or securing their own safety. Such phenomena are characteristically collective, and this is where language belongs.[32] The collective consequences can be opposite to the private actions. Keller takes as an example some German terms referring to women. On the whole, they tend to become pejorative, and one might think that this reflects a low opinion toward women. But actually the opposite is true. Due to the remnants of the courtly tradition one actually elevates women: to be on the safe side one goes rather higher than lower on the expression level. This way terms that are left behind take on 'lower' readings.

The Scottish moral philosophers of the eighteenth century took on the notion from Mandeville and built their social philosophy on it (it is really surprising that they are unknown to linguists, although they explicitly referred to language).[33] 'Nations stumble upon establishments, which are indeed the result of human action, but not the execution of any human design', wrote Adam Ferguson in 1767 (Keller 1990: 54). Dugald Stewart asked: 'Whence has arisen the systematical beauty which we admire in the structure of a cultivated language.' Since we do not know the historical facts, we have to replace them by conjecture; hence the name *Theoretical or Conjectural History* (ibid.: 55). When individuals follow their own interests thereby contributing to the common good, they are, as it were, led by an invisible hand

(Adam Smith, Wealth of Nations 1776) (Keller 1985: 56). Mandeville gave the impetus for conjectural history, later renamed invisible-hand explanation on the basis of Smith's exposition.

This kind of explanation is of the social sciences variety (Keller 1985: 91), and it is real *theory*, a kind of genetic explanation (92), or a genuinely cultural model (179). The laws are not the problem, but the premises; we reconstruct *them* (ibid.: 101), and this is what happens through abduction also. The unpredictability inherent in it is of course a nuisance for economists and theoretical linguists. But it is even more embarrassing; it shows that theoretical linguists are not theoretical after all. In phenomena of the third kind essence, function and becoming go together, as in any feasible dynamic approach, cf. the semiotic one. Invisible-hand explanation does not explain the genesis, but it is a functional explanation (ibid.: 120), and explanation in the strict sense (101). Keller's final point (on this) is that if one is interested in the fact of language change (a special case of sociocultural change) and its explanation, it is imperative to take it as a phenomenon of the third kind (193), and that there is in fact no other way known to explain language change (194). I think Keller is right, because we have a variant of the practical syllogism here. The main factor of language, or its use, used to be communication. Then came the idea that its evolutionary foundation must rather be mental mapping. And now comes Keller who strongly pushes language as a tool for influencing the environment, i.e., influencing the other members of the community or group toward one's own advantage (ibid.: 16, 128, 131, 192). This aspect fits between the other two, and makes sense there.

The behavioural maxims behind the invisible-hand process (à la Grice) (ibid.: 46, 122–39; also solidly there in Bruner 1990: 48, 63) work the same way, and they certainly agree with the practical syllogism in general, which points more toward the influencing part than anything else. They also agree with the rationality principles in rational explanation. The other leaking syllogism, the abductive one, lurks nicely in Keller's statement that individual competence has a character of a hypothesis, which for its part makes the communicative enterprise have experimental character (1990: 186–9).

Back to causality. Even if people follow the same maxims they do not follow them lawfully; thus, actions do not result lawfully, but they have lawful results (Keller 1985: 147–8; cf. Itkonen 1983: 59: 'We do not use people's behaviour to test our norm-sentence; rather, we use our norm-sentence to test people's behaviour'). This leads to the problem of evolution, for which our language/tradition does not have proper vocabulary; we have it only for growth and creation (ibid: 18–19). For a historical process to be an evolutionary one it has to satisfy the following conditions for Keller: (1) It cannot be teleological, (2) it must be cumulative, and (3) the dynamics of the process must derive from an interplay between variation and selection (ibid.: 179–82). Point (3) has been quite fashionable in linguistics, on the biological model, and Keller treats it well (ibid.: 182–90), as is shown through communication-as-experiment. Language is clearly a cumulative effort (ibid.: 181). But, according to Keller, language change is unambiguously not teleological, although partially goal-directed. It is not teleological, because there is no definite goal or end. This is too restricted a view of teleology, because Keller himself (ibid.: 153, 179) is close to the position (we know from above) that what is important is the potency of present possibilities. However, I repeat, he correctly points out that the Chomskyan rejection of epiphenomena (the dynamics of situated context), which are the interesting aspects of culture (ibid.: 162), means the rejection of being able to treat change at all (163–4); in the Chomskyan frame, language change cannot even be significantly formulated (191). So true, but still so fashionable.[34]

Since I have already transgressed the proper amount of metatheory at one sitting, I might as well sum it up by pointing to the following paradox: as the Scots said, we are doing *theoretical or conjectural history*. The method is philosophical, not historical. But it is hermeneutic, and thus all historical explanation must be done through it.[35] Habit change results inevitably from interpretation in the total human context. Habit is 'the essence of the dynamic logical interpretant' (Peirce: 5.486 in Shapiro 1991: 39), and linguistic signs are habits (Peirce: 4.531 in ibid.).[36] Explication of the iconic index and indexical icon added to the dynamic interpretants is the only way we can understand and explain change. We now have the tools for it all even in linguistics, and as an iron ration I would choose Itkonen (1983), Shapiro (1991), Haley (1988), Keller (1990), and Bruner (1990). Without knowing these works one has hardly any right to talk about explaining or understanding language change. The perspectives are clear – the problem is that linguists are generally not interested. The security of 'nomatterism' is easier, of course.

Notes

1. It is to be understood that my survey has an American emphasis. This is important from the point of view that in America transformational-generative grammar still dominates, whatever the (new) names used might be. The result is that 'historical theory' is inadequate there.

2. Extreme group cohesion secured most linguistics positions to adherents of the transformational-generative group, and the effects of this situation are still felt. Scholarly worth was often blatantly lacking.

3. Cf. the symbol (pp. 51ff.), which absorbs change from the environment, although otherwise it sounds as if the position mentioned were almost true. It is upside down, another favourite metaphor.

4. Even the synchronic theory is questionable here, witness, e.g. Sullivan (1989) who 'shows that these basic postulates of "the" [Government and Binding] theory are invalid logically, empirically, or both. . . . Moreover, it is clear that "the" theory is not a theory of language but a theory of some parts of the structure of language. Add these shortcomings together and we come up with the real mystery: why anybody attempts to apply this approach to linguistic theory to the description of language' (66). We come to the frequently mentioned fact that this is not theory, but rather successful advertising and social success. Theory lies within proper historical linguistics. Keller correctly points out that the Chomskyan rejection of epiphenomena, which are the interesting aspects of culture, means the rejection of being able to treat change at all (1990: 162–4); in fact, in the Chomskyan frame language change cannot even be formulated in a significant way (ibid.: 191). Further, see Shapiro (1991: 4): 'The extreme schematicism of transformational-generative grammar means the almost total neglect of the changeability of languages.' Still, such a position is currently taken as the highest level of 'theory'.

5. In fact, it is viable empiricism that works (Slagle 1974), and this has become quite clear today, e.g. under the so-called 'cognitive linguistics'.

6. Itkonen is of course not alone, witness, e.g. Wildgen: 'generative grammars, logical grammars, AI-systems are variants of structuralism' (1978: 148 fn. 4).

7. Unfortunately I have to leave this out here, but the references are easily available elsewhere (e.g. a very short listing in Anttila 1989a: 54, 178).

8. Cf. the short sketch in Anttila and Embleton (1989: 158 fn. 8).

9. For further references to this, e.g. other works by v. Wright, see Itkonen (1983) and Anttila (1992) and references therein. See also Zattini (1988).

10. And we are back in the tradition, very close, e.g. to Arsène Darmesteter's 'catachresis', or Michel Bréal's 'popular logic'. The semiotic twist, however, gives new depth. The American develop-

ments are represented here, and the European naturalists are just mentioned in passing. Two sectors should be mentioned that have not been adequately appreciated: there is lively activity in semiotics in Germany, of which I list two works by Pape. The same is true of Italy, represented here only by Bonfantini and Zattini.

11. All three aspects create change by nature or definition even. Representation is synonymous with semiosis (cf. Bickerton 1990: 24: representation is a process), semiosis is sign-action.

12. The easiest locus to get acquainted with this line is Itkonen (1983), or as a substitute for the real thing, Anttila (1988a), or as a smaller substitute for the latter, Anttila (1989a: 399–411 = § 23). Further relevant material can be found in Anttila (1989b, 1989c, and 1992).

13. This is not to say that deduction has no place in phenomenology (Dougherty 1983). The (wrong) deductive-nomological method has led linguists astray after predictability as the main criterion in explanation (Shapiro 1991: 65):

> Linguistics has taken over from the philosophy of science a preoccupation with predictability (of linguistic rules, particularly), forgetting that in the case of language (as in all human domains) the best we can do is to assert an overarching rationality and constrain the range of possibilities as much as we can based on our empirical knowledge of actual changes. *The explanation of change* as an instantiation of drift *is, therefore, retrodictive, not predictive, in the time-honored manner of all philological* [read: hermeneutic] *explanations* [emphasis added – RA]. We make sense of accomplished cognitions ('re-cognize').

14. Thagard requires of an account of scientific theories practical, historical, and philosophical adequacy (1988: 34). It is obvious that the ruling theory in linguistics fails in all three. To prove that his computational account is adequate in these he reviews the defects of positivist, set-theoretic, and Kuhnian accounts (35–8). Again, transformational grammar would fare badly, because of its emphasis on syntax with the neglect of semantics and pragmatics (ibid.: 35).

15. That the same comes out in action theory is of course clear in von Wright's work, see also Zattini (1988) for hermeneutics (306, 307, 307, 311, 326), interpretation (307, 311, 326), and intentionality, action, and the practical syllogism (309, 311, 313).

16. In Peirce's system, which is as good as anybody's, and rather more so, the causality we have is interpretative or semiotic or logical causality (e.g. Pape 1988: 96). This is what sign-action means. Furthermore, logic is one of the normative sciences (below phenomenology), and its foundation is speculative grammar, which can roughly be equated with semiotics. Synonyms for speculative grammar are, among other terms, hermeneutic, formal grammar, logical syntax, and universal grammar. Clearly, the self-understanding of linguists is badly astray.

17. It is to Bruner's credit that he expressly touches upon Peirce's sign theory (1990: 46, 69, 149).

18. I will streamline my exposition so that I do not refer here directly to Peirce, to keep my references to a minimum, but instead, I will only refer to Short, Shapiro, Savan, and Pape.

19. Zattini (1988) analyses the formal identity of the abductive and practical syllogisms.

20. A sufficient selection is provided in the bibliography; in the name of better readability I will not stud every sentence of mine with a reference (or more) to these authors. Particularly exciting and important for linguistics is Shapiro (1991), and as a substitute version, Shapiro (1985). In this section I also echo Anttila (1989a: § 23: 'Genetic Linguistics and Metatheory'), which can be taken as an amalgamation and synthesis of Itkonen, Coseriu, Short, and Shapiro, under the auspices of the theory of philology. My present bibliography gives an adequate shortcut to these four authors, also through my own work listed therein.

21. Even the comparative method, the aspect apparently closest to natural-science ideals, works this way: the idea of a protolanguage is adopted first and it acts as a final cause (Anttila 1988b, 1989a: 285–6).

22. The inherent incompleteness of symbols creates a kind of paradox of change. As long as dynamic interpretants provide new rules of modifications thereof in the determination of symbols, change is essential to the function of symbols. If the symbols do not grow this way, they fade away (cf. Shapiro 1991: 118). A paradox like this proves again the primacy of change in meaning structure.

23. A surprising number of rather central terms fall under final causation and teleological considerations (or history in general), as has been pointed out particularly in Shapiro's work aimed at linguists. This is hardly surprising for concepts such as 'development, flux, growth, creation', but rather startling for 'symbol, type, general, law, function, structure, selection, natural class, acquisition, use' (sign-production and sign-interpretation), 'habit', as well as 'description' (since it is pointless without a relative goal). These terms define pragmatics as well, and thus logic gets included, since it is tied to the historical context, and since it changes with time. As Peirce said, that is logical which it is necessary to admit in order to render the universe intelligible. It is clear that synchronic linguistics cannot be talked about without the above terms. The theoretical primacy of history is thus vindicated, once again.

24. Bickerton (1990: 79) gives a good account of the evolutionary basis of iconic indexicality in the evolution of representation, i.e. ultimately symbols. The semiotic substance of these features comes out nicely also in his discussion of a painting of the battle of Lepanto (ibid.: 18).

25. These iconic indexes can still be seen under the current alphabetic symbols, if we want to. E.g., the horns of the snail are still there in F (tilt it 90° left), or the waves of water in M (although unduly sharp), and the oxhead in A (turn it upside down).

26. Rhyming slang thrives even in Australia, witness a recent headline

referring to an important sailing victory: *We beat the Septics! (Yank → septic tank → Septic)*.

27. Anttila (1977) roughly combined analogy and abduction, ending with the practical syllogism. In general, this has been criticized by transformational-generative grammarians. For abduction see also Bonfantini (1987) and *L'abduzione, Versus* 34 1983).

28. Vaught (1986) is a very interesting plea for an analogical relation between the two objects and two interpretants, joining them, and keeping them at a distance. In this way meaning is perfectly analogical (proportional). To stress this, and to satisfy those who like 'scientific' terminology I have rephrased this, to echo terminology that linguists love, as 'meaning is schizoantikeimenic and schizo-semasic' (Anttila 1991: 46). Somehow analogy sounds better.

29. For the enormous amount of literature during the past decade on analogy in the computational paradigm, see Melis' references, and scan the journals *Brain, Brain and Language, Cognitive Psychology, Communication and Cognition, Memory and Cognition*, and so on. Melis' article appeared in a special issue called *Metaphor and Analogy*.

30. In fact, his last chapter (§ 7) is called 'Metaphoric Growth'. I am mainly concerned with § 6: 'Vehicle Interpretation: the Index of Figural Displacement'.

31. Cf. with Bickerton (1990: 86):

> Moreover, the paradox of consciousness – that the more consciousness one has, the more layers of processing divide one from the world – is like so much else in nature, a trade-off. Progressive distancing from the external world is simply the price that is paid for knowing anything about the world at all.

32. The concept derives from Bernard de Mandeville's fable about the bees who were pursuing private gain through all kinds of vices. While doing this they paradoxically contributed toward the common good by boosting the national economy.

33. Apart from Keller (and his colleagues Nerlich and Helmut Lüdtke) Itkonen (1983: 300–2) is about the only exception, although he does not zero in on the language part.

34. Hostility to theory of change and its true explanation is not limited to Chomskyans, note e.g. Lehmann (1990) who hails from American structuralism. One senses that even an attempt at theory and explanation is just obfuscation. Semiotics is put on the level of deconstructionism, whereas in reality transformational grammar belongs together with it. Even more surprising is that the hermeneutic centrality of philology and its importance for historical linguistics totally escapes most linguists.

35. There is this old question: does a falling tree make a noise when there is nobody there to hear it? This is the problem of the pure index. But in history we have to interpret the indexes. Delobelle (1990) is a recent discussion of this in terms of the synchrony/

diachrony axis. Let's say we have a physical event, a bullet hitting a wall, A → B (2):

$$
\begin{array}{ccc}
A_{subj} & & B_{subj} \\
1 \downarrow & 2 & \uparrow 3 \\
A_{obj} & \longrightarrow & B_{obj}
\end{array}
$$

Behind the bullet (2) is a subjective action (1), and to interpret it (3), we have to guess at the rationality behind (1). Only (2) is a spatiotemporal event. This agrees perfectly with Itkonen (cf. Anttila 1989a: 407–8), or with semiotic-logical causality (1 and 3) vs. natural-science causality (2) (cf. Pape 1988: 328).

36. For any law to be real, there then have to be actual effects, interpretations. Note that this is not true in the Chomskyan paradigm, where what *never* happens can be taken as the rule! (Itkonen 1983: 309).

References

ANDERSEN, HENNING (1973) 'Abductive and deductive change', *Language* 49: 765–93.

ANTTILA, RAIMO (1977) *Analogy*. The Hague: Mouton.

ANTTILA, RAIMO (1988a) 'Causality in linguistic theory and in historical linguistics', *Diachronica* 5: 159–80.

ANTTILA, RAIMO (1988b) 'The type and the comparative method.' In ALBRECHT, J. et al., (eds) *Energeia und Ergon: Studia in Honorem Eugenio Coseriu* Vol. 2, Gunter Narr: Tübingen, pp. 75–83.

ANTTILA, RAIMO (1989a) *Historical and Comparative Linguistics*. Amsterdam and Philadelphia: Benjamins.

ANTTILA, RAIMO (1989b) 'Pattern explanation: survival of the fit', *Diachronica* 6: 1–21.

ANTTILA, RAIMO (1989c) 'Collaterality and Genetic Linguistics.' Proceedings of the Charles Sanders Peirce Sesquicentennial International Congress, Harvard, September.

ANTTILA, RAIMO (1991) 'Field Theory of Meaning and Semantic Change.' Linguistic Agency of the University of Duisberg (LAUD) A301. University of Duisburg. Also in KELLERMANN, GÜNTER and MORRISSEY, MICHAEL, D (eds.) *Diachrony within Synchrony: Language History and Cognition*. Duisburger Arbeiten zur Sprach- und Kulturwissenschaft, 14. Frankfurt, etc.: Peter Lang, 1992, pp. 23–83.

ANTTILA, RAIMO (1992) 'Historical explanation and historical linguistics.' *Explanation in historical linguistics* (GARRY W. DAVIS and GREGORY K. IVERSON, eds.), 17–39. Amsterdam and Philadelphia: Benjamins.

ANTTILA, RAIMO and EMBLETON, SHEILA (1989) 'The iconic index: from sound change to rhyming slang', *Diachronica* 6: 155–80.

BICKERTON, DEREK (1990) *Language and Species*. Chicago and London: University of Chicago Press.

BONFANTINI, MASSIMO A. (1987) *La semiosi e l'abduzione*. Milan: Bompiani.

BONFANTINI, M. A. and KLOESEL, CHRISTIAN J. W. (eds) (1988) *Peirceana*. Special issue, *Versus* 49. Milan: Bompiani.

BRUNER, JEROME S. (1990) *Acts of Meaning*. Cambridge and London: Harvard University Press.

COATES, RICHARD (1987) 'Pragmatic sources of analogical reformation.' *Journal of Linguistics* 23: 319–40.

COLLINGWOOD, ROBIN G. (1946) *The Idea of History*. Oxford: Oxford University Press.

COSERIU, EUGENIO (1979) 'Humanwissenschaften und Geschichte. Der Gesichtspunkt eines Linguisten', *Årbok 1978*. Oslo: Det Norske Videnskaps-Akademi, pp. 118–30.

COSERIU, EUGENIO (1980) 'Vom Primat der Geschichte.' *Sprachwissenschaft* 5: 125–45.

DELOBELLE, ANDRÉ (1990) 'Permanences et changements', *Cahiers de l'Institut de Linguistique de Louvain* 16: 199–214.

DIESING, PAUL (1972) *Patterns of Discovery in the Social Sciences*. London: Routledge.

DOUGHERTY, CHARLES J. (1983) 'Peirce's phenomenlogical defense of deduction.' In FREEMAN, E. (ed.) *The Relevance of Charles Peirce*. La Salle, IL: Monist Library of Philosophy, The Hegeler Institute.

GELLNER, ERNST (1968) *Words and Things*. Harmondsworth: Penguin.

GOUDGE, THOMAS A. (1965) 'Peirce's Index', Transactions of the Charles S. Peirce Society, London, Vol. 1, pp. 52–70.

HALEY, MICHAEL CABOT (1988) *The Semeiosis of Poetic Metaphor*. Bloomington and Indianpolis, IN: Indiana University Press.

HELMAN, DAVID H. (ed.) (1988) *Analogical Reasoning: Perspectives of Artificial Intelligence, Cognitive Science, and Philosophy*. Dordrecht: Kluwer.

ITKONEN, ESA (1978) *Grammatical Theory and Metascience*. Amsterdam: Benjamins.

ITKONEN, ESA (1983) *Causality in Linguistic Theory: A Critical Investigation into the Philosophical and Methodological Foundations of 'Non-Autonomous' Linguistics*. London and Canberra: Croom Helm; Bloomington, IN: Indiana University Press, 1984.

KAPITAN, TOMIS (1989) 'Peirce and the Structure of Abductive Inference.' Proceedings of the Charles Sanders Peirce Sesquicentennial International Congress, Harvard, September.

KELLER, RUDI (1985) 'Towards a Theory of Linguistic Change.' In BALLMER, T. T. (ed.) *Linguistic Dynamics: Discourses, Procedures and Evolution*. Berlin: Mouton de Gruyter, pp. 211–37.

KELLER, RUDI (1990) *Sprachwandel: Von der unsichtbaren Hand in der Sprache*. Tübingen: Francke.

LEHMANN, WINFRED P. (1990) Review of ANTTILA, R. *Historical and Comparative Linguistics* (1989a), *Studies in Language* 14: 249–51.

MARTIN, REX (1977) *Historical Explanation: Re-Enactment and Practical Inference*. Ithaca and London: Cornell University Press.

MELIS, E. (1989) 'Grundlagen von Analogiebildung – Zu Perspektiven ihrer Rechnerstützung.' *Communication and Cognition* 22: 87–110.

NERLICH, BRIGITTE (1989a) 'Elements for an integral theory of language change', *Journal of Literary Semantics* **18**: 163–86.

NERLICH, BRIGITTE (1989b) *Linguistic Evolution*. Special Issue, *Lingua* 77/2. Amsterdam: North-Holland.

PAPE, HELMUT (1988) 'Einleitung.' *Naturordnung und Zeichenprozess: Schriften über Semiotik und Naturphilosophie* by Charles S. Peirce (KIENZLE, B. trans.) Aachen: Alano Verlag/Rader Publikationen, pp. 11–109.

PAPE, HELMUT (1989) *Erfahrung und Wirklichkeit als Zeichenprozeß: Charles S. Peirces Entwurf einer Spekulativen Grammatik des Seins*. Frankfurt: Suhrkamp.

ROMAINE, SUZANNE (1982) *Socio-Historical Linguistics: Its Status and Methodology*. Cambridge and New York: Cambridge University Press.

SAVAN, DAVID (1980) 'Abduction and Semiotics.' *The Signifying Animal* (RAUCH, I. and CARR, G. F. eds). Bloomington, IN: Indiana University Press.

SAVAN, DAVID (1988) *An Introduction to C. S. Peirce's Full System of Semeiotic*. Toronto: Toronto Semiotic Circle.

SHAPIRO, MICHAEL (1976) *Asymmetry: An Inquiry into the Linguistic Structure of Poetry*. Amsterdam: North-Holland.

SHAPIRO, MICHAEL (1983) *The Sense of Grammar: Language of Semeiotic*. Bloomington, IN: Indiana University Press.

SHAPIRO, MICHAEL (1985) 'Teleology, Semeiosis, and Linguistic Change', *Diachronica* **2**; 1–34.

SHAPIRO, MICHAEL (1991) *The Sense of Change: Language as History*. Bloomington, IN: Indiana University Press.

SHORT, THOMAS L. (1981a) 'Semiosis and Intentionality.' TCSPS **17**: 198–223.

SHORT, THOMAS L. (1981b) 'Peirce's Concept of Final Causation.' TCSPS **17**: 369–82.

SHORT, THOMAS L. (1982) 'Life among the Legisigns.' TCSPS **18**: 285–311.

SHORT, THOMAS L. (1984) 'Some Problems Concerning Peirce's Conceptions of Concepts and Propositions.' TCSPS **20**: 20–37.

SHORT, THOMAS L. (1988) 'The Growth of Symbols', *Cruzeiro semiótico*, no. **8**: 81–7.

SLAGLE, UHLAN VON (1974) *Language, Thought, and Perception: A Proposed Theory of Meaning*. The Hague: Mouton.

SULLIVAN, WILLIAM J. (1989) 'Four postulates of government and binding theory.' In BREND, RUTH M. and LOCKWOOD, DAVID G. (eds) *The Fifteenth LACUS Forum*. Lake Bluff, IL: Linguistic Association of Canada and the United States, pp. 57–68.

THAGARD, PAUL (1988) *Computational Philosophy of Science*. Cambridge and London: MIT Press.

VAUGHT, CARL G. (1986) 'Semiotics and the Problem of Analogy: a Critique of Peirce's Theory of Categories.' TCSPS **22**: 311–26.

VON WRIGHT, GEORG HENRIK (1971) *Explanation and Understanding*. London: Routledge.

WILDGEN, WOLFGANG (1987) 'Dynamic aspects of nominal composition.' In BALLMER, TH. T. and WILDGEN, W. (eds) *Process Linguistics: Exploring the Processual Aspects of Language and Language Use, and the Methods of their Description*. Tübingen: Neimeyer, pp. 128–62.

ZATTINI, IVAN (1988) 'La logica dell'azione e la storia', In BOERI, RENATO (ed.) *Il pensiero inventivo*. Milan: Edizioni Unicopli, pp. 304–27.

Chapter 3

Typology and reconstruction

Bernard Comrie

1 General considerations

The reconstruction of proto-languages is one of the most traditional tasks of historical-comparative linguistics, indeed the reconstruction of Proto-Indo-European is rightly considered one of the triumphs of nineteenth-century linguistic science. Although typology can trace its ancestry back even further than historical linguistics, it is only relatively recently that it has burgeoned to gain acceptance as a fully-fledged sub-discipline of linguistics. What, then, is the possible relationship between these two sub-disciplines? In order to answer this question, it is necessary to have some understanding of what kinds of questions typology tries to answer. While different linguists might give somewhat different answers, I will assume that the following constitute a plausible sub-set of possible answers.[1]

First, typology is concerned with the question of what constitutes a possible human language. There are two distinct but interrelated ways in which one might approach this question. The first is empirical, i.e. we try and place constraints on possible human languages by examining and generalizing across what we find in attested languages. The second is theoretical, i.e. on the basis of limited observations of attested languages we construct hypotheses about probable constraints on human languages, which we are then free to test against data from other languages. Although the empirical and theoretical approaches are often contrasted, even considered antagonistic, in effect they only reflect different degrees of emphasis, since any generalization we make from the set of observed languages to human language in general is necessarily theoretical, and any theory designed to be measured against the facts of languages is necessarily empirical.

And advances in linguistic typology suggest indeed that there is a need for fruitful cooperation between more empirical and more theoretical approaches.

There are several ways in which typology may delimit the class of human languages. For instance, it may say that every human language has to have some specified property, e.g. that it must have consonants. Or it may specify that every human language must lack some specified property, e.g. sounds integrated into the phonemic system with an air-stream mechanism that involves trapping air between the tongue and the lower lip (cf. Pike 1943: 101). Or it may specify a constraint on the co-occurrence of properties, e.g. that a language can have nasalized vowels only if it also has non-nasalized vowels; such restrictions are often referred to as implicational universals. It should be noted that some linguists draw a distinction (not made here) between the study of language universals and language typology, whereby language universals would be concerned strictly with properties that must be present in every language, while the study of restrictions on co-occurrence of properties would form part of the subject matter of language typology.

Second, typology is, or at least may be, concerned with the plausibility of various properties of human language, an area of study that sometimes goes under the name of universal tendencies or statistical universals. Empirical evidence can come from patterns of cross-linguistic distribution that diverge markedly from random. For instance, very few languages have a basic word order where the object appears before the subject, i.e. where the most neutral way of saying 'the cat ate the mouse' would be one of the following: 'ate the mouse the cat', 'the mouse ate the cat', 'the mouse the cat ate'. By contrast, basic word orders in which the subject precedes the object are very widespread, i.e. one of the following: 'the cat the mouse ate', 'the cat ate the mouse', 'ate the cat the mouse'. Thus, we might argue that the pattern whereby the subject precedes the object is more plausible, or less marked, typologically, without, however, saying that the opposite pattern is excluded (which would clearly be empirically incorrect). In one sense of the term 'markedness', unmarked would correspond to what we are here calling 'more plausible'.

In principle, the distinction between absolute statements and statements of tendencies is an important one, but in practice the situation is by no means so straightforward. Of course, if we know that some language is an exception to a typological generalization, then we know that that generalization is at best a tendency. Suppose, however, that someone has proposed a typological generalization to which no exception is known. It is always conceivable that such a generalization might be overthrown by data from some as yet undescribed language; indeed this is precisely what happened with the generalization about subjects typically preceding objects in unmarked word order, which was until quite recently widely held to be an absolute universal. In this respect, it is important to bear in mind that the number of linguistic properties with which we are dealing is immense. Given that we are dealing with such a large number of properties, it is not inconceivable that a few such properties might have very skewed distributions, even given the large number of languages to which we have access. If a putative absolute universal has a principled basis, i.e. can be shown to follow from some more general property of language or cognition, then it has a better chance of being indeed exceptionless with respect to possible human languages, though again this does not guarantee absolute reliability.

How does all of this relate to reconstruction in historical-comparative linguistics? The end-product of a reconstruction is a characterization of a language that is hypothesized to have been spoken in the past.[2] This reconstructed language can be tested against the same typological generalizations as are applicable to attested languages. Thus, we can ask of a particular reconstructed language whether it is consistent with what we believe to be constraints on possible human languages, and if the answer is negative then we should seriously reconsider the reconstruction. We can also ask of a particular reconstruction whether it is plausible, though here we are on more dangerous ground since 'implausible' does not mean the same as 'impossible', and there are even some instances where a typologically implausible reconstruction might, for other reasons, be readily acceptable. For instance, all languages of the Khoisan family of southwestern Africa have clicks as part of their regular phoneme inventory, although clicks are otherwise virtually unknown as part of the regular phoneme inventory of languages. Standard procedures of reconstruction, in particular the comparative method, would lead us to postulate clicks in Proto-Khoisan, and presumably no one would reject this reconstruction on grounds of typological implausibility, given that every descendant of Proto-Khoisan has clicks.

One limitation on the application of typology, in particular of implicational universals, in the evaluation of reconstructions is that any reconstruction is necessarily partial: the evidence from attested languages enables us to build up a partial picture of their ancestor, but there will always be properties of the ancestor that we are unable to reconstruct because evidence for them has been lost from all descendant languages. For instance, examination of the modern Romance languages would not lead us to conclude that Latin has a six-case system. Thus, a reconstruction tells us things that the proto-language had, but does not necessarily tell us what things it did not have. It there is an implicational universal 'if p, then q', and we reconstruct a language that has p but lacks q, this could in principle be due to the attested languages' having lost all traces of q but still retaining enough evidence to reconstruct p when the proto-language in fact had both p and q.

There is an important assumption implicit in the foregoing, namely that there has been no change in the range of potential typological variation in human language since the time at which such reconstructed languages are assumed to have been spoken and the present day. In fact, for the time-depth at which we work in most reconstructions this is a plausible assumption. Proto-Indo-European, for instance, is usually assumed to have been spoken some 4500 to 6500 years before the present, and most other reconstructed proto-languages involve similar or shallower time-depths. This is a short period compared with the overall history of human language: the most conservative estimates would date the latest possible time for the origin of human language to around 35,000 years before the present (i.e. the time of the start of the major migrations that carried Homo sapiens to most parts of the world), with 100,000 years before the present being closer to the consensus date (i.e. the appearance of Homo sapiens). Thus if there are typological generalizations that characterize languages attested today, they are probably equally true of languages spoken up to 10,000 years ago; at any rate, this assumption will be made in what follows.

As an illustration of how typology can be used to constrain reconstructions, we may consider a simple example involving a conflict between the comparative method, as strictly applied, and typological possibility or plausibility. First, let us take an example where there is no conflict. In both European and Syrian varieties of Romany, a language (or more accurately group of languages) of the Indo-Aryan sub-branch of the Indo-Iranian branch of Indo-European, there are two sibilant phonemes, s and š. Yet if we look at correspondence sets between European and Syrian Romany, we find that there are three, with no evidence of complementary distribution between any pair of them. Given this, strict application of the comparative method requires setting up three sibilant phonemes in Proto-Romany, as in Table 3.1 (Anttila 1989: 245–6). Now, there is nothing typologically implausible about three sibilant phonemes in a single language, indeed the system hypothesized for Proto-Romany is exactly the same as that attested in Sanskrit. Actually, the comparison goes further in this case: Sanskrit is an ancient language of the Indo-Aryan sub-branch, and in cognates we find exact correspondence between the reconstructed Proto-Romany sibilants and the attested sibilants of Sanskrit, so that here the Sanskrit data serve as independent confirmation of the correctness of the reconstruction of Proto-Romany.

TABLE 3.1   Romany sibilants

European Romany	Syrian Romany	Proto-Romany
s	s	*s
š	s	*ś
š	š	*š

A different situation is provided by vowel correspondences in Chukchee and Koryak, two closely related languages of the Chukotko-Kamchatkan family of north-eastern Siberia. Chukchee is a dialectally relatively homogeneous language, while Koryak is dialectally much more divided, indeed some varieties that are sometimes considered dialects of Koryak are perhaps more accurately to be considered separate languages, for example Alutor. Both languages have a system of vowel harmony, whereby the vowels are divided into two sets of three such that all the vowels in a given word must belong to one and only one set: in words with recessive vowels, these are i, u, e_1; in words with dominant vowels, the correspondents are e_2, o, a; e_1 and e_2 are clearly distinguishable morphophonemically. In addition, there is a schwa vowel $ə$, which is clearly sometimes phonemic in Chukchee and possibly sometimes phonemic in Koryak, although the schwa will play no role in the following discussion. In general, a given vowel of Chukchee appears also in cognate Koryak items, except that some instances of e_1 appear as a, the precise number of such correspondences varying from dialect to dialect until one reaches Alutor, the variety most distinct from Chukchee, in which all e_1's correspond to a, indeed where the division between the two sets of vowels is lost completely so that there are just three (non-schwa) vowels i, u, a. Let us suppose that we take Chukchee and three different varieties of Koryak with different distributions of e_1 and a, and that we have correspondences as in Table 3.2. Now, strict application of the comparative method would require us to set up for Proto-Chukotko-Kamchatkan five distinct vowel phonemes, one for each correspondence set, in the phonetic area from mid-front vowel to low central vowel. Typologically, such a system is highly implausible, especially given that the reconstruction has no corresponding richness of back vowels. And indeed, as far as I am aware no investigator of Chukchee and Koryak has been led to posit such a system for Proto-Chukotko-Kamchatkan. Rather, all have assumed that we have here a case of lexical diffusion, with a rule shifting e_1 to a whose domain becomes more extensive as one moves further away from Chukchee.

TABLE 3.2 Correspondences between Chukchee and three Koryak dialects

Chukchee	Koryak-1	Koryak-2	Koryak-3
e_1	e_1	e_1	e_1
e_1	e_1	e_1	a
e_1	e_1	a	a
e_1	a	a	a
a	a	a	a

In the core of this article, we will examine two sets of data from the reconstruction of Proto-Indo-European phonology. The choice of these data-sets is not accidental. The proto-language of the Indo-European family is the one that has been subject to most intensive investigation within historical-comparative linguistics, so a wealth of data are available for testing against general methodological principles; yet despite (or perhaps because of) the amount of work that has been done on reconstructing Proto-Indo-European, there remain areas of great controversy, in particular surrounding the phonation types (e.g. voicing, aspiration) of Proto-Indo-European and concerning the relation between the phonemically distinct vowel qualities and the laryngeal consonant phonemes of Proto-Indo-European. The choice of phonology rather than syntax, even though much of the recent work in typology has been syntactic, follows not so much from any question of principle as from the greater ease with which specific questions can be formulated and even, at least to some extent, answered with respect to the reconstruction of Proto-Indo-European phonology.

In discussing Proto-Indo-European, it is important to bear in mind that the term Proto-Indo-European is usually taken to cover a considerable span of time leading to the break-up of a single language into the various individual branches of the Indo-European family, and that during this period Proto-Indo-European was changing. In particular, it is useful to distinguish between Early and Late Proto-Indo-European. Our reconstruction of Late Proto-Indo-European proceeds essentially by application of the comparative method, and may be equated more or less with the classical reconstruction of Brugmann (1897–1916). Our reconstruction of Early Proto-Indo-European, given the absence of comparative data to set against those from the reconstruction of Late Proto-Indo-European, relies heavily on internal reconstruction and includes, for instance, the hypotheses set forth by the laryngeal theory (discussed further in section 3 below).

2   Phonation types in Proto-Indo-European

By the term phonation type we understand such distinctions as that of voiced versus voiceless, aspirated versus unaspirated, breathy versus creaky versus plain voice, all of which are concerned with the state of the vocal cords in producing sounds (Ladefoged 1971: 7–22). More specifically, we shall be concerned with the status of voice and aspiration in reconstructed Proto-Indo-European, although as will become clear below the notion of breathy voice will also play a role. The definitions of the relevant phonetic categories are as follows. Voice involves vibration of the vocal cords during the production of a sound, while voicelessness refers to the absence of such vibration. Aspiration refers to a period of voicelessness immediately after the pronunciation of a voiceless consonant. Breathy voice involves, articulatorily, holding the vocal cords further apart during voicing than is the case for normal voicing, with the result that more air escapes during the articulation of the given sound.

In the classical reconstruction of Proto-Indo-European, four distinct phonation types are reconstructed, namely voiceless unaspirated (e.g. *t*), voiced unaspirated (e.g. *d*), voiceless aspirated (e.g. *th*) and 'voiced aspirated' (e.g. *dh*; the careful reader will note that the combination 'voiced aspirated' is inconsistent with the phonetic definitions given above, a point to which we shall return). The three-way opposition among voiceless unaspirated, voiced unaspirated and 'voiced aspirated' is well established in that a number of branches of Indo-European have distinct reflexes of the three types, e.g. in

Sanskrit (Indo-Iranian branch) they show up as voiceless
unaspirated, voiced unaspirated and 'voiced aspirated' respectively, in Greek (sole representative of the Hellenic branch) they
show up as voiceless unaspirated, voiced unaspirated and
voiceless aspirated respectively, in Latin they show up as
voiceless unaspirated, voiced unaspirated and either voiceless
fricative (word-initially and, for the velars, in all positions) or
voiced unaspirated (other than word-initially for the labial and
dental) respectively. Compare Sanskrit *trayas*, Greek *treĩs*, Latin
trēs 'three' for **t*; Sanskrit *damas*, Greek *dómos*, Latin *domus*
'house' for **d*; Sanskrit *bharāmi*, Greek *phérō*, Latin *ferō* 'I
carry' for **bh*. Less certain is the status in Proto-Indo-European
of the voiceless aspirated phonation type. The strongest evidence
for a distinct voiceless aspirated phonation type comes from the
Indo-Iranian branch, where the putative type shows up as
voiceless aspirated stops in the Indo-Aryan sub-branch (including
Sanskrit) and as voiceless fricatives in the Iranian sub-branch,
presumably reflecting voiceless aspirated stops in Proto-Indo-
Iranian. Given this, it is conceivable that the development of a
distinct voiceless aspirated type could reflect an innovation of
Indo-Iranian, rather than an inheritance from Proto-Indo-
European that has been lost in most of the other branches. In the
other branches there are either inconsistencies in the correspondences to Proto-Indo-Iranian voiceless aspirated stops (e.g.
putative Proto-Indo-European **th* appears in Greek now as *t*,
now as *th*) or the putative opposition between voiceless
unaspirated and voiceless aspirated stops has been lost. On the
basis of these observations, the currently most widespread
reconstruction of Proto-Indo-European operates with only three
phonation types for stops, which we may continue provisionally
to call voiceless unaspirated, voiced unaspirated and 'voiced
aspirated'.

In what follows, we will not be concerned with the evaluation
of the three-term reconstruction from the viewpoint of the
comparative method; for a discussion of this, reference may be
made to Szemerényi (1989: 69–71, 150–3, 159–63), who concludes
on balance that the four-term reconstruction is preferable,
though as noted above this seems to be a minority position
among scholars actively working in this area. Rather, we are
concerned whether typological considerations can provide criteria
that might enable us to resolve the controversy. The relevant
factor is a claim that has been made in the typological literature
(e.g. Hopper 1973) that it is impossible for a language to have
voiced aspirated consonants unless it also has voiceless aspirated

consonants, i.e. corresponding to the implicational universal: If a language has voiced aspirated consonants, then it must also have voiceless aspirated consonants. If this generalization is correct, then the three-term reconstruction of Proto-Indo-European phonation types as voiceless unaspirated, voiced unaspirated and 'voiced aspirated' could be rejected out of hand, as violating a typological constraint on possible languages. If one accepts this typological constraint, then there are two ways one might proceed. The first is to return to the four-term reconstruction of Proto-Indo-European phonation types; the typological argument is, incidentally, adduced (though in an ancillary role) by Szemerényi (1989: 151) as an argument in favour of this reconstruction. The second is to question the phonetic definition of the three types in the three-term reconstruction. One phonetic redefinition of the three-term system that has gained quite widespread support recently, as the so-called glottalic theory, would reinterpret the triple *t–d–dh* as *t–t'–d*, where *t'* represents a glottalized (ejective) stop and where aspiration is absent, at least as a phonemically distinctive feature (e.g. Hopper 1973). Again, it is not our intention to evaluate the glottalic theory as such.

Let us now turn directly to the point that is of greatest interest to us here, namely the typological evaluation of the *t–d–dh* three-term reconstruction of Proto-Indo-European phonation types. As noted above, the older interpretation of this triad involving 'voiced aspirated' stops is in any event in need of phonetic reinterpretation, since the notion of 'voiced aspirate' is phonetically untenable. In the modern Indo-Aryan languages that have so-called 'voiced aspirated' stops, the usual phonetic realization to which this term corresponds are stops with breathy voice, and this provides at least a plausible phonetic reconstruction for Proto-Indo-European, i.e. the three-term phonation-type system might have been: voiceless (e.g. *t*), plain voiced (e.g. *d*), breathy-voiced (e.g. *dh*; note that we may continue to use the same symbolization). The typological question can now be reformulated as follows: Is it possible for a language to have breathy-voiced stops without also having voiceless aspirate stops? It should be noted that establishing a relationship between breathy-voiced and voiceless aspirated stops is not implausible; for instance, Chomsky and Halle (1968: 326) subsume them both under a general phonetic term 'heightened subglottal pressure'.

The most obvious evidence to use in answering the typological question just posed are the data from the Indo-Aryan languages, and no doubt the ready availability of these data influenced the original negative answer to this typological question. Most Indo-

Aryan languages have the four-way opposition *t–d–th–dh*, though a few have reduced phonation type systems. Sinhala (spoken in Sri Lanka) has lost the opposition of 'aspiration' altogether, i.e. it has only the *t–d* opposition, and is therefore irrelevant to our concerns. More relevant information is provided by Panjabi (Bhatia 1975), which has simplified the four-way system to three by losing the breathy-voiced vowels (with concomitant phonologization of tonal oppositions; compare Hindi *koṛa* 'whip' and *ghoṛa* 'horse' with Panjabi *kōṛa* and *kòṛa*, respectively, where the macron indicates mid tone and the grave accent indicates low tone); Panjabi thus has the system *t–d–th*. Evidence pointing in the same direction can be seen in the way in which some varieties of Malayalam borrow words of Indo-Aryan origin. Malayalam is a Dravidian language of southwestern India and like most Dravidian languages has no phonation-type phonemic oppositions in its native lexicon. However, Malayalam has borrowed intensively from Indo-Aryan, primarily Sanskrit, to a much greater extent than any of the other major Dravidian languages. While some speakers have incorporated the four-way phonation type system of Indo-Aryan into their speech, others have a reduced phonation type system, with the breathy-voiced stops the least likely to be maintained distinct, usually being replaced, for these speakers, by either plain voiced or voiceless aspirated stops.[3] All of these data from South Asian languages would seem to confirm the generalization that breathy-voiced stops presuppose the existence of voiceless aspirated stops.

However, there are two methodological problems with these data. First, the data all come from a genetically and areally very restricted subset of the world's languages, so one might well entertain doubts about their more general validity. Secondly, the quantity of evidence is rather meagre, because the only crucial cases are languages with voiceless aspirated stops but lacking breathy-voiced stops, in comparison with the absence of languages having breathy-voiced stops but lacking voiceless aspirated stops. Especially given the small amount of data, one might well feel more justified in arguing that the relation between breathy-voiced and voiceless unaspirated stops is one of markedness rather than of a strict implication, i.e. that languages are more likely to have voiceless aspirated stops than to have breathy-voiced stops, without there being a strict constraint against a language having breathy-voiced stops but lacking aspirated voiceless stops; the evidence available is too meagre to permit any kind of statistical discrimination of the two possibilities. And if the relationship is one of markedness rather than one of implication, then at best the reconstruction of Proto-Indo-European as having the three-term phonation type opposition t–d–dh is less likely, but by no means excluded. One might compare with this the observation that, while voiceless obstruents are less marked than voiced obstruents, whence specifically p is less marked than b, this does not deny the possibility of languages like Arabic that have b but no p.

In fact, South Asia is not the only part of the world in which breathy-voiced stops are found. Stewart (1989: 231–9) gives a detailed account of the occurrence of essentially similar sounds in some African languages, especially but not exclusively languages of the Kwa branch of the Niger-Congo family. In these Kwa languages, the opposition is referred to as one of fortis versus lenis, where 'voiced lenis' corresponds to 'breathy-voiced'. Some of these languages, such as Ebrié, have the four-way opposition of phonation type expected from the intersection of the two binary features voiceless/voiced and fortis/lenis. However, some of the languages, such as Mbatto, have lost one of the four series, and in each attested case it is the voiceless lenis stop type that is lost, i.e. these languages show precisely the opposite pattern from that found in South Asia (ibid.: 1989: 238). Indeed, Stewart goes on to propose precisely the opposite marking value from that suggested by the South Asian data; presumably more independent cases will need to be investigated to resolve this discrepancy. But at any rate, as Stewart explicitly notes in his presentation (ibid.: 238–9), the similarity of the phonation types in Mbatto to those in the three-way t–d–dh phonation type reconstruction of Proto-Indo-European strongly suggests that typological considerations cannot be adduced to rule out, or even to characterize as implausible, this particular aspect of the reconstruction of the Proto-Indo-European phonological system. The reconstruction with three phonation types, voiceless, plain voiced and breathy-voiced, is fully consistent with what is known from language typology.

3 Reflections on the Proto-Indo-European vowel system

The nature of the vowel system of Proto-Indo-European is an area of great current controversy. The traditional (Late Proto-Indo-European) reconstruction posits five vowels (i, e, a, o, u), each occurring both long and short, plus a sixth vowel, ə, the so-called schwa, occurring only short. This reconstructed vowel system survives almost intact into Ancient Greek, especially in those dialects which, unlike Attic, do not shift ā to ē; the schwa is reconstructed on the basis of correspondences between i in Indo-

Iranian and *a* in most other branches (including Hellenic). In addition to these monophthongs, this reconstruction also assigns to Proto-Indo-European a rich array of diphthongs, since each vowel can combine with each of non-syllabic *i̯* (*y*), *u̯* (*w*), *l*, *r*, *m*, *n* to form a set of falling diphthongs. Since the liquids and sonorants can also appear as syllabic nuclei, the set of syllabic (syllable-nucleus) segments is further extended to include *l̥*, *r̥*, *m̥*, *n̥*. (Note that in Indo-European linguistics, it is customary to use a subscript circle to indicate syllabicity, a convention retained here.) Yet much subsequent work has tended to reduce drastically the number of vowels posited for Early Proto-Indo-European, in the extreme case reducing the vowel inventory to just the one vowel *e*!

First, since the syllabic and nonsyllabic varieties of the sonants (*i*, *u*, *l*, *r*, *m*, *n*) do not contrast phonemically, syllabicity being predictable from the phonological environment, they can plausibly be eliminated from the inventory of vowels, i.e. there are phonemes /y, w, l, r, m, n/ which have syllabic allophones in the appropriate environments. But the major reduction in vowel inventory size was made possible by the work of Saussure (1879). The basis for Saussure's radical revision of the reconstruction of the Proto-Indo-European vowel inventory is the phenomenon of ablaut, a morphophonemic alternation that characterized Proto-Indo-European and is found, in more and less clear forms, in the various branches of the family. In essence, ablaut involves an alternation among a basic vowel *e* (*e*-grade), the vowel *o* (*o*-grade), and the absence of any vowel (ø, zero-grade).[4] Ablaut alternations are found in particularly clear form in Ancient Greek, as can be seen in the alternation between accusative singular *patéra* 'father', accusative singular *eupátora* 'born of a noble father' and genitive singular *patrós* 'father', all with a derivational suffix *-ter* and its ablaut variants *-tor*, *-tr*. The alternation *e–o–ø* can also combine with a sonant to give diphthongal ablaut series, as in the following first-person singular forms of the Ancient Greek verb 'leave': present *leípō*, perfect *léloipa*, aorist *élipon*, where the verb stem shows the alternants *leip–loip–lip*. Note that in *leip* and *loip*, the *i* is non-syllabic, whereas in *lip* it is syllabic, this following naturally from the non-phonemic status of syllabicity in Proto-Indo-European. In examples of this type, one might assume, by following through internal reconstruction (and thereby removing morphophonemic alternations from the proto-language), that the only proto-vowel represented in examples so far is *e*, with *o* as a morphophonemic derivative thereof.

Some ablaut alternations, however, seem to fall outside this general pattern. For instance, on the basis of Ancient Greek forms like *títhēmi* 'I put (present tense)', *thōmós* 'heap', *títhemen* 'we put (present tense)', it proves necessary, on the traditional reconstruction, to set up the ablaut series *ē–ō–ǝ*, *ā–ō–ǝ* and *ō–ō–ǝ*, the so-called long-vowel ablaut series. (Note that in the *ō–ō–ǝ* serie, *ō* occurs both where one finds *e* and where one finds *o* of the basic ablaut series.) On the basis of alternations like Sanskrit *janitar-* 'parent', *jāta-* 'born (past participle passive)', where Sanskrit *ani* represents Proto-Indo-European **enǝ/onǝ* and *ā* represents **n̥*, it proves necessary to set up ablaut series like *enǝ–onǝ–n̥*, or more generally *eRǝ–oRǝ–R̥*, where *R* is any sonant. Continuing to use *R* as a cover symbol for any sonant, the patterns can be set out as in Table 3.3. In this table, type (ii) is, of course, just a special case of type (i).

TABLE 3.3   Ablaut patterns in Proto-Indo-European

(i)		e	o	ø
(ii)		eR	oR	R̥
(iii)	(a)	ē	ō	ǝ
	(b)	ā	ō	ǝ
	(c)	ō	ō	ǝ
(iv)		eRǝ	oRǝ	R̥

Saussure noticed that in types (iii) and (iv), vowel length and schwa are in complementary distribution and suggested that both should be regarded as reflexes of a sound that we can represent as *H*, a type of sound that has come to be known as a laryngeal, whence the theory initiated by Saussure is known as the laryngeal theory. Under this hypothesis, lines (iii) and (iv) of Table 3.3 can be rewritten as Table 3.4, in which type (iv) is now a special case of type (i) of Table 3.3. Note that schwa is hereby reanalysed as a syllabic laryngeal, paralleling the syllabic sonants, whereas long *e*, *a*, *o* are effectively reanalysed as diphthongs with *H* as second, non-syllabic component.

TABLE 3.4   First reanalysis of ablaut patterns in Proto-Indo-European

(iii)	(a)	eH	oH	H̥
	(b)	aH	oH	H̥
	(c)	oH	oH	H̥
(iv)		eRH̥	oRH̥	R̥H

Type (iii) remains unusual in that in the *e*-grade, alongside *e* both *a* and *o* are found in some lexical items. This anomaly can be removed if one makes the assumption that what originally distinguished (a), (b) and (c) within (iii) was not the quality of the vowel, but rather the quality of the laryngeal, i.e. there were three distinct laryngeals, one with *e*-like quality (H_e), one with *a*-like quality (H_a) and one with *o*-like quality (H_o). Type (iii) of Table 3.4 can now be reanalysed as in Table 3.5, whereby types (a)–(c) are all special cases of line (d), which is in turn a special case of type (i) of Table 3.3.

TABLE 3.5 Second reanalysis of ablaut patterns in Proto-Indo-European

(iii)	(a)	eH_e	oH_e	$H̥_e$
	(b)	eH_a	oH_a	$H̥_a$
	(c)	eH_o	oH_o	$H̥_o$
	(d)	eH	oH	$H̥$

We can get from the representations of (iii) in Table 3.5 and (iv) in Table 3.4 to those in Table 3.3 by means of small number of very straightforward rules, corresponding to sound changes in the historical development of Proto-Indo-European under the laryngeal theory. In particular: the laryngeals assign their quality to an adjacent *e* (though not to an adjacent *o*); the sequence of a vowel (or syllabic sonant) plus a following laryngeal is replaced by the long equivalent of that vowel (or syllabic sonant); the syllabic laryngeal becomes *ə*. This line of analysis also provides a solution for certain other problems in Proto-Indo-European phonology. Although most Proto-Indo-European lexical roots have the shape *Ce(R)C*, where C stands for any consonant, a certain number begin with a vowel, where this vowel may be not only *e*, but also *a* or *o*, for instance **es-* 'be', **aug-* 'grow', **okʷ-* 'eye'. We can now assume that originally these words began with a laryngeal, and that the difference in vowel quality is not original but derives from different initial laryngeals, i.e. **H_ees-*, **H_aewg-*, **H_oekʷ-*. The quality of the vowel will be affected by that of the adjacent laryngeal, as already implied by the first rule we formulated above. Subsequently, laryngeals before a vowel were lost, without occasioning lengthening of the adjacent vowel. If we follow this analysis through to its logical conclusion, then we eliminate the vowels *a* and *o* from the inventory of Proto-Indo-European and end up with a system having only one vowel, namely *e*.

Although the basic argument of the laryngeal theory rests on reconstruction, some aspects of the theory found independent validation when Hittite was deciphered early in the twentieth century, since Hittite, a language of what is now called the Anatolian branch of Indo-European, has an *h* in some of the positions where the laryngeal theory posits a laryngeal consonant. Hittite does not, however, present any direct evidence for more than one laryngeal consonant.

This hypothesis of a one-vowel system for Early Proto-Indo-European is radically different from the traditional reconstruction of Late Proto-Indo-European, but what interests us here is not so much this question as whether the new reconstruction is typologically plausible, or even typologically possible. A further question that we can ask is whether the changes we have posited in going from this one-vowel reconstruction to the multi-vowel systems of the oldest attested Indo-European languages are plausible, especially given that under this analysis there are some exceptions, to be discussed below, to the regular operation of the sound changes posited.

Let us take first the question whether a one-vowel system is typologically possible or plausible. Before confronting the question directly, it is necessary to consider an implication of the notion of the incompleteness of reconstruction as discussed in section 1. In a sense, what our reconstruction says is not that Early Proto-Indo-European had only one vowel, but rather that none of the vowel oppositions posited for Late Proto-Indo-European was present in Early Proto-Indo-European; it is quite conceivable that in Early Proto-Indo-European there may have been other vowel oppositions of which no, or insufficient, traces survive in the attested languages. Under this scenario, there might have been no stage of Proto-Indo-European that lacked vowel oppositions, and the apparent one-vowel reconstruction would be a reflection of the incompleteness of our reconstruction. An analogy may make this clearer. In Proto-Slavonic, there was an opposition between rising (acute) and falling (circumflex) tone on certain vowels. In standard Serbo-Croatian, there is an opposition between rising and falling intonation on certain vowels. However, there is no connection between the opposition in Serbo-Croatian and that in Proto-Slavonic, even though Serbo-Croatian is a linear descendant of Proto-Slavonic. The opposition in Serbo-Croatian arose when the accent was shifted one syllable closer to the beginning of the word in all words except those that originally had initial accent; these shifted accents show up as rising tone, while falling tone is the reflex of an original, unshifted word-initial accent.

But if we interpret the reconstruction literally as requiring a proto-system with only one vowel, then the question of the typological possibility of such a system arises directly. Obviously, if we could find a clear case of an attested language with such a system, then the problem would be solved in favour of the typological possibility of such a reconstruction. Unfortunately the situation is by no means so clear. A number of languages have been put forward as candidates for one-vowel status, but in all cases there are residual problems. Perhaps the most famous are the Northwest Caucasian languages (Abkhaz and the closely related Abaza, East and West Circassian, Ubykh); solutions that have been suggested for the vowel systems of these languages are summarized, with bibliographic references, by Hewitt (1981: 205–7). For at least some of the Northwest Caucasian languages, most scholars are agreed on at most a two-way phonemic vowel opposition /ə/–/a/, with all other vowel qualities being allophones of one or other of these two, and the question that arises is whether the schwa can also be eliminated. Allen (1956) argued that if one allows word accent, which is phonemic, in Abaza to be stated independent of the occurrence of a vowel, then it is possible to dispense with schwa in phonemic representations, since schwa is then predictable in terms of a rule that inserts schwa where an accent has no other vowel bearer and a rule that inserts schwa to break up inadmissible consonant clusters. Part of one's attitude to this analysis for Abaza centres on whether one accepts the possibility of unattached word accents in more abstract phonological representations. Turning to another part of the world, Foley (1986: 49–52) shows how the apparent seven-vowel system of the Papuan language Iatmul (spoken in northern Papua New Guinea) *i, e, ɨ, ə, a, o, u* can readily be reduced to *i, ə, a*, treating [i, e, u, o] as allophones of one or other of the non-low vowels; the [ɨ] can then be eliminated since its occurrence is always predictable, leaving only /ə/ and /ɑ/. Finally, since Iatmul *a* is phonetically noticeably longer than *ə*, one might remove the sole remaining vowel quality distinction, leaving Iatmul with a single vowel quality and phonemic vowel length. In Comrie (1991) a similar analysis is suggested for another Papuan language, Haruai, with at first sight the same seven-vowel system as in the case of Iatmul.[5] In Haruai, [i] and [u] are best analysed as allophones of /y/ and /w/; [ɨ] is always predictable, therefore nonphonemic; some occurrences of [e] that are not obviously allophones of /ə/ can be shown to derive morphologically from the sequence /əyə/, and an overall analysis that derives all such [e]'s from this sequence encounters no more problems than would an analysis that does not take this step; the same holds, though with a weaker basis in morphological terms, for the relation between [o], /ə/ and /əwə/; finally, there is morphological evidence for deriving some instances of [a] from /əə/ (a sequence of two schwas, typically with an intervening morpheme boundary, rather than a long schwa), and an overall analysis that derives all [a]'s from this sequence encounters no more problems than would an analysis that does not take this step. Thus there are certainly some attested languages that are plausible candidates for one-vowel status, although none of those known to me can be described as an unequivocally clear case.

Let us suppose, for the sake of argument, that each of these cases and other similar cases that have been proposed turns out not to be a valid instance of a one-vowel system. Where would this leave the typological status of the one-vowel reconstruction of Proto-Indo-European? Certainly, it would indicate that the language hypothesized by this reconstruction is typologically rare, but would it actually exclude the possibility of such a language? The problem is the general one of bridging the gap between the claim that no such language is attested and the claim that no such language is possible. As indicated in section 1, I do not believe that this gap can be bridged purely by statistical arguments, since we know of too many cases where distribution of phenomena across the world's languages is heavily skewed, to such an extent that it is not surprising that a particular language should have one feature that is rare or even unique among attested languages: in the case of Early Proto-Indo-European, this might happen to be its vowel system. It is thus insufficient simply to say that no attested language is known to have a one-vowel system; rather one must claim that it is a principle of language that no language can have a one-vowel system. (Notice that if true this places heavy constraints on possible diachronic changes. For instance, a language with a two-vowel system would not be able to undergo a change neutralizing the opposition between its two vowels, even if the change in question were otherwise a perfectly natural change.) If the proposed ban on one-vowel systems does not follow from some more general principle of language, then it is hard to see how it can be justified, why there should be such a restriction on vowel systems; indeed, if the ban cannot be shown to follow from some more general principle, we would be in no better a position operationally than in trying to justify the ban in terms of cross-linguistic statistical distribution. Somewhat surprisingly, given the extent to which the ban on one-vowel systems seems to be accepted among linguists, I am not aware of any serious attempt to derive the ban from more general principles.[6] Thus, while the typological evidence suggests that one-vowel systems are at best very rare, it does not provide unequivocal motivation for saying that they are impossible. My own assessment of the statistical distribution of vowel inventory sizes would be that there is a rather narrow range within which nearly all languages fall, namely 3–7 qualitatively distinct vowels; as one goes much above or below this range, the number of languages with a given number of qualitatively distinct vowel phonemes falls off rapidly, so that languages with very few or very many vowels are going to be statistically rare and may even be absent from a particular corpus.

Let us now turn to the typological plausibility of the sound changes postulated in order to get from an earlier stage of Proto-Indo-European with three laryngeal consonants and one vowel to the later stage with no laryngeal consonants and three qualitatively distinct vowels. The general phenomenon whereby consonants produced in the guttural region, i.e. including uvulars, pharyn-geals and glottals, affect the pronunciation of adjacent vowels is widely attested cross-linguistically; a recent survey of some of the evidence from Semitic is included in McCarthy (1991). If the guttural consonants are subsequently lost, then even allophonic distinctions occasioned by guttural consonants can become phonemicized. Thus the general hypothesis of distinct vowel qualities arising in Proto-Indo-European through the loss of laryngeal consonants is typologically quite plausible. None the less, potential problems arise in tracing the details of the proposed development in Proto-Indo-European.

A useful survey of the problems is provided by Szemerényi (1989: 127–50), who concludes (147) that Proto-Indo-European had only one laryngeal consonant (which has the reflex *h* in Hittite) and that the differentiation of vowel quality must have been original. Kinds of evidence that lead him to this conclusion are as follows. On the laryngeal theory, Hittite is supposed to show a postvocalic *h* where the other Indo-European languages have a long vowel; while this works in many instances, e.g. Sanskrit *pā-*, Hittite *pahs-* 'to protect', there are other instances that Szemerényi cites as exceptions,[7] e.g. Latin *pō-tāre* 'to drink', Hittite *pas-* 'to swallow'. If a root in Latin or Ancient Greek shows an initial *a* or *o*, then Hittite should show an initial laryngeal (as reflex of *H_a* or *H_o* respectively), as in Latin *ante* 'before', Hittite *hant-* 'front', but again there are exceptions, e.g. Latin *aqua* 'water', Hittite *aku(wa)-* 'to drink'. Putative initial *He* usually disappears without trace in Hittite, as in Hittite *es-* 'to be', *ed-* 'to eat', for (under the laryngeal theory) Proto-Indo-European $*H_ees$-, $*H_eed$-; but if one takes this to be the regular development, then there is a problem with forms like Hittite *henkan* 'fate', which would suggest an irregularly retained initial $*H_e$. Some roots show the vowel *a* or *o* with little or no plausibility of positing a laryngeal, e.g. $*nas$- 'nose', $*bhardhā$ 'beard', $*ghostis$ 'stranger'. We seem thus to be faced with two possibilities: either we reject the laryngeal theory because of the number of exceptions or we accept it but are faced with a residue of unexplained developments in individual roots. At this point, however, typological comparison again proves useful, since we can examine other languages that have lost consonants in the guttural region, often with concomitant changes in vowel quality, and see if the kinds of exceptions required by the developments assumed in the laryngeal theory are similar to those found in other cases.

The data to be used here for comparison come from the historical development of Maltese, the language of Malta. Historically, Maltese is an off-shoot of North African vernacular Arabic, though with considerable influence, especially in lexicon, from Sicilian and Italian; we shall be concerned here only with the Arabic component of Maltese. Classical Arabic and most varieties of vernacular Arabic have a rich set of gutturals, including in particular the uvulars *q*, χ and γ, the pharyngeals *ħ* and Ω and the glottals $\ref{}$ and *h*. Arabic *q* shows up as /$\ref{}$/ in Maltese, though still written *q* in standard Maltese orthography. The voiceless uvular and pharyngeal fricatives are merged, the result being written *ħ* and pronounced as pharyngeal or uvular according to dialect. Likewise the voiced uvular and pharyngeal fricatives are merged, the result being written *għ*, although the pronunciation of this as a uvular fricative is retained by only a smaller number of speakers on the island of Gozo; for nearly all speakers, *għ* is realized in most environments as lengthening of an adjacent vowel, for many speakers with concomitant pharyngealization of that vowel, and we shall use representations here for such speakers, with pharyngealization indicated by a subscript dot, e.g. *ghazel* ['a̩zel] 'net', *xagħar* [ʃa̩r] 'hair'. Word-finally, *għ* is realized as [ħ] after a long vowel, e.g. *smiegħ* [smɪħ] 'hearing', but as zero after the short vowel *a*, in which latter case the orthography writes an apostrophe instead of *għ*, e.g. *sema'* ['sema] (variant *sama'* ['sama]) 'he heard'. The vowels *i* and *u* are diphthongized to [aj] and [ow] respectively (with numerous dialect variants) by a preceding *għ*, e.g. *ghid* [a̩jd] 'festival', *ghuda* [o̩wda] 'wood'. The Arabic glottal stop does not survive as a distinct phoneme in Maltese, while the Arabic *h* has a number of developments roughly paralleling those of *għ* (but without diphthongization of *i* and *u*). The details of the development of Arabic ɣ/ʕ and *h* in Maltese are set out in Schabert (1976: 45–50); their loss provides a typological comparison to the loss of the laryngeals in Indo-European, a comparison that is the more useful in that with Maltese and Arabic we are dealing with two attested languages, rather than having one of the poles of comparison a reconstruction.

Let us take first of all the disappearance of *għ*. The regular development can be seen in forms like *għazel* /'azel/ 'he chose', *jagħzel* /'jazel/ 'he chooses', *xagħar* /'ʃar/ 'hair', *ixgħel* /'iʃel/ 'ignite!'. There are, however, certain morphological exceptions to this generalization. For instance, in the third person singular feminine past tense of verbs with *għ* as their final consonant, the vowel *e* of the person-number-gender suffix *-et* is neither pharyngealized nor lengthened, so that *semgħet* 'she heard' is pronounced simply /'semet/, although the phonological environment is of the same type as in *ixgħel* above. In word-final position after a short vowel, as noted above, *għ* has a different, phonologically conditioned reflex, namely zero, so that *sema'* (variant: *sama'*) 'he heard' is simply /'sema/ or /'sama/; the fact that this verb does have *għ* as its third consonant can be seen in the third person plural *semgħu* ['semow] 'they heard', where the *għ* has occasioned diphthongization of the third person plural suffix *-u* (but note the absence of pharyngealization, paralleling the pronunciation of *semgħet*) and in the related noun *smiegħ* /smiħ/ 'hearing', with [ħ] as the regular reflex of word-final *għ* after a long vowel. But exceptionally, in the verb *zebagħ* /'zebaħ/ 'he painted', the *għ* is pronounced as [ħ],[8] although, for the dialect of St. Julian's investigated by Schabert (1976: 117), other forms of the verb at least have the option of being conjugated like verbs with *għ*, rather than *h*, as their final consonant, e.g. *zebgħet* /'zebat/ (corresponding to standard /'zebet/) 'she painted'. Finally, there is one verb that is lexically exceptional, namely 'to give', which in Arabic has ʕ as first consonant of the root. In Maltese, this consonant has disappeared completely from the past tense (e.g. *ta* /taː/ 'he gave'), while in the non-past tense, in dialects that normally retain pharyngealization of vowels, variants with a long pharyngealized vowel, with a long non-pharyngealized vowel and with a short non-pharyngealized vowel are all found, i.e. *jagħti* 'he gives' varies freely among /'jati/, /'jaːti/ and /'jati/.

For variant reflexes of Arabic *h*, a few examples from initial position will suffice. The most usual reflex is lengthening (in the relevant dialects, also pharyngealization) of the following vowel, as in *hedded* /'ẹddet/ 'he threatened'. Pronouns, however, usually show no reflex whatsoever of the original h, e.g. *hu* /'uː/ 'he' and /'aww/, a common pronunciation of written *hawn* 'here'. There are, however, lexical exceptions to the general rule, so that Arabic *haraba* 'he fled' shows up in Maltese as *harab* /ħarap/, where the orthography reflects the exceptional reflex.

Turning next to the influence of guttural consonants on vowel quality, interesting data are provided by Maltese verb forms (Berrendonner et al. 1983: 181–5). In the third person singular masculine of the past (so-called perfect) in Arabic, there are three possible vocalisms, *a–a* as in *kataba* 'he wrote', *a-i* as in *fariħa* 'he rejoiced' and *a–u* as in *jamuna* 'he was handsome'. Maltese has traces of the third of these types, with *o* as the regular development of *u*, e.g. *qorob* /'ʔorop/ 'he approached', but no trace of the distinction between the first and second types; the third type will play no role in what follows. Corresponding to the merger of the first two types, Maltese usually shows the vocalism *i-e*, as in *kiteb* /'kitep/ 'he wrote', though this vocalism should probably more strictly be given as *i–i*, since when stress shifts to the second vowel it shows up as *i*, e.g. *ma kitibx* /maki'tipʃ/ 'he didn't write'). If in Arabic there was an emphatic consonant (indicated here by a dot under the consonant symbol) in the root, then this is reflected in Maltese by a different vocalism, namely *a–a*, e.g. *talab* /'talap/ 'he requested', cf. Arabic *ṭalaba*, and this rule takes precedence over all the other cases discussed. If the verb root contains one of the three guttural consonants *q*, *ħ* or *għ*, then this has the effect of lowering the adjacent vowel(s) to *a*, so that for an initial guttural we find *qatel* /'ʔatel/ 'he killed', for a final guttural *seraq* /'seraʔ/ 'he stole', for a medial guttural *daħal* /'daħal/ 'he entered' (the last corresponding to Arabic *daxala*, with no emphatic consonant). Although this is the general rule, there are lexical exceptions, e.g. *heles* /'ħeles/ 'he got free', *xeħet* /'ʃeħet/ 'he threw', *għereq* /'ereʔ/ 'he drowned' (in which both first and third consonants are guttural), all with the pattern *e–e*; Berrendonner et al. (1983: 183) even note one example that has two different irregular realizations: *qered* /'ʔeret/~*qired* /'ʔiret/ 'he destroyed'. While *xeghel* [ʃel] 'he ignited' is an exception in the standard language, Schabert (1976: 88) notes that the dialect of St Julian's has the etymologically expected realization [ʃal].

These Maltese data show that in cases where guttural

consonants are lost, sometimes with changes in the quality of adjacent vowels, there are often idiosyncratic developments, and this in a case where we have access (via Classical Arabic and most modern Arabic vernaculars) to the original state before the loss of the gutturals and before the phonologization of the changes in vowel quality. The idiosyncrasies discussed include loss of a guttural where it should have been retained, retention of a guttural where it should have been lost and irregular developments of vowel quality. The analogy to be drawn for Proto-Indo-European is obvious: it should not surprise us, in a change from a system with several gutturals (laryngeals) and few (or no) oppositions of vowel quality to one with few (or no) gutturals and several oppositions of vowel quality, if we find a residue of exceptional instances of retention or loss of gutturals or of development of vowel quality. Of course, this still leaves some questions open, in particular as to whether any cross-linguistically recurrent sub-regularities can be found within these idiosyncrasies, but typological evidence suggests that the mere occurrence of exceptions should not in itself be a bar to our acceptance of a development as hypothesized for Proto-Indo-European by the laryngeal theory.

4 Conclusions

What contribution can typology make to reconstruction in historical-comparative linguistics? If one takes typology to be the study, both empirical and theoretical, of patterns of cross-linguistic variation, then typology can answer questions that are of great importance to historical linguistics, especially given that for the time-depths at which most reconstructions are carried out it is unlikely that there would be any major typological difference between human language at the time the reconstructed language was spoken and now. Typology can be used to justify the possibility of a given reconstruction by uncovering analogues in attested languages. Typology can be used as an argument against a particular reconstruction by showing that there are either principled or strong empirical arguments that the reconstruction reflects an impossible language type, although the strength of such arguments will always depend on the level of development of typology, since typological generalizations may also turn out, as the result of a broader or deeper understanding of language, to be incorrect. Special caution must be taken in regard to arguments of typological plausibility: possibly every language is

implausible in at least one area of its grammar, and there is no
reason to believe this is any less true of reconstructed languages.

Notes

1. For a more detailed discussion, see Comrie (1989). esp. chs 1–2.
2. Another view of reconstruction sees a reconstruction as a convenient
   formulaic summary of the relations among the attested genetically
   related languages. As far as I can see, reconstructions in this sense
   have no theoretical interest, and I will have nothing further to say
   about this conception of reconstruction.
3. These remarks on Malayalam are based on my observations of the
   speech of Suchitra Sadanandan, a speaker of the Thiyya dialect.
4. The presentation of ablaut here relies heavily on Anttila (1989:
   266–73).
5. Note that Comrie uses the symbol ö for ə.
6. One attempt that can be rejected immediately is the claim that, since
   phonemic oppositions always require an opposition between two
   elements, the existence of one vowel phoneme in a language
   necessarily requires the existence of at least one other vowel phoneme
   with which it is in contrast. It is perfectly possible for the phonemic
   opposition to be between the presence of an item and the absence of
   that item, as in the English minimal pair *steam–stream*, so that in a
   language with only one vowel phoneme the occurrence of this vowel
   would contrast with its absence.
7. Here and below, it should be noted that for some of Szemerényi's
   exceptions others have proposed alternative etymologies that would
   avoid the irregularities in vocalism, as pointed out to me by Rex
   Wallace. My concern here is not with the facts of individual items, but
   rather with the general problem of how to deal with exceptions of this
   kind.
8. As will have been noted in other examples, Maltese has a general rule
   of word-final devoicing, so that [ħ] appears here simply as the
   unvoiced equivalent of *gh*.

References

ALLEN, W. S. (1956) 'Structure and system in the Abaza verbal complex.'
   Transactions of the Philological Society, pp. 127–67.
ANTTILA, RAIMO (1989) *Historical and Comparative Linguistics*, 2nd edn.
   Amsterdam: John Benjamins.
BERRENDONNER, A., LE GUERN, M., and PUECH, G. (1983) *Principes de
   grammaire polylectale*. Lyon: Presses Universitaires de Lyon.
BHATIA, TEJ K. (1975) 'The evolution of tones in Punjabi', *Studies in the
   Linguistic Sciences* 5, 2: 12–24.
BRUGMANN, KARL (1897–1916) *Grundriß der vergleichenden Grammatik
   der indogermanischen Sprachen*. Strassburg: Trübner.

CHOMSKY, NOAM and HALLE, MORRIS (1968) *The Sound Pattern of English*. New York: Harper & Row.

COMRIE, BERNARD (1989) *Language Universals and Linguistic Typology*. 2nd edn. Oxford: Basil Blackwell and Chicago: University of Chicago Press.

COMRIE, BERNARD (1991) 'On Haruai vowels.' In PAWLEY, ANDREW (ed.) *Man and a Half: Essays in Pacific Anthropology in Honour of Ralph Bulmer*. Auckland: The Polynesian Society, pp. 393–7.

FOLEY, WILLIAM A. (1986) *The Papuan Languages of New Guinea*. Cambridge: Cambridge University Press.

HEWITT, B. G. (1981) 'Caucasian languages.' In COMRIE, B. *Languages of the Soviet Union*. Cambridge: Cambridge University Press, pp. 196–237.

HOPPER, PAUL (1973) 'Glottalized and murmured occlusives in IE', *Glossa* 7, 141–66.

LADEFOGED, PETER (1971) *Preliminaries to Linguistic Phonetics*. Chicago: University of Chicago Press.

MCCARTHY, JOHN (1992) 'Semitic gutturals and distinctive feature theory.' In COMRIE, BERNARD and EID, MUSHIRA (eds) *Perspectives on Arabic Linguistics III*. Amsterdam: John Benjamins, pp. 63–91.

PIKE, KENNETH L. (1943) *Phonetics: a Critical Analysis of Phonetic Theory and a Technic for the Practical Description of Sounds*. Ann Arbor: University of Michigan Press.

SAUSSURE, FERDINAND DE (1879) *Mémoire sur le système primitif des voyelles dans les langues indo-européennes*. Leipzig: Teubner.

SCHABERT, PETER (1976) *Laut- und Formenlehre des Maltesischen anhand zweier Mundarten*. Erlangen: Palm & Enke.

STEWART, JOHN M. (1989) 'Kwa.' In BENDOR-SAMUEL, JOHN (ed.) *The Niger-Congo Languages*. Lanham, MD: University Press of America and Summer Institute of Linguistics, pp. 217–45.

SZEMERÉNYI, OSWALD (1989) *Einführung in die vergleichende Sprachwissenschaft*, 3rd edn. Darmstadt: Wissenschaftliche Buchgesellschaft.

Chapter 4

On the phonetic basis of phonological change

Patricia Donegan

1 The nature of phonological change

1.1 Sound changes are changes in speakers' phonetic abilities

The distinction in N. American English between the low labial vowel [ɒ] of *caught, dawn, hawk* and the low non-labial vowel [ɑ] of *cot, Don, hock* is an old one, going back to early English *aw* versus short *o*. But in dialects of Canada and various parts of the United States of America, the [ɒ] is pronounced [ɑ], and the two sets of words are no longer distinguished. This sound change [ɒ] > [ɑ] was a historical event, but it remains a synchronic constraint that characterizes the phonetic capacities of the speakers of the innovating dialect: without additional learning, they cannot perceive or pronounce the [ɒ] of other speakers, and even if they learn to perceive it, they often continue to pronounce it as [ɑ] (at least in unguarded moments) or as some other substitute, e.g. [o] or [oɑ] or [ɑǫ]. It is significant that children learning the conservative dialect also typically at first cannot perceive and pronounce [ɒ]. When they learn to perceive it, they still use [ɑ] or [o] or [oɑ] or [ɑǫ] until they learn also to pronounce it. Thus speakers of the conservative dialect acquire a phonetic ability that speakers of the innovating dialect do not.

But some adult speakers of dialects with [ɒ] in fact never learn to perceive it or to pronounce it without substitution. They are innovators, though their innovation lies in *not* doing something their fellow speakers *do* do, namely learn to perceive and pronounce [ɒ]. And some speakers, having learned to hear and say [ɒ] as children, may move to an innovative dialect area and, under peer influence, lose the ability to even to hear [ɒ] as distinct from [ɑ]. One such person, whose childhood distinction of [ɒ] and [ɑ] was well attested in a linguist's diary, later forgot ever having distinguished *caught* from *cot* himself, and even refused to believe that anyone else could do so. After hearing it demonstrated by a perfect commutation test, he suspected a trick, and demanded a replay. At last he said, 'I get it: you're saying [koɑt]!' (for *caught*). But in fact the subjects had said only [kɒt] for *caught*. The sceptic, having finally heard [ɒ], could reproduce it only as the substitute [oɑ].

1.2 Phonological processes respond to universal phonetic difficulties

The phonetic qualities that cause a vowel like [ɒ] to be difficult to perceive as such, and also difficult to pronounce as such, are rather simple. [ɒ] is a maximally open vowel produced with the lips narrowed by rounding. Opening the mouth wide conflicts with rounding the lips. The conflict attenuates one or the other acoustic impression, and it also makes it hard to produce both acoustic impressions simultaneously. The difficulty is obviously universal, and so are the possible remedies: either to give up the low or the labial feature, or to sequence them in a diphthong. That is,

(1)   *Low vowels must be non-labial*, i.e. [ɒ] → [ɑ]
(2)   *Labial vowels must be non-low*, i.e. [ɒ] → [o]
(1+2) [ɒ] → [ɑǫ]
(2+1) [ɒ] → [oǫ][1]

Besides being heard in children learning [ɒ] in English and other languages, substitution (1) is standard in the North American dialects already mentioned, (2) in British Received Pronunciation (RP) (Gimson 1962: 109ff.), (1+2) in some southern United States dialects (cf. Hall 1942, Kurath and McDavid 1961), and (2+1) in northern United States urban areas (Labov et al., 1972). Since the sequenced articulation of diphthongs takes more time, often the diphthongizations are limited just to long or contextually lengthened vowels.

Since [o] shares with [ɒ] the conflict of rounding and openness, but has only medium opening, we would predict parallel but less frequent substitutions for [o], and all of them in fact occur: (1) IE short *o > Sanskrit [ʌ] (written *a*, e.g. *dáma-* 'house'); (2) OE long [o:] > late ME [u:], e.g. *fool*; (1+2) British RP and Middle Atlantic [o] → [ʌǫ] (and often [ʌǫ] → [ɛǫ], e.g. *snow*); and (2+1) Germanic long *o: > Old High German [uə] (spelled *uo*, e.g. *buoch* 'book', but still pronounced [uə] in conservative German dialects). As the hierarchy of difficulty would suggest, none of these substitutions affects [o] unless it also affects [ɒ]. So if [o] is raised to [u], [ɒ] is raised to [o].

There are parallel substitutions for the palatal vowels [æ] and [e]. Since it is difficult to combine a palatal tongue position with an open jaw, one can be given up:

(3) *Non-high vowels must be non-palatal*, i.e.

    [æ] → [ɑ], e.g. British and Northeastern US *can't, past*;

    [e] → [ʌ], e.g. New Zealand dialects *let, said*;

or

(4) *Palatal vowels must be non-low*, i.e.

    [æ] → [e], e.g. English Vowel Shift *meat*;

    [e] → [i], e.g. English Vowel Shift *meet*; and again in *meat*.

Or the conflicting features can be sequenced:

(3+4) [æ] → [ɑɛ̣], e.g. Southern US dialects *bad*;

        [e] → [ʌi̯], e.g. Australia, NZ, North Carolina *bay*.

(4+3) [æ] → [eɑ], e.g. Northern urban US dialects *bad*;

        [e] → [iʌ], e.g. Old High German *hiar* 'here'.

The low round palatal vowel [œ] combines the difficulties of [ɒ] with those of [æ], and adds the conflicting acoustic effects of tongue fronting and lip rounding. Such vowels are rare, learned late, and historically, lost early. Even the easiest of the labiopalatals, the high front rounded vowel [y], is usually unrounded (e.g. OE *mȳs* > ME *mīs* 'mice'), or diphthongized (e.g. MHG *myːzə* > NHG [moi̯zə] 'id.').

But even the optimal palatal vowel [i] and the optimal labial vowel [u] present difficulties. For children, even simple palatalization or labialization can be difficult, and since it is children who learn languages, it should not be surprising that there are languages like Adyghe, Kabardian, and others of the northwest Caucasus (Catford 1977), Gude (Hoskison 1974), or Marshallese (Bender 1971) in which the only high vowel phoneme is non-palatal and non-labial [ɨ] – i.e., in which both depalatalization and delabialization apply. Furthermore, since the optimal vowel would be maximally audible, like [ɑ], high vowels are not optimal. So we find languages in which they are lowered; e.g. Squamish, Alabama, and Amuesha lack high vowels (Maddieson 1984). And in English and many other languages, we find diphthongizations of [i] and [u] that lower their nuclei to [ɛi], [ɔu̯]; or depalatalize or delabialize them to [ɨi], [iu̯]; or that do both, to [ʌi], [ʌu̯], and lower again to [ɑi], [ɑu̯]. Of course, this was the path of early English long [iː] and [uː] as in *mice* and *mouse*.

We are left with what Hellwag called the Prince of Vowels, [ɑ], which would seem to present no difficulties at all: it is optimally open and has no conflicting features like palatality or labiality. If a child can say only one vowel, that vowel is [ɑ]. Or if a language has only one vowel, we would expect it to be [ɑ]. And we might expect that [ɑ] would always remain [ɑ]. But we find that [ɑ] sometimes does undergo substitution, acquiring either palatality ([ɑ] → [æ]) or labiality ([ɑ] → [ɒ]), or losing some of its sonority ([ɑ] → [ʌ]). These changes frequently occur in languages where short and long [ɑ] are distinguished lexically, but where the spoken length is disturbed by prosodic changes like stress timing, which lengthens and shortens vowels to fit their rhythmic context. A common response to this is the superimposition of a tense-lax distinction on the long-short distinction. But since tenseness in vowels is an intensification of palatal or labial colouring (Donegan 1978), it is inapplicable to vowels like [ɑ], which are neither palatal nor labial. For example, Latin long vs. short vowels became proto-Romance tense vs. lax vowels, but Latin long and short [ɑ] merged. The imposition of palatal or labial colour on long or short [ɑ] – or on both, so that the tense-lax difference would be possible – could reinforce a threatened length distinction and prevent lexical mergers. For example, OE long ɑ:, in words like *stān* 'stone' and *rāp* 'rope', became [ɒ:] (long open ǫ) in early ME, while short ɑ remained [ɑ]. Later, in Middle English, long ɑ: (from lengthened ɑ, as in *mate*) was fronted to ę [æ], while short ɑ remained [ɑ]. Hock (1986: 144) cites Modern Persian as a language where both labialization and palatalization have applied, one to long ɑ: ([ɑ:] > [ɒ:]), and the other to short ɑ ([ɑ] > [æ]).

Since the disadvantage of combining high sonority with either palatal or labial colouring remains, we should expect [ɑ] to be less susceptible to such colouring than higher vowels are. And we do find that, other things being equal, [ɑ] → [ɒ] implies that, in the same speakers, [ʌ] in the system → [o]. Similarly, [ʌ] → [o] implies [ɨ] → [u] (Donegan 1978). Cross-language comparison of changes reveals, then, that opposite substitutions have opposite implicational conditions on their application – e.g. the more sonorant a vowel is, the more susceptible it is to delabialization, but the less sonorant a vowel is, the more susceptible it is to labialization. Far from making us conclude that 'anything can happen' and there are no phonetic motivations, careful comparison of changes confirms – and indeed often reveals – their phonetic motivations.

1.3   Phonological processes are not physical slips

It is important to realize that these systematic substitutions that result in phonetic change do not occur by 'accident'. The vocal tract itself cannot select a substitution to resolve a phonetic difficulty; it must be the brain, or the mind, that chooses a substitute that is both regular and perceptually similar to its input. The substitutions that occur are motivated by vocal and perceptual constraints, but they apply in the mind. It is the mind that gives the instructions that produce a substitution. It is likewise the mind – not the ear or the mouth – that learns to perceive and pronounce the difficult segment or sequence. Only the mind can attend (or not attend) to the appropriate cues in perceiving sounds as the same or different, and only the mind can consistently give the appropriate neuromuscular instructions to produce the 'output' of the substitution. The processes are mental, because it is the mind that, having insufficient control of the body, determines or discovers a regular substitute. And it is the mind that, in learning to control articulation and perception, learns the abilities or 'keys' that turn off the substitutions.[2]

But the mental nature of processes does not require us to assume that phonological processes are learned through the observation and comparison of forms, as morphology must be learned. Unlike morphology and morphophonology, which are conventional, phonological processes are motivated by the demands of the body, not the results of analysis.

2   The phonological system as the representation of phonetic abilities: phonetic change is phonological

The set of *phonetic constraints and responding substitutions* that speakers are born with can be represented as a set of phonological processes. Each process replaces a class of sounds which presents a difficulty to the speaker with another class which lacks that particular difficulty. These processes represent the speaker's inabilities. What the speaker learns, in learning the phonology of a particular language, is the required set of *abilities to perceive and pronounce*. That is, in learning to perceive and pronounce the required segments and sequences, he acquires the abilities or 'keys' to turn off the processes which would eliminate these sounds or sequences. We can represent these learned abilities as inhibitions of phonological processes. The set of constraints and substitutions – phonological processes – is universal. What a linguistic community shares is the set of learned inhibitions of these processes.

In our first example, the conservative speakers who distinguish /ɒ/ from /ɑ/ have learned to inhibit the process represented by (1). When a 'phonetic change' takes place, speakers fail to learn the 'key' that turns off the process that is involved. In the case of an optional or variable change, speakers learn to inhibit the process and pronounce its input, but their learning is imperfect. Then using this ability or key requires special attention or effort, so they may fail to do so in certain prosodic or stylistic circumstances.[3]

Any difficulty that is not mastered is avoided automatically by substitution. The phonetically motivated, universal processes which the speaker continues to apply (either obligatorily, or as options) after he has acquired the adult form of the language are responsible for the phonological substitutions of the language. If, through some failure of learning, or through some relaxation of the requirements of the community (even if only in limited contexts), a speaker continues to make a substitution that was not generally accepted at an earlier time, he may appear to have 'added' a phonological process to the language. Such substitutions, when context-sensitive, may create variant pronunciations without changing the phonological form, because the speaker can attribute the variants to their occurrence in a particular environment. For example, the de-rhotacization of syllable-offset *r*, in Eastern New England and Metropolitan New York *ear*, *care*, *door* [iə̯, keə̯, dɔə̯] (Kurath and McDavid 1961: 171), does not change their phonemic status as /ir, ker, dɔr/, where they are pronounced with [r] before a vowel. But this 'added' r-deletion also does not represent an invention, or the creation of some new linguistic operation. The innovator has not 'made a change' in his own linguistic system. In a sense, he has done nothing. He has simply continued to submit to a constraint that other speakers overcome, because he has failed to acquire the ability to inhibit the resulting substitution.

2.1 Phonology is not conventional

Unlike the 'natural' theory being described here, most theories of phonology, structuralist and generative, are conventionalist theories. They regard phonological substitutions as grammatical conventions that are discovered, or learned, by speakers on the basis of their analysis of language data. These conventionalist theories – generative phonology, in particular, and its autosegmental, metrical, and lexical variants – do not distinguish *in kind* between phonological processes, which are based entirely on phonetic and prosodic features, and morphophonological rules.[4]

Morphophonological rules are purely conventional, or traditional. They may resemble phonological processes because they can be expressed, in part, in phonological features. But they apply only in connection with grammatical processes and in terms of lexical and grammatical categories, not prosodic ones. And they apply only in terms of phonemes, or classes of phonemes that may be phonetically arbitrary (e.g. in English, velar softening relates 'hard' /k, g/ to 'soft' /s, ǰ/).

This means that morphophonological rules do not represent constraints on pronunciation.[5] That is, their inputs are not difficult or unpronounceable. In English, for example, there are obligatory morphophonological rules that make k → s in words like *electric* + *ity* [ilɛk'trɪsɨti], and that make t → null in words like *chaste* + *en* ['čɛɪ̯sn̩]. But any English speaker who can pronounce *persnickety* [pr̩'snɪkɨti] or *Boston* ['bɒstn̩] could perfectly well pronounce *electric* + *ity* as [ilɛk'trɪkɨti], or *chaste* + *en* as ['čɛɪ̯stn̩]. Rules like these may have their historical origins in alternations of phonemes that were originally phonetically motivated, but they no longer represent limitations on what the speaker finds pronounceable. Instead, they have become conventions or traditions to which the speaker conforms in order to make his speech grammatical. (For further discussion and examples, cf. Darden 1989.)

The absence of this distinction between phonetically motivated and conventional substitutions – and the consequent assumption that phonological substitutions are conventional – create a gap between phonetic change and phonology that is virtually impossible to reconcile. Scholars like Labov, Ohala, Janson, and others have documented phonetic change and explored the reasons for such change, but they have not explained how the phonetic changes are implemented in speakers' phonological systems, or how they affect these systems. For example, Labov, Yaeger, and Steiner, in their 1972 vowel shift study, documented a remarkable number of vowel changes in many dialects of English, compared these changes to vowel shifts in the histories of other languages, and attempted to specify generative rules by which these changes were taking place. But the status of these rules in the innovating speakers' phonological systems, the question of why or how speakers would adopt such rules, and the ways in which the rules affected the speakers' phonological representations were not addressed.

It is sometimes assumed that changes are introduced 'in the phonetics' of the innovating speakers, and that other speakers invent a rule in imitation of the innovators. But this leaves in question the nature of the change in the innovators' *phonetic* processing.

Conventionalist theory, where phonological rules (like morphophonological rules) must be learned, fails to explain systematically how phonetic motivation is related to the adoption of new phonetic targets, how phonetic rules are acquired, or what it means for these new rules and targets to become phonological.

2.2 The identity of phonology and phonetics

While conventionalist phonology has obscured the difference between phonology and morphophonology, it has seemed to exaggerate the distinction between phonology and phonetics, and to assign much of the detail of pronunciation and change to the phonetic component. But phonology *is* phonetic processing; it is thus the mental (or central-nervous-system) aspect of phonetics.[6] Although certain phonetic *events* may occur in the vocal tract of the speaker, or in the air, or in the ear of the hearer, phonetic *processing* is a matter of the perception and the production of sounds, and it is thus fundamentally mental. Indeed, when we speak and hear in our imaginations, even though no physical articulations or sounds actually occur, the constraints remain the same as they are in actual speech. The nature of articulations and the acoustic or perceptual character of sounds, of course, affect speakers' categorizations. Such physical factors also motivate the alterations or substitutions speakers make. But the categorizations and alterations themselves are mental. The relationship between the physical events and the mental processes is what makes phonetics different from physiology or acoustics.

Thus, phonology must include matters of 'phonetic detail'. Unless we are willing to believe that differences between sounds in different languages or dialects are the result of differences in their speakers' vocal tracts, we must regard such differences as results of the processing of speech. Articulatory parameters such as speech rate and jaw mobility, or the particular gestures used to implement features like voicing or implosion in obstruents or frontness (palatality) in vowels may vary from speaker to speaker. Such differences may be idiosyncratic and vary randomly from speaker to speaker, making little difference in the perceptual quality, in which case they are irrelevant to phonology. But if such differences turn out to be consistent across speakers within particular communities, and particularly if they are associated with differences in the applications of substitutions, then they are part of the phonology.

Correspondingly, a systematic innovation in a speaker's

pronunciation, even if it is only a small difference of articulatory target, or a difference in the timing of articulatory gestures, must result from a difference in the processing of speech. It cannot be accomplished by the vocal tract itself, but must result from some specific relaxation of the requirements of the language in favour of some requirement (whether fortitive or lenitive) of the speaker. If phonology were a matter of conventional or merely traditional substitutions, we would have to explain how substitutions become 'phonologized', or 'grammaticized'. But if phonology is phonetic processing, through a set of systematic substitutions with direct phonetic motivation, then any phonetic change *occurs in the phonology*, by the application of a substitution that other speakers inhibit.

2.3   The identity of phonological and phonetic features

If phonological processes specify phonetic detail, and if the conditions on such processes are sensitive to phonetic detail, such detail must be reflected in the system of phonological features. And, since phonological processes have both articulatory and perceptual motivations, the features in terms of which they operate must integrate these. One can conclude that phonological features are the mental connections speakers draw between particular gestures or commands to the vocal organs and the perceived effects of those gestures or commands. There is no distinction, in this view, between phonetic features and phonological features.

Phonological features, then, are universal. Segments specified with the same features ought to be the same from language to language, articulatorily and acoustically (allowing, of course, for individual variation). But segments said to have the same features often are not the same from language to language. For example, English initial voiceless stops are said to be aspirated. Yet speakers of Hindi and other Indian languages with aspirated voiceless consonants never borrow English initials as aspirates. This simply suggests that features currently in use do not include sufficient detail, and are thus inadequate to account for phonological substitutions (or for phonological change). This is not surprising, considering their origins in the minimal feature set sufficient to specify only the phonemic oppositions occurring in languages (Jakobson et al. 1963). Feature sets in general use typically continue to specify 'contrasts observable at the systematic phonetic level', even though 'there is no clear evidence showing that the set of features required for specifying phonetic contrasts is the same as that required for specifying the natural classes of sounds required in phonological rules' (Ladefoged 1971: 1).

Distinctions *could* actually be represented by speakers in terms of sounds. It is only because speakers treat similar sounds identically with respect to particular substitutions that we can claim that features are part of the actual processing of speech. That is, the only real evidence for the psychological or linguistic reality of phonological features is their function in synchronic or diachronic phonological substitutions (cf. Keating 1988)[7]. Substitutions may specify features that are non-distinctive, and they are often, in turn, conditioned by features which are non-distinctive. For example, in some of the southern United States dialects noted earlier (s. 1.2), /æ/ and /ɒ/ diphthongize to [æɛ̣] and [ɒɒ̣] only when lengthened (before voiced stops or fricatives, in mono-syllables), even though length is not distinctive. In fact, features which are not distinctive in *any* language (e.g. release of stops) may affect the application of processes. Release, for example, blocks assimilation of an apical stop to a following non-apical in English (*bad cat* [bæg˺ kʰæt] but not *[bægᵊ kʰæt]). It also blocks assimilation (deletion) of stops after fricatives or nasals in words like *fast*, or *hand*. Thus a non-distinctive feature controls processes that neutralize feature values that are distinctive.

It would seem, then, that feature theory must concern itself with substitutions and their conditioning factors and with the relationship between the features relevant in processing and their phonetic correlates. Ladefoged (1980) has identified some seventeen articulatory and fifteen acoustic parameters that can specify the actual sounds of languages, but he notes that these parameters are not in a direct or one-to-one relationship to phonological features. There is, in fact, no reason to assume that the relationship between phonetic parameters and phonological features would be simple, if features are speakers' ways of relating articulation to perception. But until the relationships between phonological features and articulatory and acoustic parameters can be established, phonological features will be inadequate to account for phonological substitutions or change.

2.4 The scope of phonology

In the view I am expounding, phonology is a system of processes embodying the entire faculty for perceiving and pronouncing speech (or misperceiving and mispronouncing it), plus those 'keys' – inhibitions of the processes – that the speaker acquires in learning to pronounce a language. Strictly speaking, the inhibitions would be sufficient as a description of what is language-particular, and a more parsimonious kind of phonological description is hard to imagine. But the point of recognizing the identity of phonology and phonetics is not to eliminate the universal or the predictable from language descriptions. Our aim is not parsimony; it is understanding, and clearly, we can understand phonology – the discrepancy between what we say and what we think we are saying – only if we understand the processes that cause that discrepancy.

The focus of structuralist and generative phonology on rigorous justification of descriptions of languages has eliminated or marginalized anything 'external' (child speech, baby talk, foreign-isms, singing, verse, etc.) and has limited discussion of anything not 'distinctive' or 'standard' (allophonics, individual and dialectal variation, etc.) Many 'phonetic realization rules', or 'default specifications' are omitted or consigned to a separate phonetic component. This is understandable: what possible relevance can the 'default' phonetic process that raises low labial vowels have to a description of Japanese, for example, which has no low labial vowels? But the result is phonological descriptions that end just when they are getting interesting, ignoring the details of rhythm and phonetic nuance that are most characteristic of the truly unique 'accent' of its speakers. And they stop short of the very questions that that unique 'accent' poses, e.g. why Japanese speakers who learn English words should perceive and pronounce [ɒ] as [o].[8]

Under the influence of this focus on the minimal relevant characteristics of speech, the role of phonetics in phonology was reduced to providing descriptions of phonemic distinctions or distinctive features. But it is clear that phonemes are not the sums of their distinctive features, and that phonological processes do not operate only in terms of phonemes and distinctive features. Before structuralism, the standard handbooks of phonetics covered such 'non-distinctive' features as syllabication, and also the phonological processes that are responsible for free and contextual variation. Whether we call it phonetics or phonology, all this is essential to understanding how speakers of any language perceive and produce speech, and how they are prepared for situations that could never have been anticipated in language learning: having to pronounce foreign words, or the results of tongue slips or Pig Latins, or having to cope with extraordinary tempos, or noise, or fatigue, or a dentist's tools in one's mouth. Obviously, no minimalist description of a language will ever tell us what pronunciations the language could have in the next generation. But phonology should.

3 The phonetic basis of phonemic systems

3.1 Fortitions and lenitions

The phoneme inventory and the phonemic forms of a language arise, in each learner, in the interaction between two sets of phonetic demands (cf. Stampe 1987). One set of demands works to limit the inventory of 'possible' – intentionally pronounceable and perceivable – segments in a language; these demands are represented by fortition processes. *Fortitions* are typically context-free or dissimilative, and they apply to optimize individual segments in some way; they overcome difficulties that are associated with simultaneous combinations of conflicting features, or they optimize a feature of the individual segment. Delabialization and depalatalization, as exemplified in (1) and (3), and raising, as exemplified in (2) and (4), are examples of fortitions.

The other set of demands on the speaker works to make the 'possible' segments pronounceable in the different contexts in which they appear: these are represented by lenitions. *Lenitions* apply to optimize sequences of segments; they overcome difficulties associated with sequential combinations of features. Assimilative processes, like vowel nasalization before nasals and consonant palatalization before palatal vowels, are examples of lenitions.

It is in the speaker's phonetic interest to have as few distinct segments as possible to produce or perceive or remember, and to allow fortitive processes to constrain the possibilities. Therefore, in languages like Japanese or Spanish, with five-vowel systems /i, e, a, o, u/, fortitive processes – like unrounding (1) or depalatalization (3), or raising (2) or (4) – eliminate /æ/ and /ɒ/. These processes are part of the speaker's native *incapacity*, since they represent things the speaker has *not* learned and does not have to learn. They represent the inability to pronounce or perceive their inputs (low palatal or low labial vowels), and the requirement that the speaker substitute their outputs.[9]

In applying, fortitions limit the possible segment inventory, so the speaker encodes forms lexically only in terms of a limited set of relatively optimal 'possible' segments. Obviously, some processes must be overriden to acquire *any* language: a lexicon cannot be built of just the least marked segments, /t/ and /ɑ/. A child learning English must acquire the abilities or keys that turn off processes (1) through (4) – first, in perception, as he learns to attend to the difference between words like *hat* and *hot*, even though he might at first still pronounce them alike, and eventually, in production, as he learns to pronounce them differently. A child learning Japanese must, of course, limit or turn off some substitutions, but he need not turn off (1)–(4), and so does not acquire the same abilities.

But at the same time, the speaker may need to alter the optimal or 'possible' segments left by the fortitions, when these segments are combined in real-time utterances, and he will thus allow certain lenitive substitutions to apply. In a language with no /ɒ/, a speaker may produce [ɒ] when /ɑ/ appears adjacent to labial consonants, as in (5):

(5)   *Back vowels between labials must be labial.*

A context-sensitive lenition like this does not alter the set of 'possible' segments – the phoneme inventory – because the existence of a phonetic motivation for the substitution in a particular context makes it possible for both speaker and hearer to discount or ignore the effects of the substitution.

The possible outcomes of the conflicting effects of the fortition (1) and the lenition (5) are illustrated in the chart below. In conservative United States dialects, neither applies, as in A, below. In the innovating dialects I know of, only (1) applies, as in B, or both (1) and (5) apply, as in C. But one would not be surprised to find a dialect like D, where (1) does not apply, but (5) does. Donegan and Stampe (1979) established, on the basis of optional fortitions and lenitions, that all fortitive processes must apply before all lenitive ones: fortitions first, lenitions last.

Dialect:			cot	caught	bobble	bauble
A.	(1) does not apply:		/kat/	/kɒt/	/babəl/	/bɒbəl/
	(5) does not apply:		[kat]	[kɒt]	[babəl]	[bɒbəl]
B.	(1) applies:		/kat/	/kat/	/babə/	/babəl/
	(5) applies:		[kat]	[kat]	[bɒbəl]	[bɒbəl]
C.	(1) applies:		/kat/	/kat/	/babəl/	/babəl/
	(5) does not apply:		[kat]	[kat]	[babəl]	[babəl]
D.	(1) does not apply:		/kat/	/kɒt/	/bɒbəl/	/bɒbəl/
	(5) applies:		[kat]	[kɒt]	[bɒbəl]	[bɒbəl]

The forms in / /'s represent forms that are perceived and stored in long-term memory; those in [ ]'s represent forms as spoken.

3.2   The interaction of fortitions and lenitions creates phonemic representations

Whenever they can, speakers hear and remember 'impossible' sounds – sounds that are eliminated from the phonemic inventory

by fortitive constraints – as 'possible' sounds, so in dialects where
(1) applies, only /ɑ/ appears in phonemic forms. (Similarly,
English speakers perceive and remember sounds like [ɛ̃] in words
like bend [bɛ̃nd] as /ɛ/, or [t̪] in words like eighth [ɛɪt̪θ] as /t/.) If
possible, speakers do this by undoing the effects of lenitive
processes to arrive at representations which the fortitive constraints do not rule out. The phoneme inventory of a language is
thus the result of the interaction of the typically context-free
fortitive processes and the context-sensitive lenitive processes.
And the phonemic form of a word is the result of undoing
subconsciously, in perception, enough lenitive processes to arrive
at a form that is not ruled out by the obligatory fortitions. This is
why speakers and hearers are typically unconscious of allophony.

Learning the phonemic system of a language, then, involves
only learning which processes are not allowed to apply. A learner
of dialect A need only realize that [ɒ] sounds different from [ɑ] in
a single word, like caught, where its presence is unattributable to
assimilation, to overcome process (1) – unrounding – in
perception. On doing so, he can begin to lexicalize low labial
vowels differently from low non-labials, and he marks (1) for
eventual mastery in production. (Overcoming a process perceptually is of course necessary for overcoming it articulatorily, but
it is not sufficient, which is why learners' perceptions and lexical
representations are often more advanced than their productions.)
Learners of dialects B and C do not recognize the [ɑ]/[ɒ]
difference, even in perception, and have not learned to
pronounce [ɒ] as an intentional, or permissible, sound. Thus they
lexicalize all low non-palatal vowels as /ɑ/.

But the B speakers, though subject to (1), can and do
pronounce [ɒ], by assimilation (5), in words like Bob, Mom,
bomb, bobble, etc.[10] These [ɒ]'s are not perceived or remembered
as different from the vowels of Don and cot. The B speakers
apparently discount the labiality of these [ɒ]'s as an effect of the
labials in the environment. In fact, such speakers may be quite
unconscious of any difference between their vowels in dog [dɑg]
and Bob [bɒb], although A speakers, who maintain the original
distinction, may notice the 'wrong' vowels in these words.

Learners who hear words like bobble, with [ɑ] in potentially
labializing environments, mark process (5) – labiality assimilation
– for eventual mastery (suppression) in production. Speakers of
dialect C seem to overcome this process.

Speakers of dialect A also overcome (5), and thus they
eliminate (5) as a way of accounting for [ɒ] in labial environments. The recognition that (5) does not apply in bobble means

that (5) does not account for the occurrence of the [ɒ] in *bauble*. So when words like *bauble* [bɒbəl] are encountered, the [ɒ]'s in such words are perceived and remembered as /ɒ/'s.

Learners of dialect D overcome (1) and thus distinguish between /ɑ/ and /ɒ/, but they do not need to overcome (5). Thus (5) remains as a way of accounting for the labiality of the [ɒ] in either *bauble* or *bobble*. But since (1) has been overcome and /ɒ/ is, consequently, a 'possible' sound – a phoneme – there is no need to undo (5) in the perception or lexicalization of either of these words; both [ɒ]'s can represent /ɒ/'s. (See Donegan 1985 for further discussion.)

3.3 Morphophonemics: undoing substitutions to make morphological connections

When the undoing of further processes in perception will also allow the expression of a morphological relationship, this too occurs, if, but only if, the speaker makes the morphological connection. To take a very simple example, *handbag*, usually pronounced ['hæm̩ˌbæg], can be perceived phonemically (and possibly lexicalized) as /'hæm̩ˌbæg/ by undoing only the lenition which nasalizes vowels, since /hæm̩ˌbæg/ is a sequence of possible sounds (phonemes) in English. But ['hãmˌbæg] can also be perceived as /'hændˌbæg/ (by undoing the lenition which assimilates a sequence of alveolar stops to a following labial, and that which degeminates stops), and it will be thus perceived if the speaker recognizes that it represents the morphemes *hand* and *bag*. Both /'hæm̩ˌbæg/ and /'hændˌbæg/ are possible phonological representations of *handbag*. /'hæm̩ˌbæg/, the most superficial possible phonological representation, is the phonemic representation – and thus we recognize its homophony with *ham bag*. /'hændˌbæg/, also a possible sequence of phonemes is, further, a morphophonemic representation. (See Stampe 1987 for further discussion.)

The term 'morphophonemic' is used here to refer to representations that are accessible through the undoing of phonological processes past the point where an acceptable phonemic representation is achieved. Arriving at a morphophonemic representation requires the undoing of one or more additional derivational steps in order to reveal a relationship with another form of the same morpheme. The term may also refer to the effect of a process which makes a different phonemic interpretation possible – e.g., the alveolar assimilation process that affects /'hændˌbæg/ has morphophonemic effects when nd → mb, where /m/ and /b/ are phonemes. This is not the same as 'morphophonological', a term which refers to rules that appear to be partly phonological but are morphologically conditioned – or to representations that are not accessible through the undoing of purely phonological processes (see section 2.1).

4 Sound change and learnability

In the conventionalist view, the optimal grammar is the optimal combination of lexical forms and phonological rules. Because the phonetic forms of a language change over time, the optimal grammar to be derived from the phonetic forms will change. Conventionalist phonology appears to assume that segment inventories and phonological forms are acquired through the performance, by learners, of distributional analysis of remember-ed phonetic forms and through comparative evaluation of alternative grammars or grammar-and-lexicon combinations. (For a discussion of the improbabilities of this assumption, see Donegan 1985.) But there is an alternative explanation of how a child, who hears only phonetic forms, can arrive at adult-like *phonemic* representations as well as adult-like *phonetic* forms. The phonemes and the phonological forms of a language are not the results of grammatical analysis, but of automatic phonological processing.

In this theory of acquisition advocated here, the phonemic system of a language arises within the learner as a way of categorizing the elements of speech for storage in long-term memory. No distributional analysis, and no direct comparison of unrelated forms like *bobble* and *bauble* or *cot* and *caught* are required. Lexical representations are achieved and revised one word at a time, with reference to what one has learned about which processes apply and which do not. The learner goes from remembering less about each word to remembering more, from less mastery of perception and production and more reliance on 'defaults' to greater mastery, and from perceiving differences to producing them.

5 Changes in phonological representations

Phonological change begins with changes in pronunciation. Because the speaker perceives in terms specified by the phonological processes that apply in his speech, changes in learners' phonemic inventories or phonemic identities result 'automatically' from changes in the application of phonological processes in the speakers around them. Let us examine some examples of how phonetic changes – changes in the application of phonological processes – result in changes in speakers' phonological representations.

5.1 Loss of phonemes – merger of lexical classes

Perhaps the simplest example of a change in representation by the application of a phonological process is that of merger. Examples include the merger resulting from the unrounding of labiopalatal vowels, which took place not only in English (Brunner 1965), but also in Yiddish (Sapir 1915), and the German dialects of Darmstadt and Upper Austrian (Keller 1961). In these cases, a fortitive process,

(6)   *Palatal vowels must be non-labial*

was allowed to apply, with the result that /y/ and /ø/ were pronounced [i] and [e].[11] As the application became more widespread and general, learners stopped hearing [y] and [ø], and thus did not find it necessary to produce them, so /y/ was eliminated in favour of /i/, and /ø/ was eliminated in favour of /e/. The fortition became a constraint on the inventory.

Similarly, in the United States dialects where *caught* and *cot*, *dawn* and *Don*, *auto* and *Otto* are homophonous, the application of (1) is responsible for the merger of /ɒ/ with /ɑ/. This process or constraint, applying in all styles and at all tempos, means that the speaker does not learn to distinguish [ɑ] from [ɒ] at all.

At first, such a substitution may be introduced as an option. The innovating speakers, in that case, maintain the lexical distinction, with only an optional surface neutralization. But if the process applies to substitute [ɑ] for [ɒ] with sufficient frequency, a subsequent generation of speakers may find it unnecessary to inhibit the process by mastering the pronunciation of [ɒ]. For them, the unrounding is obligatory, and there is no phoneme /ɒ/, but only /ɑ/, because when a fortition is obligatory for a speaker, it affects his lexical representations, ruling out the input as 'impossible'. Such fortitive processes may constrain perception as well as pronunciation, so that speakers do not even perceive the distinction in the speech of those who retain it.

As noted in section 3.2, while the context-free fortition acts as a constraint on the phoneme inventory, eliminating /ɒ/ in favor of /ɑ/, a context-sensitive labiality assimilation can account for the phonetic instances of [ɒ], as in [mɒm], [pɒp], [bɒb] for *mom*, *pop*, *Bob*, if these occur. But it can only do so as long as the learner does not notice forms like invariant [bɑm] *bomb*, or [bɑbəl] *bobble*, which would make the labiality assimilation untenable.

5.1.1 The Labov–Yaeger–Steiner paradox

Labov et al. (LYS) (1972) reported on a rather puzzling situation which they encountered with a speaker (in central Pennsylvania) who appeared to merge [ɑ] and [ɒ] in reading or judging minimal pairs. They found that this speaker maintained a firm distinction between words with /ɑ/ and words with /ɒ/ – like *cot* and *caught* – in casual or connected speech, but lost the distinction in reading minimal pairs, and denied its existence when asked about the pairs directly. LYS pursued this apparent paradox of 'reported mergers' and found other instances where speakers distinguished in connected or casual speech forms which they merged in careful or closely monitored speech – and which they judged to be 'the same'.

Surprise at this state of affairs results from a number of assumptions: (a) We assume that if speakers produce a consistent difference between minimal pairs in casual speech the pairs must be represented as different in long-term memory. That means the words have different phonemic representations. However, it is often assumed (b) that speakers' careful pronunciations, as in reading word-lists, are more like their lexical representations than pronunciations drawn from connected speech. And (c), we assume that speakers make same/different judgements on the basis of their lexical representations, rather than on the basis of connected-speech forms. Accepting (a), that if a speaker makes a consistent distinction in connected speech, he maintains the distinction in the lexicon, let us examine assumptions (b) and (c).

Many optional phonological substitutions (alveolar place-assimilation, flapping, flap deletion, 'monophthongization' of [ən] to [ṇ], etc.) are characteristic of casual speech. It is our attention to substitutions of this kind that makes it appear (b) is true: that careful speech forms, to which these substitutions do not apply, are closer to speakers' lexical forms. But there are some optional phonological substitutions – fortitions – that apply only in slow or careful or exaggerated speech, as when *prayed* is overpronounced as [pəˈrɛi̯d] (cf. Donegan and Stampe 1979). If such optional substitution neutralizes a phonemic distinction, we may find that speakers actually merge, in careful speech, forms that they distinguish in connected speech. E.g., *prayed* becomes homophonous with *parade*. It appears that LYS's Pennsylvania speaker applied the low-vowel unrounding fortition only option-ally, in careful speech. He produced both a low back-rounded vowel /ɒ/ and a low back-unrounded vowel /ɑ/ in casual speech, but only the unrounded /ɑ/ in careful or reflecting speech. The careful speech forms [hɑk] and [kɑt] of /ɒ/-class words like *hawk* and *caught* are thus 'farther from' the lexical forms, than the casual forms [hɒk] and [kɒt] would be. Therefore (b) is not always true.

Assumption (c) is that speakers make same/different judgements on the basis of lexical representations. Speakers often do make such judgements on the basis of lexical forms when an optional merger affects connected speech. For example, *latter* and *ladder* may be judged as different even by speakers who pronounce both as [læDɻ] in connected speech. This occurs because speakers ordinarily base their judgements on careful pronunciations, to which the merging process does not apply. But in the case of an optional neutralization, there are two possible phonological representations for the neutralized form: the lexical representation is the representation *before* the substitution applies, but the output of the substitution is interpretable as a different phonemic form. Thus, speakers may also recognize that *latter* and *ladder* are pronounced the same, ['læDɻ], by noticing that *latter* can be pronounced 'with a d instead of a t'. When the merger applies only in careful speech, the sameness judgement is particularly apt to reflect the merger, rather than the different lexical forms. So although *caught* is [kɒt] in connected speech for LYS's speaker, it is [kɑt] – just like *cot* – in careful speech. Unfortunately, LYS did not report on the Pennsylvania speaker's ability to perceive the *cot/caught* distinction in the speech of others. We would expect that this speaker could perceive it.

In the section in which this paradox is presented, many of LYS's informants appeared to be considering their careful speech in same/different judgements, or to be marginally aware of dual possible pronunciations (which suggest dual phonemic interpretations). Unfortunately, I cannot account here for all of the puzzles LYS presented. My intention is simply to point out that optional *careful-speech* fortitions and resultant dual phonemic perceptions must both be considered when evaluating and accounting for speakers' judgements.

5.2   Changes in the phonemic forms of words

The application of a process that is lenitive and context-sensitive but that does not create alternations may, of course, change the phonemic representations of some words without changing the phoneme inventory. In many dialects of English where /ɑ/ and /ɒ/

both exist, /ɑ/ has become [ɒ] after [w] (and before a tautosyllabic liquid), as in *wall, squall, war, quart,* [wɒl, skwɒl, wɒr, kwɒrt]. Learners encountering invariant [ɒ] in [wɒl] might attribute it to an assimilation if [ɒ] were ruled out of the phoneme inventory by a fortition. But since, in most dialects, this fortition is suppressed to allow words like *caught* [kɒt], and since these forms involve no variation or alternations with /ɑ/, there is no reason for language learners to interpret the [ɒ] here as anything other than /ɒ/.

There are, however, more interesting cases of changes in the phonemic representation of a class of words because of the addition of a lenition process. The case of 'intrusive r' in English seems to be such a case. It is well known that 'r-insertion' occurs only in dialects in which syllable-final r is de-rhotacized. In RP, for example,

(7)   *r in a syllable-fall[12] (before consonant or pause) loses its r-colouring, becoming ə̣.*

De-rhotacizing [r] leaves a non-syllabic schwa, which may coalesce with a preceding syllabic schwa. Thus, we find final [ə] or [ə̣] phrase finally or before consonants, as in

A.

butter	[bʌtə]	*favour*	[fɛi̯və]
hear	[hɪə̣]	*pour*	[pɔə̣].

But pre-vocalically, where [r] can begin the syllable, [r] appears:

B.

butter it	[bʌtər ɪt]	*favour it*	[fɛi̯vər ɪt]
hear it	[hɪr ɪt],	*pour it*	[pɔr ɪt].

In RP, and other dialects which have 'intrusive r', words that have final schwa when pronounced alone or before consonants, e.g.

C.

India	['ɪndiə]	*idea*	[ai̯'dɪə]	*drama*	['drɑ:mə],

are pronounced with 'linking' r when they occur before words that begin with a vowel:

D.

India and Pakistan	['ɪndiər ən ˌpɑːkɪ'stɑːn],
drama and music	['drɑːmər ən 'mjuːzɪk]
idea of	['ai̯dɪər əv].

This innovative [r] may also occur – though 'less frequently' after final /ɑː/ or /ɔː/, as in

E.
Shah of Persia   [ˈʃɑːr əv ˈpɜːʃə]
law and order   [ˈlɔːr ənd ˈɔːdə]   (Gimson 1962: 203ff.).

Gimson describes this 'intrusive r' as occurring by analogy. In generative phonology, the insertion of r in these dialects has been described as a 'rule inversion' (Vennemann 1972: 216). This means that speakers of dialects which have an 'r-deletion' rule (r in syllable-offsets is de-rhotacized) reinterpret the resulting data and create a new rule, one which inserts r after certain word-final vowels. (It would be possible to say the insertion occurs after word-final schwa; insertion after final /ɑː/ or /ɔː/ may depend on the pronunciation of these vowels with centering glides, as [ɑə] or [ɔə].) But neither 'analogy' nor the creation of an inverted and perhaps more general rule can explain the *difficulty* of pronunciations without the intrusive r. Gimson says that pronunciations like *I saw it* /aɪ ˈsɔːr ɪt/, or *drawing* /ˈdrɔːrɪŋ/, are 'generally disapproved of', and that 'it is likely that many RP speakers have to make a conscious effort to avoid the use of such forms'. He says, in fact, that they may have to insert a glottal stop or pause to do so (1962: 204). Attempts not to analogize or generalize would not create such a pronunciation difficulty for the speaker.

So instead, we might take the following view.[13] In these dialects, the lenition, (7), applies obligatorily. Therefore speakers find final r's difficult or impossible to pronounce, and they produce alternations like those between the A and B forms above. Learners can account for such alternations by 'undoing' the lenition (7), and they thus arrive at underlying forms with final /r/'s. Words like *hear* and *favour*, with a final [ə] or [ə] are interpreted as having final /r/ to account for the B forms. The A forms are pronounced before pause or consonant because of (7), and the B forms occur before a vowel, since the r can be syllabified with the following vowel.[14]

But learners may also undo the r-to-schwa lenition in perceiving words like *India* and *drama*, which have final schwas that did not originate in r's: thus, /ɪndiər/, /drɑmər/. And if words like *draw* and *Shah* – and even *baa* – are pronounced with schwa offglides [drɔə], [ʃɑə], [bæə] they too can be interpreted as having final vowel-plus-/r/: as /drɔr/, /ʃɑr/, /bær/. But then, before vowels, where de-rhotacization does not apply, these /r/'s will actually be pronounced. (This may happen even though the words are often pronounced [drɔː], [ʃɑː], etc., since these may be perceived as assimilated forms of [drɔə], [ʃɑə], which are in turn perceived as de-rhotacized forms of /drɔr/, /ʃɑr/).

The 'intrusive r' does not, then, intrude because the speaker makes up an r-insertion rule. Instead, the r appears by analysis, when speakers assume that, because some final schwas represent /r/'s, other final schwas do so as well. Assuming that final schwas are /r/'s allows certain vowels to be eliminated from the phoneme inventory: the long vowels /əː/, /ɑː/, and /ɔː/ (just those that cannot be analyzed as vowel plus /i̯/ or /u̯/) would be represented as /ər/, /ɑr/, and /ɔr/; and the diphthongs described as /iə̯/, /ɛə̯/, /ɔə̯/, /uə̯/ would be /ir/, /ɛr/, /ɔr/, /ur/. Lexical postvocalic /r/'s are required in any case, but having /r/ rather than length or /ə̯/ means that fortitive constraints can be maintained which eliminate distinctive length or offglides other than /i̯/ or /u̯/. Speakers without intrusive r must overcome these constraints to acquire long vowels and final /ə/'s.

Thus *Shah*, *draw*, *baa*, and *India* are hard to pronounce without r, in linking environments like *Shah of*, *draw it*, because there is, in these environments, no reason to de-rhotacize their final /r/'s. The change is a matter of perception: speakers with intrusive r's perceive final [ə]'s as /r/'s, by attributing them to the application of (7). Speakers without intrusive r's can perceive final schwas as /ə/'s (or they can ignore them, as the results of a lenition that centralizes the offsets of long low vowels) in words where alternations do not reveal the presence of /r/'s.[15]

5.3 Addition of phonemes to the inventory, process 'loss'

New applications of lenitive substitutions may not only cause changes in the phonological forms of words; they may also result in changes in the phoneme inventory. Further, the innovative application of one lenition may, in obscuring the environment for another lenition, cause that 'earlier' lenition to cease to apply.

Old High German (OHG) umlaut is a well-known but instructive example of both these results (cf. Stampe 1987: 294). This context-sensitive palatality assimilation (a lenition) might be stated:

(8) *A vowel is palatalized if a high palatal vowel follows in the same metrical foot.*

This created OHG forms like *betti* 'bed' and *stein* 'stone' (cf. Gothic *badi*, *stains*). Assimilated (short or long) /u/ and /o/ became [y] and [ø], as /a/ became [e]. For example, in OHG, *muːs* 'mouse' alternated with *müːsi* 'mice', *fuot* 'foot' with *füösi* 'feet', and *gast* 'guest' with *gesti* 'guests'. Twaddell (1938) points out that the [y] and [ø] outputs of umlaut were indicated in spelling only in Middle High German, after the palatal environment which occasioned the umlaut had been eliminated. But the [e] result of umlaut was spelled in OHG. Since OHG had an /e/ phoneme, it was possible for speakers to perceive the [e] result of umlaut as the phoneme /e/. (Speakers did not need to undo the umlaut lenition, except to connect alternants.) And, as the spellings indicate, the OHG scribes did perceive this umlaut-product, [e], as /e/.

OHG had no /y/ or /ø/ phonemes, however. We can say that [y] and [ø] were ruled out of the phonemic inventory by fortitive constraints against labiopalatal vowels:

(9)   *Labial vowels must be non-palatal.*
(10)   *Palatal vowels must be non-labial.* See (6) on p. 114.

In perceiving [y] and [ø], speakers apparently undid the umlaut process which created them; in effect, they discounted their palatal quality as an effect of the following palatal vowel, and perceived and spelled [y] and [ø] as /u/ and /o/. Only when a later change,

(11)   *Unstressed vowels must be non-palatal.*

reduced the unaccented palatal vowels which occasioned the assimilation did speakers begin to perceive and spell [y] and [ø] as separate phonemes.

Such re-phonemicization must take place in the learners of the language. During a time when the vowel reduction was variable or optional, learners encountered phonetic forms like [muːs] 'mouse', [myːsi] ~ [myːsə] 'mice'. They could interpret these as /muːs/ and /muːsi/ by undoing both the vowel reduction (11), and the palatality assimilation (8). But at some point, the reduction (11) became sufficiently exceptionless to make the unstressed palatal vowel impossible for learners to perceive. Learners encountering only phonetic forms like [muːs] and [myːsə] no longer had reason to interpret the plural suffix as other than /ə/. Therefore, they could no longer discount the palatal quality of [y] as the result of an assimilation to a final /i/. At that point, learners had to forgo the fortitive processes (9) and (10) that had constrained the phoneme inventory, and learn to produce, perceive, and remember labiopalatal vowels. They were, in other words, forced to admit /y/ and /ø/ as phonemes. Thus, the obligatory vowel reduction process (11), by completely obscuring the motivation for the umlaut assimilation (8) resulted in speakers' having to overcome the fortitions that had eliminated labiopalatal vowels.

At this point, the vowel pairings created by umlaut became usable in morphological marking, and they eventually acquired significance in marking plurals, subjunctives, diminutives, etc. Even when the fortition represented by (10) or (6) re-asserted itself in some German dialects, unrounding the labiopalatals as described in section 5.1, the pairings, though entirely arbitrary from a synchronic point of view, retained their morphological significance (cf. Sapir 1921, ch. 8).

5.4 Phonemic split and complementary distribution

When changes in the application of lenitions make a fortitive constraint untenable, as in the MHG case, the phoneme inventory changes. And when a fortition applies obligatorily, as in American dialects where /ɒ/ > /ɑ/, the fortition changes the phoneme inventory. It is change in the application of fortitions that allows (or creates) the change in the inventory.

The fortitive constraints in these two examples, *labial vowels are non-palatal* and *low vowels are non-labial*, are context-free; this is typical of fortitions. But a fortitive change may apply context-sensitively, applying only in stressed syllables, in lengthening contexts, at intonation peaks, in dissimilative environments, etc. For example, in most British and American dialects, early Modern English [ʌi̯] became [ɑi̯] and [ʌu̯] became [ɑu̯] – that is, the following fortitions applied:

(12)   *A non-palatal syllabic that precedes a palatal glide must be low.*

(13)   *A non-labial syllabic that precedes a labial glide must be low.*

If an obligatory fortition constrains phonemic representations, a fortition that becomes obligatory will change speakers' phonemic representations as (12) and (13) did. This may happen even when the fortition applies only in specific environments.

In certain United States and Canadian dialects, the vowel corresponding to Middle English long i: is represented in some contexts by [ɑi̯] and in others by [ʌi̯].[16] The distribution is often described, somewhat over-simply, as [ʌi̯] before voiceless consonants and [ɑi̯] elsewhere. The rule has been called 'Canadian Raising' (Chambers 1973), but it is not limited to Canadian dialects, nor is it necessarily a raising – no evidence has been offered that [ɑi̯] is basic and [ʌi̯] is derived. I follow Stampe (1972) and Gregg (1973) in suggesting that the United States and Canadian dialects which retain [ʌi̯] have not quite completed the Great Vowel Shift change of ME i: to /ɑi̯/, and that 'Canadian

Raising' is actually the result of lowering the [ʌi̯] reflex of ME i:
to [ɑi̯] only in certain environments, rather than generally.[17]
Gregg adduces evidence for this view from Anglo-Irish, in which
ME i: remains /əi̯/, and from Scottish and Scotch-Irish, in which
[ʌi̯] and [ɑi̯] apparently diverged early, and underwent a
phonemic split.

This alternation (or split) is clearly related to the process by
which vowels are lengthened in open syllables or before voiced
(lenis) consonants. Long vowels are, ceteris paribus, more
susceptible to lowering than their short counterparts (Donegan
1978), and basically, /ʌi̯/ is lowered to [ɑi̯] where it is lengthened,
and it remains [ʌi̯] where it is short. The conditions that create
sufficient lengthening to condition the quality change apparently
differ from dialect to dialect. They include not only the voicing
and continuance of the following consonant, but also the number
and accentuation of following syllables within the accent-group.

For speakers who have no quality difference in words with /ɑi̯/,
we expect a length difference between the vowels of *write* [rɑi̯t]
and *ride* [rɑːi̯d], as between those of *kit* [kɪt] and *kid* [kɪːd]. Thus
fly, *ride*, *tide*, *gibe*, *drive*, *tithe* (with final [ð]), *rise*, etc. have long
vowels, while *write*, *tight*, *ripe*, *life*, *blithe* (with final [θ]), *rice*,
etc. have short. In the North American dialects with an [ʌi̯]–[ɑi̯]
alternation, the words in the first set have [ɑi̯], and those in the
second have [ʌi̯].[18]

For some Michigan, Minnesota, and New York speakers, the
vowel in words like *cider*, *spider*, and *idle*, as well as in *miter*,
title, is [ʌi̯]. In these disyllables, the nucleus is mid, regardless of
the voicing of the following consonant, because the presence of a
following unstressed syllable within the stress-group, or foot,
shortens the first syllable (cf. Lehiste 1971a, b). The stressed
nucleus is thus not lengthened in words like *spider* and *pilot* (as it
would be in *spied* or *pile*). Because their phonetic shapes do not
provide the conditions for lengthening, these disyllables have not
undergone the length-dependent lowering.

Note that these words, though disyllabic, are monomorphemic.
In words (or phrases) of similar shape but bimorphemic
structure, like *glider*, *slider*, *tidal*, *pile it*, the vowel of the stressed
syllable in these dialects is [ɑi̯]. But why should *spider*, *idle* and
pilot have [ʌi̯], while *slider*, *tidal* and *pile it* have [ɑi̯]? The
obvious answer is that the two-morpheme forms with [ɑi̯]
maintain the same vowel that their one-syllable bases have. That
is, [ɑi̯] occurs in the derived forms, *slider*, *tidal*, *pile it* because it
occurs in the one-syllable base forms, *slide*, *tide*, *pile*. This might
be expressed formally by having a morpheme boundary condition

the stressed-vowel change.

But this response leaves us with a further problem: the [ʌi̯] ~ [ɑi̯] alternation is usually regarded as allophonic, and allophonic alternations or changes do not ordinarily depend on morpheme identity. And we would not expect them to. If, as has been repeatedly observed (by Sapir 1921, Bloomfield 1933, Swadesh 1934, and others), speakers are not aware of allophony, we would expect them to make allophonic changes under conditions that are purely phonetic (and prosodic) – not morphological. But the lowering of [ɑi̯] in these disyllables does seem to depend on morphemic identity.

The explanation seems to be that, in becoming obligatory, the lowering, a fortition, changed the phonemic forms of the words in which it applied. When the process,

(12')   *A long non-palatal syllabic that precedes a palatal glide must be low.*

was optional (as it may have been at some point in history), then /rʌi̯d/ could be pronounced [rʌi̯d] or [rɑi̯d]. But when (12') became obligatory, then

/rʌi̯d/, always pronounced   [rɑi̯d], became   /rɑi̯d/ *ride*, while
/rʌi̯t/, pronounced   [rʌi̯t], remained /rʌi̯t/ *write*.

With affixation and flapping,

/rʌi̯t – ər/ becomes [rʌi̯Dɹ̩], and
/rɑi̯d – ər/ becomes [rɑi̯Dɹ̩].

The lowered vowel, being phonemic, now no longer depends on a particular phonetic environment. The evidence for the phonemic nature of the change is that the words with lowered nuclei retain these low nuclei even when an affix makes them disyllabic and shortens the stressed vowel. It is notable that forms like *pilot* and *pile it* may constitute minimal pairs in such dialects. It is also worth noticing that 'Along came a sp[ʌi̯]der' does not rhyme with 'and sat down bes[ɑi̯]de her' for these speakers.

Vance (1987) argues that the difference between [ɑi̯] and [ʌi̯] is phonemic, at least in some dialects. He notes the ease with which 'naive' informants who use [ɑi̯] and [ʌi̯] are able to attend to this difference and make judgements about it. This ease is contrasted with the difficulty of training ordinary speakers to detect allophonic differences like that between front vs. back [k] and clear vs. dark [l]. Vance also points to the irregularities in the distribution of [ɑi̯] and [ʌi̯], and to some minimal pairs (like *idle/idol*). He notes that the difference between an /ɑi̯/–/ʌi̯/

distinction and the presence of /aɪ̯/ in all environments seems to involve lexical diffusion, and that changes that occur by lexical diffusion are always phonemic (cf. Chen and Wang 1975, Krishnamurti 1978).

Once a speaker has determined that two sounds, like [aɪ̯] and [ʌɪ̯], are different phonemes and must be represented differently in long-term memory, his representations of individual words that contain either sound will depend on the pronunciations of the speakers from whom he learns each word. It does not matter whether the other speaker makes a distinction or not: if the new word is heard with [aɪ̯], the learner will remember /aɪ̯/, and if the new word is heard with [ʌɪ̯], the learner will remember /ʌɪ̯/. This means that the pronunciations of speakers who make a distinction will, for the most part, agree with those of speakers for whom the alternation is automatic. It also accounts for the discrepancies and occasional indecisions among the speakers Vance questioned. (Hearing multiple variants may create indecision in the learner, although it will not necessarily do so.)

The distribution of [aɪ̯] and [ʌɪ̯] is somewhat different in Baltimore, Maryland, from the distribution in the dialects Vance discussed. In monosyllables and monomorphemic disyllables, the following consonant phoneme predicts the variant: [ʌɪ̯] occurs before voiceless consonants, and [aɪ̯] occurs before voiced consonants or finally: so *tight*, *miter*, and *title* have [ʌɪ̯], and *tide*, *spider*, *idle*, and *tie* have [aɪ̯]. Even in polysyllables, the difference seems to be predictable: before an unstressed syllable, the following consonant is predictive, as above: *glycogen* and *nitrogen* have [ʌɪ̯], but *gyroscope*, *hibernate*, and *hydrogen* have [aɪ̯]. Before a stressed syllable, the vowel is [aɪ̯]: *hypotenuse*, *isosceles*, *vituperate*, *iconic* (*bicycle* and *bifocals*, with secondary stress on the second syllable, fall into this category), although here there are some exceptions: *nitrate*, *python*, have [ʌɪ̯] before a secondary stress, and *psychotic*, *licentious*, *micrometer* are at least possible with [ʌɪ̯] before primary stress, where [aɪ̯] is expected.

Yet the same ability to identify the difference that Vance noted as evidence of phonemic status also exists for Baltimore speakers. Although *raider* and *rater*, *kiddie* and *kitty*, with medial flaps, are homophones, *writer* and *rider* with identical medial flaps are not.[19] In this dialect, as in Vance's, it seems that [aɪ̯] and [ʌɪ̯] are different phonemes, in spite of the fact that here they are in complementary or near-complementary distribution. This in turn suggests that an obligatory fortitive constraint, even if it is context sensitive, may affect the phoneme inventory.[20] This supports the idea that it is the obligatory application of fortitions (along with the possibility of perceiving via lenitions) – rather than the distributional analysis of a mass of remembered phonetic forms – that creates the phoneme inventory. (Cf. the discussion in s. 4.)

6 Summary

The examples presented here were chosen to show that every phonological change – from a 'low-level' nuance of pronunciation to a radical restructuring of perception – can be understood as the failure by speakers to overcome a phonetic constraint that past speakers did overcome. Such a constraint, manifested as a substitution, was already a part of a dynamic mental system of phonetically motivated substitutions that constitute the phonology. It is this same robust and subtle system that, from the close of the babbling period in infancy, and throughout the life of the individual, provides a perceptually and/or articulatorily optimal substitute for any unpronounceable utterance. (Recall that this unpronounceability extends even to the phonemic representations of the native language – in English, can't /kænt/ cannot be pronounced without aspiration or vowel nasalization, and in connected speech it is ordinarily [kʰæ̃ʔt].) Whether the unpronounceability is due to the intrinsic difficulty of the intended utterance, or its tempo, or its novelty (as in foreign words, or the results of tongue-slips or Pig-Latins), or whether it is due to the speaker's condition (fatigue, nervousness, or the dentist's hands in his mouth), the phonology instantly puts the appropriate substitute at the 'tip of one's tongue'.

The pioneers of phonology – Baudouin, Passy, Jespersen, Sapir, Meillet, Jakobson – recognized that all sound change (as opposed to analogical change) is simply a failure of new speakers to overcome some aspect of this inner system of 'phonetic tendencies'. The problem of how sound changes become part of the phonology, and the problem of how to impose 'naturalness constraints' on phonological descriptions, are pseudo-problems that have arisen only because modern linguistics, obsessed with economical descriptions, has separated phonology from phonetics. But they are inseparable: the phonology is the phonetics, and phonological change is phonetic change.

Acknowledgement

Sincere thanks to Ann Peters, Ken Rehg, and David Stampe for all their help. Errors, of course, are my own.

Notes

1. For the sake of brevity, I omit 'intermediate' substitutions that involve only tense/lax differences (e.g. [ɒ] → [ɒ̆] → [ɑ]) or diphthongizations limited to just the onset or the offset of the vowel (e.g. [ɒ] → [aɒ̞] → [aɒ̞], or [ɒ] → [ɒɒ̞] → [aɒ̞]).
2. Some learners easily acquire keys that elude others. For example, some children learning English get the vowels nearly right, making few substitutions, almost from the beginning, while others make do with a small set of substitutes for a rather long time: contrast Amahl Smith (Smith 1973) and Joan Velten (Velten 1943). Such differences may be idiosyncratic, or they may depend on developmental factors or on the learner's prosodic system.
3. E.g., US speakers learn to distinguish *latter* [lætɾ̩] from *ladder* [lædɾ̩], but they do not do so in ordinary speech, and producing the distinction is perceived as requiring special effort.
4. The distinction goes back to Baudouin de Courtenay (1895), who called the morphologically conditioned alternations of morphophonology 'correlations', as opposed to the phonetically motivated 'divergences' of what is here called phonology. (The division between 'post-lexical' and 'lexical' rule applications is not presented as a difference between rules with and without synchronic phonetic motivation.)
5. Morphonological rules are insensitive to prosodic factors like tempo and intonation, and to physical states like drunkenness or tiredness. They never affect or depend on non-distinctive features; rather, they always substitute one phoneme for another. See Donegan and Stampe (1979) for further characterization of the difference between such conventional rules and phonological processes.
6. Cf. Keating's remarks that phonetics is being viewed, more and more, as 'largely the same sort of creature as the phonology, that is, a formal system of rules', and that 'it is too early to decide the exact division of labour between phonological and phonetic rules' or even 'what is at stake in positing such a division' (1988: 288, cf. 287–91). I am arguing that there is no such division.
7. In word pairs like *divine/divinity*, *verbose/verbosity*, *profound/profundity*, etc., there is a relationship between 'long' and 'short' phonemes /aị̯/, ɪ/, /oụ̯/, ɑ/, and /aụ̯/, ʌ/. But no evidence has ever been presented that this relationship is *synchronically* phonological and based on features, rather than morphological and based simply on conventional pairings of phonemes. If the change of a feature in one member of the pair implied anything about the pronunciation of the other member, one might make an argument for a feature description that unifies the pairs. For example, if the dialectal fronting of /ɔụ̯/ to /ɛụ̯/ in *verbose* and /aụ̯/ to /æụ̯/ in *profound* implied anything about the pronunciation of /ɑ/ in *verbosity* or /ʌ/ *profundity*, one might argue for a feature relationship between /oụ̯/ and /ɑ/, or between /aụ̯/ and /ʌ/ – but arguments for a synchronic phonetic basis have not stood up to scrutiny (see, for example, Manaster-Ramer 1981).

8. The admissibility theory of classical generative phonology at least made an attempt at such prediction. But, as Greg Lee has pointed out, it implied that an inadmissible word like *Gdansk* would be pronounced by English speakers as [stɑnsk].

9. In Arabic, or Brunei Malay, with three vowels /i, a, u/, /e/ and /o/ are ruled out, as well as /æ/ and /ɒ/. Thus, (1) and (2) apply to non-high vowels, and (3) and (4) result in high, instead of non-low, vowels.

10. This is like the pronunciation of nasalized vowels before nasals, by speakers who cannot pronounce such vowels 'intentionally' in non-nasal environments.

11. In English, the unrounding of mid vowels preceded that of high vowels, and the unrounding of short vowels preceded that of their long counterparts.

12. 'Fall' indicates decreasing sonority. A syllable-fall includes the syllabic and extends to the end of the syllable. A measure-fall includes the stressed syllabic and extends to the end of the measure, or foot (Donegan and Stampe 1978).

13. This is a proposal of David Stampe's.

14. Speakers of dialects like Southern United States or Hawaiian English, with no linking r's at all, need not have a difference in the application of (11) or any other substitution. They appear, instead, to have a difference in the syllabification of r, so that r does not re-syllabify across a word boundary, with the result that the r's do not appear before vowels:

hear   [hɪə̯]   *hear it*   [hɪə̯ ɪt]
mother [mʌðə]   *mother is* [mʌðə ɪz]

15. As Gimson notes (204), "Spelling consciousness remains an inhibiting factor" in this development. The syllable final r's that occur in unconventional spellings sometimes represent these 'intrusive' r's. Louisa May Alcott's 'Marmie' in the New England speech of her *Little Women* would have been ['mɑːmi], and A. A. Milne's 'Eeyore' in *Winnie-the-Pooh* is, of course, ['iːyɔə̯] or ['iːˌyɔː], which is how the donkey says his own name.

16. This alternation is remarkably widespread. It occurs not only in Canada and certain northern states of the US, but also in Maryland, Virginia, the Carolinas, and Georgia. It seems to underlie the distinction between the [ɑɪ̯] of *tight* (< [əɪ̯]) and the [ɑə̯] of *tide* (< [ɑe̯] < [ɑɪ̯]) in much of the Southern United States. It is also characteristic of Hawaiian English.

17. Like Stampe, I regard the [ʌu̯]–[ɑu̯] alternation, too, (as in *clout/cloud*) as a result of lowering. Gregg notes only that ME *ū* > əu in Scots, Scotch-Irish and Canadian is a 'parallel but somewhat different case' (1973: 144).

18. It has been claimed that the slight lengthening that occurs before voiced consonants even when unstressed syllables follow produces a quantity distinction between *writer* [rɑɪDr̩] and *rider* [rɑɪːDr̩] for some speakers. Such a lengthening would also distinguish *kitty* [kɪDi] and *kiddie* [kɪːDi]. I know of no studies that confirm either

128 ON THE PHONETIC BASIS OF PHONOLOGICAL CHANGE

distinction. The degree of lengthening in such disyllables is far less
than in monosyllables, and may in fact be negligible (cf. Lisker 1975;
Lehiste 1971b).

19. The news that I was running an experiment to test whether Ohio
speakers could perceive the difference between words like *rider* and
writer puzzled my Baltimorean family, even when I pointed out the
sameness of the t and d pronunciations in these words. Although all
the speakers I asked agreed that *kitty* and *kiddie* were homophones,
the idea that *rider/writer* were similarly indistinguishable, in Ohio,
was met with disbelief all around. On the other hand, the Ohio
speakers thought that I was setting them a completely impossible
discrimination task.

20. The status of [ɑi̯] and [ʌi̯] in these dialects has been briefly indicated
here. It merits further investigation because it calls into question the
distributional criteria by which phonemes have always been established (though these criteria have never been altogether satisfactory).

References

BAUDOUIN DE COURTENAY, JAN. (1895) 'An attempt at a theory of
phonetic alternations.' In STANKIEWICZ, E. (ed. and trans., 1972) *A
Baudouin de Courtenay Anthology*. Bloomington: Indiana University
Press.

BENDER, BYRON W. (1971) 'Micronesian languages', *Current Trends in
Linguistics* 8: 426–65.

BLOOMFIELD, L. (1933). *Language*. New York: Henry Holt.

BRUNNER, K. (1965) *An Outline of Middle English Grammar*. JOHNSTON,
GRAHAME (trans.) Oxford: Oxford University Press.

CAMPBELL, A. (1959) *Old English Grammar*. Oxford: Oxford University
Press.

CATFORD, J. C. (1977) '"Mountain of Tongues." The Languages of the
Caucasus'. *Annual Review of Anthropology* 6: 283–314.

CHAMBERS, J. K. (1973) 'Canadian raising.' *Canadian Journal of
Linguistics* 18: 113–35.

CHEN, M. and WANG, W. S-Y. (1975) 'Sound change: actuation and
implementation', *Language* 51: 255–81.

DARDEN, BILL J. (1989) 'The Russian palatalizations and the nature of
morphophonological rules.' In WILTSHIRE, CAROLINE et al. (ed.) *Papers
from the 25th Annual Regional Meeting of the Chicago Linguistic
Society*, 41–55. Chicago: Chicago Linguistic Society.

DONEGAN, P. (1978) 'On the natural phonology of vowels.' Dissertation.
Ohio State University. Published 1985, New York: Garland.

DONEGAN, P. (1985) 'How learnable is phonology?' In DRESSLER, W. and
TONELLI, L. (eds), *Papers on Natural Phonology from Eisenstadt*.
Padova: Cooperativa Libraria Editoriale Studentesca Patavina.

DONEGAN, P. and STAMPE, D. (1978) 'The syllable in phonological and
prosodic structure.' In BELL, A. and HOOPER, J. (eds) *Segments and
Syllables*. Amsterdam: North-Holland, pp. 25–35.

DONEGAN, P. and STAMPE, D. (1979) 'The study of natural phonology.' In DINNSEN, D. (ed.) *Current Approaches to Phonological Theory*. Bloomington, IN: Indiana University Press.

DONEGAN, P. and STAMPE, D. (1983) 'Rhythm and the holistic organization of language structure.' In RICHARDSON, JOHN et al. (eds), *Papers from the Parasession on the Interplay of Phonology, Morphology, and Syntax*. Chicago: Chicago Linguistic Society, pp. 337–53.

GIMSON, A. C. (1962) *An Introduction to the Pronunciation of English*. New York: St Martin's Press.

GREGG, R. J. (1973) 'The diphthongs ʌi and ai in Scottish, Scotch-Irish and Canadian English', *Canadian Journal of Linguistics* 18: 136–45.

HALL, J. (1942) *The Phonetics of Great Smoky Mountain Speech*. *Morningside Heights*. American Speech Monographs and Reprints, No. 4. New York: King's Crown Press.

HALLE, M. (1962) 'Phonology in generative grammar', *Word* 18: 54–72.

HOCK, H. H. (1986) *Principles of Historical Linguistics*, Berlin, Mouton.

HOSKISON, JAMES (1974) 'Prosodies and verb stems in Gude.' *Linguistics* 141: 17–26.

JAKOBSON, R., FANT, G. and HALLE, M. (1963) *Preliminaries to Speech Analysis: the Distinctive Features and Their Correlates*. Cambridge: MIT Press.

JANSON, T. (1983) 'Sound change in perception and production', *Language* 59: 18–34.

JOOS, M., (ed.) (1957) *Readings in Linguistics*. Washington, DC: American Council of Learned Societies.

KEATING, PATRICIA (1988) 'The phonology-phonetics interface.' In NEWMEYER, F. J. (ed.) *Linguistics: the Cambridge Survey*. Cambridge: Cambridge University Press, pp. 14–36.

KELLER, R. E. (1961) *German Dialects: Phonology and Morphology*. Manchester: Manchester University Press.

KIPARSKY, P. (1988) 'Phonological change.' In NEWMEYER, F. J. (ed.) *Linguistics: the Cambridge Survey*. Cambridge: Cambridge University Press, pp. 30–46.

KRISHNAMURTI, BH. (1978) 'Areal and lexical diffusion of sound change'. *Language* 54.1–20.

KURATH, H. and MCDAVID, R. I. JR (1961) *The Pronunciation of English in the Atlantic States*. Ann Arbor: University of Michigan Press.

LABOV, W. (1981) 'Resolving the neogrammarian controversy', *Language* 57: 267–308.

LABOV, W., YAEGER, M. and STEINER, R. (1972) 'A quantitative study of sound change in Progress. Report on NSF Project No. 65–3287.' Philadelphia: US Regional Survey.

LADEFOGED, P. (1971) *Preliminaries to Linguistic Phonetics*. Chicago: Chicago University Press.

LADEFOGED, P. (1980) 'What are lingusitic sounds made of?' *Language* 56: 485–502.

LASS, R. (1980) *On Explaining Language Change*. Cambridge: Cambridge University Press.

LEHISTE, I. (1971a) 'The timing of utterances and linguistics boundaries.' *Journal of the Acoustical Society of America* **51**: 2018–24.

LEHISTE, I. (1971b) 'Temporal organization of spoken language.' In HAMMERICH, H. H. et al. (eds) *Form and Substance: Phonetic and Linguistic Papers Presented to Eli Fischer-Jorgensen*. Copenhagen: Akademisk Forlag, pp. 159–69.

LISKER, LEIGH (1957) 'Closure duration and the intervocalic voiced-voiceless distinction in English', *Language* **33**: 42–9.

MADDIESON, I. (1984) *Patterns of Sounds*. Cambridge: Cambridge University Press.

MANASTER-RAMER, ALEXIS (1981) How Abstruse is Phonology? Dissertation. University of Chicago.

MANDELBAUM, D. G. (ed.) (1949) *Selected Writings of Edward Sapir*. Berkeley, CA: University of California Press.

OHALA, J. (1974) 'Phonetic explanation in phonology.' In BRUCK, A. et al. (eds) *Papers from the Parasession on Natural Phonology*. Chicago: Chicago Linguistic Society, pp. 251–274.

POSTAL, P. (1968) *Aspects of Phonological Theory*. New York: Harper.

SAPIR, E. (1915) 'Notes on Judeo-German phonology', *The Jewish Quarterly Review*, n.s. **6**: 231–66. (Reprinted in Mandelbaum 1949, pp. 206–12.)

SAPIR, E. (1921) *Language*. New York: Harcourt, Brace & World.

SMITH, N. V. (1973) *The Acquisition of Phonology: a Case Study*. Cambridge: Cambridge University Press.

STAMPE, D. (1969) 'The acquisition of phonetic representation.' In BINNICK, R. I. et al., (eds) *Papers from the 5th Regional Meeting of the Chicago Linguistics Society*. Chicago: Chicago Linguistics Society, pp. 443–54.

STAMPE, D. (1972) A Dissertation on Natural Phonology. Dissertation. Published 1980, New York: Garland. University of Chicago.

STAMPE, D. (1972) 'On the natural history of diphthongs.' In PERANTEAU, P. et al. (eds) *Proceedings of the 8th Regional Meeting of the Chicago Linguistics Society*. Chicago: Chicago Linguistics Society, pp. 578–90.

STAMPE, D. (1987) 'On phonological representations.' In DRESSLER, W. and PFEIFFER (eds) *Phonologica 1981*. London: Cambridge University Press, pp. 287–300.

SWADESH, M. (1934) 'The phonemic principle', *Language* **10**: 117–29. (Reprinted in Joos 1957, pp. 32–7.)

TWADDELL, W. F. (1938) 'A note on Old High German umlaut', *Monatshefte für Deutschen Unterricht* **30**, 177–81. (Reprinted in Joos 1975, pp. 85–7.)

VANCE, T. (1987) '"Canadian Raising" in some dialects of the northern United States', *American Speech* **62**: 195–210.

VELTEN, H. V. (1943) 'The growth of phonemic and lexical patterns in infant language', *Language* **19**: 192–281.

VENNEMANN, T. (1972) 'Rule inversion', *Lingua* **29**: 209–42.

Chapter 5

Internally and externally motivated change in language contact settings: doubts about dichotomy

Nancy Dorian

1 Introduction

'Dichotomy', writes paleontologist Stephen Jay Gould, 'is the usual pathway to vulgarization. We take a complex web of arguments and divide it into two polarized positions' (1984: 7). Gould was writing with special reference to 'the false antithesis between nature and nurture', but his point is equally well taken in the case of many other simplistic dichotomies, including some which are dear to linguists. The competence vs. performance dichotomy has not proved altogether easy to establish and maintain, for example, although at first blush it may seem to be a convincing and even obvious distinction.

And it is much the same with less far-reaching dichotomies. Despite the fact that a distinction between active vs. passive skills is at the heart of most language-proficiency testing and also forms the division around which foreign language classroom teaching is usually organized, in the natural state it is not at all easy to demonstrate that such a distinction exists. Among people who have grown up with modest or inconsistent exposure to a language which is the first and/or dominant language of a good many persons within the first and second ascending generations of their own families, I have found in fieldwork that self-identification as a speaker or a non-speaker cannot be considered reliable and that the utility of direct testing hinges to a considerable extent on the good will and the equanimity of the individual. Short of devising a behaviourist experiment in which the subjects are rewarded with some equivalent of food pellets for producing as speech what they are able to act upon when spoken to (and in which they are starved in the absence of speech), I cannot think of any way to set a convincing boundary between active and passive skills.[1]

Dichotomies have the effect of nudging us in the direction of an either/or discrimination. The responsibility for this may lie with the user of the dichotomy, but it is certainly encouraged when the terms of the dichotomy are themselves antonyms, as is the case with *internal* and *external* in the phrases 'internally motivated change' and 'externally motivated change'. If I complain of the built-in pitfall in this dichotomous terminology, it is because I fear I have fallen victim to it myself on occasion, at least in the initial stages of considering some particular outcome of a language-contact situation; it constitutes a hazard one needs to be aware of.

In what follows I would like to consider certain weak points of the way in which the notion of internally vs. externally motivated change is commonly applied in the assessment of developments in a contracting language which is in intense contact with an expanding language. This is the kind of setting in which I have worked myself, and by drawing on my own research and on the literature of this research area it is possible to illustrate a number of potential problems.

2 Comparison in terms of single features

Language structures are complex, and the forms which linguistic influence takes may be correspondingly so. There is a danger in looking for cross-linguistic influence in terms of the waxing or waning of rather obviously parallel structures, since the total map of cross-linguistic influence may be much more complex than that. Grammatical gender in a Scottish Gaelic dialect which is in intense contact with English can serve as an example.

As is well known, English does not have grammatical gender. Inanimate nouns are not assigned to gender classes (apart from the metaphorical categorization of inanimates like cars and ships as feminines, among some speakers) and pronoun reference for them is normally the neuter *it*.

Scottish Gaelic does have grammatical gender, and traditionally all nouns require pronoun reference in terms of assignment to masculine or feminine gender categories. There is no neuter.

In the absence of a neuter third person singular pronoun in Gaelic, there is of course no possibility of an absolutely direct item-for-item influence from expanding English on contracting Gaelic. But in the isolated East Sutherland dialect of Gaelic which I studied over a fifteen-year period it was easy to document a strong tendency to extend the use of the masculine third person pronoun /a/ 'he' at the expense of the feminine third person pronoun /i/ 'she', with Gaelic /a/ increasingly parallelling English *it* in generality. The increase in the generality of /a/ was so great, in fact, that a workable rule of thumb for the use of pronoun reference as an indication of nominal gender assignment could be formulated as follows: If all pronoun references to a given noun are masculine, that noun may or may not be a traditionally masculine noun; but if even one fluent speaker uses the feminine pronoun *regularly* in replacement of a given noun, then that noun is almost[2] certain to be a traditionally feminine noun.

It seems straightforward in this case to judge that English influence has weakened pronoun replacement as a gender signal in East Sutherland Gaelic (ESG), and I would not hesitate to make that judgement myself. The risk comes in going on from there to an assumption that contact with English has weakened nominal gender assignment in ESG overall, which is *not* true. It is not true because the form of English which has most influenced ESG has properties not present in standard English, and the effect of one of them actually strengthens nominal gender assignment in ESG. This points to a second problem in assessing language-contact influence.

3   Comparison in terms of a standard form of the expanding language

Unless one has personal experience of a contact setting, it is all too easy to read of influence from 'English', 'Spanish', or any other language very well known in a standardized form, and to assume that what we know as the standard form can be used in assessing the source, direction, and degree of the influence. In the case of third person singular pronoun replacement, there is no difference between standard English and the form of English with which ESG speakers were most in contact, but this is not the case in other respects. Important to the question of retention or loss of grammatical gender in ESG as a reflection of heavy contact with English is the fact that it was east-coast Scots rather than any other British form of English which most influenced ESG.

When the East Sutherland fishing communities came into forced existence, in the early years of the nineteenth century,[3] the Sutherland estate planners deliberately brought in Scots-speaking fishermen from the so-called 'northeast' to serve as models for the reluctant new fisherfolk. Original contact with these Scots speakers from Morayshire, Banffshire, and Aberdeenshire was reinforced over the years by the following facts:

many East Sutherland fishermen hired out to northeastern fishermen during the herring season; all East Sutherland fishermen marketed their herring catches in the northeast ports during some phases of the herring season; East Sutherland fisher girls spent time in those same ports as gutters and packers; and East Sutherland fishermen usually bought their boats secondhand from northeast fishermen. Over the decades some few northeast fisherfolk moved with their families into the East Sutherland fishing communities; some few also married in. Because of all this, northeast varieties of Scots long represented the 'English' with which the Gaelic speakers of East Sutherland had the most direct and sustained contact.

Northeast Scots has no more sign of grammatical gender than standard English. It does, however, make much more use of diminutives, in particular of the diminutive suffix -*ie*: *wifie*, *mannie*, *hoosie* (house), *boatie*, etc., are everyday usages, often with a reinforcing attributive adjective to give *wee wifie*, *wee hoosie*, and so forth. Diminutive -*ie* can be added to virtually any monosyllabic noun, in this form of Scots, and this happens with a freedom and frequency which is startling to speakers of many other forms of English.[4]

One way in which ESG reflects the influence of English of this Scots variety is in a corresponding freedom of occurrence for diminutives. Originally I took the extreme freedom of diminutive formation to be a pan-Gaelic phenomenon, but I discovered when I tried to find morphological diminutives in a western dialect of Gaelic that this was not so. Not only did Gaelic speakers from the Isle of Mull, in the Inner Hebrides, not use many diminutives in free conversation, they also did not produce them in elicitation contexts which had quite reliably produced them in East Sutherland. One Mull speaker told me, in fact, that the way ESG speakers attached diminutives liberally to body-part terms sounded childish to him, like a form of babytalk.

Gaelic diminutives are like the Scots diminutives in -*ie* in that they are formed by means of suffixation, but the Gaelic diminutive suffix has distinct forms for each of the two genders, and assignment is governed strictly by grammatical gender.[5] The masculine diminutive suffix takes the form /-an/, and the feminine takes the form /-ag/.

Because of the extreme frequency of diminutive suffixes in Scots-influenced ESG, nominal gender assignment gets an enormous boost in the dialect. In fact, one of the methods I used to test the hypothesis that any noun for which even a single fluent speaker regularly used a feminine pronoun replacement would prove to be a traditional feminine was to ask a half-dozen or more fluent speakers for the diminutive of that noun. If the noun was in common use and susceptible of diminutive formation, this proved to be an excellent way of determining its gender. However few of the fluent speakers might use /i/ 'she' in reference to the noun in question, there would be near-uniformity among fluent speakers on a diminutive suffix /-ag/ for that noun. While pronoun replacement was a fading signal of gender assignment in ESG, diminutive formation remained a strong one. One curious indication of this is that the imperfect last speakers (semi-speakers) of ESG, among whom no feminine pronoun replacement at all survives (i.e., they refer to all nouns with /a/ 'he'), err in the direction of the *feminine* diminutive suffix as compared with fluent speakers, using /-ag/ not only for most traditionally feminine nouns, if they use the diminutive form at all, but for a good many traditionally masculine nouns as well.[6]

There are thus two possible sources of error in assessing the impact of expanding English on gender in the receding Gaelic of East Sutherland. The first would be to look in too limited a fashion at pronoun replacement as an indication of the state of grammatical gender in ESG, noting its weakness and drawing the obvious parallel to English but overlooking the counterbalancing strength of diminutive formation as a signal of grammatical gender in ESG. The second would be to overlook the primacy of Scots as the source of 'English' influence in ESG, failing to recognize the prominence of morphological diminutives in this form of English and so overlooking the contribution of English influence to what proves to be a particularly strong signal of grammatical gender in ESG.

4 Intersection of the convergence vs. divergence dichotomy with the external vs. internal motivation dichotomy

Intersecting to some degree with the concept of a dichotomous external vs. internal motivation in language contact settings is yet another dichotomous concept, that of convergent vs. divergent change.

In convergent change, at least one of the languages in contact becomes more like the other with respect to certain features. In divergent change, at least one of the languages in contact becomes less like the other with respect to certain features than it can be shown to have been previously. Since change is assessed precisely in terms of a comparison with features of the other language, there is a natural tendency to assign convergent change to external motivation and divergent change to internal motivation.

This tendency may be natural, but it is risk-laden. There is always the possibility that internal pressures within the language structure were lining up in favour of such a change already, and the still more likely possibility that internal pressures have combined with external influence from the other language, in the contact setting, to produce the change. (Thomason and Kaufman refer in this connection to 'the untenable position that an external cause excludes an internal one' (1988: 61).)

Research on the German language in the United States context (i.e., in contact with English) offers a certain perspective on these problems thanks to two factors. The first is that the two languages are genetically moderately closely related and have some structural features in common even when they are not in contact with one another. The second is that Old World German is relatively well studied, both as to its history and as to its numerous and generally quite distinctive dialects. Because of these factors, researchers have been fairly cautious, by and large, in their assessment of the role which English plays when a variety of German spoken in the United States shows features which depart from Standard German norms in the direction of parallel features of English. None the less it can be argued that the degree of caution which the situation actually requires is still greater, in some cases, than the degree of caution which has been exercised.

4.1   Changes convergent with English in the US German verb

In commenting on the German spoken in the state of Wisconsin, Eichhoff (1971: 53) makes the following statement:

> Not only are there numerous English loan words in all Wisconsin German dialects (and in 'standard German' as spoken in Wisconsin), but also the phonology, morphology, and syntax of the dialects show the effect of contact. In Sauk County Low German, a Hanoverian dialect, the auxiliary *sein* was completely replaced by *haben*, resulting in such sentences as *Hast du gewesen?* instead of German *Bist du gewesen?* Sentences like *Tust du ihn sehen?* can be heard in northern Germany, to be sure, but their frequency of usage has increased considerably in Wisconsin under the influence of English.

In connection with the second of the Sauk County verbal phenomena mentioned, Eichhoff seems on the face of it to include a usefully cautious note. He acknowledges that sentences with *tun* in an auxiliary function can be heard in northern

Germany, and he attributes only an increase in the frequency of such constructions to the influence of English.

In fact, such constructions can be heard in many parts of Germany, with some local variations on the uses to which they are put. Because this is a relatively small syntactic matter, it is not treated in some of the more general discussions of German dialects, which tend to emphasize phonological and morphological features. But one dialectologist notes the use of *tun* as an auxiliary to be especially frequent, in the Altenburg dialect of Thuringia, in connection with sentences which correspond to Latin concessive sentences; in the Nürnberg dialect of Bavaria, he states that more or less every present indicative and imperative can be paraphrased by means of *tun* + infinitive; and in Rappenau it is rather all verbs of action which can be paraphrased in the same way, in the present tense (Weise 1910: 219–20). *Der Sprach-brockhaus* calls the construction a 'paraphrase, especially dialectal', without mentioning any regions, but note is made of 'idiosyncratic dialectal forms' of the construction[7] (1964: 706). In an actual northern German dialect text representing North Saxon, I found ten instances of auxiliary *tun* + infinitive (Keller 1961: 369–76). All were in the present tense, and all were interpretable as iterative: four carried the clear sense of 'whenever', and the other six referred to an action which is repeated several times in the story (digging for a buried treasure; wooing a duplicitous princess; applying salve to a magically elongated nose).

There are clearly a number of possible models in Old World German for the use of *tun* + infinitive, and despite the relative caution of Eichhoff's statement about its use in the Sauk County German of Wisconsin, the reader is missing a great deal of critical information. Some idea of Hanoverian usage is needed, and nineteenth-century Hanoverian usage at that. As for Sauk County usage, would additional examples also typically be in the interrogative? In the present tense? What would be the incidence in a given (present-tense) stretch of discourse relative to the number of words overall?

The need for far more caution than even Eichhoff's hedged statement demonstrates is clear from one US German dialect in which this construction has been thoroughly studied. Huffines, a seasoned investigator of Pennsylvania German (PG), gathered enough data from both sectarian (Anabaptist) and non-sectarian speakers of PG to document the use of *tun* (Pennsylvania German *du*) plus infinitive, and her findings were very sharply at odds with what the most authoritative and frequently consulted normative grammar of PG had led her to expect (Huffines 1991: 131–3). The authors of that grammar, Buffington and Barba, describe PG *du* + infinitive 'as an emphatic form . . . often used when asking questions and in negative statements' (1965: 26). If this were the case, there would be a clear parallel to English use of dummy-verb *do*, but no obvious parallel to any of the Old World uses of *tun* + infinitive mentioned by Weise or exemplified by the North Saxon dialect text. If that remained the case even when other dialect usages were investigated, then the case for direct English influence would be very strong.

What Huffines actually found was quite different. She established three separate groups of native-speaker sources: non-sectarians (thirteen speakers), Mennonites (ten speakers), and Amish (nine speakers). The age range of the speakers selected as sources was quite wide in each group. Further, she used three different techniques in data gathering: English-to-German translation tests, free conversation, and elicited but unconstrained description of a set of pictures. She was not testing specifically for the *du* + infinitive construction, and she could not perfectly predict for any set of data just what features of her speaker-groups or of the testing techniques might prove relevant to differences in their PG; hence the carefully designed sample and tests.

In the event, Huffines found greater use of *du* + infinitive among sectarians of both varieties than among non-sectarians. Neither group used the construction in the way Buffington and Barba claimed, however. Sectarians and non-sectarians both used the construction fairly routinely in the present tense, to convey an iterative sense. The sectarians, however, used it in several other ways as well: (1) in iterative contexts even when the iterative sense was otherwise expressed by an adverb or a temporal clause (e.g. 'sometimes I make yogurt'); (2) in pro-form functions (e.g. 'they still do'; 'I know some people do'); and (3) with verbs which do not have iterative aspect (e.g. 'know', 'like').

Huffines concludes that the iterative sense of *du* + infinitive in the present tense is no longer strong among the sectarians, as indicated by its use in conjunction with adverbs and temporal clauses which in themselves convey the iterative notion and by extension of its use to non-iterative verbs. She sums up as follows:

> PG *du* does not parallel functions or assume the role of English *do*.
> All groups provide uniform and unambiguous evidence of that fact.
> PG *du* is not used with any special frequency in the formation of

questions or negatives, and it is not used emphatically. In sectarian communities a subtle semantic shift is occurring. The loss of iterative meaning results in the increased availability of *du* to perform functions more similar to the English model. The use of *du* as a pro-form is such a function (Huffines 1991: 133).

The degree to which English influence has operated in these developments is clear only for the emergence of *du* in pro-form function. It's true that *du* + infinitive in its present-tense iterative sense has no parallel in English, and true that among sectarians that particular usage has faded. None the less it's not clear that simple lack of an English parallel is the major factor in this development. Huffines points out in an earlier paper that the construction 'appears always to have been restricted to the present tense', and that the extension of adverbial *als* (originally used only with past tense, in the meaning 'used to') to present-tense contexts, among sectarian speakers in particular, may have been a more important factor in the shift away from exclusively iterative present-tense occurrence of *du* + infinitive than the absence of an English parallel (Huffines 1986: 150–2). That is, in addition to traditional past-tense structures with *als* like *mei Dad hot als en Brein gemacht* 'my dad used to make a brine', sectarian PG speakers use *als* in present-tense structures like *ich schteh als uff baut finef Uhr* 'I get up (usually) about five o'clock'. Sentences with both *als* and *du* + infinitive also occur: *maryets duhn ich als hinaus geh* 'morning I (usually) go out';[8] but with the highly favoured iterative-past adverb *als* increasingly available for use in the present tense as well, the simplicity of *als* as a single-element iterative signal usable in both tenses must have exercised a certain pull. Cross-tense uniformity was achieved by extending the temporal range of *als*, and *du* + infinitive remained a purely present-tense option.

The development of pro-form use of *du* is a more clearcut matter, by contrast. There was no native verbal pro-form usage to compete with *du* in this function, and the English and German words are transparently cognate, often also translation equivalents. The analogy to the English construction seems obvious enough, and no alternative explanations for the development of a pro-form function for *du* suggest themselves. (The restriction of the change to sectarians is congruent with others of Huffines' findings: fluent non-sectarian speakers are much the more conservative in the German which they speak, but more loss of German is taking place among them; the sectarians' German is much less conservative in its structure, but the language is surviving much better among them. See Huffines 1989 for her well-reasoned explanation of this difference.)

The meticulousness of Huffines' methodology matches the sophistication of her findings, where *tun* + infinitive is concerned. She is able to refute entirely the more blatant English influence of *do* asserted by Buffington and Barba; but on finding that an original PG sense not matched by anything in English is weakened among sectarian speakers, she is able to establish that a somewhat less obvious (if only because the construction is less frequent in English) parallel to English *do* is emerging in the contact setting, the pro-form.

4.2   Changes convergent with English in the US German case system

The manifestations of case in the nominal and pronominal systems of varieties of German spoken in the United States have attracted a fair amount of attention, because the US German case systems are often not those of the standard language. This is a difficult matter to pronounce on, however, since many Old World German dialects also do not display the case system of the standard language. In a 1965 paper, Shrier explored the nominal and pronominal case systems of 55 dialect locations in the German-speaking parts of Europe; the results reveal a very complex situation. A good many regional dialects which have a two-way case distinction for the masculine definite article, for example, none the less have no case distinction at all for the masculine *in*definite article; and while a great many locations have only a two-case system for the masculine definite article, some of them show a system in which the nominative is distinguished from a merged dative/accusative, whereas others show a system in which the nominative and accusative are merged as against a distinctive dative (Shrier 1965: 423–4).

Under such circumstances the US German varieties may well show case systems which are aberrant from the point of view of Standard German because of the regional dialect or dialects which underlie them, quite apart from any influence of English.

In reporting on case usage in the German of New Braunfels, Texas, Eikel (1949: 279–81) notes that both the nominal and pronominal systems show loss of the dative case, accusative forms appearing where dative forms would be required in the standard language. After a disclaimer to the effect that the descriptive linguist is not obliged to explain the phenomena which he records, Eikel offers a moderately cautious statement about likely causes of this development:

This use of the cases may follow a pattern inherited from the parent dialects of Germany; secondly, New Braunfels German has been forced to follow the English pattern of syntax. Of these two reasons I consider the second much more important since the older people use the dative more freely than does the present generation (1949: 281).

The persuasiveness of his reasoning here is reduced, however, by the account which he gives of the town's use of German and especially of the teaching of German in the schools: the First World War was a watershed, marking the first departure from universal use of German and from the regular teaching of German in all grades of the school, including a first grade in which children were 'started off in German', presumably to ease them into some use of English (Eikel 1949: 278–9). Eikel reports that German instruction began again a few years after the First World War, and that a six-week summer school in German was conducted by the New Braunfels schoolboard during the decade before 1939; in 1939 German instruction was dropped entirely and definitively (ibid.: 279). But it seems probable that German in the more standard form fostered by the schools never recovered from the instructional hiatus and the negative affect brought about by the First World War, in New Braunfels as in many other German-American communities (Kloss 1977: 285, 294–5). The older generation was almost certainly more conversant with Standard German; the greater use of dative forms by older speakers may have had as much or more to do with their extensive schooling in German as with some earlier and less aberrant stage of the local speech form.

Eikel's willingness to recognize the possibility of Old World dialect influence in the local New Braunfels case system was lost altogether en route to Uriel Weinreich's reference to his paper. Weinreich states baldly, footnoting Eikel's *American Speech* paper, that 'German speakers in Texas, under the influence of English, neglect the distinction between dative and accusative in certain constructions' (1964: 43). Since Weinreich's book is doubtless much more widely read than Eikel's original article, it's not surprising that other scholars of language-contact phenomena, seeing Weinreich's unqualified statement, take these manifestations of case in Texas German to be a clear case of convergent change towards English and cite it in that connection (King 1985: 214).

Once again one can turn to Huffines for both a thorough and a cautious treatment of case in a US German language variety. Using the same methods and the same three groups of

Pennsylvania-German-speaking sources, she established with reference to case that there is a sharp difference between nonsectarian and sectarian speakers, and that the nonsectarians are again the more conservative. Nonsectarians used common case (a merged nominative/accusative form which is the norm for the PG nominal system) and dative in the noun phrase, but a three-way nominative vs. accusative vs. dative system for personal pronouns. For the sectarians, Huffines sums up the rather different situation as follows (1989: 223):

> The sectarians use accusative and common case forms to express dative functions almost exclusively. The Mennonites produce some dative forms, most of which are fossilized remnants. Other datives were given by the oldest members of the Mennonite group. The Amish group uses even fewer dative forms than the Mennonites, and several of them were given by the [one] Old Order Amish informant. It is clear from their uniform linguistic behavior that the sectarians have a firmly established norm. There is little variation among speakers. Their norm has adopted a one-case system for nouns and a two-case system for personal pronouns, and there is evidence for the possible future inclusion of the English genitive -s on nouns to express possession.[9] The nominal system as a whole reflects an English model.

The object forms of the modern English personal pronouns are historically datives rather than accusatives; it is the original accusative forms which died away in English. As a result, some of the related PG dative forms, in particular those of the third person, have shapes which are phonologically much more similar to the English object forms than are the PG accusative forms: PG accusative /in/, dative /im/ (unstressed /əm/) and English *him*; PG accusative /si/, dative /ir(ə)/ and English *her*; PG accusative /si/, dative /in/ (unstressed /ən/) and English *them*.[10] In edging towards an English model, then, sectarian PG speakers might in theory have embraced the set of PG object pronouns which sound more like their English equivalents, following English in eliminating historical accusatives in favour of the historically dative object forms. This has clearly not happened. The direction of change has been towards the English system in the number of slots for pronominal forms (i.e., subject and undifferentiated object only), but not towards English in terms of phonological resemblance. Neither English nor dialectal German provides a model for complete loss of subject vs. object oppositions in the personal pronoun, so that the development of a pronominal common case paralleling the nominal common case was quite unlikely. The evident weakening of dative case in the nominal system of sectarian PG speakers has probably spilled over into a parallel weakening of the pronominal dative, however, despite the phonological resemblance between the PG dative pronouns and the English object pronouns.

4.3 Divergent change and external motivation

The usual assumption, as noted above, has been that where change was convergent, in language contact settings, the motivation would very likely be external. Associating *divergent* change with external motivation would seem counter-intuitive on the face of it.

None the less one scholar has recently made a strong case for the appearance of divergent change under external motivation. Woolard (1989) points out that an overuse of glottalization, phonemic for Xinca but not for Spanish, by imperfect last speakers of Xinca in Guatemala is not unrelated to the overwhelming presence of Spanish in their environment. Campbell and Muntzel, who reported the phenomenon of imperfect Xinca speakers who 'go hog-wild, . . . employing the "exotic" [excessively glottalized] version' of Xinca, suggested that it arose from imperfect learning of the ancestral language and had 'nothing to do with Spanish' (1989: 189). Woolard counters that the overuse of a marked or 'exotic' phenomenon in Xinca 'has everything to do with Spanish; sounds are overgeneralized precisely because they do not appear in Spanish' (1989: 363).

Woolard further points to the sociolinguistic analogue of vowel centralization in the speech of young people on Martha's Vineyard, especially those who made a late but firm decision to remain islanders (Labov 1963):

> In that example, we can interpret the accentuation and extension of local dialect features as distinguishing island-identified speakers from other speakers, summer people and tourists. The divergent change is a sociolinguistic commentary on the relations of islanders and outsiders (Woolard 1989: 364).

She notes that such divergent change as a symbolic act can only be 'an act of differentiation internal to the minority speech community' at least where two different languages are concerned; minority-language speakers' interactions with members of the majority-language population will take place in the language of the majority, who for their part will not normally learn or use the minority language. It is in interactions among speakers of the minority language that divergent change can carry special symbolic weight (ibid.: 364–5).

5   Partially parallel features: a test case

There are two ways of expressing the pronominal possessive in
the Gaelic of East Sutherland. One has a partial parallel in
English and the other does not. Thinking in terms of an external
vs. internal motivation dichotomy, I had expected to find that
the final imperfect speakers of ESG, that is, the semi-speakers,
would make increasing use of the Gaelic construction which has a
partial English parallel and make correspondingly less use of the
construction which does not. What I found was the opposite. The
semi-speakers used very few of the constructions for which there
was a partial parallel in English, and they had gone over very
largely – entirely, for some speakers – to the construction with no
parallel at all.

In assessing the reasons for this development, I soon came to
the conclusion that it was quite a complex situation in which the
presence or absence of an English parallel was a rather small
part. I had been misled by simplistic dichotomous thinking into
overestimating the importance of an expanding-language parallel
and underestimating the web of semantic, syntactic, morphological,
and even phonological factors which came into play within the
contracting language.

The ESG pronominal possessive construction without a parallel
in English consists of the preposition /ig/ 'at', conjugated for
person and postposed to the noun. The definite article, preceding
the noun, is obligatory in this sort of pronominal possessive
construction. A sample paradigm, using a feminine noun in initial
voiceless velar stop, /kʻəːr/ 'sheep' (plural /kʻəːriç/), follows:

nə kʻəːriç am	my sheep	nə kʻəːriç an'	our sheep
nə kʻəːriç ad	your (sg.) sheep	nə kʻəːriç agi	your (pl.) sheep
nə kʻəːrɪç ig	his sheep	nə kʻəːriç ɔkʻ	their sheep
nə kʻəːriç ɛkʻ	her sheep		

This structure is multiply alien to English, since English does not
compound prepositions and pronouns, conjugating the result for
person, and does not permit the combination of article and
possessive in one and the same noun phrase.

The other pronominal possessive construction is like English in
that a free-standing possessive pronoun is used, and as in English
it precedes the noun; no definite article appears. This construction is unlike English, however, in that some of the possessive
pronouns act as mutating elements, requiring a change in the
initial consonant of the noun which follows them (and which they
modify). In the paradigm which follows, the noun used is also a

feminine which begins with a voiceless velar stop (since gender and the phonological class of the initial consonant affect declensional paradigms), /kˈas/ 'foot' (plural /kˈasən/):

mə xasən	my feet	nə[11] kˈasən	our feet
tə xasən	your (sg.) feet	nə[11] kˈasən	your (pl.) feet
ə xasən	his feet	ə(n) gasən	their feet
ə kasən	her feet		

It was because /mə xasən/ seems to parallel *my feet* quite well, apart from the initial mutation, whereas /nə kˈəːriç am/ (literally 'the sheep at-me') is unlike anything in English, that I had anticipated semi-speakers' gradual extension of the former pattern and gradual abandonment of the latter.

In retrospect this was an almost laughably simple-minded expectation. For a start, the semantic complexity involved here is revealed by the use of two different nouns to illustrate the two possessive options, rather than the use of the same noun twice over. For fluent speakers of ESG the two possessive constructions are not semantically equivalent. The free-standing pronouns are typically used with nouns which belong to certain semantic classes: body parts (like /kˈasən/); nuclear-family kin, plus 'grandmother' and 'grandfather'; the commoner items of clothing; objects likely to be carried regularly on the person (e.g. 'knife', 'pen'); the four daily meals of rural Scotland ('breakfast', 'dinner', 'tea', and 'supper'); and the two-member class of large, privately owned transport, that is, 'boat' and 'car' (the former originally much the commoner, since the ESG speakers were fisherfolk). It may be that some additional classes could be discerned; 'memory', 'mind', 'voice', 'life' and (to a lesser extent) 'name' all show a tendency to take the free-standing possessive pronoun, for example, suggesting an extension of the 'body part' class to non-physical aspects of the self. The classes mentioned are the most obvious ones, at any rate, and most of them are of high frequency in ordinary discourse.

Over against the very high frequency of occurrence of such semantic classes as body parts and nuclear-family kin must be set the fact that the vast – and vastly extendable – category of 'other nouns' typically appears with the conjugating-preposition type of pronominal possessive.[12] That is, the conjugating prepositions are the unmarked choice in expressing pronominal possession. The fact that contemporary borrowings from English, including nonce-borrowings, will appear with the conjugating preposition if a pronominal possessive is used, has major consequences for a language spoken exclusively by bilinguals, since those bilinguals are accustomed to pressing English nouns into service at need. An ESG speaker sent me a tape-recorded message in which she used the phrase 'in your college', for example; she borrowed the word she had heard me use (not an English word otherwise familiar among the Gaelic speakers of the East Sutherland fishing villages), adapted it well to Gaelic phonology (/kʰɔlaǰ/), and supplied the conjugating preposition for the possessive, to get /s ə xɔlaǰ ad/ 'in the college at-you'.

Among the syntactic factors which seem likely to have favoured the semi-speakers' marked leaning toward the conjugating-preposition possessive construction is one in terms of which the conjugating prepositions actually resemble English more than the free-standing possessives do. This is the expression of emphasis. Although English uses suprasegmental markers of pronominal emphasis, whereas ESG uses suffixation, the pronoun itself is the element marked for emphasis both in English and in the conjugating-preposition possessive construction of ESG. If one wanted to emphasize that a particular sheep or a particular foot was one's own, in English, the pronoun *my* would carry the markers of stress, pitch, duration, and so forth. In ESG the conjugating preposition /am/ would add the emphatic suffix /-əs/ to express the same emphasis (/ə xəːr aməs/ 'MY sheep'); but the emphasis would have to attach to the noun rather than to the pronoun in the case of the free-standing possessive pronoun construction, since the possessive pronoun cannot take an emphatic suffix while the noun can (/mə xasəs/ 'MY foot'). Even though it is the person which is being emphasized and not the foot, the emphatic element must be displaced to the noun when it is in construction with the free-standing possessive pronoun.

There is ample indication that fluent ESG speakers are more given to using the emphatic suffix in conjunction with the conjugating-preposition pronominal possessives than in conjunction with the free-standing possessive pronouns. For example, in sixteen freely spoken tape-recorded ESG narratives or messages which I have transcribed, plus one short text taken down from dictation, there are 110 instances of free-standing first-person singular possessive pronouns, versus 52 conjugating-preposition first-person singular possessives. (The proportions, incidentally, are revealing of the extreme frequency of occurrence of the semantic classes which take the free-standing possessive pronouns.) Among the former there are only three which include an emphatic suffix (3 per cent); among the latter there are 14 (27 per cent).

From a morphological point of view, the conjugating prepositions formed on /ig/ have the advantage that none of the elements in the paradigm overlaps with any other morpheme or word in the language, except for /ig/ itself, which is both the simple preposition 'at' and the third-person singular masculine conjugated form 'at-him'; and those two forms are obviously related to one another in sound and sense. With the free-standing possessive pronouns the story is very different. Not one of the forms is unique to this paradigm; the morphemes with which they are homophonous are all grammatical morphemes unrelated to them in meaning. Here is a partial inventory of the overlap:

/mə/ possessive pronoun 'my'; conjunction 'if'
/tə/ possessive pronoun 'your (sg.)'; preposition 'of'; verb-complement particle; particle of the dependent past tense
/ə/ possessive pronoun 'his'; possessive pronoun 'her'; adverbial particle; non-prepositional relative pronoun; numerical particle (in counting); definite article (masc. dat. and gen.; fem. nom. and dat.); verbal particle; variant /əh/ 'her' before some vowel-initial nouns (see note 13); (with numerical particle (in counting) before vowel-initial numbers)
/nə/ possessive pronoun 'our'; possessive pronoun 'your (pl.)'; definite article (pl.); conjunction 'or'; negative particle; comparative particle; prepositional possessive 'in'; conditional 'if'; (with variant /nəh/ 'our', 'your' before some vowel-initial nouns (see note 11); definite article (pl.) before vowel-initial nouns in the plural)
/ən/ possessive pronoun 'their'; positive interrogative particle; definite article (masc. nom.); prepositional relative pronoun

Not all of the items which are pronounced alike are spelt alike, but this is irrelevant for ESG since most speakers are either illiterate in Gaelic or very minimally literate.

One effect of all this homophony, especially homophony involving grammatical rather than lexical morphemes, is that ESG speakers show little awareness of the possessive pronouns as full-fledged *words*. If asked what their words for 'my' and 'your' are, speakers may offer ESG /mə/ and /tə/; but if asked what their words for any of the other English equivalents to the possessive pronouns are (e.g. 'our' or 'her' or 'their'), speakers cannot think of anything at all to offer. One very thoughtful fluent speaker who had been doing some work on a house which bore the name 'Our Home' in English mentioned to me with some puzzlement that he did not think there was a Gaelic word for 'our', although that seemed odd to him; he had not been able to imagine a parallel house name in Gaelic. I asked him to say 'our mother' and 'our hands', and he produced the first person plural possessive pronoun with no trouble, of course. But this possessive would not in fact be used with the noun /taxi/ 'home' in Gaelic – it would take the conjugating-preposition form of possessive. The failure of ESG /nə/ 'our' to equate fully, in privileges of occurrence, with English *our*, and the considerable number of grammatical morphemes of the shape /nə/, are no doubt factors in blocking ESG speakers from identifying a word 'our' (and similarly 'his', 'her', 'your' (pl.), and 'their') in their language; but my sense is that purely phonological attributes actually have more to do with it, since after all /mə/ and /tə/ do not have the same privileges of occurrence as 'my' and 'your', either, and there are quite a few grammatical morphemes homophonous with /tə/ in particular. Apart from /mə/ and /tə/, none of the free-standing possessive pronouns contains any consonant which is not a dental nasal; all of the others consist of schwa or of schwa plus dental nasal: /ə/, /ən/ or /nə/. These possessive pronouns are too much like one another, in addition to being identical in sound to various other grammatical morphemes.

Yet another phonological factor which may operate in the case of all the third person possessive pronouns is the fact that these are deletable within the noun phrase when the element which precedes them ends with a vowel; when that happens, any mutation which they trigger is the only indication of their underlying presence. None of the forms of the conjugating preposition based on /ig/ can ever be deleted in a possessive construction, by contrast, so that there is no opportunity to overlook their physical shape or to avoid their physical presence.

Perhaps partly because of their phonological distinctiveness among the free-standing possessive pronouns, the possessives /mə/ and /tə/ are very much more frequent in occurrence than the others. The next most frequent are the other two singulars /ə/ 'his' and /ə/ 'her'; none of the plural possessives can really be considered common, even among the oldest and most proficient speakers.

Several other complications appear in connection with the use of the free-standing possessive pronouns. One is that they are much more likely to appear with nouns in the singular than with nouns in the plural, with the partial exception of nouns which occur naturally in pairs (e.g. eyes, ears, hands). Another is that they appear freely with nouns of the appropriate semantic classes only if there are no postponed attributive-adjective modifiers in the noun phrase. This second factor means that adding a specifying adjective (except for the very few that precede the noun) may bring about a shift from free-standing possessive pronoun to conjugating-preposition possessive. In the ESG equivalent of the following brief dialogue, there would typically be such a shift:

Speaker 1:   Where's my jersey?
Speaker 2:   Which jersey?
Speaker 1:   My black jersey.

Speaker I would most likely use /mə fɛčan/ 'my jersey' in the first line, but most likely /ə bɛčan tu am/ 'my black jersey' (lit. 'the jersey black at-me') in the third. There are no syntactic conditions which would cause the reverse – that is, a shift away from /am/ and over to /mə/, in connection with a noun which usually takes a conjugating-preposition possessive.

There is, however, one special set of phrases which so vastly favours the free-standing possessive pronouns that speakers who have opted for a plural conjugating-preposition possessive with a body-part noun in the plural (a common enough choice if both noun and possessive are indeed plural) will overwhelmingly revert to the free-standing possessive pronoun of the same person with the same plural noun, when one of these phrases comes into play. These are fixed phrases, and just how many of them there actually are in ESG is impossible to say, since I cannot be sure that my inventory of them is exhaustive. In the course of the fifteen-year period of my fieldwork I simply ran into perhaps twenty or thirty of them, and they were always immediately recognizable by the fact that most speakers so unhesitatingly and unvaryingly used the free-standing possessive pronouns within them, regardless of what person and number they were in and regardless of whether the noun was singular or plural. An example of the scope of the difference between possessive options with a noun in a phrase of this type as compared with the same noun not in a phrase of this type is easily extracted from my field notebooks. In one set of tests, eight fluent speakers were asked to give the Gaelic for 'Their feet are wet' – body-part noun, but plural, and with a third-person plural possessive. All eight gave versions with the conjugating preposition for 'their feet' (/nə kʻasən ɔkʻ/), although two of the eight offered a version with the free-standing possessive pronoun as well. On a different occasion, in a different year, nine fluent speakers (five of them the same, four different) were asked to give the Gaelic for 'They were on their feet all night'. In this instance, with the fixed phrase 'on (their) feet', all nine fluent speakers used the free-standing pronoun with the same body-part noun, again plural, again with third-person plural possessive (/ə gasən/); just one speaker offered a version with conjugating-preposition possessive as an alternative.

Since these fixed phrases are moderately numerous and occur with some frequency, they might in theory serve to reinforce the durability of the free-standing possessive pronouns in ESG and increase their chances of survival among the semi-speakers. Furthermore, because there is some tendency even among fluent speakers for the less common of the conjugating prepositions to separate into their constituent parts (e.g. /fɔ/ 'beneath them' into /fo/ 'under' and /aĭ/ 'them'), while there is also some general preference among semi-speakers (and to a very much lesser extent also among the youngest of the fluent speakers) for analytic structures rather than synthetic ones, it might be supposed that the incidence of dissolution of the conjugating prepositions would increase markedly among these weak speakers. In these two features of ESG there would seem again to be some reason to look for retreat of the conjugating preposition possessives among the last imperfect speakers and extension of at least the highest-frequency free-standing possessive pronouns ('my' and 'your (sg.)').

There is in fact a very evident tendency for conjugating prepositions to dissolve into their constituent parts in the usage of semi-speakers. This can happen even with some of the high-frequency representatives of the type, ones that never show the slightest tendency to dissolve among fluent speakers. The conjugating prepositions formed on /ig/ 'at' are almost never involved, however, and this must reflect the fact that in the absence of a verb 'to have' Gaelic most commonly expresses the notion of 'having' something by means of a construction which uses the verb 'to be' and a form of conjugated 'at': /ha kˈəːriç ãn'/ 'we have (keep) sheep'. The conjugated forms of /ig/ are more frequent in occurrence by far than any other conjugating-preposition forms, and even most semi-speakers control them well.[13]

There is a crucial difference in the level of proficiency at which imperfect control of the free-standing possessive pronouns turns up and the level of proficiency at which imperfect control of the conjugated forms of /ig/ (apart from the second-person plural) turns up. Only the best of the semi-speakers get the first- and second-person singular free-standing possessive pronouns right (those being the only ones which semi-speakers ever use), at least if consistently showing the obligatory mutation of the initial consonant of the following noun is considered part of getting them right. In the case of the conjugating-preposition possessives formed on /ig/, only the very worst of the last imperfect speakers ever get the forms *wrong*. In what proved to be pretty much the plumbing of a bottom line in productive capacity, I tested two terminal speakers who are more nearly good passive bilinguals than actual 'speakers' of any sort. They did give defective forms of 'at-them' in their attempts to produce the sentence 'Their feet are wet'. One apparently lacked the third-person plural conjugating proposition /ɔkʿ/ and gave the analytic equivalent in the form of preposition and personal pronoun instead, /ig e:jəs/ 'at THEM' (emphatic form); the other wandered murkily among three completely incorrect and unintelligible versions, two of which did however include the personal pronoun of the third-person plural, /aǰ/ 'they' (non-emphatic form).

Probably the frequency features of the competing possessive forms cancel each other out: the extreme frequency in daily discourse of some of the nouns which usually evoke the free-standing possessive pronouns, and the extreme frequency of the conjugated forms of /ig/ in the meaning 'have'. But the free-standing possessive pronouns are phonologically and syntactically less stable, and furthermore they are intricately linked with obligatory initial consonant mutations in the nouns which follow them. The possessives which represent conjugated forms of /ig/ appear with far more individual nouns, as the unmarked class of pronominal possessives; they are also both phonologically and syntactically stable, compared to the free-standing possessive pronouns, and they have no link at all with the intricacies of initial consonant mutation. And finally there is even one structural sense in which they actually resemble English more than do the free-standing possessives: any emphasis expressed in the noun phrase attaches to them as pronominal elements, whereas in noun phrases which use the free-standing possessive pronoun the emphasis cannot attach to the pronominal element but must be displaced to the noun.

Once all the factors which are likely to play some part in the semi-speakers' extension of the conjugating-preposition possessives and abandonment of the free-standing possessive pronouns are teased out in this fashion, it seems thoroughly naive on my part ever to have imagined that the simple presence or absence of a near-parallel in English could constitute a decisive factor. Yet I

did entertain that notion at one point and was initially surprised
by the contrary data.

6 Conclusion

The competing pronominal possessive constructions of ESG seem
to me an especially instructive case of the weakness of simplistic
dichotomous thinking, not merely because it proved to be
mistaken thinking here, but also because of the number and
complexity of the factors which most likely play a role in the
outcome of this competition. It strikes me as highly improbable
that brief fieldwork, even if intensive, or fieldwork with only a
handful of sourcepeople, even if long-term, could bring to light
the full range of differences – semantic, syntactic, morphological,
and phonological – in fluent-speaker use of the two different
possessive constructions of ESG and the resultant differences in
their frequency and generality. Yet without a reasonably clear
view of these matters, it would be very difficult to evaluate
realistically the data from the semi-speakers and the ultimate
explicability of those data.

It is difficult enough to achieve rich data for contemporary
studies of language contact settings. If the questions of direction
and degree in cross-linguistic influence are being raised for
languages which were in contact in the past, or for languages
which have already been in contact over a long period, the
difficulties will be greater still. It is impossible to know just what
form(s) of Old World German arrived with the settlers in most
New World German-speaking communities, for example, or what
range of variation existed within them. Nor can it be assumed
that the English with which New World German came into
contact was always the standard variety; 'English influence' in
such German may not always have been in the direction that
speakers of standard English would expect, and its existence may
be correspondingly hard to detect.

Precisely because there will seldom be the ideal breadth and
depth of material on which to base an assessment of change in
terms of external or internal motivation, it is useful to consider
the hazards of casually invoking that tempting but overly simple
dichotomy.

Notes

1. It should be noted that passive skills are very often inadvertently
   tested in a real-world fashion by parents who use a language which

they share but believe that their children do not: they discover that the children have found the hidden presents or spent the stash of change whose existence and location they discussed in the language the children 'didn't know'.

2. The hedge 'almost' recognizes the existence of occasional idiosyncratic gender assignments. Some nouns belong reliably to one gender in one or two of the three ESG-speaking communities and to the other gender in the other(s). Much more rarely, a single speaker or a single family (within the sample of about 44 fluent speakers whom I worked with) maintains a gender assignment different from that of all the others.

3. This was the result of mass evictions of tenant pastoralist-farmers from inland districts, in favour of large-scale sheep farms considered to be potentially much more lucrative than tenants paying very low rents. It took place throughout the Highlands and Islands in Gaelic Scotland, and the phenomenon as a whole is known as the Highland Clearances.

4. I'm obliged to Professor Kenneth Jackson for pointing out to me (personal communication) the exceptional frequency of diminutives in Scots.

5. In the rare but high-frequency nouns with feminine sex reference but masculine grammatical gender, e.g. /pərn:ax/ 'woman' and /pāū:ntərax/ 'widow', diminutive suffixation is not normally used; but when a fluent ESG speaker is persuaded to form one just on a 'suppose you did anyway' basis, the experimental formation proves to be in line with grammatical gender, not natural gender. I had expected the reverse and was surprised to find grammatical gender prevailing in these unnatural but analogically very ordinary productions.

6. See Dorian 1981: 126 for an instance of this result in one set of tests.

7. 'Umschreibung, bes. mundartlich'; 'eigenartige mundartl. Formen'.

8. The examples are all drawn from Huffines 1986.

9. In the usage of sectarians, nine of 73 possessives appeared with -s, but in the translation task only; in free conversation and the picture descriptions, no genitive -s appeared in 26 sectarian instances of the possessive construction (Huffines 1989: 219).

10. Other persons are either irrelevant for comparison with English (second-person familiar, singular and plural) or neutral (PG first-person singular /mir/, unstressed /mər/ and accusative /mɪç/ are both unlike English in having a final consonant; the PG first-person plural forms are identical for dative and accusative, /ʊns/).

11. The third-person singular feminine takes the form /əh/ before some vowel-initial nouns: e.g. /əh ō:īç/ 'her throat'; the first- and second-person plural take the form /nəh/ before some vowel-initial nouns: e.g. /nəh a:r/ 'our father', 'your (pl.) father'. Not all vowel-initial nouns which otherwise appear with the free-standing possessive pronouns will appear with /əh/ in the third-person singular feminine, however, and even fewer will appear with /nəh/ in the first-person and second-person plural. Though I made some serious efforts to find

a general principle which could explain which vowel-initial nouns of the appropriate semantic classes (see below) could appear with /əh/ and which could not (and lesser efforts of the same sort with /nəh/), and which vowel-initial nouns therefore theoretically shifted over to the corresponding conjugating prepositions /ɛk'/, /ān'/ and /agi/, I never succeeded in my quest. If there are general principles of that sort, rather than just lexical conditioning, I did not uncover them.

12. There is a different sort of frequency-of-occurrence factor which might be invoked here, namely the frequency of the general semantic-class distinction which emerges in the distributional pattern for the free-standing vs. the prepositional pronouns. In fact that distinction is unique; it plays no role elsewhere in the language. Although this fact may be of no significance in determining which of the prepositional choices is more likely to persist in the late stages of the dialect's existence, it probably does play a role in lessening the chances that two distinct prepositional options will continue to exist under such circumstances.

13. The second-person plural is an exception. This form is no longer used by most semi-speakers, who know none of the conjugating prepositional forms and usually do not even know the pronoun of the second-person plural itself. They scandalize fluent speakers just a little older than they by speaking to their parents in the second person singular, unheard of for fluent speakers yet tolerated by the aged parents concerned, who seem to recognize that the entire second-person plural usage is more or less lost to these last speakers of the language.

References

BUFFINGTON, ALBERT F. and BARBA, PRESTON A. (1965) *A Pennsylvania German Grammar*. Allentown, PA: Schlechter.

CAMPBELL, LYLE, and MUNTZEL, MARTHA C. (1989) 'The structural consequences of language death.' In DORIAN, NANCY C. (ed.) *Investigating Obsolescence: Studies in Language Contraction and Death*. Cambridge: Cambridge University Press.

DORIAN, NANCY C. (1981) *Language Death: The Life Cycle of a Scottish Gaelic Dialect*. Philadelphia, PA: University of Pennsylvania Press.

EICHHOFF, JÜRGEN (1971) 'German in Wisconsin.' In GILBERT, GLENN G. (ed.) *The German Language in America*. Austin, TX: University of Texas Press.

EIKEL, FRED, JR (1949) 'The use of cases in New Braunfels German', *American Speech* 24: 278–81.

GOULD, STEPHEN JAY (1984) Review of *Science and Gender*, by Ruth Bleier. *New York Times Book Review*, 12 August, p. 7.

HUFFINES, MARION LOIS (1986) 'The function of aspect in Pennsylvania German and the impact of English', *Yearbook of German-American Studies* 21: 137–54.

HUFFINES, MARION LOIS (1989) 'Case usage among the Pennsylvania German sectarians and nonsectarians.' In DORIAN, NANCY C. (ed.) *Investigating Obsolescence: Studies in Language Contraction and Death*. Cambridge: Cambridge University Press.

HUFFINES, MARION LOIS. (1991) 'Pennsylvania German: convergence and change as strategies of discourse.' In SELIGER, HERBERT W. and VAGO, ROBERT M. (eds) *First Language Loss*. Cambridge: Cambridge University Press.

KELLER, R. E. (1961) *German Dialects*. Manchester: Manchester University Press.

KING, RUTH (1985) 'Linguistic variation and language contact: a study of the French spoken in four Newfoundland communities.' In WARKENTYNE, H. J. (ed.) *Papers from the Fifth International Conference on Methods in Dialectology*. Victoria, B.C.: University of Victoria.

KLOSS, HEINZ (1977) *The American Bilingual Tradition*. Rowley, MA: Newbury House.

LABOV, WILLIAM (1963) 'The social motivation of a sound change', *Word* 19: 273–309.

SHRIER, MARTHA (1965) 'Case systems in German dialects', *Language* 41: 420–38.

DER SPRACH-BROCKHAUS (1964) (7th edn) Wiesbaden: F. A. Brockhaus.

THOMASON, SARAH GREY, and KAUFMAN, TERRENCE (1988) *Language Contact, Creolization, and Genetic Linguistics*. Berkeley: University of California Press.

WEINREICH, URIEL (1964 [1953]) *Languages in Contact*. The Hague: Mouton.

WEISE, OSKAR (1910) *Unsere Mundarten*. Leipzig: B. G. Teubner.

WOOLARD, KATHRYN A. (1989) 'Language convergence and language death as social processes.' In DORIAN, NANCY C. (ed.) *Investigating Obsolescence: Studies in Language Contraction and Death*. Cambridge: Cambridge University Press.

Chapter 6

How real(ist) are reconstructions?

Roger Lass

> tempus edax rerum, tuque, invidiosa vetustas,
> omnia destruitis vitiataque dentibus aevi,
> paulatim lenta consumitis omnia morte
>
> Ovid, *Metamorphoses* XV.234–6

1   Reversing time

Most of what historical linguists do these days seems less strictly
historical than theoretical. We interpret, try to explain, apply
synchronic theory to historical data, use language history to
illustrate or justify (non-historical) theoretical positions. We do
not usually ask where our 'data' comes from, or what its status is.
Yet these are important matters; the more idealizing and
'Galilean' (Botha 1982) our methodology, the further we get
from our sources and the more we content ourselves with simply
citing 'the handbooks', the greater the risk of seduction by
corrupt or improperly understood materials.

We normally, for instance, invoke Grimm's and such epony-
mous laws as virtually 'factual' material; yet their content, like
the bulk of our knowledge of language history, is based not on
'raw facts' but on deliberate reconstructions of past states, not
done (or re-done) by the users, but accepted as part of a
tradition.[1] Reconstruction, however, is a theoretically loaded and
complex operation. It might be useful to ask some fairly basic
questions about the status of reconstructed entities, given their
role as foundation-stones of the whole edifice; in particular, the
results of comparative method, which is perhaps the most
important component of our underlying body of (apparent)
knowledge.

Very few of us, I suspect, have during our training been made
to ask basic and naive questions about what it is that we do when
we reconstruct (or more to the point, what our 'authorities' have
done). What is the epistemic status of reconstructed entities?
How much of the mass of accepted 'classical' reconstruction is
really justified? How much on the other hand is dogma whose

rational basis (if any) is buried so far in the past of our subject
that nobody except the linguistic historiographer can (or wants
to) recover it? What are the relative roles of realism and
conventionalism in establishing historical knowledge? This chapter
is a minor 'rational reconstruction' of some of the most important
underlying tenets of comparative method and related techniques.

To reconstruct is to reverse time, and make the products of
that reversal accessible: as objects of intellectual contemplation,
portions of the historical record, sources of new knowledge.
'Reversing time' is not the trivial exercise of reading a
documentary sequence backwards (Shakespeare, Wyatt, Chaucer
. . .); it is rather denying in theory that time is irreversible. While
this may be true literally of the 'arrow' of physical or
thermodynamic time, for us historians it must be false as a matter
of principle (or at least occupational definition). We take it that
time can be made (*ceteris paribus* as always) to disgorge what it
has eaten. It is not *a priori* clear, however, how much we can
make it disgorge, or in what condition. How in fact do we
recover what has been lost? What are the time-reversing
technologies in linguistics, the ways for making what is (*ex
hypothesi* only apparently) lost re-emerge? What are the
epistemological, methodological, empirical, aesthetic justifications
for these technologies?

Here we come to the central epistemological problem: realism
vs. conventionalism. Certain kinds of historical 'truth' are
apparently largely conventionalist, the products of notation or
procedure (Lass 1986 and below). Truth in reconstruction is both
relative and constrained, though there are still satisfactory – if at
times rather hermetic and self-referential – ways of telling
whether the output of a reconstructive operation is a (reasonably
useful) 'true' picture of a linguistic past.

I distinguish here between reconstruction proper and explanation (even though explaining is a kind of reconstruction: 'causes'
or 'reasons', rather than objects or processes: see Lass 1980: ch.
1). This chapter treats a still more restricted aspect (if the
primary one), for the most part excluding the 'interpretation' of
documented entities (whether metalinguistic descriptions or
forms in texts). Here reconstruction is creating state descriptions
and accounts of transitions between states, where either the
states or transitions are missing from the record.

We have to reconstruct because things we want or need are not
there (section 2 below). There are two basic types of missing
objects: 'ancestors' and 'missing links'. The reconstruction of
ancestors is perhaps most familiar: given a set of reflexes

(segments, formatives, etc.) we extrapolate an ancestor ('proto-segment', 'proto-formative', etc.) from which they can be derived in some regular and principled way.[2]

The reconstruction of missing links is less straightforward; it is a matter of filling gaps in the record, e.g. between a protoform and its first attested reflex, or even between objects in a record where there are no apparent gaps. The interesting question here is what constitutes a gap, and the answer is a theoretical one: gaps can in fact be created by a theory that demands them. I have dealt with this in some detail in Lass (1978); here my concern is mainly with the ancestor problem. The strictly 'historical' (narrating, chaining attested links and producing missing ones) and the 'comparative' (devising ancestors) are two sides of the same coin, but the present focus is on the latter: the background and fundamental properties of that kind of reconstruction usually called 'comparative'.

2   The genetic hypothesis

The whole historical enterprise rests on the idea that it is possible to produce an ancestor for a set of reflexes presumed to have a common origin (cf. Meillet 1967). Familiar as this is, it is not self-evidently true that ancestors can be produced otherwise than out of a hat, or that there even are such things. The underpinning of the claim that reconstruction is possible is a set of interlocking assumptions, which for convenience I call the 'genetic hypothesis':

   (i) Languages change over time.
  (ii) In doing so, they often change into other languages.
 (iii) Therefore some languages are genetically related to other languages.
 (iv) Given the appropriate procedures and auxiliary assump-tions, these relationships can be used to reconstruct two kinds of non-attested objects: (a) stages under (i) lost because of gaps in the record; and (b), stages antecedent to the record itself.
  (v) Conversely, the procedures and auxiliary assumptions (iv) can be used to test whether (iii) is true of any pair of n-tuple of languages or linguistic items.
 (vi) These procedures and auxiliary assumptions can in some way be 'justified'.

The two classes under (iv), 'ancestors' and 'missing links', are equally important; a reconstructive technology must allow us to access both history proper and prehistory. This is because the record fails us in at least four crucial respects: (1) no language has a complete sequence of texts from its beginnings to the present; (2) no language is recorded in its earliest stages; (3) most of the world's languages have documentary histories of negligible length, or none at all; and (4) virtually all documentary records have serious gaps, or at least because of the inbuilt conservatism of orthographic traditions fail to register significant transitions.

So 'prehistory' must be reconstructable simply because it is relative, not absolute. Even if we could reconstitute gapped textual records, inability to recover prehistory would deny most languages a history at all. Consider a language first recorded in 1968. The year 1967 would be 'prehistoric' for it, no matter how long it had actually been spoken; its 'history' would at this moment span less than three decades. Whereas another (related) language with texts dating back to the third century BC would have a history of over two millennia; but it could be the case that both were of equal or near equal antiquity.[3]

So while our information-base is severely constrained by the available time-depth in sequences of texts, this must not prevent us from getting back to some period preceding the earliest records. Our ability to push back the time-barrier however is not unlimited; there are no signs that we can ever get back to 'the origin of language' by reconstruction, any more than we can by observing the first utterances of children raised in isolation (*pace* Herodotus and James IV). In every reconstructive venture we keep going back to a language from which the one in question descended, and then finally to a point where we simply have to stop. We lack the technology to recover a protolanguage for man.[4]

So much for prehistory; we can now return to the basic assumptions. It can be shown (though nobody usually bothers to do it) that some form of reconstructability is entailed by genetic relationship, at least to a certain time-depth. I will look at this in the next two sections. But first, why does the possibility of genetic relation follow from the mere fact of change?

Given enough time, the implication is trivially true: if by internal change one language can become another, 'different' one (Latin > Old French > Modern French, Dutch > Afrikaans, etc.), then (panchronically) some languages are genetically related to some others. The comparative end of historical linguistics simply develops this insight, by invoking a particular theory of mutation that allows us to recover the more distant linkages assumed in (i)–(iii). The key is the set of auxiliary assumptions (iv), which define the procedures and techniques of reconstruction. Or to put it more accurately, that give rise to the projective techniques that lead to the extrapolation of 'common ancestors'.

3   Projection: basic principles

Linguistic reconstruction is a 'palaeontological' operation, if not quite the same as in (biological) palaeontology proper. The usual task for zoological reconstruction, more or less a paradigm case, is rebuilding an animal from some *disjecta membra* that we believe have a common source. Reconstructing linguistic proto-entities isn't quite like that, i.e. fleshing out a 'whole' from 'remnants'. (Except in the odd sense that the structural features of the daughters of a protolanguage can in part be considered 'remnants of' those of the mother.) It's rather more like either projecting an ancestor (what kind of fish do we need to give us an amphibian?); or filling in a missing but patently necessary stage (what comes between crossopterygian fishes ('coelacanths') and amphibians?[5] These two activities are, as the examples suggest, quite different. In the first case we don't necessarily invoke a specified or coherent notion of 'change'; in the second we don't extrapolate or 'project'. In both we do allow for (even radical) transformation; but defining its limits can be a problem.

The 'projective' phase of comparative reconstruction (Lass 1978) extrapolates from static correspondences to an ancestor, though with a strong concern for likely transition types and directions of change (section 5 below). A biological parallel to the projection of linguistic proto-entities: on the basis of modern bony fishes and amphibians, could we project, in fair and recognizable detail, something like a coelacanth? One difference should be immediately apparent: it's rather rarer in linguistics than biology to find a 'living fossil' that corroborates a reconstruction after the fact. There are not many discoveries in comparative linguistics with the dramatic impact of fishing up a *Latimeria* off the South African coast (the decipherment of Hittite may come close).

Projection is the first step in comparative (or for that matter internal) reconstruction.[6] In projecting we assume that (for whatever reason) some set of items represents the terminal nodes of a rooted genetic tree, whose topmost node is missing. The task is to project, by method or intuition (or both) this missing node.[7] That is: given a set of correspondences (an 'equivalence class' as defined below), develop a label for the set. The status of the label may be problematic; I return to this in section 4.

Let us begin with an absurdly simple case: reconstruct the initial segment in the Indo-European word for 'mouse', using as data L *mūs*, Skr *mūḥ*, Gr *mūs*, OE, OHG *mūs*, etc. Given semantic constancy and (intuitive) 'likeness' of form, we assume reconstructability *a priori*, and set up a class with a label chosen to stand for the putative relationship. The content of the class is {L m, Skr m, Gr m, OE m . . .}, and we assign a label 'E' = 'equivalence', which in this instance happens to be identity. In a case this simple, we could derive the class-label from the internal invariance, and redefine E{m, m, m, . . .} as 'm', i.e. m{m, m, m, . . .}. The next stage marks 'm' as '*m', indicating some particular (non-attested, reconstructed, hypothetical, etc.) status. More on this below.

'Equivalence' in this sense is of course another name for 'cognateness', a relational (and historical) notion defined over the members of an equivalence class. Substituting C = 'cognate' for the cover-symbol derived from the class-content, we say: given a class C{x, y, z}, where the label C is defined according to a set of fairly standard procedures, for any x, y, z ∈ C it is the case that:

(1) i. $xCy \supset yCx$ (symmetricalness)
    ii. $(xCy$ and $yCz) \supset xCz$ (transitivity)

The relation defined over this set can be (and usually but not always is) given an ontological interpretation: 'C' is not only a set-theoretic relation but a genetic label. The set C is convertible to a graph (an oriented tree) whose originating node is labelled C and whose branches are x, y, z:

(2)

The relational label is conventionally phylogenetic (cf. the etymology of *cognate*); and usually strictly monogenetic as well. (By definition any genealogy representable as a well-formed tree is of course monogenetic; recalcitrant or 'non-arboriform' genealogies, whether of languages or individual items, imply more complex origins, e.g. of a Schmidtian 'wave' type: cf. note 6.) The base assumption – in fact the warrant for any reconstruction – is that all non-identities in the set-members represent an original identity. In cases where (on other grounds) we know that a present identity represents a historical non-identity (i.e. a merger) only the existence of some non-merged items will allow a reconstruction. Identities project to identities by default, and non-identities project to identities *ex hypothesi*.

The relational, class-defining label C thus has a dual interpretation: taken as defining monogenesis, the abstract relation is hypostatized into an 'entity'. And the relation between this hypostasis and the rest of the set is now 'ancestor-of', which unlike 'cognate-to' is asymmetric and non-transitive. My own view is that the proper interpretation of the originating node (and indeed the whole content of the set) is realist; but even if this seems obvious it has not always been taken to be so, and requires supporting argument (section 4).

Cognation and ancestor relations may be, and usually are, much more complex. Set-internal evidence can suggest grouping sub-sets of C into sub-trees with their own labels. For example, given the set C{Gr *kardíā*, L *cord-*, OE *heorte*, Go *haírtō*, OIc *hjarta*}, the subset C' {OE, Go, OIc} is a subtree of the tree labelled C, defined by the sub-equivalence C{k-} ≡ C' {h-}. But this is a lower-level cladistic problem, and not our concern here.

Before looking at projection proper, we must distinguish between macro- and micro-projection: the category instantiated by C can (so far) be anything from a segment to a language, as the relation is defined over domains of any size. So L *cord-*, OE *heorte* are 'cognate' in the same sense as Latin and Old English as wholes. But the latter cognateness is procedurally derived from demonstrations of lexical cognateness, and these in turn rest on a strictly segmental basis.

Projecting a mother-node for a genetic tree now looks rather simple (say at the segmental level): given a set of reflexes (whose identity as such a set is established by relatively independent assumptions and tests, assign a symbol to the set representing the monogenesis of the relation holding among its members, and prefix it with an asterisk. Assuming that the asterisked symbol *C has phonetic content (on why this is necessary see section 4), we must now ask what kind. How idealized (crude) is it? What descriptive or theoretical level does it represent? We will see that the only reasonable level is something like ('broad') surface-phonetic.

It is important to note that the projection of mother-nodes by comparison of reflexes is essentially self-justifying; the system is set up in such a way that if a comparison gives a 'reasonable' projection, this is *prima facie* evidence for cognation. The principles guaranteeing this are:

(i) 'Sound Laws' (= correspondences) are to be regular, i.e. replicable across some substantial portion of a lexicon. This rules out adventitious similarities in both semantics and phonetic shape like L *deus*: Gr *theós*, Kannaḍa *ondu* [wʌndu] 'one': E *one*. As well as sporadic correspondences due to borrowing: e.g. regular E /f/: L /p/ in *father*: *pater*, *fish*: *piscis* is a 'correspondence', but E /p/: L /p/ in *paternal*: *paternalis*, *piscatorial*: *piscator* is not. (Or it is a default correspondence, the identity due to movement of a whole item with its own history into a language with a different – even if at some point related – one.) The methodology here involves pseudo- or semi-quantitative notions like 'systematicity' or 'pervasiveness', as well as qualitative ones like 'core' vs. 'non-core' lexis.[8] This proviso rules out adventitious resemblances like those often found in onomatopoeias: if there was an inherited IE root for 'cuckoo', English *cuckoo*, Fr *cou-cou* could not be cognate; English would have to have **huhoo*.

If correspondences are not fully regular, the irregularities should be specifiable as sub-regularities (context-sensitive restrictions and the like); or in the last resort we can invoke escape-hatches like analogy, folk-etymology, borrowing, the special properties of systematically 'aberrant' classes like names, hypo-coristics, onomatopoeias; or in the post-Neogrammarian age (see section 6 below) lexical diffusion, rule-abortion, etc. We might call this 'Verner's Principle', after the elegant, paradigm-defining procedural model in Verner (1875).

(ii) Parallel innovation ('convergence') is to be avoided in favour of single innovations pushed back to an earlier date, unless there is clear (normally external) counter-evidence. For example, the similar vowel shifts in English, German, Dutch (E *house*, G *Haus*, Dutch *huis* with original */u:/, E *bite*, G *beissen*, Dutch *bijten*, with original */i:/) cannot, in the face of documentary evidence, be pushed back to pre-separation West Germanic; nor can they be ascribed to contact (Awedyk and Hamans 1989). Whereas the lenition of intervocalic stops in various modern Romance dialects can probably be pushed back to Vulgar Latin allegro styles (Dressler 1975).

Principle (ii) is also partly a 'simplicity' principle (convergence is 'multiplying entities'); but there is more to it. Both (i) and (ii) are partly conventionalist methodological dictates, even if they embody what might loosely be called 'empirical hypotheses'. There is nothing in the data itself – as of course there never is – that guarantees them to be either rational or empirically sound. This is particularly the case for (ii). But they do give useful results, in some cases testable. We could for instance match predictions made by projection against a 'surviving proto-language'; or make predictions and have them justified (given luck) by a later discovery or a reinterpretation of known material. This is especially true of (i), which in this way has become increasingly trusted as one of the major sources of information about language change and filiation.

Checking predictions against an 'attested protolanguage' can be illustrated by projecting a Latin intervocalic */g/ on the basis of French, Spanish zero, Italian /dʒ/ (Fr *lire*, Sp *leer*, It *legere*) and matching against L /legere/, etc. Enough (relatively) reliable cases of this kind, and we begin to trust our methods. Justification (of sorts) by subsequently uncovered information can be illustrated by the discovery in Hittite of segments (apparently) matching the hypothetical laryngeals that grew out of Saussure's 'coéfficients sonantiques' (1879), and the later development of laryngeal theory. (There are of course problems here: cf. Szemerényi 1989: s. VI.4.)

The two foundational principles rest in turn on broader assumptions; one, matching (i), is eventually an empirical hypothesis about the nature of phonetic change; the other, matching (ii), is a basic assumption about good method ('playing fair'), on occasion empirically supportable.

(i′) *The Regularity Hypothesis*: Sound change is regular (in more or less the Neogrammarian sense: but see section 6).

(ii′) *The Coincidence-Barring Requirement*: convergent development is bad, not to be invoked except under severe compulsion (cf. Lass 1984).

To these we can add, as a guarantor of the warrantability of reconstruction, the Saussurean principle of *l'arbitraire du signe*: there is no necessary connection between substance and form, and this allows (in general) whatever 'mechanical' processes occur in change to be reasonably well insulated from semantics.[9]

4   The reality problem: what do we project?

The onotological commitment assumed by comparative method, judging from positions that have been taken in the literature, is anything from none at all to naive realism. Both extremes are untenable, but if we're going to err, it's better to do it on the realist side. This is also more philosophically consistent both with actual practice, and linguists' covert assumptions.

The grossest distinction between the two positions was nicely put by Meillet, who came down on what I take to be the wrong side, perhaps for the wrong reasons. In a passage in his *Introduction* (Meillet 1964: 42) he says that 'les "restitutions" ne sont que les signes par lesquels on exprime en abregé les correspondances'. What comparative method produces is not (47) 'la restitution de l'indo-européen tel qu'il a été parlé; *c'est un système défini de correspondances entre les langues historiquement attestés*' (emphasis Meillet's).

Reconstruction utilizes an uninterpreted algebra; it presupposed no particular ontology, only maximal convenience of statement. It aims solely to produce formulas that subsume classes of reflexes. This position unfortunately is anti-historical as well as non-linguistic; and Meillet failed to note that between it and the admittedly absurd proposition that one could reconstruct a language 'tel qu'il a été parlé there might be a reasonable middle ground. If the reconstructive enterprise is to make any sense, there must be some compromise between devising uninterpreted algebras and writing fables in the protolanguage.

The distinction between producing abstract cover-symbols or set-labels and reconstruction proper was insightfully focused nearly three decades ago in an important, perverse, and generally neglected study by Leon Zawadowski (1962). He contends (contrary to much of the tradition, but in spirit rather like a formalized version of Meillet) that the primary historiographic act is the setting up of strictly content-free labels for correspondence sets. These are pure signs of relatedness, with no 'object' interpretation; they allow us to establish regular cognation and the like, and filter out 'irregularities'. Such a procedure leads to 'a very comprehensive grammar *free of reconstruction in any sense*' (Zawadowski 1962: 11; emphasis original). This is 'the comparative grammar of attested relations', where 'the asterisk formulae are . . . simply formulae of observed correlations' (cf. Meillet's 'signes' above).

Zawadowski is obsessed with attaining 'certainty', and dismissive of 'hypotheses' (one recalls Newton's *hypotheses non fingo*!). The output of the procedure described above, where e.g. '*374' stands for the set {L *cord-*, Skr *śṛd-*, Go *haírt-*}, etc. is 'absolutely certain'; or it is 'at least as certain as the attested elements are. There can be no question as to their more or less hypothetical character' (ibid.). The procedure is 'observational' only, and therefore as good as the ('non-theoretical') observation that goes into it. This much is either epistemically complacent or trivial. But Zawadowski's hierarchy of 'certainties' is of interest, as general epistemological issues do arise, as well as questions about what the whole game is in aid of.

If now we extrapolate from the correspondences (say with some kind of 'genetic hypothesis' in mind), we can interpret the asterisked object as not merely a correspondence-set, but a 'source element' (10). This is an abstract proto-morpheme, devoid of phonetic substance; and like the first labelling, 'purely relational and unquestionably certain'. Such an object, e.g. *374, represents an abstract proto-formative. It is 'a relational genetic element'; and a set of such statements is a 'comparative grammar of relational reconstructions' (or 'quasi-reconstructions').

Here is the first equivocation: even this stage is not as 'abstract' as he makes it out. The set in question – while not phonetically specified – cannot be merely relational, since its members are selected on covert semantic grounds (as well as phonetic ones: see below). This introduces an 'uncertain' element if any forms in a set are not simple synonyms or near-synonyms. For example, L *porcus*, OE *fearh*, G *Ferkel* are not problematical as members of a 'pig' set; but the 'source' relation of these to OE *furh* 'furrow', Lith *paršas*, L *porca* 'field-drain' – though the evidence is good – is harder to manage under Zawadowski's 'emptiness' assumption.[10]

The next step is 'letter asterisk notation'; instead of *374 we produce say *k̥rd-. (He does not tell us precisely where the particular 'letters' come from, which is the second equivocation.) This can still be a pure mnemonic for a correspondence class, and we then get a 'comparative grammar of attested relations (or that of relational reconstructions) in letter asterisk notation' (13). Only the notation has changed, the symbol sequence is still free of any representation of 'substance'.

But, says Zawadowski, this is not the usual interpretation of formulas like *k̥rd-; 'this notation is usually meant to convey assertions about *the phonic substance* of the presumable source phones' (13; emphasis original). Such an interpretation assigns the formulas a radically different character; though he does not put it this way, it hypostatizes a relation into a thing. With this hypostasis, we take an epistemic leap backwards: from 'certainty' to 'probability'. The 'comparative grammar of substance reconstruction' deals only with 'a greater or lesser degree of probability', because it is hypothetical, based on judgements of 'natural' derivability and the like. But this is 'the traditional comparative grammar'.

The interesting point is his disjunction between the purely 'relational' forms of comparative grammar and the reconstruction of substance. Representations like *374, *k̥rd- can be taken as alternative one-to-one mappings from the set of attested relations; it is only when the algebra is 'substantially' interpreted in terms of some function like '*k → [k]' (a mapping from the set of 'letter asterisk notations' into the set of phones) that we enter a new ontological realm (14).

One might question the adequacy of such non-substantial

reconstructions (15), since obviously 'the functional elements of languages' are substantial, and a substanceless reconstruction is bound to be 'incomplete'. But, says Zawadowski, 'a complete description of the source language is not the aim of comparative grammar';

> what is intended primarily is to discover prehistoric . . . relations between the attested languages and . . . their elements . . . and detect hidden relations present in the attested period. Relational reconstruction does this very well. A reconstruction of substance is of much less use; its use consists mainly in the fact that a definite phonetic value of prehistoric entities is an aid for the intuition in the process of research.[11]

While his taxonomy is illuminating, and in essentials correct, his conclusions are rather shakier. In particular, the claims that (a) the primary aim of comparative grammar is simply to discover relations and not 'entities', and (b) that substantial reconstruction is less useful than relational, are untenable. Nobody would deny that discovering 'hidden relations' is a vital part of the historiography of language families, but it is only a preliminary. An unembodied relation is a heuristic promissory note for a history, not itself something historical. Linguistic evolution is in the end the evolution of speech forms, and forms at some significant level must be substantially embodied (not least because this is our only access to them historically). Particularly so because the data on which the 'relational' groupings are based in the first instance is unintelligible without the assumption of substance underlying the relations. We cannot even take the first steps in relational reconstruction without some kind of phonetic sorting, which is a covert attribution of substance to the set being defined.

Consider for instance the equivalence-class {L *dent-*, Go *tunpus*, Lith *dantìs*, Old Irish *det*, Oscan *dunt-*}, all with the sense 'tooth'. If substance is not at issue, why restrict the reconstruction-base for PIE to this sort of material, and omit Tocharian *kam* 'tooth'? Surely the omission of the latter (regardless of its eventual identification with a different set (E *comb*, Polish *zǫb* 'tooth', Gr *gómphos* 'peg', etc.)) rests initially on a 'substantial' intuition – despite the semantics.

To clarify this I turn to another view, similar in some ways to Zawadowski's, outlined in Kuryłowicz (1964). Can there be any rigorously defined middle ground between purely abstract mnemonics for correspondence classes and 'substantial' reconstructions, of whatever degree of detail, something more 'linguistic' and historical than the former, but more abstract, perhaps less conjectural than the latter? Kuryłowicz adopts what we might call 'abstract systemic relationism'. This is the notion that (phonological) reconstruction is by definition non-phonetic, but purely 'linguistic', i.e. what we recover is points in systems of formal intralinguistic relations. Kuryłowicz is writing here about internal reconstruction, but his remarks apply to (external) comparison as well, since the point at issue is substance.

He claims (ibid.: 11) that seeking an articulatory explanation – or even description – of a change like the Grimm's Law spirantization is beside the point:

> Physiological speculations . . . do not grasp the *linguistic* essence of these changes, the shift of the *internal* relations of the elements in question being the only pertinent fact. Once we leave language *sensu stricto* and appeal to extralinguistic factors, a clear delimitation of the field of language research is lost. [Emphasis original.]

Instead of phonetic elements, we have points in a purely abstract system (12):

> the accumulating deviations from the traditional pronunciation are not linguistic changes . . . It is only owing to certain *identifications* within the phonemic system that they have become pertinent . . . The point in time of such a coalescence is . . . the moment of linguistic change in the literal sense, when purely articulatory features are being *phonemicized*.

Carried to its logical conclusion, this would mean that if the (impossible?) change below were to occur, it would not really be a 'linguistic change':

(4) i u   y u
      e o →   ø ɣ
        ɑ   ɒ

(In both systems roundness is non-distinctive, back and front vowels of the same heights have opposite values for it, and the open vowel, though back, has the rounding of the front series.) This methodological decision limits our purview to those cases alone where systems change; yet probably the majority of actual changes are sub-systemic – and these are the source of all systemic transformations.

The narrowing of reconstruction (and hence of the locus of 'significance' in linguistic history) to formal relations rather than substance is incoherent. Kuryłowicz' 'relations' are ultimately cast in terms of particular features, and thus are covertly phonetic; the distinction will not hold in detail any more than Trubetzkoy's between 'phonetic' and 'phonemic' content (1939).

There is a simple but telling argument-in-principle against all relational, abstract, algebraic, etc., approaches to the concerns of linguistic history and reconstruction. I refer for the moment not to any kind of 'empirical testability' of outputs, but simply to what *must* characterize them if they are to mean anything at all. Whether this is all 'true' or not is another – in principle independent – question. It also may not have an unequivocal answer, but this should not be too worrying: no historical questions really do. The basic argument is similar to one Kiparsky mounted over two decades ago (1968) against 'fully abstract morphophonemics'. If the system of underlying representations (initiation points of derivations or segment inventory) is totally 'abstract' or non-phonetic, all mappings between 'deeper' and more 'superficial' or 'underlying' and phonetic levels of representation, and all class-groupings and particular morphophonemic relations, are arbitrary.

This holds *a fortiori* for history, where our concern is not with mappings between 'abstract' and 'concrete' representations, but between one concrete or phonetically specified representation and another. If 'IE */p/' is simply a cover-symbol or uninterpreted label for sets like L *ped-*, Skr *páda-*, E *foot*; and 'IE */t/' is the same for L *tenuis*, OIr *tanae* 'I stretch out', E *thin*; then there is no particular reason why one should consistently yield reflexes like [p, f] and the other ones like [t, θ]. Protosegments must be assumed to have some kind of phonetic content if their reflexes are to be intelligible.[12] Without such an assumption (and this is not merely an aid to the intuition) it would have been impossible to posit laryngeals or 'labiovelars' for Indo-European, or even to discuss the classical problem of the 'guttural series' (see section 5 below).

The reconstructing historian is making claims about substance whether he thinks he is or not. Zawadowski's hierarchy is rather more like a set of heuristics or an account of a historian's private, pre-publication operations, than a taxonomy of types of (completed) 'historical grammars'. When we reconstruct a */k/ we are not merely labelling the initials of cognate forms of the (putative) PIE word for 'heart'; nor on the other hand are we specifying the exact location of the dorso-velar closure, the voice-onset timing, and so on. But we are saying that we would be very surprised indeed if we met a speaker of PIE and his initial in 'heart' were

[p]; less trivially, that certain features (fairly gross, but no less specific) are integral to the reconstructed entity, and not others; and these features, whatever role their carrier happens to play in an oppositional system, are phonetic. In short, reconstruction – at least in phonology, where it has shown itself to be most useful – must in some sense be 'realist'. Protophones, protophonemes, etc., are not relational terms or set-labels, but 'entities', even physical ones. It is their (assumed) phonetic content, and this alone, that guarantees the possibility and ultimate rationality of projective reconstruction, and derivatively of history, rather than mere 'demonstration', in Zawadowski's sense, of filation. We will see below how this realist assumption alone can lead to the positing of rational constraints on reconstruction.[13]

5 Projection: procedures and constraints

The essential projective techniques are familiar to anyone who has ever studied historical linguistics. But there are a number of hidden assumptions that need exposure, and interesting points of method that arise. Much seems to be learned as tradecraft from other practitioners, and little is usually laid out in a really explicit way, at least in terms of potential conventionalism, and the extent to which the procedures 'force' realities to arise from technical operations.[14] The materials discussed in this section are not new; the reconstructive problems have been 'solved' already. My concern is rather with unpacking the assumptions lying behind these familiar solutions, as a kind of object lesson in 'constructivist' historiography.

Given a reasonably obvious set of correspondences, what determines a projection? Except in the limiting case of identity of reflexes, projection cannot be based on a purely 'mechanical' procedure or algorithm. For example, in Skr múḥ, L mūs, OE mūs, projecting the initial is no problem: PIE */m/, since the set contains only /m/.[15] But even simple non-identities may present some hidden difficulties; take for instance the familiar Grimm's Law correspondences among the velars:

(5) a. OE here 'army, troop, war', OHG heri, Go harjis, OIc herr; OCS kara 'struggle'; Lith karias 'army', OPr karia-woytis 'military review'; MIr cuire 'horde'; OPers kara- 'army', Gr koíranos < */kórjanos/ 'army leader'.

   b. OE heorte 'heart', OS herta, Go haírtō, OIc hjarta; L cord-; OCS srĭdĭ̄ce; Lith širdìs; OIr cride; Arm sirt; Skr śr̥d-.

   c. OE *hlyst* 'listening, (sense of) hearing', OFris *hlest*, OIc *hlust*; OCS *slyšati* 'to hear'; Lith *klausýti* 'to hear'; MIr *clos*, gen sg *cloiste* 'hearing', W *clust*; Skr *śruṣṭí* 'obedient'.

The initial consonant reflexes spread over a range glottal-velar-palatal-alveolar ('palatal' = high, non-anterior, non-back); this does not immediately suggest a projection. But the tradition is uniform in reconstructing IE */k/[16] for these and related sets, and it is worth asking why. The arguments converge from a number of directions; and it is this convergence that ultimately 'convinces', typically for good historical argument.

   First, compare these sets with a simpler one, from the labial series:

  (6)　OE *fearh* 'pig', G *Ferkel* 'piglet', Afrikaans *vark*[17] /fark/ 'pig'; OCS *prasę* 'pig'; Li *paršas* 'castrated pig'; L *porcus* 'pig'; MIr *orc* 'pig'

Here there are three reflexes, two labial and one zero; and the dialectal spread concentrates /f/ in Germanic (which we have other, independent reasons for considering a coherent genetic grouping), and zero in Celtic; whereas all other independently defined branches have /p/. Therefore we project */p/ initially on the grounds of:

(a) *Simplicity*. Zero or */f/ would require multiple convergent innovation throughout IE, with only a small grouping on the western fringe retaining the original. This is not impossible, but unlikely given the geography. In any case the guiding principle is avoiding convergence (cf. section 3 above).[18]

(b) *'Majority rule'*. Another aspect of the same thing: if most branches of a family have the same reflex, it is *a priori* likely to have been original. This suggests an implicit 'inertia' clause: anything is less likely to change than not, so if lots of languages in a family have X, X was probably always the case. This may or may not be empirically sound, but it is an intuition many historical linguists seem to have, and deserves inclusion for that reason if no other.

(c) *Phonetic 'naturalness'*. Prothesis of an articulated segment (i.e. not a glottal) is highly unlikely, whereas aphaeresis is well documented. And we know of many cases where historically attested labials have tended to weaken or drop, while other series have remained intact.[19] Our intuitive (or 'inductive') judgement of likelihood, based on pseudo-statistics of recurrence of change-types, is the guiding principle here, apparently, as well as (in some but not all cases) stipulations derived from knowledge of the kinds of articulatory or perceptual processes involved.[20]

But (6) is not that easy, because the majority rule principle is less clearly applicable, and the convergence problem therefore less obviously soluble. There are, however, constancies which can generate a projection. First, Germanic always has /h/, and Latin, Greek, Celtic always /k/. The difficult cases appear to be Indic, Slavonic, and Armenian with sibilants, either palatal or alveolar, and Baltic, with both (Lith *širdìs*, *klausýti*).[21] On just this evidence the non-convergence principle argues (weakly) for */k/.

The phonetic arguments are stronger. For one, what we know about the sources of /h/ in a wide variety of languages (cf. Lass 1976: ch. 6) suggests that a glottal segment is less likely to be original than just about any other kind, as glottals typically arise as lenitions (losses of articulation) of oral obstruents (so for Uralic, Dravidian, and other IE /h/). A proto-*/h/ is generally a last resort.[22] In addition (on both historical and synchronic grounds), velars seem to be the most responsive to conditioned articulatory shifts of all articulatory series: especially to palatalization and (subsequent) assibilation. Shifts of the type [k] > [ʃ], [s], etc. are well documented, whereas [ʃ], [s] > [k] are not. There is an environmental asymmetry: velars palatalize in front environments, but palatals do not typically become velar in back environments. Lenition and palatalization evidence therefore converges on */k/.[23]

These are 'process-segmental' arguments, focusing on the narrow segmental domain and what is on the one hand (virtually) impossible (e.g. labial prothesis) and on the other what is highly likely (lenition, velar palatalization). They are simply low-level instantiations of 'uniformitarian' principles (Lass 1980: ch. 1 and appendix, 1986). These strategies, however, do not always work, and there are others, not usually defined explicitly, that we can use. These will at times make us violate other principles – hopefully in good causes.

A useful beginning for complex correspondences, which gives a natural lead-in to others, is what I will call the 'Maximal Coding Principle'; it says:

Maximal coding principle. In cases where phonetic naturalness, non-convergence, etc., do not give a satisfactory result, project a segment that codes enough of the disparate properties of the reflex-set so that a strategy of phonetic 'decomposition' will yield the set-members relatively naturally.

Some discussion may be useful here. Consider these forms:

(7) (a) L *qui-s* 'who?'; Gr *tí-s*, Osc *pi-s*
    (b) L *qui-d* 'what?'; Skr *ci-d* 'indef. particle'; OCS *či-to* 'what?'
    (c) Go *hwā-s* 'who?', OE *hwā*; Skr *ka-ḥ*; li *kà-s*; OCS *ko-*

These are obviously formations off a single deictic root, (a, c) masculines of different vowel grades, (b) a neuter. But the initial raises a problem. Of course it has been 'solved'; it is the nature of the solution that is interesting. The consensus is that the initials go back to a PIE 'labiovelar',[24] normally reconstructed as $*/k^w/$.

Clearly the anti-convergence, majority-rule directive has been bypassed; the only groups that show both labial and velar components are Germanic and the Latin-Faliscan branch of Italic (note the Oscan labial). Given the range velar (and glottal by previous argument = velar reflex) – palatal-labial-labiovelar (not to mention Greek dental), the majority rule principle is weakly applicable if at all. Even if we tried (say choosing velars) we would still have to find a 'natural' way of keeping (7) distinct from (5), where we obviously do have an original velar.

So we can reconstruct the kind of question that (at least implicitly) must have been asked in deriving the accepted protoform: what sort of segment could – componentially speaking – give us what we have? One possibility, an original palatal, can in any case be eliminated on the basis of sets like Skr *kaḥ*, OCS *ko-* vs. Skr *cid*, OCS *čito*; palatals are to be derived from palatalized velars. The other main groups of reflexes are distributed among three types: velars, labials, and ones with both a velar and a labial component. Taking these as our primary choices, the obvious solution is to project a segment simultaneously coding all the possibilities; the attested *qu-*, *hw-* types suggest the answer. If the original has both a labial and a velar component, then the two basic (simple) reflex types derive from dropping one or the other.[25] Thus we code the cross-dialect spread of reflexes into a single protosegment, rather in the same way as we encode in synchronic underlying structures (if we do the kind of grammars that allow them) the maximal information that will naturally generate the members of the surface paradigm, paraphrase class, etc. we are describing.

But the distinction from synchronic 'underlying forms' is important. Some synchronic grammars that allow derivations do not constrain underlying forms to be (surface-canonically) well formed. In fact much of what goes on in certain types of generative grammars (in terms of 'rescue rules', absolute

neutralizations, the use of filters, etc.) is designed precisely to
remove the garbage produced by something very like a maximal
coding principle (or maximal coding plus some kind of 'simplicity').
But reconstruction cannot allow this kind of freedom: whatever we
reconstruct must be phonetically well formed. We require at least
this constraint:

> *Phonetic legality condition.* No segment type may be recon-
> structed that is not phonetically attested in a modern language;
> or (if we need a weaker version) not consistent with our
> present knowledge of the capabilities of the human vocal tract.

To return to PIE */kʷ/. The daughter languages show fairly
extensive convergence, at least insofar as there has been a
widespread move from the original type, if not always in the
same direction. Since we cannot invoke the majority rule
principle, we resort to a kind of reconstruction-by-reconstitution,
i.e. actual building from *disjecta membra* (section 3).

But */kʷ/ is not really the most obvious choice, given the
reflexes; and this suggests another constraint. Taken at face value
this symbol would mean a velar stop with labialization, the latter
presumably a superimposed approximant articulation ('secondary
stricture'). If this were the case, our 'dissolution' scenario ought
to eventuate in either velar stops or labial approximants: e.g. we
would not expect Oscan /p/. And if we look at more data
involving this putative */kʷ/, we find that where Greek does not
have /t/ it has /p/: e.g. *leíp-ō* 'I leave' (cf. L *li-n-qu-ō* with nasal
infix); Vedic Sanskrit *kṛnóti* 'he does', Irish *creth* 'poetry', Welsh
peri 'do', *prydydd* 'poet'. Not Greek *leíw-ō* or some post-
diagamma reflex, Welsh *weri*, etc.

This would suggest that perhaps L *qu-*, Germanic *hw-* ought to
be 'aberrant', not the type of the source segment; the other
reflexes, uniformly simple stops, usually velar or labial, would
derive most naturally from a double stop articulation, i.e. */k͡p/.
The actual derivations of Oscan, Celtic /p-/, and so on, would be
simpler; we would not need to transfer the stop closure from the
'primary' velar stricture to the 'secondary' labial, then delete the
velar.

What stops us? Why has nobody seriously suggested this? The
main reason is probably the background of most earlier workers
in Indo-European – very few of them would likely have been
familiar with segments of the [k͡p] type, precisely because they
were Indo-Europeanists. And this suggests a justification. Double
stop articulations like this are not widespread in the world's
languages; the majority of them appear to occur in West African

languages of various genetic affiliations (e.g. Ibo, Yoruba, Idoma, Margi). No contemporary IE language as far as I know has [k͡p], and no attested older one has tempted anyone to claim seriously anything of the sort. This leads us to a primary, typologically based constraint on the content of reconstructions:

Family consistency condition. No segment type ought to be reconstructed for a protolanguage that does not occur in at least one attested descendant.

Like all uniformitarian constraints, this is neither logically necessary nor grounded in theory. It is methodological or conventionalist: a critical tool, designed to impoverish reconstructive technology. It also expresses (within limits) an interesting fact about cross-language segment distributions: certain phonetic types are apparently highly restricted, both genetically and areally. The total inventory of possible segments is not 'randomly' spread over the world's languages, but often skewed by family and place.

An overall constraint on reconstruction can be developed in the form of a theoretically uninterpreted but inductively binding version of 'markedness' theory: the construction of an 'index of oddity', keyed to specific families and/or areas.[26] For instance the number of languages in the world with front rounded vowels appears to be both low and concentrated. In the sample in Maddieson (1984), only 26 out of 317 languages (about 8 per cent) have them. This looks like the classic picture of a 'marked' category. But this 8 per cent is overwhelmingly concentrated: Indo-European and 'Ural-Altaic' (= Uralic, Turkic, Tungus and a few others) account for 74 per cent of the total. The rest are scattered in Kwa, Austro-Tai, and Uto-Aztecan, with the only other cluster of any size in Sino-Tibetan (16 per cent). In the groups that have them, they tend to be the norm rather than the exception; the largest IE concentration is in Germanic, and Yiddish is the only language in that group none of whose dialects seem to have any.

Similarly, clicks are, cross-linguistically, extremely rare, but highly concentrated in sub-saharan Africa: in Khoi and San languages, where they appear to be original, and in southern Bantu langauges (e.g. Zulu, Xhosa) that have been in intimate contact with Khoisan. So a reconstructed proto-click in a Khoi or San language (or a 'post-proto' click in a Bantu language of the Nguni group) is unproblematical. Whereas if a click were proposed to fill a 'problematic' place like that of the IE labiovelars, this would be extremely dubious, probably rejectable out of hand. We can then propose another constraint:

> *Oddity condition.* The rarer a segment-type is, the more
> evidence we need to reconstruct it. Except if it is widely
> distributed either in the family concerned, or in the geographi-
> cal area in which the language in question occurs.[27]

The Index of Oddity again is of no theoretical import; like the
other constraints it is simply a device for recognizing the
existence of cases where the 'marked' is as it were the 'unmarked'
condition. It blocks the reconstruction of (cross-linguistically)
'odd' segments just in case they are not common in the family or
area involved, but allows them if they are 'family universals'
(Lass 1975). Thus the Oddity Condition is really the obverse of
the Family Consistency Condition. Segmental reconstruction
does not proceed in a vacuum, nor is it constrained only by the
dictates of some general theory; genetic and areal typology play a
major legislative role.

6 'Lawfulness' of change: the neogrammarian effect

The term 'law' has been used in two basic senses in historical
linguistics: as 'sound-law' (e.g. the equivalence L /p/: E /f/ is
'lawful', determined by a *Lautgesetz* or 'law of mutation'); and in
a historicist sense as 'evolutionary law', governing directionality
of change (Zipf's Law, Mańczak's Laws of Analogy, etc.).

The claim that phonetic change is lawful in the first sense, that
it follows the Osthoff and Brugmann *Ausnahmslosigkeit* formula,
is locally false, and globally close to true; the other claim, that
change follows directional laws, is locally sometimes (adventi-
tiously) true, and globally false.[28] I deal here only with the first
kind of claim.

There are really two questions involved in basing reconstructive procedures on the hypothesis that sound change is 'regular',
proceeding 'mit blinder Notwendigkeit' (Osthoff and Brugmann
1878): an empircal one (is it?) and a methodological one (ought it
to be?). These intersect: operating on the principle that sound
change is regular (except when compromised by equally regular
processes, or last-ditch aberrations like analogy and borrowing),
we get 'good' results. The hypothesis is (weakly) confirmed by
the possibility of reconstructing protoforms, the fruitfulness of
these objects for further research, their occasional testability, the
pleasing or 'insightful' shapes of the resultant histories, etc.

The regularity hypothesis is the indispensable foundation of
historical/comparative linguistics; virtually everything we know

about (for example) the history of IE languages, their interrelations and prehistory, is based on the painstaking application of techniques and argument based on Neogrammarian methodology and assumptions, which are virtually our only *entrée* to linguistic prehistory (and much of history as well). Without it, there would be no such thing as a reliable etymology. Despite all this, however, the hypothesis is dead wrong as a picture of phonological change. It is not a correct claim about the mechanism of change, and makes wrong predictions about the kinds of *état de langue* that exist in the world. But, paradoxically, it is also a true picture of perhaps the bulk of the standardly utilized data: it is micro-wrong, but macro-right. To put it another way, the Neogrammarian hypothesis is correct for Neogrammarian (parts of) languages, and wrong for non-Neogrammarian ones. These apparent contradictions can be brought into some kind of peaceful coexistence by making some fairly sharp distinctions.

Now on the face of it the Neogrammarian claim is the best sort: the stronger a theory is, in the sense of forbidding more states of nature, the more empirical content it has. And this one has enough content for it to be falsifiable, and for the falsifications that emerge to be themselves theoretically interesting.

We obviously know a lot of things that most nineteenth-century historians did not; the importance of variability as input to change, the role of the lexicon in the diffusion of innovation, and so on. But even without this 'variationist' and 'diffusionist' perspective, the evidence to refute the strong regularity hypothesis has always been available, even if it has often been bypassed by arguments based on 'dialect borrowing' and the like (cf. Chen 1972). One micro-level example will indicate the problem and its (partial) solution.

Consider the typical reflexes of ME /o, au, a:/ in my variety of New York English:

(8)	ME	NYC	e.g.
	/o/ before voiceless stops	ä	cop, cot, lock
	/o/ before voiced stops, /m, n/	α:	cob, cod, log, bomb
	/o/ before voiceless fricatives, /ŋ/	ɔ:	off, cloth, moss, moth, long
	/au/	ɔ:	fault, brought, law
	/a:/	ɛɪ	mate, cave, cane

The bulk of the lexicon shows these correspondences, and

allows proper Neogrammarian reconstruction, giving these
developments:

(9) ME   NYC

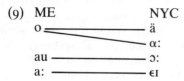

With a certain comparative perspective (not relevant here) and
fairly uncontroversial details from what is known about the
history of English vocalism, the scenario is fairly easy to
reconstruct (for details Lass 1980: ch. 5):

(10) 1. ME /a:/ > /ɛ:/ > /e:/ > /ɛɪ/ (Great Vowel Shift and
         its aftermath: sixteenth to nineteenth century).
      2. ME /o/ > /ɔ/ > /ɒ/ (sixteenth to seventeenth century)
      3. ME /au/ > /ɔ:/ > /ɒ:/ (as 2)
      4. /ɒ/ (from 2) > [ɒ:] before /ɣ/, voiceless fricatives (late
         seventeenth-early eighteenth century)
      5. /ɒ:/ > /ɔ:/ (nineteenth century)
      6. /ɒ/ > /ɑ/ (US, eighteenth to nineteenth century)
      7. /ɑ/ > [ɑ:] before voiced stops, /m, n/ (nineteenth
         century?)
      8. /ɑ/ > /ä/ (nineteenth century?)[29]

If we take these changes, all between c. 1450 and 1850, as
'exceptionless', we get the following incorrect predictions:

(a) ME /o/ before voiceless fricatives, /ŋ/: *tong(s)*, *prong*, *fossil*,
    offal, *coffer*, *posset*, *cosset*. Expected /ɔ:/, actual /ä/.
    Expected development via 2, 4; actual development involves
    failure of 4, leading to application of 6, 8.
(b) ME /o/ before voiced stop: *dog*. Expected /ɑ:/, actual /ɔ:/.
    Expected development via 6, 7; actual development involves
    misapplication of 4, i.e. treating /g/ as if it were /ŋ/.
       These two developments are idiosyncratic American ones;
    but these categories show earlier, more widespread 'aberra-
    tions' of the same kind:
(c) ME /au/: *palm*, *calm*, *balm*, *psalm*. Expected /ɔ:/, actual
    /ɑ:/. Expected development via 3, 5; actual development
    involves existence of early doublets in /æ/ < ME /a/, which
    lengthens and falls in with ME /a/ before /r/ (*far*).
(d) ME /a:/: *father*. Expected /ɛɪ/, actual /ɑ:/. Problematic:
    failure of Great Vowel Shift in late ME /a:/ < /a/ lengthened
    in open syllables; apparent *ad hoc* treatment of probable

short /a/, lengthened before /ð/, hence the same development as in (c).

What does such an apparent mess have to say about 'regularity' and its use in reconstruction? A despairing view might be that the whole 'lawfulness' idea is inept except in some statistical sense; etymology becomes a science where consonants count for little and vowels for nothing, as Voltaire suggested. But the global success of Neogrammarian method argues against this, as does our natural impulse to fight chaos.

This is of course a pseudo-problem, arising entirely from failure to distinguish mechanisms and results, and a vulgar idealization of sound change as 'instantaneous'. At this point we invoke the 'sociolinguistic' dimension to extricate ourselves from the problem of failed correspondences, by simply admitting into our background assumptions the following:

 (i) Sound change is implemented primarily by cumulating output variation, in some particular direction (Hockett's (1965) drift of 'local frequency maxima', Weinreich et al.'s (1968) 'orderly heterogeneity', mediated through Labovian variation).

 (ii) Therefore all change scenarios are played out in time: 'change' has duration ((i) plus Chen 1972 adding the 'time dimension', and the 'diffusionist' tradition).

(iii) To individual variation (i) and time (ii), we add the lexicon as a fundamental determinant; the environment of a mutation (always?) includes lexical tagging, at least until the change has gained a certain momentum (Chen 1972; Ogura 1987, etc.).

(iv) Any change, at any point in the variation sequence, the time-course, the process of lexical diffusion, can abort (Lass 1981).

 (v) Any pair of n-tuple of changes can overlap, or 'compete' for given environments (Wang 1969; Newton 1971).

These claims are now uncontroversial, even banal. But they are important, because they give us an explicit warrant for reconciling even the strong version of the Neogrammarian hypothesis with both messy data and the results of recent work. The operation of change along the variational and lexical dimensions shows that the earlier we catch a change, the more 'irregular' its reflexes look. Institutionalization of change, like anything else, takes time.

The reason that regularity has (say since Verner) been taken for granted is that 'microdialectal' reflexes of the kind I have been looking at have not been the primary material for language history. The usual procedure, dictated partly at least by the interests of the major earlier scholars, has removed the problem in advance. As long as comparative reconstruction in IE, for instance, stuck largely to language-sets like {Greek, Latin, Sanskrit}, {Old Prussian, Latvian, Lithuanian}, etc., and to an institutionalized standard form in each case, the language-splits and major changes were far enough back in time for the worst irregularities to be removed by supervening analogy, completion of diffusion, etc. And the material used was largely written, i.e. normalized and with the variation filtered out, confined in the main to representation of lento forms in more formal registers (cf. Dressler 1975).[30]

Sound change in fact *is* Neogrammarian: as long as we use Neogrammarian materials to study it. Especially written materials, which in the nature of things tend to belong to relatively formal, hence non-innovating registers.[31] Though from one perspective Grimm might have seemed a bit naive in first calling his phonology not *Lautlehre* but *Lehre von den Buchstaben* (1819), this is what comparative and other forms of historical linguistics have been for the greater part of their history.[32]

This may be what has made comparative method so stunningly successful; it characteristically enters the historical sequence at a point where the 'irregularity' problem has largely been taken care of. This the source of the endemic naive equation of correspondences and changes that continues to bedevil us if we are not careful (cf. Lass 1978). It is really only within the past two decades or so that Neogrammarian *regelrecht* correspondences have come to be naturally interpretable as the end results of long-term processes of much messier change, involving variation, and often lexeme-specific mutation.

The proper formulation now might be something very different in the letter but akin in spirit to the original Osthoff and Brugmann claim: sound changes *tend to become* exceptionless, given enough time (*ceteris paribus* – as usual). And the closing hedge involves all those factors mentioned above. This means that instead of the Neogrammarian Principle, we have what might better be called the Neogrammarian Effect: exceptionless correspondences are what tend finally to emerge from the untidy business of actual implementation.

Does this empirically well-founded view imply a complete reassessment of language history and reconstruction? Should comparative method be taken as reliable only if restricted to 'old' changes, and unusable for new or nascent ones? Should we scrap the regularity hypothesis for recent change, and admit two different kinds of language history, one with a small and one with a great time-depth?

This would be misguided and counterproductive, a case of missing forests because we have at long last developed techniques for looking at trees, and become obsessed by their fine detail. While local microhistory may be (even largely) about variation and diffusion, macrohistory is not. After all, in the end it does not much matter how Grimm's Law came about if one's particular interest is in the global history of Germanic; it does not matter that *dog*, as well as *prong* and *tong*, have the wrong vowels if one is talking about the overall history of ME /o/ in New York English. There is still a legitimate generalization in each case:

(i) PIE */p, t, k/ > PGmc */f, θ, x/ – no matter how. It is irrelevant that there may have been an intermediate stage of voiceless aspirates, or whatever. Here of course there's no problem, since the mess has already been cleaned up. But it still makes sense to talk of 'the change' as spirantization of voiceless stops.

(ii) ME /o/ > NYC [ä] before voiceless stops, [ɑ:] before voiced stops and /m, n/, [ɔ:] before /ŋ/. This is the 'basic shape' of the history: only it does not get realized everywhere in all its details. (If I walk from Edinburgh to London and lose a shoe at York, my 'achievement' is still the whole walk, not the loss of a shoe.)

The opposite approach would get us into the sterility of *chaque mot a son histoire*: all trees, no forests. A forest has its own special shape, even if odd trees die from time to time.

7 Envoi: what is a protolanguage?

As Meillet said (section 4 above), reconstruction does not give us back a language 'tel qu'il a été parlé'; but it is not an uninterpreted algebra without substantive content either. If it's something in between (and this is surely not a case of *tertium non datur*), what is it likely to be? Presumably an 'idealization' of some kind; but one that approaches as closely as possible to an object that could purport to be a representation of a natural language, at some degree of abstraction or idealization permissible in a synchronic description.

Since a protolanguage is a summation over a set of individual reconstructions, it must be an object governed, initially, by a set of uniformitarian constraints, as always synchronically based. Here are some candidates:

(i) *Absolute constraints.* A protolanguage must not show any properties 'known' (inductively) to be illegal for a natural language, or lack any that are 'known' to be necessary (= defining). For example, it may not have more (phonemic) nasals than non-nasal stops, more fricatives than stops, only non-low vowels, must have at least one low vowel, (probably) at least three stops one of which is coronal and one velar, etc.

(ii) *Local constraints.* A protolanguage must not (or ought not) have any properties that on a well-motivated Index of Oddity (section 5) do not occur in any of its daughters, or at least in its linguistic area.

(iii) *Judgement constraint.* In cases of doubt, the properties of a protolanguage must be (inductively) controlled by the best available judgements of overall likelihood. For example, if only one coronal fricative is to be reconstructed, and there are doubts about what it is, it is */s/.

These conditions are simply additive micro-level projections of the general uniformity conditions binding on micro-level reconstructions at the segmental level, as suggested in section 5. In a sense then, a protolanguage as a whole is an idealized summation over a set of local reconstructions. Starting from the necessary base of individual segmental reconstructions, we expand, if possible, to the paradigmatic plane (the system of 'units' our reconstructed protocategories produce). From there we move to the syntagmatic plane; once we have enough protomorph(eme)s we have a phonotactics; once we reconstruct morphologically complex forms we have a morphology and morphotactics; and from there we may, with luck, get to at least the outlines of a protosyntax.[33]

In a way, the thrust of this chapter has been that linguistic historiography is a partly conventionalist operation whose results make no sense except under a realist interpretation, and which cannot be carried out as a rational empirical pursuit without conventionalist underpinning. This kind of paradox is built in to the historical enterprise, and should not bother anybody. We use uninterpreted and problematic tools to 'recover' items whose very recovery presupposes a realist ontology – even, for the kind of items that have been our concern here, a physicalist one. One of the marks of the real is its ability to cast shows (*Republic*, VII.

514ff.); we recover the shadows of phones, and through them the shadows of phonemic systems, morphs, morphemes . . . and the rest is method.

Notes

1. Grimm's Law is a nice case in point. What it 'actually was' depends now on whether one believes in the traditional IE stop system, or some version of post-Gamkrelidze/Ivanov 'glottalic theory' (cf. Vennemann 1989, pt III), with ejectives as part of the inventory. On the old interpretation, the initial correspondence in L *decem*: E *ten* represents devoicing of IE */d/ to /t/; on the new, IE */t'/ went from ejective to plain stop with no voicing change. Other IE groups offer even more striking cases. If the dental series was not */t, d, dh/ but /t, t', d/, the origin of the Greek voiceless aspirate in *'tí)thēmi* 'I place' is more complex than simple deaspiration or shift from breathy-voice to voiceless aspirated; while that in OCS *děti* 'lay', *dějati* 'do' is simpler, representing no change at all. (Assuming a root */dhe(:)-/ (old style), */de(:)-/ (new style).)
2. By 'regular' I mean using techniques with some coverage and theoretical support, not *ad hoc* devices. This excludes ploys like etymology by *lucus a non lucendo* ('War is called *bellum* because it's ugly'). It also forces the evaluation of regular correspondences as superior to intuitively attractive but unprincipled resemblances (section 3 below).
3. The languages are Iruḷa, first identified by Zvelebil in 1968, and Tamil (cf. Zvelebil 1970: 12). Both appear to belong to the same (South Dravidian) sub-family.
4. Or even to achieve really convincing reconstructions of 'superfamilies' supposedly ancestral to reasonably well reconstructed families. For example, a relation between Uralic and Dravidian has been mooted since the time of Caldwell (1856), and now both are supposedly members of the monstrous 'Nostratic' superfamily. Constructs like Nostratic, however, are not 'proto-languages' in the traditional sense, and a 'Nostratic etymology' is not the same thing as a Proto-Indo-European etymology, at least in my estimation (but see Bomhard 1984 for the opposing view). In this chapter I will not be concerned with reconstructability at any level higher than that of the 'normal' or conventional protolanguage.
5. In palaeontology there is a special problem: certain kinds of change seem habitually to involve fine sequential 'linkages', while others at least appear to be saltatory. Thus we get fairly clear 'graded' sequences between tokens of lower-level taxa (varieties, species, even genera), but often little or nothing between higher-level ones (orders, classes, phyla). This has been construed as a problem for evolutionary theories of natural selection exclusively based on cumulative micromutation, and the basis for arguments for evolution by 'hopeful monsters', or at least the incorporation of some

macroevolutionary machinery in current (neo)Darwinian theory. (See Ayala 1983, Turner 1983.)

6. Internal reconstruction is in essence nothing more than comparative method applied to 'cognates' within one language, under the assumption that all non-suppletive allomorphs of a morpheme are cognate. For discussion see Lass (1977).

7. Genetic stemmata are normally assumed to be trees in the graph-theoretic sense (no circuits, a single originating vertex). Graphs portraying aspects of the internal histories of single languages (showing mergers, etc.) may be 'semitrees', 'vines', etc. (cf. Stewart 1976: 95ff.). This problem is by and large micro-taxonomic; we run into it when dealing with apparent 'fusion-languages' like Dutch, or difficult subgroupings like 'Northwest IE'. It does not normally arise in reconstruction proper on the intralinguistic level.

8. This may give rise to difficulties when a regular morphological process has been superseded by borrowing. Thus in certain kinship and body-part terms, English has a native Germanic noun and a borrowed adjective: both cognate: *father: paternal, mother: maternal, heart: cardiac, head; cephalic, tongue: lingual* (L *lingua* < */dingwa/), etc.

9. There are of course cases of non-insulation, such as onomatopoeias, semantically bound 'expressive gemination' in animal names (OHG, *snecco* 'snail', cf. OE *snægel*), special systems for hypocoristics (Dahlstedt 1978), etc. So-called 'sound symbolism' may also enter here as well, if there is such a thing.

10. OE *fearh* 'pig', *furh* 'furrow' do in fact belong to a single 'relational' set (respectively < *o*-grade */pork-/ and zero-grade */pr̥k-/, of a single IE root, presumably with a sense like 'dig'). The Lithuanian and Latin forms also continue the *o*-grade, and G *Ferkel e*-grade.

11. For further discussion of the possibility of making a rigorous distinction between establishing protoforms and investing them with content, see Collinge (1970: 70f.).

12. The same argument holds for 'non-phonetic' phonologies like that of Foley (1977). Foley claims that his 'phonological' categories are not phonetic, but cannot explain why for instance the abstract category 'velars' always seems to surface as things like [k, g, x].

13. For a programmatic rejection of realism in reconstruction see Allen (1953). The realist position I take here is strictly 'external'; phones, etc. are construed as 'objects in the world', not 'mental realities'. I see no need for any kind of psychologism, mental representationalism or 'psychological reality' in historical linguistics. For argument, see Lass 1987, forthcoming).

14. There are explicit accounts in some textbooks, notably Anttila (1972) and Hockett (1958), and most recently and sophisticatedly, Hock (1991). The best really detailed methodological discussion is probably still in Hoenigswald (1960, 1973). But certain philosophical points have not yet been sufficiently explored.

15. Of course there are cases where identity does not – in a larger

perspective – reconstruct as identity. For example, Gothic /α/ in *akrs* 'field', *ahtau* 'eight' (and most other Germanic sets like this) project to Proto-Germanic */α/, but non-Germanic evidence shows that this represents a merger of two IE categories (cf. L *ager*, *octō*). Much depends on the size of the data-set in cases like this; 'mouse' is a simple default for illustration.

16. Or rather the 'traditional tradition', not the 'glottalic', (cf. note 1), which I do not subscribe to. For some useful critical discussion see Szemerényi 1989: s. VI.9.

17. We can assume that the older /v/ suggested by the spelling <v>, and still attested in some varieties of Dutch, is a development from Germanic /f/; we do not have to invoke /v/ as another reflex.

18. H.-H. Lieb (personal communication) suggests that the admixture of empirical evidence or expectation in this apparently conventionalist principle actually dilutes it and makes it approach the empirical. All the conventionalism here is in a sense 'tainted' with realism. I agree that to some extent this is the case; but the important point is the presence of conventionalist elements to any degree, and their role as (in the absence of 'data', or the presence of corrupt or ambiguous data) at least *faute de mieux* sources of what we have to call 'historical knowledge'.

19. So S. Dravidian /p/ > /h/ in Kannada (Ka *hoogu* 'go', Tamil *poo-*), Japanese */p/ > [h, ɸ] and zero; perhaps also the labial-free state of some Salishan languages.

20. On the theoretical importance of the notion of 'natural recurrence' see Anderson and Ewen (1987: ch. 1).

21. The *satem* palatalization (which of course is what this is) has uneven results in Baltic; Lithuanian appears to be largely *satem*, but is *centum* in some cases, particularly (but not exclusvely) in onset-clusters. This is presumably a matter of the temporal stratification of the lexicon, with non-*satem* forms older.

22. Of course in some version of laryngeal theory PIE has a 'proto-*/h/', but the effects of putative laryngeals normally suggest that whatever else they were they were not pure glottals: at least those laryngeals that either lengthen or 'colour', not simply the silly ones inserted to make sure all IE initial syllables are /CV-/.

23. Comparison of labials and velars shows a Germanic/Celtic convergence: the Celtic initial zero for */p/ as in *porcus*: *orc* probably presupposes a prior *[h]. This may go back to an areal link between the two groups (a Bronze-Age 'Northwestern IE' community). There are also lenition convergences in Greek and Armenian for IE */s/, but anti-convergence arguments weaken in proportion to the 'naturalness' or expectability of the change-type involved (Lass 1984).

24. This term is of course ill-formed if interpreted like 'labiodental'; nobody's vocal tract is built that way. The proper term would be 'labialized velar' (if the velar stricture is 'primary'), 'labial-velar' if it is not.

25. The Greek dental before a front vowel represents not a mere 'decomposition' of the original, but an assimilation: since both labials and velars are grave, we have assimilation of a grave consonant to a nongrave vowel.

26. In my opinion, this is the only intelligible interpretation of markedness (Lass 1975, 1980: ch. 2). Despite the seriousness with which many linguists with otherwise impeccable credentials take the idea, I have found no reason in the past decade to change my mind. For a recent intelligent and wide-ranging discussion of markedness by a believer, see Croft (1990: ch. 4).

27. One obvious place to invoke this would be for the IE laryngeals. At least some proposals, e.g. for pharyngeals (Lehmann 1952: 108) could probably be excluded by the index.

28. That is, while there are sequences in language histories that can be interpreted as 'directional' (in nearly any direction!), counter-examples are numerous enough to falsify nearly all such claims (cf. Lass 1975, 1980: ch. 2 on directionality predictions made by believers in markedness and 'naturalness').

29. The chronology of these later changes has not been worked out, but they cannot reasonably be any earlier than the nineteenth century.

30. The (necessary) restriction of much pioneering work to early written records probably filters out numerous apparent violations of *Lautgesetze*. In an institutionalized orthography many odd reflexes can show up only by accident (e.g. if they happen to occur in rhymes), or through extra-textual evidence (orthoepists, etc.). The fact that in my dialect *dog* and *log* do not have the same vowel would be invisible in non-rhymed texts, and require specific metalinguistic evidence, as here, to be recorded at all.

31. Except of course if we use 'naive' materials which coexist with standardized writing systems, e.g. letters, diaries, and the like.

32. Whether Grimm meant *Buchstab* in the abstract and sophisticated sense of the medieval use of *littera* (cf. Abercrombie 1949) is uncertain; but he did coin the term *Lautverschiebung*.

33. There are problems with the reconstruction even of morphology, in that for instance stem-class memberships may be unstable or variable as far back as one can go. For example, it is not possible to reconstruct a full Proto-Germanic etymon in the usual sense for the word 'tooth'; the Germanic reflexes show both zero-grade (Go *tunþus*) and *o*-grade (OHG *zand*, OE *tōþ*) in the root, and stem-assignment is also variable: Gothic has a *u*-stem while most of the other dialects show a consonant-stem (cf. Lass 1986).

References

ABERCROMBIE, D. (1949) What is a letter? *Lingua* 2. pp. 12–22.

ALLEN, W. S. (1953) 'Relationship in comparative linguistics', *Transactions of the Philological Society (TPS)* 52–108.

ANDERSON, J. and EWEN, C. (1987) *Principles of Dependency Phonology*.

Cambridge: Cambridge University Press.

ANTTILA, R. (1972) *An Introduction to Historical and Comparative Linguistics*. New York: Macmillan.

AWEDYK, W. and HAMANS, C. (1989) 'Vowel shifts in English and Dutch: formal or genetic relations?' *Folia Linguistica Historica* 8: 99–114.

AYALA, F. J. (1983) 'Microevolution and macroevolution.' In BENDALL, D. S. (1983) *Evolution from Molecules to Men*. Cambridge: Cambridge University Press, 387–402.

BOMHARD, A. (1984) *Toward Proto-Nostratic*. Amsterdam: Benjamins.

BOTHA, R. P. (1982) 'On "the Galilean style" of linguistic inquiry', *Lingua* 58: 1–50.

CALDWELL, R. (1875) *A Comparative Grammar of the Dravidian or South-Indian Family of Languages*. London: Harrison.

CHEN, M. (1972) 'The time dimension: contribution toward a theory of sound change', *Foundations of Language* 8: 457–98.

COLLINGE, N. E. (1970) *Collectanea Linguistica*. The Hague: Mouton.

CROFT, W. (1990) *Typology and Universals*. Cambridge: Cambridge University Press.

DAHLSTEDT, K.-H. (1978) 'On reduced phonological structures: Hypocorisms in the dialect of Anundsjö.' In *Sign and Sound. Studies Presented to Bertil Malmberg on the Occasion of his Sixty-fifth birthday, 22 April 1978 (Studia Linguistica)* 32: 18–35.

DRESSLER, W. U. (1975) 'Methodisches zu Allegro-regeln.' In DRESSLER, W. U. and MAREŠ, F. V. (eds) *Phonologica 1972*. München: Fink, pp. 219–34.

FOLEY, J. (1977) *Principles of Theoretical Phonology*. Cambridge: Cambridge University Press.

GRIMM, J. (1819) *Deutsche Grammatik*. Göttingen: Dieterich.

HOCK, H. H. (1991) *Principles of Historical Linguistics*, 2nd edn. Berlin: Mouton de Gruyter.

HOCKETT, C. F. (1958) *A Course in Modern Linguistics*. New York: Macmillan.

HOCKETT, C. F. (1965) 'Sound change.' *Language* 41: 185–204.

HOENIGSWALD, H. (1960) *Language Change and Linguistic Reconstruction*. Chicago: University of Chicago Press.

HOENIGSWALD, H. (1973) *Studies in Formal Historical Linguistics*. Dordrecht: Reidel.

KIPARSKY, P. (1968) 'How abstract is phonology?' Bloomington: Indiana University Linguistics Club.

KURYŁOWICZ, J. (1964) 'On the methods of internal reconstruction.' In LUNT, H. 'Proceedings of the 9th International Congress of Linguists'. The Hague: Mouton, pp. 9–36.

LASS, R. (1975) 'How intrinsic is content? Markedness, sound change, and "family universals".' In PULLUM, G. and GOYVAERTS, D. (eds) *Essays on the Sound Pattern of English*. Ghent: E. Story-Scientia, pp. 475–504.

LASS, R. (1977) 'Internal reconstruction and generative phonology', *Transactions of the Philological Society (TPS)*, 1–26.

LASS, R. (1978) 'Mapping constraints in phonological reconstruction:

on climbing down trees without falling out of them.' In FISIAK, J. (ed.), *Recent developments in historical phonology*. The Hague: Mouton, pp. 245–86.

LASS, R. (1980) *On Explaining Language Change*. Cambridge: Cambridge University Press.

LASS, R. (1981) 'Undigested history and synchronic "structure".' In GOYVAERTS, D. (ed.) *Phonology in the 1980s*. Ghent: E. Story-Scientia, pp. 525–44.

LASS, R. (1984) 'Survival, convergence, innovation: a problem in diachronic theory.' *Stellenbosch Papers in Linguistics* 12: 17–36.

LASS, R. (1986) 'Words without etyma: Germanic "tooth".' In KASTOVSKY, D. and SZWEDEK, A. (eds) *Linguistics Across Historical and Geographical Boundaries. In Honour of Jacek Fisiak on the Occasion of His Fiftieth Birthday*, I. Berlin: de Gruyter, pp. 473–82.

LASS, R. (1987) 'Language, speakers, history and drift'. In KOOPMAN, W. F.v.d.

LASS, R., O. FISCHER and R. EATON, *Explanation and Linguistic Change*. Amsterdam: Benjamins, pp. 151–76.

LASS, R. Forthcoming. 'What are language-histories histories of?' In LIEB, H.-H. (ed.) *Prospects for a new structuralism*.

LEHMANN, W. P. (1952) *Proto-Indo-European Phonology*. Austin: University of Texas Press.

MADDIESON, I. (1984) *Patterns of Sounds*. Cambridge: Cambridge University Press.

MEILLET, A. (1967) *The Comparative Method in Historical Linguistics*. Paris: Champion.

MEILLET, A. (1964) *Introduction à l'Étude Comparative des Langes Indo-Européennes*. University, Alabama: University of Alabama Press.

NEWTON, B. (1971) 'Ordering paradoxes in phonology', *Journal of Linguistics* 7: 31–53.

OSTHOFF, H. and BRUGMANN, K. (1878) *Morphologische Untersuchungen auf dem Gebiete der Indogermanischen Sprachen*, Vol. I. Leipzig: S. Hirzel.

SAUSSURE, F. DE (1878) *Mémoire sur le Système Primitif des Voyelles dans les Langues Indo-européennes*. Leipzig: Teubner.

STEWART, A. H. (1976) *Graphic Representation of Models in Linguistic Theory*. Bloomington, IN: Indiana University Press.

SZEMERÉNYI, O. (1989) *Einführung in die Vergleichende Sprachwissenschaft*. Darmstadt: Wissenschaftliche Buchgesellschaft.

TURNER, J. R. G. (1983) '"The hypothesis that explains mimetic resemblance explains evolution": the gradualist-saltationist schism.' In GRENE, M. (ed.) *Dimensions of Darwinism. Themes and Counter-themes in Twentieth-century Evolutionary Theory*. Cambridge: Cambridge University Press.

TRUBETZKOY, N. S. (1939) *Grundzüge der Phonologie*. Travaux du Cercle Linguistique de Prague (TCLP), VII.

VENNEMANN, T. (1989) (ed.) *The new sound of Indo-European: Essays in Phonological Reconstruction*. Berlin: Mouton de Gruyter.

VERNER, K. (1875) 'Eine Ausnahme der ersten Lautverschiebung.' *Zeitschrift für vergleichende Sprachforschung auf dem Gebiete der Indogermanischen Sprachen* Vol. 23, No. 2, pp. 97–130.

WANG, W. S.-Y. (1969) 'Competing changes as a cause of residue', *Language* 45: 9–25.

WEINREICH. U., LABOV, W. and HERZOG, M. (1986) 'Empirical foundations for a theory of language change.' In LEHMANN, W. P. and MALKIEL, Y. (eds) *Directions for Historical Linguistics. A symposium.* Austin, TX: University of Texas Press, pp. 95–196.

ZAWADOWSKI, L. (1962) 'Theoretical foundations of comparative grammar', *Orbis* 11: 6–20.

ZVELEBIL, K. (1970) *Comparative Dravidian Phonology.* The Hague: Mouton.

Chapter 7

Why UG needs a learning theory: triggering verb movement

David Lightfoot

For more than a decade generativists have viewed the linguistic genotype or 'Universal Grammar' (UG) as consisting of principles and a set of option-points or parameters. Correspondingly, language acquisition proceeds as children set those parameters, sometimes characterized as switches with ON and OFF positions. And languages change over time as parameters come to be set differently. The notion of a parameter has stolen the limelight, but particular parameters are surprisingly evanescent. That is, for only very few parameters can one point to a solid basis of evidence, a clear understanding of how a particular parameter-setting interacts with other elements of various grammars, and a plausible screen-play for how the parameter might come to be set in the appropriate fashion. Our analytical performances do not match the script very closely. That script is offering too simplistic a view of language acquisition, and the discrepancy between script and performance could bring us some bad reviews.

I shall discuss one of the most tantalizing topics in the current theatre of research, the V2 phenomenon. I hope to show that the loss of this phenomenon in the history of English suggests that parameter setting is not a simple matter and that substantial ideas are needed about how parameters come to be set. If UG consists of principles and parameters, then one needs a distinct type of theorizing to connect more directly with acquisition, dealing with what it takes to set parameters; this does not follow from the nature of the parameters themselves and therefore reflects a distinct theory of acquisition or, properly construed, a learning theory.

The V2 phenomenon, some analyses and degree-0 learnability

The V2 phenomenon in its most familiar form has a finite verb occurring in second position, following a category of arbitrary grammatical/thematic/semantic function. The phenomenon is often (although not always) restricted to matrix clauses. Paardekooper (1971) linked the non-occurrence of V2 in Dutch embedded clauses to the presence there of an overt complementizer, usually *dat*. Den Besten (1983) embedded this insight into generative analyses by positing a transformation moving the finite verb to a position in COMP; this movement would be blocked if the COMP position were already filled by an overt complementizer. This analysis, in turn, has been incorporated into standard wisdom, along with the more recent notion (due to Travis 1984) that it can be seen as movement of a head if COMP is the head of a clause. In that case, the verb moves first to I(nflection). If, following Stowell (1981) and Chomsky (1986), I and C(OMP) are each heads which project to a maximal phrasal category, the structure of a V2 clause would be as in (1), where the verb moves first to I and then V+I moves to C.

(1) $_{CP}[Spec\ _{C'}[[V_i+I]_j\ _{IP}[NP\ _{I'}[_{VP}[.\ .\ .\ e_i]\ e_j]]]]$

Spec of CP may be filled by any phrasal category through what is often referred to misleadingly as a 'topicalization' operation; this yields the familiar V2 phenomenon of Dutch, German, the Scandinavian languages, etc. Principles of UG force heads to move locally and therefore preclude movement of an uninflected (infinitive) verb directly to C. The inflected verb (V+I) cannot move to C if C is already filled, e.g. by a complementizer in an embedded clause. This yields straightforwardly what have been taken to be core features of the V2 phenomenon, and this analysis will provide a vocabulary with which we can discuss some interesting issues. In (2) I provide some simple examples of V2 structures in Dutch.

(2.a) $_{CP}[Den\ Haag_i\ [bezoek_j+t]_k\ _{IP}[hij\ _{VP}[e_i\ e_j]\ e_k]]$
The Hague visits he
'he is visiting The Hague'

(2.b) $_{CP}[in\ Den\ Haag_i\ [bezoek_j+t]_k\ _{IP}[hij\ _{VP}[e_i\ het\ museum\ e_j]\ e_k]]$
'in The Hague he is visiting the museum'

(2.c) $_{CP}[Peter_i\ [bezoek_j+t]_k\ _{IP}[e_i\ _{VP}[Den\ Haag\ e_j]\ e_k]]$
'Peter is visiting The Hague'

If one considers some non-V2 languages, one sees some of the parameterization. For example, French allows finite verbs to move to C only if the initial element is +wh and the subject NP is pronominal (3).

(3.a) $_{CP}$[pourquoi [all$_i$+ez]$_j$ $_{IP}$[vous e$_j$ $_{VP}$[e$_i$ à Paris]]]
         why go you to Paris
         'why are you going to Paris?'

(3.b)   *$_{CP}$[à Paris$_k$ [all$_i$+ez]$_j$ $_{IP}$[vous e$_j$ $_{VP}$[e$_i$ e$_k$]]]

English, on the other hand, allows only a narrow class of finite verbs to move to C, namely 'auxiliaries', i.e. elements base-generated under I and the aspectual markers *have* and *be*; and they move to C only if the initial element is +wh or a negative (4).

(4.a) $_{CP}$[what$_i$ have$_j$ $_{IP}$[you e$_j$ $_{VP}$[seen e$_i$]]]

(4.b) $_{CP}$[never have$_j$ $_{IP}$[you e$_j$ $_{VP}$[seen such a mess]]]

(4.c)   *$_{CP}$[what$_i$ [discuss$_j$+ed]$_k$ $_{IP}$[you e$_k$ $_{VP}$[e$_j$ e$_i$]]]

(4.d)   *$_{CP}$[never [discuss$_j$+ed]$_k$ $_{IP}$[we e$_k$ $_{VP}$[e$_j$ such a thing]]]

This suggests that, unlike French, English verbs do not move to I, as argued in a slightly different framework by Emonds (1978). This predicts correctly, for example, that English verbs must occur adjacent to their complements (5), whereas French verbs may be separated from their complements through movement to I (6).

(5.a)   she always $_{VP}$[reads the newspapers]

(5.b)   *she reads always the newspapers

(6)   elle lit$_i$ toujours $_{VP}$[e$_i$ les journaux]

Other parameters may be involved, of course, but these are some clear cases: verbs may or may not move to I; and any element may occur in Spec of CP and require I-to-C movement (Dutch, German, Swedish) or only categories bearing certain features may occur there (English, French). On the basis of the latter parameter, Rizzi (1990a) distinguished 'full' and 'residual' V2 languages; we shall return to this distinction later.

A more basic issue is: what exactly does the V2 parameter consist of? That is, under what conditions do finite verbs move to C in Dutch, Swedish, etc? Under what conditions do arbitrary phrasal categories occur in Spec of CP? What is the relation between these two properties? And how do children acquire the relevant parameter settings? Although we have a plausible descriptive framework, these questions continue to tantalize us and there are no entirely satisfactory answers.

What requires explanation in the V2 languages, whether underlying verb-object (like Swedish) or object-verb (like German and Dutch), is the obligatoriness of I-to-C movement in all main clauses and the obligatoriness of what is often called 'topicalization', i.e. the movement of a phrasal category to Spec of CP, in declarative main clauses. Some element of UG will be needed to explain the obligatoriness of the processes. Since children generally do not have access to negative data, the Dutch child cannot 'learn' that, say, I-to-C movement is obligatory directly on the basis of the ungrammaticality of *in Den Haag hij het museum bezoekt 'in The Hague he visits the museum'. If that datum is not available to the child, there can be no consequence or inference or learning based on it. One must leave open the possibility that this learning might take place if children have indirect access to such data: that is, failure to hear such a simple expression might lead the child to deduce its ungrammaticality and thus to acquire some specific device which will block its derivation. This cannot be ruled out in principle but there are reasons to be sceptical of appeals to indirect negative data (Lightfoot 1991: ch. 1). If one is eventually forced to appeal to negative data, one would expect to find that this kind of deductive learning would emerge in children somewhat differently than the usual parameter-setting, perhaps later or after a stage of misgeneralization. Certainly an argument will be required that children do have indirect access to negative data under, one hopes, narrowly prescribed circumstances.

None the less, one finds several proposals in the extensive V2 literature postulating language-specific devices, and in such a way that they implicitly (but never explicitly, as far as I know) presuppose indirect access to negative data. For example, the proposals of den Besten (1983), de Haan and Weerman (1986), Haider (1986), Koopman (1984) and others each postulate some element in C which must, given some principle of UG, 'attract' I (or the finite verb) to that position, but the evidence for this element is the obligatoriness of the movement, i.e. the ungram-maticality of structures where movement has not taken place. In the absence of an appropriate learning theory whereby children have access to the appropriate negative data, the proposal simply re-states the problem. Platzack's (1986) proposal suffers from the same defect when he postulates different projections in V2 and non-V2 languages. His idea is that S is a projection of I in

English and other languages which do not have V2 properties, and a projection of C in V2 languages. He also allows grammars to differ in terms of whether the subject NP is base-generated as part of the projection of I or part of the projection of C. Then a principle of UG, his 'Case assignment rule', forces a verb to move to C in grammars where the projection of I does not include the subject NP. This postulates major differences in projection-types and the evidence for the particular projection-scheme for a V2 language is the obligatoriness of I-to-C movement and the ungrammaticality of structures where I fails to move to C, and again there is no discussion of how the child would have access to such data. It is unclear how one might treat grammars (like those of earlier forms of English) allowing verbs to move to C as an option, and the proposal also fails to account for the necessity of topicalization in declarative main clauses, a point to be taken up below.[1]

The same sort of attainability problem arises with the quite different proposals of Safir (1981) and Evers (1982). Safir has UG require that verbs (and other heads) be uniquely governed, and he makes the structure of German such that verbs must move to C in main clauses in order for this requirement to be satisfied. Evers keys movement of the finite verb to the assumption that the tense element has a scope-bearing property and must c-command the clause; in embedded clauses the verb does not need to move because the matrix verb determines the scope of tense. In each case the child has to learn something specific about V2 languages: Safir's child must learn the structural properties which entail that a verb in a base-generated main clause I position (assuming that verbs move to I in all clause-types) fails to be uniquely governed in the appropriate sense (unlike, say, equivalent verbs in French). Evers' child must learn that C is the only position which c-commands the clause, unlike in English, French, Italian, etc. In each case the evidence is not explicitly discussed but it would appear to be the ungrammaticality of structures where movement to C has not taken place. Also, neither Safir nor Evers discuss the relationship between movement to C and topicalization.

One solution to the problem of an appropriate triggering experience for the proposed analysis would be to make the V2 phenomenon unmarked. So, if, for example, one postulates that I moves to C by attraction to some element there, one might argue that generating that element in C reflects the unmarked situation; English and French children, on the other hand, are exposed to positive data which show that the attractive element is absent, namely the occurrence of the finite verb in some other position. This might lead one to expect English and French children to go through an early V2 stage, just as Hyams' (1983) English children go through an early pro-drop stage reflecting the alleged unmarked status of the null-subject option in her analysis. I know no evidence along these lines.

A striking feature of the basic properties of V2 languages is the correlation between the topicalization process and the obligatory movement of I to C. A fundamental shortcoming of many analyses is that while they offer some account for why the finite verb must be in some C-like position, they have nothing to say about why some other phrasal category must occur in initial position. Since the I-to-C movement is a common option in many languages which are not V2, it is unlikely that the obligatoriness of the movement would entail obligatory topicalization. Indeed, some verb-subject-object languages seem to have obligatory verb fronting without any obligatory topicalization; so, for example, Welsh seems to have underlying I-subject-verb-object order and surface verb-subject-object order in all clause-types by virtue of the verb moving obligatorily to I (Harlow 1981; Sproat 1985), but there is no requirement that another phrasal category be moved forward. It is possible, of course, that the verb must be not just at the front of the clause but actually in C to entail topicalization, but it is hard to see why the obligatoriness of the movement should require topicalization, i.e. why topicalization should not be required in English or French when a verb happens to be in C.

However, the reverse relationship might be more plausible: topicalization might entail verb movement, perhaps by a kind of predication requirment. So Taraldsen (1986), developing work by Cinque and Kayne, argued interestingly that a topicalized argument phrase must be locally licensed and that a verb in C effectively turns the position filled by the topic into an argument position by yielding a predicate structure; so verb movement has the effect of providing a local licensing environment for a displaced argument phrase, which in turn permits its trace to be construed as a variable. He offered some intriguing evidence based on the absence of V2 effects with bare wh- words introducing root interrogatives in certain northern dialects of Norwegian. Also, it is a theory of the right type in that UG forces movement to C in order to license initial argument phrases; in that case, the child has to learn that Dutch and German sentences begin with some argument phrase of arbitrary function. Hellan and Koch Christensen (1986: introduction) noted that the V2 phenomenon occurs in those languages which allow long distance anaphors, which are sometimes argued to be sensitive to predication; they went on to speculate that the common denominator of these languages may be some sort of predication sensitivity. However, there are two fundamental problems. First, it seems unnatural to construe expletives like Dutch *er* and German *es* as elements requiring predication, just as they cannot be taken as topics. Second, topicalization does not entail verb movement in languages that are not V2 (English, French, etc.). If one keys this to a *structural* difference in the position of the topicalized element, then the requirement of a certain kind of predication relationship becomes unclear.

Rizzi (1990a), none the less, builds on this idea of V2 languages fulfilling a predication requirement. He distinguishes 'residual' V2 structures which occur in non-V2 languages, like English subject-auxiliary inversion and French subject clitic inversion, and he compares them with the 'full V2' phenomenon which determines the order of constituents in all main (and some embedded) clauses in Dutch, German and the Scandinavian languages. The distinction lies in the features of the head of CP, [+C, −I] in the case of a residual V2 construction and a kind of hybrid [+C, +I] in the case of full V2 languages (7). Rizzi interprets the feature +C as 'propositional' and +I as 'predicational'. Thus a [+C, −I] category designates a proposition, projecting to the familiar CP of non-V2 languages and of non-V2 clauses in V2 languages, [−C, +I] designates a predication, projecting to IP, and [+C, +I] is the hybrid category characteristic of V2 langauges, being both propositional and predicational. For Rizzi this is the category of V2 clauses in full V2 languages. The inflected element [−C, +I] moves to the head of the CP, necessarily in the case of a full V2 language because of a universal principle that the tense specification must c-command all other +I categories in a given clause.

(7.a)   Residual V2

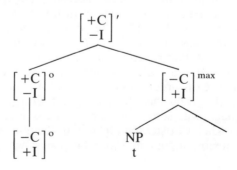

(7.b)   Full V2

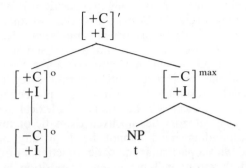

The moved element properly governs a subject trace in (7.b) under the 'minimality' assumptions of Rizzi (1990b), because the trace is within the immediate projection of $[+I]°$, i.e. $[+I]'$; in (7.a) 'the moved head and the host are disjoint feature bundles, hence in no sense can the moved head be said to govern the subject trace within its (immediate) projection' (1990b: 385). This accounts for the symmetry of subject-object extractability in full V2 languages, while subjects are relatively immobile in non-V2 languages where a subject trace would generally fail to be properly governed; this difference between V2 and non-V2 languages was the central puzzle addressed by Rizzi's paper. Furthermore, different kinds of functional heads license different kinds of specifiers: so a $[+C]$ head licenses an operator or trace in a A-bar chain and a $[+I]$ head licenses a subject in the specifier position. So the hybrid case $[+C, +I]$ allows its specifier to be a wh phrase or trace by virtue of being $+C$ (8) or the subject of predication by virtue of being $+I$ (9).

(8.a)   wer ist [e gekommen INFL]
        'who has come?'

(8.b)   wer hat Johann gesagt [e ist [e gekommen INFL]]
        'who did Johann say has come?'

(9)   Maria ist [e gekommen INFL]
        'Maria has come'

A comparable approach, which does not involve notions of predicate formation, was adopted in Lightfoot (1991: ch. 3) and can be stated in terms of constraints on phrase structure. Suppose that Dutch children learn that sentences begin with an arbitrary phrasal category, NP or PP and so on, which has no fixed functional or thematic role. Since the category is utterance-initial, it cannot be a complement of some head and must therefore be a specifier, since these are the only two positions in which a phrasal category may occur in D-structure; this assumes the familiar strong form of X-bar theory which claims that a head X projects to a X' which may also contain a complement, and the X' projects to a XP which may also contain a Specifier. Lexical specifiers always project to another phrasal category which must have a head, presumably C in this case, projecting to CP; UG dictates that a lexical specifier requires a lexical head. Since the initial phrasal category has no fixed thematic or functional role, the corresponding head cannot be I or any other element associated with a particular thematic, functional or case-assigning role, and therefore will be an empty position at D-structure, which is subsequently filled as another head moves to that position. The only element which is local enough to move to the empty head position and head-govern its trace is I (with its associated verb). Under this approach, principles of UG dictate that an initial XP be locally licensed in a fashion which in turn requires obligatory movement of a verb to C. Universal 11 of Greenberg (1966: 83) says: 'inversion of statement order so that verb precedes subject occurs only in languages where the question word or phrase is normally initial. This same inversion occurs in yes–no questions only if it also occurs in interrogative word questions.' If languages generally do not move verbs to the front unless they also front interrogative phrases, then it is plausible to interpret a moved verb as licensing the initial phrase. If children acquiring a V2 language learn that utterances begin with an element of arbitrary functional or thematic role, then it would follow from UG that the inflected verb must occur in second position, specifically, let us assume, in C, in order to license the initial phrasal category. This analysis provides a different answer to Rizzi's puzzle. (10.a) is well-formed in a full V2 language, because the subject trace is properly governed by the inflected verb in C (details omitted); but (10.b) is ill-formed in English because *did* is not sufficiently lexical to act as a proper governor for the subject trace.

(10.a) $_{CP}$[wie$_i$ bezoekt $_{IP}$[e$_j$ Den Haag]]

(10.b) $_{CP}$[who$_i$ did $_{IP}$[e$_i$ visit The Hague]]

An alternative account, adopted by Aoun, Hornstein, Lightfoot & Weinberg (1987), would construe (10.b) as a violation of the doubly filled COMP filter, which requires COMP to contain no lexical material other than the head. This filter is 'unlearned' in

Dutch when children are exposed to structures like (10.a).[2]

Although current theoretical mechanisms explain certain aspects of the V2 phenomenon, some things remain mysterious. Nonetheless children attain these V2 languages readily, more readily in fact than children acquire the 'residual' V2 constructions in English. I have shown in Lightfoot 1991 ch. 3 that simple data from matrix Domains suffice to trigger underlying object-verb order in V' for Dutch and underlying verb-object for Swedish, and children do not need rich or complex data in order to learn that verbs move and from where they move. A crucial element in this account was that the X-bar schemata of UG require that verbs occur alongside their complements at D-structure; therefore Dutch children have ample evidence that verbs move syntactically, because they encounter plenty of utterances where verbs and complements are not adjacent (e.g. (2.b) above). Furthermore, there is ample evidence from unembedded Domains that Dutch verbs *follow* their complements underlyingly; therefore Dutch children do not need access to embedded Domains to establish the underlying position of the verb. So the underlying position of the verb is readily attainable by a 'degree-o learner', i.e. a child who sets her parameters only on the basis of simple, unembedded structures.

Not only is this a possible and theoretically pleasing account, but acquisitional data strongly suggest that something along these lines is correct, that there are simple, unembedded indicators which enable the child to adopt an object-verb setting and to posit the relevant verb movement operation. Clahsen and Smolka (1986) identify four stages in the acquisition of German verb movement properties (11).

(11.a) *Stage 1 (25–29 months)*: no fixed order between sentence constituents; all verbal elements (including verbal complexes) occur in first/second and final position with a preference for final position.

(11.b) *Stage 2 (31–33 months)*: verbal elements with particles occur regularly in final position; other finite verbs occur in both first/second and final position.

(11.c) *Stage 3 (36–39 months)*: all and only finite verbs occur in first/second position; verbal complexes with finite and non-finite parts appear in discontinuous positions.

(11.d) *Stage 4 (41–42 months)*: as soon as embedded sentences are produced, their finite verbs are in final position.

Strikingly, from the earliest relevant stage children identify sentence-final position as one of the possible positions for verbs, including finite verbs despite the fact that they are almost never heard in this position in main clauses. At stage 3 there is a dramatic increase in the frequency of V2 structures: in stages 1 and 2 they are used in only 20–40 per cent of the utterances but at stage 3 they are used in 90 per cent; Clahsen and Smolka (1986: 149) report that this increase takes place explosively, within a month for all the children studied. Children seem at this stage to have the object-verb D-structure order and an operation moving a finite verb obligatorily to a C-like position; in simple clauses there are two positions for verbs, and verbal elements with the suffix -t and modals occur in second position while infinitives and verbs with other inflections occur sentence-finally. To this extent the adult system is in place (Clahsen 1990). Importantly, when they begin to use embedded structures (stage 4), the finite verbs are invariably in final position and there seems to be no 'experimentation' or learning based on embedded clause data. Clahsen and Smolka go further and make stronger claims: they take 'move V' to operate from the earliest stage, initially affecting verbs and verbal complexes of all types, affecting only simple verbs at stage 2, and affecting finite simple verbs at stage 3. This is exactly what one would expect if children are degree-0 learners, and not at all what one would expect if children were sensitive to embedded Domains as they set grammatical parameters. If children are degree-0 learners, as these and other facts suggest, then learning theory is implicated; degree-0 learnability could not follow from the principles and parameters that make up UG and could only follow from some conditions on the way that parameters are set, i.e. from some sort of learning theory. Thus a condition of degree-0 learnability would exist alongside Berwick's (1985) Subset Principle, which must also be construed as part of a learning theory (the Subset Principle says that children first adopt parameter settings which yield smaller sets of sentences). For some arguments for degree-0 learnability, see Lightfoot 1991: chs 3 and 4.

In short, it seems reasonable to suppose that in so-called V2 languages, where verbs move to I and then to C, the underlying position of the verb is degree-0 learnable whether it precedes its complement, as in the Scandinavian languages and in Yiddish (den Besten and Moed-van Walraven 1986), or follows them, as in Dutch and German. Furthermore, the relevant parameters are set early, and with no apparent difficulty. From the earliest stages children manifest both object-verb and verb-object order, reflecting two verbal positions, whereas English-speaking children are more consistently verb-object at the two-word stage. In addition, Dutch and German children seem not to make the kinds of errors that English-speaking children make in acquiring inverted forms; at least, such errors are not part of the common lore of language acquisition and colleagues report that they do not occur. So, failure to invert (12.a) or copying instead of substitution (12.b) are not typical childhood forms, whereas the equivalent forms are standard for English-speaking children (13). Failure to invert with an initial *why*, for example, often persists in 7 year-olds (13.c), but apparently not in other languages; see Davis (1987) for extensive discussion of the acquisition of English auxiliaries.

(12.a) *wat Jan moet schoenmaken?
        'what Jan must clean'
        'what must Jan clean?'

(12.b) *kan hij kan de vloer schoenmaken?
        'can he can the floor clean'

(13.a) what John must clean?

(13.b) can he can clean the floor?

(13.c) why John must clean the floor?

There is a puzzle here. The acquisition of English auxiliary verbs, the only elements to occur in V2 contexts, is clearly data-driven and involves a significant amount of learning. For example, Newport et al. (1977) showed that a child's ability to use auxiliaries results from exposure to non-contracted, stressed forms in initial position in yes–no questions: the greater the exposure to these subject-auxiliary inversion forms, the earlier the use of auxiliaries in medial position. Richards (1990) demonstrates a good deal of individual variation in the acquisition of English auxiliaries. Nothing in any of the accounts mentioned so far would make English V2 constructions (i.e. subject-auxiliary inversion) in any way hard to attain. This makes Weinberg's (1990) account interesting because she argues that subject-auxiliary inversion involves marked and highly data-driven operations, thereby explaining why it is attained late in English. However, the equivalent V2 constructions in Dutch are at least as marked from her perspective (probably more so, because the 'doubly filled COMP filter' has to be relaxed beyond what is required in English grammars), but the work of Clahsen and others suggests strongly that these constructions are acquired early and without the kinds of errors that English-speaking children produce. So the puzzle remains.

The triggering experience and change

The approaches of Rizzi and Lightfoot to V2 phenomena have the virtue of making the presence of the finite verb in C conditional on a certain kind of initial element; in this regard they seem to be theories of the right type. Presumably both analyses would invoke the same triggering experience; that is, hearing utterances which begin with phrasal categories with arbitrary grammatical functions and thematic roles followed by a finite verb, Rizzi's child determines that the verbal head is both propositional and predicational (his 'hybrid' case), and my child determines that there is an 'extra' projection beyond IP. Given the scant ideas we have about possible triggers for particular parameters, we cannot know whether the trigger that both analyses need would more plausibly set a parameter relating to predication relations or a parameter relating to structural projections. Since both analyses make the same claims, I assume, about the triggering experience, they would also make the same predictions about the loss of full V2 properties historically. In languages which have lost full V2 properties, like English and French, Rizzi and I would expect a period when the arbitrariness of the initial phrasal category gradually declines and comes to be predominantly the subject of the clause. Such a statistical shift would not reflect a change in people's grammars but just a change in the way that grammars were used. However, one would suppose that the statistical changes eventually would reach a point where the primary linguistic data would trigger a different grammar, and, whatever the nature of the parameter, one would expect the loss of V2 to take place rapidly and catastrophically, reflecting the new parameter setting.

Such are the expectations; what are the facts? The second prediction seems to be correct. It seems to be the case that V2 constructions dropped out of English and French rather suddenly. Schmidt (1980) shows that V2 forms are standard in Chaucer but disappear rapidly after 1400; this view is echoed by van Kemenade (1987). From Old English through Chaucer, finite verbs occurred quite uniformly in C when preceded by an initial *þa* or *þonne* (literally 'then', but used effectively as sentence connectives); in a study of Chaucer's prose in the *Treatise on the Astrolabe* (written for his young son and therefore in a conversational style) and the *Equatorie of Planets*, Schmidt

(1980: 191) noted only one case of *tho/thanne* which was not followed by inversion (although *Mandeville's Travels*, translated from a French source, was less consistent in this regard, and the 'very formal', non-narrative prose in Chaucer's translation of *Boethius* shows still less inversion). However, Schmidt's study of early fifteenth-century prose (*Book of Margery Kempe* and Malory's *Tale of King Arthur*) showed a very different pattern, and after *than*, the environment historically most conducive to inversion, she found only eighteen cases of inversion in 88 clauses (20 per cent) (ibid.: 250). She offers more data supporting the rapid, catastrophic disappearance of V2 forms after 1400. The lack of a good, continuous prose tradition prior to the mid-fourteenth century suggests some caution, but Vance (1990) has also argued that V2 constructions disappeared rapidly in French in the fourteenth century: when movement of finite verbs to C ceased to be obligatory, instances of verbs preceding subjects dropped out quickly.

On the first prediction, that the loss of V2 should have been preceded by a steady increase of utterances beginning with subject + verb and a decline of non-subject + verb (while remaining V2), I can offer some supporting evidence from English but it is far from conclusive. One is bedevilled here again by the lack of a continuous prose tradition. However, Bean's 1983 study of the *Anglo-Saxon Chronicle* shows 28 per cent of matrix clauses showing subject-verb order in the first three sections, which were probably written in 891, and 41 per cent in the last three sections, which are presumed to have been written contemporaneously with the events they describe (respectively 1048–66, 1122–4, and 1132–40). This increase in subject + verb order is significant but not enormous. Gerritsen (1984: 110) reports that modern Dutch, German and Norwegian, all V2 languages, show about 60 per cent subject + verb order in conversational modes. Similarly, Jörgensen (1976) reports spoken Swedish showing 62 per cent of initial subjects in interview contexts and 73 per cent in more formal radio broadcasts of news and commentary (thanks to Kjartan Ottósson for this reference). These figures suggest that the Chronicle may be showing an artificially high number of non-subject + verb sequences, perhaps due to what many commentators have called its 'vivid style'. If this is correct and if as few as 40 per cent or even fewer non-subject + verb sequences suffice to set the relevant parameter in the V2 mode, then even the later sections of the Chronicle remain well above that threshold. Recall, however, that Old English showed V2 obligatorily only when clauses were introduced by interrogative or negative phrases; otherwise V2 was just one option, albeit a prevalent one (see Stockwell 1984 for discussion), unlike in Dutch, German and Norwegian, where V2 is generally obligatory. This may reflect an important difference in the grammars and thus in what experience is required to set the relevant parameters.

So there is some uncertainty about what it takes to set parameters in the V2 mode and about how those requirements ceased to be met in English by the beginning of the fifteenth century.[3] However, we do know that there were two major steps in the loss of the old V2 system and the evolution of the 'residual' system of modern English. We know that English ceased to be a full V2 language in Rizzi's sense by the early fifteenth century. From this time verbs ceased to occur generally in C, occurring there only when preceded by certain kinds of elements, particularly a +wh feature. When the full V2 properties were first lost, initial negative phrases also ceased to trigger V2 on any regular basis (compare *never did I see such a mess*, etc.). Schmidt (1980: 209) claims that V2 declines in frequency with initial negative phrases, being re-established in the sixteenth century. If correct, this suggests that wh- and negative features do not have to be treated in parallel as triggers for V2 properties; after all, initial negatives are structurally distinct and occur where wh-elements may not, e.g. in embedded contexts like: *that seldom/ under no circumstances would she contemplate such issues*. In any case, the first step is the restriction of V2 forms to certain environments, namely sentences introduced by interrogative (or negative) phrases. In those environments verbs continued to move to C obligatorily, as in earlier English. The restriction of V2 to a narrow class of environments seems to have been complete by the early fifteenth century.

Modern English, however, shows a further restriction: only certain verbs occur in V2 forms, namely the modals, *have* and *be*. Since Emonds (1978), this lexical restriction has been viewed as following from the fact that modern English lacks the V-to-I operation, raising a verb into a position in which it acquires various inflectional features (for tense, person, and number). Modal verbs are base-generated in I and are therefore free to move to C, but a verb cannot move from its D-structure position directly to C without violating the Empty Category Principle (its trace would not be properly governed). The major evidence offered by Emonds and others for this parametric distinction is that English-type languages without the V-to-I operation have their verbs strictly adjacent to their complements (14), whereas languages with the V-to-I operation (like French) allow adverbs, negatives, and floating quantifiers to intervene (15).

(14.a) *he watches always/never television on Wednesdays

(14.b) *they watch not television

(14.c) *they watch all television on Wednesdays

(15.a) il regarde toujours/seulement la télévision le mercredi

(15.b) ils regardent pas la télévision

(15.c) ils regardent tous la télévision le mercredi

By this criterion, English used to have the V-to-I operation but lost it. One finds sentences parallel to French (15) (examples from Kroch 1989):

(16.a) I wende *wel* thys nyght to have deyed. Caxton, *The Ryall Book* lines 20–25. 'I managed almost tonight to die.'

(16.b) . . . if thay do noghte all. Rolle, 'The Bee and the Stork' lines 23–24. '. . . if they don't do everything.'

(16.c) . . . that is to seyn, whyl that they liven *bothe*. Chaucer *The Parson's Tale* line 916. '. . . while they both live.'

One reflection of the loss of V-to-I is the transitional occurrence in the sixteenth and seventeenth centuries of forms like *he not spoke those words*, discussed in Visser 1969: s. 1440: 'Before 1500 this type is only sporadically met with, but after 1500 its currency increases and it becomes pretty common in Shakespeare's time.' Visser cites 57 examples but none involves an auxiliary verb. This suggests that *not* continues to occur between I and VP, as in Middle and modern English; the novel forms result from failure of the V-to-I operation (at this stage '*do* support' has yet to become categorical and 'affix hopping' may apply across the intervening negative; the forms died out as *do* became a tense carrier). The loss of V-to-I is dated as mid-sixteenth century by Kroch (1989: 222) and as early seventeenth century by Lightfoot 1991, significantly later than the restriction of V2 to interrogative and negative environments and therefore a separate and distinct change.

Before we ask why this second change took place, let us ask what triggers the presence/absence of the V-to-I operation for French/English children. It could, of course, be precisely the data that motivated Emonds to postulate the operation. This, however, is unlikely: adverbs are notoriously flexible in their distribution, being subject to a 'transportability convention'.

Adverbs such as *always* and *rarely* may occur in any of the
positions indicated in (17).

(17)   _ _ _ John _ _ _ must _ _ _ have _ _ _ watched television
        _ _ _ on Wednesdays _ _ _.

It is hard to imagine that failure to hear adverbs precisely
between the verb and its complement would trigger the absence
of V-to-I for an English-speaking child; similarly, it is unlikely
(although not impossible) that French children must hear (and
properly analyse) adverbs between a verb and its complement in
order to acquire the V-to-I operation. From a diachronic
perspective, if the V-to-I operation were triggered in this way,
then one would expect the loss of the operation to reflect changes
in the *use* of grammars prior to an actual change in grammars.
That is, one would expect the historical record to show a steadily
declining number of postverbal adverbs; as the decline reached a
certain critical point, there would be a parametric change
reflecting the categorical loss of the operation.

An alternative scenario would posit a more indirect trigger, for
example V-in-C forms. If verbs occur in C, then, since traces
must be properly governed, the verbs could only move there via I
and therefore there must be a V-to-I operation. Now the relevant
difference for French (and Dutch, German, Swedish, etc.), on
the one hand, and English children on the other is that the
former hear V-in-C forms (*regardez-vous la télévision?*, (2), (3),
etc.), while English children do not. There can be no doubt that
these forms are sufficiently robust and salient to be plausible
triggers.

If the latter scenario is along the right lines, then an
explanation for the loss of V-to-I reduces to an explanation for
the loss of V-in-C. This might be partially correct, but it cannot
be the whole story. We have seen that V-in-C forms came to be
greatly curtailed by the early fifteenth century but this had no
apparent effect on the V-to-I operation. After the curtailment of
V-in-C to interrogative contexts, V-to-I continued to operate:
one still finds forms like (16) robustly attested, negatives like *John
spoke not these words*, and interrogatives like *how great and
greuous tribulations suffered the Holy Appostyls . . .?*, all of
which involve V-to-I (and I-to-C for the interrogatives). Similarly,
the loss of general V2 in French had no effect on the attainability
of V-to-I, which persists in the present-day language even though
V-in-C forms are much rarer than in English (occurring only in
interrogatives with pronominal subject NPs).

This suggests that one needs to look for other changes in the primary linguistic data taking place between 1400 and 1600, which might have the effect of making V-to-I harder to attain. Two likely candidates are the demise of inflectional endings on the verb and the rise of periphrastic *do*. The inflectional changes were effectively complete by 1400 and helped to distinguish *shall*, *may*, *must*, and so on, as a distinct sub-class of lexical items, instances of I rather than of V (Lightfoot 1991: ch. 6). Therefore, the morphological changes took place too early to affect the primary linguistic data in the relevant period, and one cannot correlate V-to-I *entirely* with morphological properties (cf. Platzack and Holmberg 1989, who make such a correlation at least for the verb-object Germanic languages). V-to-I persisted for some time after verb morphology had become impoverished and English had lost its rich system of subject-verb agreement.[4] Furthermore, the mainland Scandinavian languages have lost their verbal morphology but retain full V2 properties and, therefore, a V-to-I operation.[5]

Periphrastic *do*, on the other hand, occurred first at the beginning of the fifteenth century and steadily increased in frequency until it stabilized into its modern usage by the mid-seventeenth century. This change has been analysed extensively and Ellegård (1953) shows that the sharpest increase came in the period 1475–1550; for discussion and analysis, see Kroch (1989) and Lightfoot (1991), both of which reproduce Ellegård's important graph showing the rise of *do* in different construction types. Each insertion of a periphrastic *do* to carry inflectional markers represents a case where the V-to-I operation has not applied, so a steady increase in the distribution of *do* entails fewer and fewer instances of V-to-I; the two operations are mutually incompatible.

The historical facts, then, suggest that lack of strong subject-verb agreement cannot be a sufficient condition for absence of V-to-I despite suggestions along these lines by some authors, but it may be a necessary condition. That is, if a language has strong verbal inflection, it will have V-to-I. Furthermore, if certain individual elements of grammar show strong inflection, then they undergo V-to-I: so English *be* is generally inflected richly and undergoes V-to-I wherever possible (i.e. whenever I is not otherwise lexically occupied).[6] However, there are some forms of English which do not inflect *be*, and in those cases *be* does not raise to I. So so-called Black English uses *George be president now*, but the usual negative is *George don't be president now* rather than *George ben't president* and the uninflected *be* does not invert with the subject: **be George president now?* and **what be*

George? (Myhill 1988). Similarly, children often use uninflected forms of *be*, but they do not invert them or use them to the left of *not*: instead they use *do*-support forms: *did it be funny?*, *do clowns be a boy or girl?*, *I don't be angry*.

Under this view, the *possibility* of V-to-I not being triggered first arose in the history of English with the loss of rich verbal inflection; similarly in Swedish. That possibility never arose in Dutch, French, German, and so on, where verbal inflection remained relatively robust. Despite this possibility, V-to-I continued to be triggered and it occurred in grammars well after verbal inflection had been reduced to its present-day level. Although V-to-I continued to be triggered, it did not apply obligatorily as it had in Old and Middle English. There were two alternatives: the use of *do* as a 'dummy' tense carrier and a *morphological* operation lowering the tense marker on to the verb ('affix hopping') . As already noted, the first option was exercised with steadily increasing frequency from the fifteenth century onwards. It is impossible to know when the second option of 'affix hopping' came into use, because any effects of affix hopping could also be produced by V-to-I. But it is worth noting that affix hopping or tense lowering could not be a syntactic operation (it would leave an unbound trace) and therefore must be a morphological operation:[7] this entails automatically that it applies only to contiguous elements (modulo Visser's transitional *John not spoke those words* examples cited above) and that it does not feed other syntactic operations (compare V-to-I, which applies across intervening adverbs and feeds I-to-C operations). In that case it is reasonable to suppose that this morphological operation is generally available, even in grammars which also have the V-to-I operation, and that V-to-I (in grammars which have the operation) applies only where necessary, i.e. where there would otherwise be a stranded affix. We know that '*do* support' was exercised increasingly during the relevant period, and it seems that it became sufficiently frequent that there was no 'need' for V-to-I. That is, with the rise of periphrastic *do* there was no longer anything very robust in the primary linguistic data which *required* V-to-I, given that the morphological operation was always available. In particular, post-verbal adverbs and quantifiers (16) were not triggers for V-to-I and they simply disappeared quietly. Under this analysis, the absence of V-to-I in modern English grammars is a result of a historical convergence: at the time that verbal inflections were simplified, verbs underwent a mitosis whereby a subset (*must*, *shall*, etc.) came to be generated under I and there was in addition an element *do* which could be analysed as a 'dummy' tense carrier generated in I and came to be used more and more frequently. As a result, V-to-I ceased to be triggered.

Now that we have some idea of how the I-to-C and V-to-I parameters might be set, we can ask why the 'residual' I-to-C operation (or 'subject-auxiliary inversion') in English should be so hard for children to attain. Weinberg's (1990) account whereby children must learn to relax the demands of the doubly filled COMP filter predicts that Dutch and German children should have even more difficulty, because the filter must be relaxed still further than in English. This seems to be contrary to the acquisitional facts discussed earlier, which suggest that Dutch and German children acquire the I-to-C operation relatively early and without the kinds of errors made by English-speaking children. The difference might arise through Rizzi's full vs residual distinction: I-to-C is harder to learn because it is restricted to a narrow class of syntactic environments in English (i.e. to sentences introduced by +wh or a negative phrase). However, the acquisition of French militates against this view. Clark (1985) and others have pointed out that young French children show a preference for verb-subject and even verb-object-subject order over subject-verb in their early utterances. It is unclear whether such forms should be analysed as cases of subject-verb inversion or as right dislocation of the subject. Whatever the analysis, this preference is surprising because other studies show that sentences with inverted subjects are quite rare in speech addressed to children, unlike in English; Lightbown (1977) noted almost total absence of subject-verb inversion in yes–no questions addressed to children. Questions with inverted subjects (18.a) occur much more in 'textbook' French than in colloquial forms, where people tend to indicate an interrogative by intonation (18.b) or with a wh-in-situ construction (18.c) or by an *est ce que* form without inversion (18.d).

(18.a) que manges-tu?

(18.b) tu manges la poire?

(18.c) tu manges quoi?

(18.d) quand est ce qu'il vient?

A common error, noted by Clark (1985), is failure to invert with subject pronouns (19), but children produce forms like (20) from an early age.

(19) où ils sont?
      que ce c'est?

(20) où est cheval?

Again, it is unclear whether (20) should be analysed as a case of
V-in-C (cf. *où est le cheval?*) or as right discussion of the subject
with a missing pronoun (cf. *où il est, le cheval?*) (Amy Pierce,
personal communication). Clark (1985) notes various types of
word-order errors made by French children but she does not note
errors with inversion comparable to those of English-speaking
children. She confirms in a personal communication that she has
not noted errors of copying (21.a) or of failure to invert with a
fronted wh- NP (21.b).

(21.a)   *vient il/Jean vient à Toulon?

(21.b)   *que tu manges?

Although French subject-verb inversion is restricted to +wh
contexts as in English and, even more narrowly, to contexts
where the subject NP is pronominal, and although the construction is attested much less robustly in what children hear, none the
less French children seem to acquire the I-to-C operation readily
and without the kinds of systematic errors noted in English-
speaking children.

If I-to-C is easy for French children to learn despite being
restricted to +wh contexts with pronominal subjects, then the
source of the difficulty experienced by English children presumably lies elsewhere, probably in the fact that only a small set of
'auxiliary' verbs may occur in C: *do, be, have* and the modals. It
has been argued that these 'functional' or 'grammatical' items are
opaque to children and are in some sense not perceived at early
ages. This may be true but it would not explain the difficulty in
moving them to C at a time when they occur in medial position,
i.e. in I. It seems that it is relatively difficult to attain an
operation which is manifested by a small class of lexical items,
even though that operation is attested widely and robustly in the
triggering experience. This would explain why English-speaking
children seem to acquire the I-to-C operation later than Dutch,
French and German children, and usually via systematic errors.

Conclusion

We have considered the loss of the V2 phenomenon in English
and examined the conditions under which the V-to-I operation
was lost and the I-to-C operation was restricted first to +wh
contexts and then to a small class of lexical items. In doing so, we
have learned something about what might trigger these operations in grammars which have them. What emerges is that the
triggering experience may be only distantly related to the data

that the operation immediately accounts for. That is, what triggers an operation in a child is by no means equivalent to the (positive) data that force a linguist to postulate that operation. This should not be a surprise: if a grammatical operation were triggered by precisely the positive data that the operation accounted for, one would expect languages to change only by the kind of arbitrary fluctuations of population genetics; there would be nothing very systematic and the historical foundations of the discipline laid in the nineteenth century would be shown to be weak. It means that a modern historical linguist cannot say that some changing phenomenon 'is due to' the new parameter setting which accounts for it, although this is often said. Rather, it manifests and provides evidence for that parameter setting; it is *due to* changes in the triggering experience which in turn entailed the new parameter setting. It may be true that UG consists of principles and parameters, but an account of language acquisition needs to show how those parameters are set. This raises substantive issues and a substantive 'learning theory' is required; that is, we need some theorizing about what it takes to set a parameter one way or another. I hope that my discussion of the triggering of the V-to-I operation has provided some relevant suggestions. In general, I believed that one can learn much about this from figuring out the conditions under which a parameter comes to be set differently at some historical stage in a language's development.

Acknowledgement

Thanks to Norbert Hornstein and Peter Coopmans for comments on a preliminary version of this chapter. This paper will also appear in A. Battye and I. Roberts (eds) *Language Change and Verbal Systems* (forthcoming).

Notes

1. van Kemenade (1987) adopts a form of Platzack's analysis in her discussion of the history of English and claims that the projection-types changed as the V2 construction was lost, but no explanation is offered and the problems with the analysis are not noted.

2. English children are never exposed to structures equivalent to (10.a). Sentences like *who has seen The Hague?* have *has* still in its I position and thus only one element in COMP: $_{CP}$[who $_{IP}$[e has $_{VP}$[seen The Hague]]]. Sentences like *what have you seen?* are immune to the doubly filled COMP filter because the COMP has no head, i.e. no index percolates to COMP (or to CP in the framework adopted here). See Aoun, et al. (1987) for details.

3. Alternative explanations have been offered for the loss of V2 constructions, seeking to make it a consequence of another parametric

shift. Some have sought to relate it to the earlier object-verb to verb-object word order change, and van Kemenade (1987: 221) relates it to the demise of the clitic status of subject pronouns, but the explanations are deficient. First, Swedish shows that a language can acquire verb-object order and maintain full V2 status. Secondly, while van Kemenade claims that the non-clitic status of subject pronouns blocks a V2 analysis of structures like XP-pronoun-verb . . ., she does not show why such pronominal structures did not become obsolete? There is no obvious reason why such structures should have driven V2 constructions to their death, rather than vice versa. After all, the pronoun forms were a small subset of all the former V2 constructions and considerations of robustness would lead one to expect V2 forms to win out over XP-pronoun-verb constructions.

4. The second person -st ending survived longer than the other endings, but it is hard to imagine that this particular ending was the key to the V-to-I operation.

5. Swedish is sometimes analysed as lacking the V-to-I operation because it has negatives preceding finite verbs in embedded clauses: . . . *om Jan inte köpte boken* '. . . if John didn't buy the book' (Platzack and Holmberg 1989). But this indicates that *inte* 'not' and other such adverbs occur to the *left* of I, and does not provide evidence against the application of V-to-I. Occurrence of verbs in C is strong evidence of movement through I, given almost any version of the proper government condition on traces.

6. *Have* is ambiguous in this regard. It shows no more inflection than regular verbs, but it none the less raises to I under certain circumstances, although some of those circumstances are subject to dialectal variation: *Kim hasn't a car* vs *Kim doesn't have a car* etc.

7. Well, tense lowering might leave an unbound (and thus illicit) trace which is subsequently erased, for example by a LF operation raising verbs to I (Chomsky 1986). Lightfoot (1991: ch. 6) criticizes this approach, which fails to explain why tense lowering affects only contiguous elements and why unstressed forms like *John did write books* (which permit the most economical derivations) entered the language along with the other periphrastic forms and then disappeared rapidly.

References

AOUN, J., HORNSTEIN, N., LIGHTFOOT D. and WEINBERG, A. (1987) 'Two types of locality', *Linguistic Inquiry* 18, 4: 537–78.

BEAN, M. (1983) *The Development of Word Order Patterns in Old English*. London: Croom Helm.

BERWICK, R. (1985) *The Acquisition of Syntactic Knowledge*. Cambridge, MA: MIT Press.

BESTEN, H. DEN (1983) 'On the interaction of root transformations and lexical deletive rules.' In ABRAHAM, W. (ed.) *On the formal Syntax of the Westgermania*. Amsterdam: Benjamins.

BESTEN, H. DEN and MOED-VAN WALRAVEN, C. (1986) 'The syntax of verbs in Yiddish.' In HAIDER, G. and PRINZORN, M. (eds) *Verb-second*

Phonomena in Germanic Languages. Dordrecht: Foris, pp. 111–35.

CHOMSKY, N. (1986) *Barriers.* Cambridge, MA: MIT Press.

CLAHSEN, H. (1990) 'Constraints on parameter setting: A grammatical analysis of some acquisition stages in German child language.' Paper presented at the Boston University Conference on Language Development.

CLAHSEN, H. and SMOLKA, K.-D. (1986) 'Psycholinguistic evidence and the description of V2 phenomena in German.' In HAIDER, G. and PRINZHORN, M. (eds) *Verb-second Phenomena in Germanic Languages.* Dordrect: Foris, pp. 137–67.

CLARK, E. (1985) 'The acquisition of Romance, with special reference to French.' In SLOBIN, D. (ed.) *The Cross-Linguistic Study of Language Acquisition.* Hillsdale, NJ: Lawrence Erlbaum Associates.

DAVIS, H. (1987) 'The acquisition of the English auxiliary system and its relation to linguistic theory.' Doctoral dissertation. University of British Columbia.

ELLEGÅRD, A. (1953) *The Auxiliary 'do': The Establishment and Regulation of its Use in English.* Stockholm: Amqvist and Wiksell.

EMONDS, J. (1978) 'The verbal complex V'–V in French', *Linguistic Inquiry* 9: 151–75.

EVERS, A. (1982) 'Twee functionele principes voor de regel "Verschuif het werkwoord"', *GLOT* 5: 11–30.

GERRITSEN, M. (1984) 'Divergent word order developments in Germanic languages: a description and a tentative explanation.' In FISIAK, J. (ed.) *Historical Syntax*, Trends in Linguistics: Studies and Monographs, 23. Amsterdam: Mouton, pp. 107–35.

GREENBERG, J. (1966) 'Some universals of grammar with particular reference to the order to meaningful elements.' In GREENBERG, J. (ed.) *Universals of language.* Cambridge, MA: MIT Press.

HAAN, G. DE and WEERMAN, F. (1986) 'Finiteness and verb fronting in Frisian.' In HAIDER, H. and PRINZHORN, M. (eds) *Verb-Second Phenomena in Germanic Languages.* Dordrecht, Foris. pp. 77–110.

HAIDER, H. (1986) 'V-second in German.' In HAIDER, H. and PRINZHORN, M. (eds) *Verb-Second Phenomena in Germanic Languages.* Dordrecht, Foris. pp. 49–75.

HARLOW, S. (1981) 'Government and relativization in Celtic.' In HENY, F. (ed.) *Binding and filtering.* London: Croom Helm, pp. 213–54.

HELLAN, L. and KOCH CHRISTENSEN, K. (eds) (1986) *Topics in Scandinavian syntax.* Dordrecht: Reidel.

HYAMS, N. (1983) 'The Pro-drop parameter in child grammars.' In Proceedings of the West Coast Conference on Formal Linguistics.

JACOBSSON, B. (1951) *Inversion in English with Special Reference to the Early Modern English Period.* Uppsala: Almqvist and Wiksell.

JÖRGENSEN, N. (1976) *Meningsbyggnaden i Talad Svenska,* (Lundastudier i nordisk språkvetenschap c7), Studentlitteratur, Lund.

KEMENADE, A. VAN (1987) *Syntactic Case and Morphological Case in the History of English.* Dordrecht: Foris.

KOOPMAN, H. (1984) *The Syntax of Verbs: From Verb Movement Rules in the Kru Languages to Universal Grammar.* Dordrecht: Foris.

KROCH, A. (1989) 'Reflexes of grammar in patterns of language use', *Language Variation and Change* 1, 3: 199–244.

LIGHTBOWN, P. M. (1977) 'Consistency and variation in the acquisition of French: A study of first and second language development' Doctoral dissertation. Columbia University.

LIGHTFOOT, D. W. (1991) *How to set parameters: Arguments from language change.* Cambridge, MA: MIT Press (Bradford Books).

MYHILL, J. (1988) 'The rise of *be* as an aspect marker in BE vernacular', *American Speech* 63: 304–26.

NEWPORT, E., GLEITMAN, H. and GLEITMAN, L. (1977) 'Mother, I'd rather do it myself: some effects and non-effects of maternal speech style.' In SNOW, C. and FERGUSON, C. (eds) *Talking to Children: Language Input and Acquisition.* Cambridge: Cambridge University Press, pp. 109–49.

PAARDEKOOPER, P. C. (1971) *Beknopte ABN-syntaxis.* Den Bosch: L. C. G. Malmberg.

PLATZACK, C. (1986) 'COMP, INFL and Germanic word order,' in Hellan and Koch Christensen (eds).

PLATZACK, C. and HOLMBERG, A. (1989) 'The role of AGR and finiteness in Germanic VO languages', *Working Papers in Scandinavian Syntax* 43.

RICHARDS, B. J. (1990) *Language Development and Individual Differences: A Study of Auxiliary Verb Learning.* Cambridge: Cambridge University Press.

RIZZI, L. (1990a) 'Speculations on verb second.' In MASCARÓ, J. and NESPOR, M. (eds) *Grammar in Progress; GLOW Essays for Henk van Riemsdijk.* Dordrecht: Foris, pp. 375–86.

RIZZI, L. (1990b) *Relativized Minimality.* Cambridge, MA: MIT Press.

SAFIR, K. (1981) 'Inflection-government and inversion', *The Linguistic Review* 1, 4: 417–67.

SCHMIDT, D. (1980) *A History of Inversion in English*, Doctoral dissertation. Ohio State University.

SPROAT, R. (1985) 'Welsh syntax and VSO structure', *Natural Language and Linguistic Theory* 3, 2.

STOCKWELL, R. (1984) 'On the history of the verb-second rule in English', in FISIAK, J. (ed.) *Historical Syntax*, Trends in Linguistics: Studies and Monographs, 23. Amsterdam: Mouton, pp. 575–92.

STOWELL, T. (1981) 'Origins of Phrase Structure', Doctoral Dissertation, MIT.

TARALDSEN, K. T. (1986) 'On verb-second and the functional content of syntactic categories', in HAIDER, H. and PRINZHORN, M. (eds) *Verb-Second Phenomena in Germanic Languages.* Dordrecht: Foris. pp. 7–25.

TRAVIS, L. (1984) 'Parameters and effects of word order variation.' Doctoral dissertation. MIT.

VANCE, B. (1990) 'Inversion and pro-drop in Middle French.' Paper presented at the First Generative Diachronic Syntax Conference, York.

VISSER, F. TH. (1969) *An historical syntax of the English language*, Vol. IIIa. Leiden: E. J. Brill.

WEINBERG, A. (1990) 'Markedness versus maturation: the case of subject-auxiliary inversion', *Language Acquisition* 1, 2: 165–94.

Chapter 8

On the social origins of language change

James Milroy

1   Introduction: the locus of change in speaker-interaction

'The drama of linguistic change', according to H. C. Wyld (1927), 'is enacted not in manuscripts nor inscriptions, but in the mouths and minds of men'. This is most evidently true of sound change: phonetic and phonological changes in language are implemented by *speakers* and they take place in *speech*. It is sound change that I am chiefly concerned with in this paper.

Sound change has always been a testing-ground of historical linguistic theory, chiefly because – in a language-internal account – sound change, more so than other kinds of change, appears at first sight to be quite mysterious: there is no obvious reason why it should happen at all. In a sound change from [a] to [o], for example, there is apparently no 'improvement' in the language – we cannot convincingly show that one of these sounds is 'better' than the other, or demonstrate that the new state of language brought about by this particular change is better or more efficient than the state that went before. Yet, it must be the case that human beings attach great importance to changes like this: if they did not, then there would be no reason why they should implement them at all.[1]

Similar considerations, however, apply to *variation within a language at a given time*. To simplify, let us suppose that Dialect A has [a] in environments where Dialect B has [o]. Again, speakers of the dialects will often attach great importance to this kind of difference. An intra-linguistic account will, however, regard this as a difference that is wholly describable in linguistic terms: the structure of the dialects can be described as differing in this particular way – it is just a fact of language. But we are also dealing here with a social fact, in that the difference (whether it is manifested as spatial or temporal) between State A and State B is *maintained* by the speakers in the communities concerned. In this case, it is a consequence of the fact that the speakers *agree* respectively on [a] or on [o] as realizations in this linguistic environment. Just as there is internal consensus of this kind within different communities at a given time, so there must also be consensus on the implementation of a change through time. The change would not take place if the speakers did not in some way agree that it should take place. To this extent, therefore, linguistic change is social, just as variability is social, and no given state of language at any time can be fully accounted for by purely intra-linguistic description.

But there is another difficulty in understanding why and how sound changes happen. This has to do with the transmission of changes from person to person, which is of course also a social matter. The difficulty is that if we take a non-social view of language states, linguistic change can appear at first sight to be *dysfunctional*. If a new form is introduced into speech, then there would seem to be more risk of miscommunication or misunderstanding than there would be if the old form had been maintained. Thus, if we take the view that communication through language is essentially a matter of successful communication of information-bearing messages from A to B and that these messages should be fully interpretable *out of context*, linguistic innovations must belong to the class of phenomena that can be miscomprehended. If we take this 'message-oriented' view of language function (Brown 1982),[2] they are therefore dysfunctional.

In fact, there has been a general tendency in historical linguistics to treat the 'message-oriented' function as if language in use can be best understood with reference to this function. This assumption seems to underlie Martinet's (1955) proposals, for example, on 'functional' change, which emphasize the importance of preserving *meaning-bearing* distinctions and avoiding 'homonymic clash' in the course of change. But if this were the only – or main – constraint involved in sound change, then there seem to be a large number of changes, such as wholesale mergers of previously distinct phoneme classes, that really ought not to have happened (because they reduce 'communicative efficiency' in this message-oriented sense). Therefore, it seems that speech-exchanges have other functions besides the context-independent transmission of information-bearing messages, and that in some circumstances these other functions may override the effects of the message-oriented function. Indeed, it must be the existence of these other (social) functions, and the interaction between the various functions, that make linguistic change possible. If this is so, we need to look more closely at the functions of spoken discourse and the situational context of speech events in order to understand the manner in which linguistic change is implemented.

The functions of spoken discourse differ from those of written language. Wyld and his contemporaries, of course, had little chance of investigating speech systematically, for the reason that they had neither the methodology or the technology to analyse naturalistic spoken discourse *in extenso*. Even the branch of linguistics that was most interested in spoken variation – dialectology – had to rely on citation forms elicited in non-conversational settings and transcribed as single words independently of sentential contexts. As for the analysis of historical data, the interest in spoken language here has focused on reconstructing earlier pronunciation on the evidence of written records and has therefore been concerned with the formal, rather than the functional, properties of language: for example, with working out the correspondences between alphabetic writing systems and the phonological systems underlying them (see the discussions by McIntosh 1966, McIntosh et al. 1986). Thus, as a result of these things, much of the generally accepted body of knowledge on which theories of change are based depends on the interpretation of written records and on citation forms rather than on the analysis of naturalistic speech.

Speech is a social activity in a sense that writing is not, and the primary locus of speech is *conversation*. Conversations take place between two or more participants in social and situational contexts. Thus, observation of speech-exchanges by linguists must in some way take account of social and situational factors affecting speech exchanges. To put it more strongly: as language use (outside of literary modes and laboratory experiments) cannot take place *except* in social and situational contexts and is *always* observed in these contexts, our analysis – if it is to be adequate – *must* take account of society, situation and the speaker/listener.

The theme of this chapter is therefore the *social* nature of language change, and the view taken is that linguistic change is one of the things that is *negotiated* by speakers in the course of speech-exchanges. As language activity takes place in social contexts, linguistic changes must be passed from speaker to speaker in these contexts. But many other things happen in speech-exchanges, and so we need to consider their characteristics quite carefully. One thing that is clear is that speakers in casual social contexts are not necessarily concerned with such matters as avoiding homonymic clash or with being maximally clear and explicit in conveying information: they are satisfied if the conversation progresses successfully, and the success of the conversation is judged in social, rather than strictly linguistic, terms. But it is the possibility of miscomprehension that is of interest here: it seems that if misunderstandings occur because of homonymic clash or for any other reason, they can be *repaired* if necessary; speakers appear to accept the results of vagueness and ambiguity on the assumption that meanings will be clarified *if necessary* as the conversation proceeds (on conversational repair see especially Schegloff 1979).

Underlying the distinction between different functions of spoken discourse, there is another more general distinction. This is the stark contrast between what is desirable in the written medium (or context-independent speech-styles such as lectures) and what is desirable in, and characteristic of, speech-exchanges in social settings (this is relevant here simply because so much of our information on linguistic change comes from written language). Redundancy, vagueness and ambiguity, which are disfavoured in writing, are wholly characteristic of everyday speech. Furthermore, many of the features that are positively dysfunctional in context-independent language are actually functional and necessary in the conduct of successful conversation: lack of explicitness, hesitation, ambiguity, incompleteness, repetition and reliance on extra-linguistic cues are themselves very important aspects of how conversation is organized. Some of these characteristics may well be implicated in different aspects of language change, but amongst the various strategies of conversation, it is the possibility of conversational *repair* that is most immediately relevant here.

Although it is true that conversational miscomprehensions are not *necessarily* corrected and that conversational breakdown can arise, the important point here is simply that conversational structure provides the means whereby miscomprehensions *can* be repaired. Miscomprehensions arising from diversity and change in language fall within the general class of miscomprehensions, and we have been interested in these from the beginning of the research programme that we carried out in Belfast between 1975 and 1982 (Milroy and Milroy 1978, etc.).

In historical argumentation we have not normally taken much account of matters of this kind, but it seems as though a perspective on conversational analysis can throw new light on the assumptions that we make as historical linguists, some of which arise from too much emphasis on the message-oriented nature of speech exchanges. For example, the claim that mutual comprehensibility between generations is a primary (or at least an important) *constraint* on linguistic change (see, e.g. Lightfoot 1979) may need to be modified. At the very least, more emphasis on conversation as the primary locus of change will enable us to think more clearly about what is meant by 'mutual comprehensibility' and to specify the other functions of discourse which may override the 'message-oriented' function. For example, the maintenance of *social identity* may in some circumstances be important enough to devalue the message-oriented function: to put it crudely, some groups in society may not particularly want to be understood by other groups.

But to return to the conversational setting as the locus of change: it is obviously unlikely that by observing conversation we will literally detect the origin of a specific sound-change and trace its adoption and diffusion thereafter. We have therefore approached the question at a somewhat more abstract, or generalized, level, which is foreshadowed in the first few paragraphs of this chapter: taking our cue from studying speakers and speech events, we approach the origin of sound-change by making a primary distinction between *speakers* and *systems*. If we appeal to this as a primary distinction, it appears that most of historical linguistics (including Martinet's functionalism) has been about systems and not about speakers – the question addressed has been: how do language systems change within themselves? In a speaker/system perspective, however, the question becomes: how do activities of speakers in social contexts feed into linguistic systems as established *changes* in the basic structural parts of language? In the remainder of this chapter, I am concerned with this question.

2 Speaker innovation and linguistic change

Historical linguists have generally rejected a predominantly social approach to change. There have been many reasons for this, but one of them is that historical linguists can certainly justify a mainly language-internal approach by various arguments, especially as such approaches have led to so many important insights. It has been quite usual to speak of historical descriptions as consisting of two types: *internal* and *external*, and of these it is the internal accounts that have been the most intellectually challenging and most highly valued. Roger Lass (1980: 121) has pointed out that when speaker-based 'external' (i.e. social) factors have been appealed to in historical linguistics, these have been 'superficial and otiose': in fact, they very often appear as *ad hoc* appeals to unanalysed social categories such as 'prestige'. What strikes me as important here, however, is the fact that if we focus on linguistic change alone (excluding other aspects of language), we can indeed propose sophisticated descriptions of attested changes and go on to propose even more sophisticated theories of change, without taking any account whatever of social factors. That is to say that it is possible to have very sophisticated language-internal theories of change. However, if we pose the more basic question why some forms and varieties are *maintained* while others change, we cannot avoid reference to society. Let me clarify this.

If we are interested in how language states can remain stable and how speech communities *resist* change, we have no alternative but to take account of social factors. Suppose we notice that the structure of Language X has remained stable for a century: it is not very interesting to point this out and then to leave it at that. We naturally want to know why it has remained stable when other states of language have changed, but in order to do this we have to study the social and speaker-based reasons that may account for the fact that it has *not* changed. In reality, languages change at given times in some ways and not in others, sometimes they change rapidly and sometimes slowly, some varieties are divergent and some convergent, and so on. To account for these different patterns, we have used an account of language change that is embedded in a more general account of language maintenance.

But what must be pointed out here is that although historical inquiries have focused almost exclusively on patterns of change, they have necessarily had to make *implicit* assumptions about the pre-existing states of language in which the changes are embedded. It's no accident therefore that much of historical description (until recently) has focused on relatively stable, fairly well-attested and mainly monolingual situations, rather than highly variable and unstable situations (such as Pidgin/Creole situations). To account for patterns of stability and maintenance, and for consensus norms in speech communities, we need to take account of the social factors that favour these things. Therefore, I am interested here in exploring the extent to which a socially based approach that gives explicit attention to linguistic mainten-ance can clarify our understanding of language change.

It is appropriate to start by recalling Weinreich, Labov and Herzog's statement of the actuation problem, which is for them 'the very heart of the matter':

> Why do changes in a structural feature take place in a particular
> language at a given time, but not in other languages with the same
> feature, or in the same language at other times? (Weinreich et al.
> 1968: 102)

This is such a challenging formulation that many historical
linguists do not address it directly – and this is hardly surprising
as, when it is formulated in this way, the actuation problem is
actually insoluble: a solution to it implies the capacity to *predict*,
not only what particular change will happen, but also when and
where it will happen. However, the probability of *any* particular
event in life actually taking place at a particular time and place is
close to zero. Weather prediction is a convenient analogy here:
we can predict from meteorological observations that it will rain
on a particular day with a high probability of being correct, but if
we predict that in a particular place it will start raining at one
minute past eleven and stop at six minutes past twelve, the
probability of the prediction being correct is vanishingly low.
Nevertheless, we would be bad meteorologists if we did not try to
improve the accuracy of our predictions, and this greater
accuracy includes the ability to specify the conditions under
which something will *not* happen in addition to the conditions
under which it *will* happen. In view of all this, we have no excuse
as linguists for not addressing the actuation problem.

The point of view adopted here is that actuation must be
speaker-based. Linguistic change originates with speakers and is
implemented in social interactions between speakers, so it is
reasonable to suggest that by systematic observation of language
in use we can come closer to understanding actuation. It is useful
therefore to observe in our analysis a distinction in principle
between *speaker* and *system*. It is important to specify when we
are talking about speakers and when we are talking about
systems, and I shall attempt to show that observing this
distinction can lead to some insights that we would be unlikely to
achieve if our approach were purely language-internal. As for
linguistic change, the speaker/system distinction leads immediately
to an associated distinction – the distinction between speaker
innovation, on the one hand, and linguistic *change*, on the other.
Innovation and change are not conceptually the same thing: an
innovation is an act of the speaker, whereas a change is
manifested within the language system. It is *speakers*, and not
languages, that innovate.

We can therefore approach the *actuation problem* in the
following way. We can describe *speaker-innovation* as *an act of*

the speaker which is capable of influencing linguistic structure. The innovation may, or may not, enter the language system: thus, part of the solution to the actuation problem will be to explain the conditions in which an innovation is unsuccessful in addition to those in which it is successful. This is one reason why it is important to associate our account of change with a prior account of language maintenance: incipient changes can be *resisted* in the speech community, and we must attempt to understand the conditions under which this happens. If, however, the innovation is successful, the reflex of this speaker-act is *change in the language system*, which of course is always observed after the speaker-act of innovation has taken place. Once a new linguistic structure is created – that is, once change has entered the system – it penetrates in an orderly fashion and constrains individual and collective behaviour in the manner that has been shown in quantitative analysis by Labov (1966) and many others. We must notice here, however, that what the graphs, diagrams and variable rule statements of the quantitative paradigm actually model is not the behaviour of speakers, nor is it the act of actuation: what they model is *the linguistic system*. This quantitative modelling of the system is, of course, much more sophisticated than the homogeneous and uniform systems that are postulated in other branches of linguistic inquiry, as it incorporates the *orderly heterogeneity* of the community 'grammar', but it is none the less a linguistic system – one which characterizes the *constraints on the linguistic behaviour of groups and individuals*. It models the effects of the linguistic system on speakers rather than the effects of speakers on the system. This is conceptually quite a different matter from the modelling of *how speakers introduce an innovation into the system in the first place.* These relationships are expressed graphically in Figure 8.1.

It seems that while investigators may observe something quite close to *speaker innovation*, they have no principled way of determining whether what they have observed is the beginning of a linguistic change in the system. As the diagram shows, what the quantitative analyst describes is a change that has already assumed a regular pattern of social variation in the community, and this of course applies even more to a historical linguist observing changes that have gone so far as to be admitted into writing systems (which are, of course, resistant to structural change). For these reasons, intra-linguistic approaches generally dismiss actuation as unobservable: it is, for example, discussed by Lass (1980: 95–6) in the following way. Suppose I have observed that a speaker utters [e] in a 'word of etymological category X' on

SPEAKER INNOVATION AND LINGUISTIC CHANGE

one day, and utters [i] in the same environment on the next day, all that I have observed (according to Lass) is a diachronic correspondence: I have no way of determining whether it is a change. There is a distinction that sociolinguists customarily make that Lass does not make here – the 'change' from one day to the next might, for example, be stylistic, an instance of *orderly heterogeneity* – but what is relevant in the present context is the absence of the speaker/system distinction: it appears from Lass's example that a change in the output of a *single* speaker might be regarded as the locus of a change in the system, whereas of course a change is not a change until it has been adopted by *more than one* speaker. Therefore, we cannot deal with actuation by positing examples like this, based on a single speaker. But if we make the distinction between *innovation* and *change*, it does appear that we *can* observe a speaker innovation (perhaps completely accidentally): the problem is that we do not know

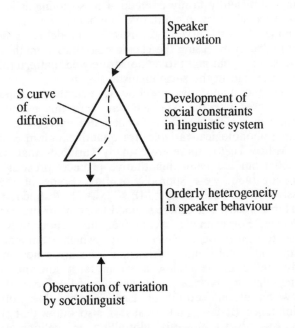

FIGURE 8.1   Model of transition from speaker innovation to linguistic change.

whether it will be a *successful* innovation – we cannot demonstrate systematically that it leads to a linguistic change until after it has spread. Yet, as we have already noted, our methods do not give us the means to deal with *actuation* and the very early stages of a change.

The distinction I am trying to make here can be further clarified by referring to some recent work by Trudgill (1986), which strongly suggests that we need methods quite different from the standard quantitative ones to study *actuation* of change (depending on speaker-behaviour) as distinct from *the effect of the system on speakers*. Returning to Norwich eighteen years after his original survey (published in 1974), Trudgill noticed that one particular linguistic feature (a labio-dental variant of /r/) was by then firmly embedded as a patterned sociolinguistic variable. In his 1968 fieldwork, however, he had noticed this feature sporadically, but had thought that it might be pathological – perhaps a speech problem experienced by a few younger speakers. Now, although actuation of this change must already have taken place when Trudgill observed it in 1968, it had not yet become sufficiently firmly embedded in sociolinguistic structure to be accessible by quantitative methods, but was near the beginning of the S-curve of diffusion (as modelled in figure 8.1, above). Therefore, using the classic quantitative methods, it was not possible at that point to demonstrate what pattern this change might have had in the sociolinguistic system.

In fact, the quantitative methodology actually predisposes us to exclude cases like the Norwich one, and this example draws attention in a clear way to a familiar difficulty. When we were selecting phonological variables for quantification in Belfast (see, e.g., Milroy 1986), there were many variables that had to be rejected from the main quantitative projects precisely because tokens of them were sporadic or rare. Some of these were recessive forms such as the MEAT/MATE distinction (Milroy and Harris 1980), but others seemed to point to the early stages of change. For example, we noticed in a pilot study that the glottal stop for /t/ (as in *water*, *what*) – which is emphatically *not* part of traditional Belfast vernacular – occurred now and again, chiefly among female adolescents. I am fairly sure that this is the leading edge of a change (the beginning of the S-curve), because I know that urban central Scots English (which has glottal stops) can influence Belfast, and because I also know that there is a trend (or 'drift') towards glottalling in colloquial English generally. So I am quite willing to predict that it will have spread by now (and if I am right, I have come a little closer to solving the actuation problem in this case). However, we could not have demonstrated all this in 1975 by using standard quantitative methods. This is because (as we noted above) the classic methods are designed to examine the effect of the system on speaker behaviour rather than *vice-versa*, and so it is hard to see how anyone relying wholly on these methods could make a systematic attempt to handle *actuation* or the very early stages of a change.

Bearing in mind this distinction between speaker and system together with our focus on language maintenance, we have attempted elsewhere to characterize the kind of social situations in which linguistic change is impeded or facilitated. Basically, this depends on the notion of speaker-links within society, which was operationalized in the Belfast research in terms of *social network* (Milroy 1987). In situations where the internal links are maximally dense and multiplex, the norm-enforcement aspect of the network model predicts that linguistic change will not take place. That is to say that speaker innovations in such situations will be resisted and will not find their way into the system as linguistic changes. This is of course an idealization, and real speech communities approximate to the ideal to varying extents: they are characterized by greater or lesser degrees of network density and multiplexity. But, from the assumption that linguistic change is impeded by strong ties, it can be argued that it is facilitated by weak ties. In our 1985 paper (Milroy and Milroy 1985) we found it quite useful to attempt to think of the problem in terms of characterizing what I may call the *idealized speaker innovator*.

The best-known attempt to determine the social characteristics of the speaker/innovator is that of William Labov. His main conclusions can be summarized as follows:

1. Speakers who lead sound change are those with the highest status in their local communities as measured by a social class index.
2. Among persons of equal status 'the most advanced speakers are the persons with the largest number of local contacts within the neighborhood, yet who have at the same time the highest proportion of their acquaintances outside the neighborhood', Labov then goes on to comment 'Thus we have a portrait of individuals with the highest local prestige who are responsive to a somewhat broader form of prestige at the next larger level of social communication' (Labov 1980: 261).

According to this account, linguistic innovation is accomplished by persons who have many ties within the community but who simultaneously have a large number of outside contacts. We have pointed out elsewhere (Milroy and Milroy 1985), following Granovetter (1973), that, strictly speaking, an individual cannot be a central member of a close-tie community and at the same time have large numbers of *close-tie* outside contacts. This is impossible because if the ties are strong ties, *they actually constitute the definition of the speaker's in-group*, not his/her out-group. Therefore, by definition out-group ties must be weak, and to speak of strong *external* ties is a contradiction. It is therefore likely that the person characterized here has large numbers of *weak ties* outside his/her community. The persons he/she knows do not necessarily also know one another, and he/she knows these persons in mainly uniplex, rather than multiplex, functions. However, it is unlikely that the kind of person described here can actually be the person responsible for innovations.

What is extremely plausible is the idea that this sociable and outgoing kind of person, who probably has a large number of weak ties, is instrumental in *diffusing* changes once they have been initiated. It is likely that, both in Philadelphia and Belfast, the groups that we will most readily identify as the carriers of change will be the *early adopters* rather than the innovators, and we have identified at least one such group in Belfast (Milroy and Milroy 1985). It is these early adopters, and not the innovators, who will be shown by quantitative methods as carrying linguistic changes between groups in the community. The initiation of a change, however, will not show up as highly patterned or significant in quantitative terms, because it will not yet be embedded in sociolinguistic structure.

So far, we have spoken of innovators and early adopters in terms of considering what personality types might be involved, but it is dangerous, I think, to go very far along that road. Therefore, in general, we have preferred to argue, not mainly in terms of characterizing a type of personality, but more abstractly in terms of characterizing the kind of social ties that can exist between individuals. In this argument, it is *weak ties*, and not strong ties, that are crucial, and the innovation is likely to be passed by individuals who are subjectively perceived as peripheral to the groups into which the change is introduced: they will have *weak-tie* links with these groups. But as it is possible to have very large numbers of weak ties (as against small numbers of strong ties), the success of innovations depends on the fact that weak ties can be numerous.

3 Weak-tie explanations

We have elsewhere argued the case for weak-tie explanations by citing some examples from our own field research which are very difficult to explain in terms of strong-tie contacts. These concern the passing of phonetic/phonological change in a particular segment (/a/) from one part of a city to another (where strong-tie contacts cannot be implicated) and the development of consensus norms in younger generation speakers who are not in close contact. Thus, although we have been working here at a higher level of abstraction from the data than would be involved in a close analysis of conversational exchanges (recall my remarks in section 1), the studies have nevertheless been carried out at a fine-grained level of linguistic analysis. Here, I would like to pass on to a higher level of generalization and consider the more general applicability of the model to broader language situations. We have suggested a general principle:

> Linguistic change is slow to the extent that the relevant populations are well established and bound by strong ties, whereas it is rapid to the extent that weak ties exist in populations (Milroy and Milroy 1985: 375).

There are many patterns of linguistic maintenance and change that have been widely observed, but which are not easy to explain in a principled way if we depend on the usual assumptions about diffusion being brought about through strong links. These patterns can be observed at many different levels of generality, and I shall mention a small number of them here. At the most general level, it can be noted that while some languages (such as English and Danish) have been structurally innovative, other related languages (such as Icelandic) remain highly conservative. In such cases we may be able to show that the conservative communities are characterized by close-knit networks and the innovatory ones by the development over history of numerous loose-knit ties, and we have attempted to demonstrate this in the case of English and Icelandic (Milroy and Milroy 1985).[3]

It can also happen that within some particular language, some dialects are innovative, whereas others are conservative. The conservative dialects are often (but not always) regionally peripheral, and therefore likely to be relatively strong-tie communities that are less exposed than centrally located dialects to influence from mainstream norms. Relevant here is the case of the Scots vowel systems (Catford 1957), in which the regionally peripheral dialects have a greater number of vowel phonemes than the central ones, the latter having innovated by merging vowel phonemes that were previously distinct. In a wide-ranging discussion of innovatory and conservative patterns in a large number of dialects of different languages, Andersen (1988) proposes a distinction between *open* and *closed* dialect communities, and further proposes that within these categories some communities are *endocentric*, whereas others are *exocentric*. It seems that endocentrism and exocentrism may have to do with psycho-social *attitudes* within the communities towards the maintenance of local identities and resistance to external influence, with the endocentric communities strong in these respects and the exocentric communities weak. However, it is not easy to see how we could undertake an empirical investigation of personal attitudes in such a wide range of relevant language situations. It does appear, however, that once we have supported a theory of weak and strong network ties by fine-grained sociolinguistic analysis in the speech community, we may be justified in projecting the model on to these more general instances. This will predict that the closed communities will be characterized by strong internal cohesiveness with relatively few weak external links, and the open ones by more loose-knit networks, with more external links. It is then a matter of adducing supporting evidence to assess the degree of network strength in the relevant communities.

There are other situations which are also clearly amenable to weak-tie explanations, and these appear as essentially language-contact situations. For example, it has been widely noted that neighbouring languages which are unrelated or distantly related may share similar linguistic changes. Trudgill (1983: 56–9) draws attention to the wide distribution of uvular /r/ in North-west European languages, and certain Balkan languages are known to share specific grammatical features even though they are very distantly related. Trudgill suggests that we come closer to an explanation for the cross-language distribution of uvular /r/ if we focus on urban centres: Paris, The Hague, Cologne, Berlin, Bergen and others, which have uvular /r/. One of the most important ways in which this innovation has been implemented is by 'jumping' from one urban centre to another. Within specific languages also, it is known that innovations tend to spread from one centre of population to another without immediately affecting the intervening countryside (which is of course more sparsely populated and probably characterized by strong internal

cohesiveness). Urban development seems therefore to be implicated in the diffusion of vernacular features within a language.
The adoption of London features by Norwich teenagers (Trudgill
1986) is a case in point, and the historical spread of /h/ dropping
(Milroy 1983) and (probably) glottal-stopping in British English
seems also to be urban. There is support for this in the fact that,
despite the long history of /h/ dropping, there are still rural (but
not urban) dialects in Southern England which do not /h/-drop
(see, e.g., Trudgill 1974). However, the occurrence of a rather
unusual phenomenon – *pre-aspiration* of post-vocalic voiceless
stops – in two distantly related languages which were in
prolonged contact in the Middle Ages – Icelandic and Scottish
Gaelic – suggests that urban situations are not the only type that
might be involved, but that these are themselves best seen as a
sub-type of contact situations in general – a situation in which
numerous weak-tie relationships are bound to arise.

As I have raised the question of language contact, it seems
appropriate to comment here that a theory of weak ties at the
level of *speaker* may help to illuminate language-contact situations
generally. What we call *close* contact situations that lead to
linguistic change seem to be characterized, not by *close* networks,
but by open ones – not by numerous strong ties, but by the
development of numerous *weak* ties. Clearly, if we do not
distinguish between speaker and system, this might appear to be
contradictory or paradoxical, because the influence on the
language situation concerned is often *strong*, rather than weak.
For example, the influence on Scandinavian and Norman French
on medieval English was strong, and the consequences of the
shift from Hungarian to German speaking in Oberwart (reported
by Gal 1979) are considerable. However, if we bear in mind the
fact that although change is observed in systems, it must be
brought about by speakers, the apparent contradiction is
resolved. When linguists speak of a close contact situation, they
are usually thinking of contact between *systems*, but what actually
occurs is contact between *speakers* of different languages: the
changes that result and which are then observed in the system
have been brought about by the speakers, who form weak and
uniplex ties when two populations first come into contact. So,
strictly speaking, it is not really *language* contact at all, but
speaker contact. In such situations the model would predict that
the innovators in close contact situations are those who form
numerous weak ties outside their own community, and not the
central members of either community.

4   Conclusions: the social modelling of language change

I shall conclude by making some general comments on the social model of linguistic change that I have been proposing. It is a social model in quite a basic sense: it assumes that, as the natural state of language is to be divergent and not convergent, the extent to which language states are maintained in reasonably stable and internally convergent forms will depend on pressures which are social rather than on strictly linguistic criteria. Thus, stable language states are maintained by relatively strong network relationships in the communities concerned – that is to say that they are maintained by speakers and not by languages. Our arguments have been based on close observation and fine-grained analysis of language use in social and situational contexts (Milroy and Milroy 1978, etc.), and we have assumed that linguistic changes are passed from speaker to speaker in conversational exchanges. We have also made use of quantitative methods, but I have suggested that these methods give us an account of the embedding of language variation in speech communities, and that patterns of change in progress are one of the things that are revealed by these methods. But these methods are necessary, because although single instances of speaker variation (including speaker innovations) can be directly observed, patterns of change in progress have to be *demonstrated* after the data has been analysed and cannot be directly observed as individual events. Thus, I am advocating quantitative methods, and not attacking them. But they do not in themselves give us access to the actuation of change, so we have tried to tackle this by observing a basic distinction between speaker-oriented approaches and system-oriented approaches, and of course traditional historical linguistics in this perspective must be characterized as system-oriented and not speaker-oriented. On the basis of this distinction we have further proposed a conceptual distinction between *innovation* and *change*: innovation is an act of the speaker, whereas change is manifested in the system. I would like to comment briefly on some possible consequences of all this for historical linguistic argumentation.

It is noticeable that, after a period of quiescence, the Neogrammarians have returned in recent years to prominent position in the theory of sound-change (see especially Labov 1981; Kiparsky 1988). It seems to me that their distinction between *blind* exceptionless change and linguistic 'borrowing' is relevant here, as it would be easy to conclude that what I have proposed accounts mainly for patterns of diffusion and contact (i.e., 'borrowing') rather than for internal spontaneous change within speech communities. I do not think that this is quite correct: it seems to me that the model I have suggested actually cuts across the traditional distinctions and may even call into question the validity of the Neogrammarian distinction. The distinction between innovation and change is not merely terminological: it has consequences for what we mean by a sound-change and for the manner in which questions about sound-change are put. In the weak-tie model *all* sound-change is socially conditioned, simply because those so-called changes that arise spontaneously are not actually changes; they are innovations, and they do not become changes until they have assumed a social pattern in the community. If, as often happens, these innovations are not adopted by a community, however small that community may be, then they do not become changes at all. Thus, we are not asking how spontaneous innovations arise, but how we are to specify the conditions under which some of these innovations, and not others, are admitted into linguistic systems as linguistic changes.

This interpretation of what is actually meant by a change differs considerably from what is usually assumed. It is usual to suppose that sound change is an internal linguistic phenomenon, perhaps explainable with reference to the mental capacities of the idealized speaker, but not a social phenomenon. It does not become social until it is observed to show a social pattern in the community, and this comes about when the community latches on to the variants that have already arisen and imposes social meanings on them. Henning Andersen's insightful account of deductive and abductive change is one of those that differ in emphasis in this way in that linguistic constraints are seen as primary: Andersen's 'implementation rules' are structurally motivated within the language system and therefore productive (Andersen 1973, 1978: 332). The present account, on the other hand, would suggest that, while all variants must be constrained by aspects of linguistic structure and may be produced by deductive and abductive generalizations (as argued by Andersen), language-internal arguments or mentally-based idealizations do not account for change (or indeed variation), although they help to account for innovations. What has to be explained is the manner in which speaker-based variants actually feed into the system as established changes (Andersen handles this aspect by postulating 'adaptive rules'). A linguistic change is a social phenomenon, and it comes about for reasons for marking social identity, stylistic difference and so on. If it does not carry these social meanings, then it is not a linguistic change: it is a random variant stuck somewhere near the beginning of the S-curve in Figure 8.1. Since our perspective differs in these ways, it is appropriate to examine it more fully.

Suppose we observe at a given time that a spontaneous innovation (for example, a common one such as palatalization of /k/ before front vowels) occurs in the speech of a small number of persons who do not have any social contact with one another, and suppose also that we can demonstrate that this really is an innovation in the community (like the glottal stop in Belfast). The question is how we are to determine whether and in what manner the innovation will feed into the system as a patterned change. It is clear that the structural conditions exist in many languages for palatalization of initial /k/ to take place: in some languages (or dialects) we can observe that it has taken place, whereas in others it has not, but has remained at the stage of a sporadic innovation that is always a potential change. At billions of moments throughout history, the change has been possible in these varieties, but has not been realized. This is the point: the likelihood of any specific event occurring at any given place or time is close to zero; therefore, no specific sound change is ever likely to happen at any particular time even when favourable structural conditions exist in the language (e.g. when it is regarded as 'natural'), and when there have been innovations which might favour the initiation of a change. It appears that for the change to take place it is necessary for the *social* conditions to be favourable.

Such conditions must have applied to the case discussed by Andersen (1973) – the attested change from sharped labials to dentals in the Teták dialects of Czech, which is explained as arising from the acoustic similarity between sharped labials and dentals. The difficulty that our account raises here is the question of why this change, which was always possible for these acoustic reasons, took place at the time and place that it did, and not at other times or places. The acoustic similarity adduced by Andersen defines the Teták innovation as one of a class of innovations that must have been possible candidates for change at any time or place, so long as the linguistic conditions (in this case, acoustic similarity) existed within the language system. The historian's problem, of course, is that in historically attested, but highly specific, instances like this, we cannot have sufficiently precise social information to explain the social conditions that favoured the change and then (in the nineteenth century) helped to bring about its recession. But it is unlikely that social identity factors were not involved, as Andersen's subsequent work would itself suggest (e.g. Andersen 1988). In sociolinguistic inquiries into present-day states of language, we can pursue these social questions more fully.

The distinction between innovation and change, if it is acceptable, may have further relevance to some general assumptions that linguists commonly make about the origin of language changes – for example the proposal that the locus of change is in child language-learning phenomena. One difference between this and a sociolinguistic model is in the nature of the information available. Whereas social dialectologists can demonstrate the patterning of change in progress in adolescent and adult populations by large-scale investigations and quantitative techniques, mentalist accounts depend on more idealized data and on theoretical positions that take little note of heterogeneous databases. It would clearly be very difficult to demonstrate, beyond reasonable doubt, which of the many innovations observed in child language (for example) will actually be accepted by speech communities and become linguistic changes, as most of the innovations observed in such circumstances (as in others) will never become changes. We are thinking here of present-day communities and assuming that innovations can be directly observed in them, but as so much of our knowledge depends on history, it should also be remembered that phonological innovations cannot be observed in historical data; what historical data normally display are changes at a late stage of development – usually late enough to be accepted into writing systems and message-oriented styles. Thus, much of historical linguistic argumentation has depended on the observation of completed changes and not directly on the origins of innovations. As for the Neogrammarian axioms, if we accept that a change is not a change until it assumes a socially regular distribution of some kind, we have no criteria for determining absolutely that there is an axiomatic distinction between *sound change* and borrowing (or contact change) because, as we have defined them, all changes must arise from contact between speakers. But we can certainly save the Neogrammarian hypothesis that change is regular, provided we allow social regularity to be counted as regular: in this perspective it is innovations that may have an irregular distribution, and change must be regular by definition. This implies, amongst other things, that phenomena of the type that appear to be irregular in an intra-linguistic account may turn out to be regular in relation to a more fully developed sociolinguistic model of social structures, processes and relationships.

Finally, we need to make a few comments on the social model of change proposed here and some suggestions as to how it might be extended. The weak-tie model is not in itself sufficient to provide a full social explanation of linguistic change. What it proposes is a set of conditions that are necessary – but not sufficient – for linguistic change to take place. There are certain things that are important socially about which social network has nothing to say. It is not about psycho-social attitudes to language or about language learning processes, and so it has nothing directly to say about these things. Similarly, it is not about social stratification, and so it has nothing to say about that either. In order to make progress towards a fuller account of the social embedding of language change, we are now trying to explore the connection between network and wider patterns of social structure (Milroy and Milroy, 1992). Ethnographers, such as Mewett (1982), have noted that social stratification is observed to develop in cohesive communities to the extent that the strong ties are weakened. This is where we also make the link, but it also appears that whereas a network approach emphasizes shared values and consensus in social groupings, social class (together with other stratificational concepts such as rank or status) involves not consensus, but conflict. It is reasonable to point out that the social models on which sociolinguists have relied have not always been noticeably sophisticated, and there has been much vagueness in the use of important socially-based concepts such as social class, language standardization and prestige. In order to reach a fuller understanding of social aspects of language change, therefore, we hope to move towards a more sophisticated understanding of society, and this will be particularly relevant to the extent that linguistic change is a social phenomenon.

Notes

1. The speaker-oriented view of language variation and change and the social embedding of these things are discussed very fully in J. Milroy *Linguistic variation and change* (1992). The article as a whole is an outgrowth of my own empirical research (mainly in Belfast, 1975–82). I am grateful to Lesley Milroy for her contributions to that research.

2. A distinction between 'message-oriented' and 'listener-oriented' discourse is proposed by Gillian Brown (1982: 77). I am using the distinction here as a 'primitive' and programmatic distinction in the

belief that this is adequate for my present purpose. In practical analysis of conversational texts, more refinement would be needed.

3. Whereas Papua/New Guinea has been called a 'laboratory' of linguistic diversity, Iceland is possibly the nearest we have to a laboratory for the study of language maintenance. The medieval situation, as discussed by Milroy and Milroy (1985) was a close-tie situation. In modern times, the consensus linguistic norms of the society have become more institutionalized and planned but what is remarkable is that there is considerable popular agreement on institutional prescriptions: for example, resistance to pan-European vocabulary such as *taxi, telephone, hotel.*

References

ANDERSEN, HENNING (1973, 1978) 'Abductive and deductive change', *Language* 49: 765–93. Reprinted in BALDI, P. and WERTH, R. N. (eds) *Readings in Historical Phonology.* University Park, PA: Pennsylvania State University Press, pp. 313–47.

ANDERSEN, HENNING (1988) 'Center and periphery: adoption, diffusion and spread. In FISIAK, J. (ed.) *Historical Dialectology.* Berlin: Mouton De Gruyter, pp. 39–85.

BROWN, GILLIAN (1982) 'The spoken language.' In CARTER, R. (ed.). *Linguistics and the Teacher.* London: Routledge, pp. 75–87.

CATFORD, J. (1957) 'Vowel systems of Scots dialects.' Transactions of the Philological Society, pp. 107–17.

DANCHEV, ANDREI (1988) 'Language contact and language change', *Folia Linguistica,* **XXII**: 37–53.

GAL, SUSAN (1979) *Language Shift.* New York: Academic Press.

GRANOVETTER, M. (1973) 'The strength of weak ties', *American Journal of Sociology,* **78**: 1360–80.

KIPARSKY, PAUL (1988) 'Phonological change.' In NEWMEYER, F. (ed.) *Linguistics: The Cambridge Survey,* Vol. I. Cambridge: Cambridge University Press.

LABOV, WILLIAM (1966) *The Social Stratification of English in New York City.* Washington DC: Center for Applied Linguistics.

LABOV, WILLIAM (ed.) (1980) *Locating Language in Time and Space.* New York: Academic Press.

LABOV, W. (1981) 'Resolving the Neogrammarian Controversy', *Language* 57: pp. 267–308.

LASS, ROGER (1980) *On Explaining Language Change.* Cambridge: Cambridge University Press.

LIGHTFOOT, D. (1979) *Principles of Diachronic Syntax.* Cambridge: Cambridge University Press.

MARTINET, ANDRE (1955) *Economie des Changements Phonétiques.* Bern: Francke.

MCINTOSH, A. (1966) 'Graphology and meaning.' In MCINTOSH, A. and HALLIDAY, M. A. K. (eds) *Patterns of Language.* London: Longman.

MCINTOSH, A., SAMUELS, M. and BENSKIN, M. (1986) *A Linguistic Atlas of*

Late Medieval English, 4 volumes. Aberdeen: Aberdeen University Press.

MEWETT, P. (1982) 'Associational categories in the social location of relationships in a Lewis crofting community.' In COHEN, A. (ed.) *Belonging*. Manchester: Manchester University Press, pp. 101–30.

MILROY, JAMES (1983) 'On the sociolinguistic history of /h/-dropping in English.' In DAVENPORT, M., HANSEN, E. and NIELSEN, H-F. (eds) *Current Topics in English Historical Linguistics*. Odense: Odense University Press.

MILROY, JAMES (1986) 'The methodology of urban language studies: the example of Belfast.' In HARRIS, J., LITTLE, D. and SINGLETON, D. (eds) *Perspectives on the English Language in Ireland*. Dublin: Trinity College.

MILROY, JAMES (1992) *Linguistic Variation and Change*. Oxford: Blackwell.

MILROY, JAMES and HARRIS, JOHN (1980) 'When is a merger not a merger?: the MEAT/MATE problem in a present-day English vernacular', *English World-Wide* 1: 199–210.

MILROY, JAMES and MILROY, LESLEY (1978) 'Belfast: change and variation in an urban vernacular.' In TRUDGILL, P. (eds) *Sociolinguistic Patterns in British English*. London: Edward Arnold, pp. 19–36.

MILROY, JAMES and MILROY, LESLEY (1985) 'Linguistic change, social network and speaker innovation', *Journal of Linguistics* 21: 339–84.

MILROY, LESLEY (1987) *Language and Social Networks* (2nd edn). Oxford: Blackwell.

MILROY, LESLEY and MILROY, JAMES (1992) 'Social network and social class: toward an integrated sociolinguistic model', *Language in Society* 21: 1–26.

SCHEGLOFF, E. (1979) 'The relevance of repair to syntax for conversation.' In GIVON, T. (ed.) *Syntax and Semantics*, Vol. 12. New York: Academic Press, pp. 107–17.

TRUDGILL, PETER (1974) *The social differentiation of English in Norwich*. Cambridge: Cambridge University Press.

TRUDGILL, PETER (1983) *On dialect*. Oxford: Blackwell.

TRUDGILL, PETER (1986) *Dialects in contact*. Oxford: Blackwell.

WEINREICH, URIEL, LABOV, WILLIAM and HERZOG, MARVIN (1968) 'Empirical foundations for a theory of language change.' In LEHMANN, W. P. and MALKIEL, Y. (eds), *Directions for Historical Linguistics*. Austin, TX: University of Texas Press, pp. 95–195.

WYLD, H. C. (1927) *Short History of English*. London: John Murray.

Chapter 9

The phonetics of sound change

John Ohala

1 Introduction

1.1 Strengthening the comparative method

One of the few solid scientific accomplishments of linguistics is the discovery of ways to reconstruct the history of languages via the comparative method. With it one first establishes sets of cognate words or morphemes in different languages and then posits an optimal route between them which consists of a hypothetical parent form and sound changes that transformed the parent forms into the attested cognates. Though not usually thought of in this way (but see Young 1819), the comparative method is a quasi-mathematical operation, involving implicit (and qualitative, not quantitative) estimations of probabilities of events and what is, in effect, the application of optimization theory. The posited reconstructed forms and the sound changes must also be within the bounds of the plausible, where plausibility is determined inductively, that is, by what the linguist has previously encountered in other human languages.

The quasi-mathematical character of the comparative method permits the linguist to treat words and their constituent sounds more or less as abstract algebraic entities without having to worry too much about their physical substance. They can be and have been manipulated like variables in an equation. Indeed, the leading historical linguists often emphasize that the reconstructed forms are simply parts of formulae for relating sets of cognates and should not be regarded as representing phonetic structure (Bloomfield 1914, 274ff; Meillet 1964, 39ff.). In addition, the inductive constraints on posited reconstructed forms and the sound changes that apply to them do not require that the linguist actually understand why languages are structured as they are or behave as they do, all that is necessary is to be aware of structure and behaviour frequently encountered. Thus, the actual phonetic substance of reconstructed forms and the mechanism of sound changes is usually of secondary importance.

In this chapter I argue that it is possible to do better historical phonology by taking into account the mechanism of sound change. This involves integrating phonetic studies with historical phonology. Of course, I am not claiming that 'complete' reconstructions of past languages are possible; just that the reconstructions can be improved by an attempt to understand the factors which give rise to sound change. In fact, my point is similar to ones made throughout the past few centuries: de Brosses (1765), von Raumer (1863), Key (1855), Osthoff and Brugmann (1878), Rousselot (1891) – to mention only a few – have all insisted and sometimes demonstrated that we could understand language change better by paying more attention to the phonetic and psychological aspects of change. This chapter, then, can be considered as an attempt to bring historical phonology up to date with current data and concepts in phonetics and psychology.

1.2 Delimiting the scope of the discussion
It is well recognized that changes in pronunciation can come about through many quite different factors, including some, such as spelling pronunciation, paradigm regularization, and fashion, which are language and culture-specific. In this chapter I consider only sound changes which have been attested independently in substantially the same form in many unrelated languages and which, therefore, are most likely to arise from language universal factors, i.e. physiological and psychological factors common to all human speakers at any time. Henceforth I will use the unqualified term 'sound change' to refer to these common, frequently encountered sound changes.

A further delimitation on the discussion to follow is that I am primarily concerned with the preconditions for sound changes, not their actual trigger and not their subsequent spread through the lexicon, through the dialect community, and from one speech style to another. Thus I will not be concerned with questions such as 'why did this sound change occur in such-and-such language at such-and-such time?' although I will suggest that such questions are for the most part fruitless pursuits.

2 Phonetic discoveries of importance to sound change
There are two major discoveries in phonetics which form the starting points for the subsequent discussion.

2.1 The first point: the infinite variability of speech

One of the major discoveries of phonetics over the past century is the tremendous variability that exists in what we regard as the 'same' events in speech, whether this sameness be phones, syllables, or words. Some variability was evident to phoneticians simply from ear analysis, for example, as exemplified by the work of Pāṇini, Amman (1700), Ellis (1889), and Sweet (1877), but more and more variation was noticed through instrumental analysis, starting in the late nineteenth century with kymographic studies and accumulating markedly with the onset of acoustic studies in the 1930s and 1940s. It is now accepted that there is infinite variation in speech – though still more or less lawfully determined. The 'same' sound is measurably different not only when spoken by the different speakers (which might be expected) but also when spoken by the same speaker in different phonetic environments or at different rates or levels of loudness (Lindblom 1963; Traunmüller 1981). The typically short list of 'allophones' given in traditional phonemic inventories of languages does not begin to give the whole story of the amount of variation present in speech.

2.2 The second point: the parallels between phonetic variation and sound change

That some of the synchronic variation in speech is similar to sound change has long been noted, for example, vowels are commonly non-distinctively nasalized before nasal vowels and that is the environment which most often gives rise to distinctively nasal vowels via sound change. But as instrumental studies and perceptual studies of speech accumulated, more and more points of similarity were noticed. In the next two sections I give some examples first from the domain of speech production and then from the acoustic-auditory domain.

2.2.1 Variation in the domain of speech production

2.2.1.1 Tonal development and consonantally induced FO differences on following vowels

Edkins (1864) and Maspéro (1912) and subsequently several other researchers noted that in East and South-east Asian languages[1] certain tonal distinctions developed out of former (subsequently neutralized) voiced vs. voiceless contrasts on pre-vocalic consonants; a higher tone developing after what had been the voiceless consonant and a lower tone after the voiced. An example from closely related dialects of Kammu, described by Svantesson (1983), is given in (1).

(1) Data showing that tone in Northern Kammu corresponds
     to a voicing contrast in Southern Kammu (from Svantesson
     1983: 69).

Southern Kammu	Northern Kammu	Translation
klaaŋ	kláaŋ	eagle
glaaŋ	klàaŋ	stone

Parallel to this is the discovery documented via acoustic analysis
for many diverse languages (see, e.g. Sato 1950; Hombert 1978;
Hombert et al. 1979) that the fundamental frequency (FO) on
vowels is higher following voiceless consonants than voiced; see
Figure 9.1.

Löfqvist et al. (1989) have discovered the apparent physiological
cause of this effect: during voiceless stops there is a higher
contraction rate for the cricothyroid muscles in the larynx, the
chief tensor muscle and the one most directly involved in
regulating the FO of voice. This increased tension of the vocal
cords may serve to insure the voicelessness of the stops by
stiffening the vocal cords.[2] The concomitant FO difference on the
following vowel is therefore probably a fortuitous consequence of
this activity directed towards maintaining the voicelessness of the
consonant, at least there is no evidence yet to suggest that the FO
perturbation is purposeful.

2.2.1.2 Spontaneous nasalization
Bloch (1920, 1965), Turner (1921) and Grierson (1922), studying
Indo-Aryan languages, have called attention to what they call
'spontaneous nasalization', i.e. the development of distinctive
nasalization on vowels in words that never had any lexical nasal
consonant (the usual source of nasal vowels). One type of
segment that reappears in many of their examples is one
characterized by high airflow, e.g. any voiceless fricative,
especially [h], aspirated stops and affricates (Ohala 1983a); see
(2).

(2) Examples of spontaneous nasalization (from Grierson 1922).

Sanskrit	Prakrit	Old Hindi	Modern Hindi	Bengali	Translation
pakṣ	pakkha	pākh	paŋkhā		a side
akṣi	akkhi-		ā̃kh		eye
uččaka-	uččaa-		ū̃čā	uɲča	high
satya-	sačča-	sã̄č			truth
sarpa-	sappa-		sã̄p		snake

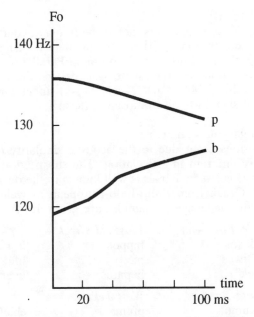

FIGURE 9.1 Average fundamental frequency values (in Hz) of vowels following English stops; data from five speakers. The curves labelled 'p' and 'b' represent the values associated with all voiceless and voiced stops, respectively, regardless of place of articulation. (From Hombert, Ohala & Ewan 1979.)

The same phenomenon exists in other languages; see Ohala (1975); Matisoff (1975). Ohala and Amador (1981, summarized in Ohala 1983a) studying both American English and Mexican Spanish, found that high airflow segments like voiceless fricatives have a greater-than-normal glottal opening which is partially assimilated by adjacent vowels which, in turn, creates an acoustic effect which mimics nasalization. Such pseudo-nasalization, they argued, is liable to be misinterpreted by listeners as actual nasalization and reproduced by them as such.

2.2.2 Variation in the acoustic-auditory domain
The preceding examples described variation found in the domain of speech production and in the conversion of articulation into sound. Variation has also been found in the perceptual domain.

2.2.2.1   [θ] and [f]
Sweet (1874: 8), among others, noted the frequent confusion and
consequent substitution of [f] for [θ] in dialectal English, e.g.
[θɪŋ] ~ [fɪŋ] 'thing'; [θɹu] ~ [fɹu] 'through'. Parallel to this is the
frequent confusion of the same sounds in the consonant
confusion study of Miller and Nicely (1955) under virtually all
conditions of signal-to-noise ratio and filtering.

2.2.2.2   Labial velars and labials
Some confusions occur due to the acoustic similarity of sounds
that are very different in articulation. The substitution of labial
(or labialized) velars by labials is well known in the development
of Classical Greek from Proto-Indo-European as well as many
other unrelated languages. Examples are given in (3)

(3.a) *Indo-European*   > *Classical Greek*
       *ekwōs   hippos   'horse'
       *gʷiwos   bios   'life'
       *yekʷr̥   hepatos   'liver'

(3.b) *Proto-Bantu*   > *West Teke*
       *-kumu   pfuma   'chief'
       Proto-Yuman   > *Yuma*
       *imalikʷi   malʸpu   'navel'
       Proto-Muskogean   > *Choctaw*
       *kʷihi   bihi   'mulberry'
       *uNkʷi   umbi   'pawpaw'
       Sungkhla (free variants)
       \khwai   \fai   'fire'
       /khon   /fon   'rain'
       Proto-Zapotec   > *Isthmus Zapotec*
       *kkʷa-   pa   'where'

Again, there are striking phonetic parallels. Durand (1955)
commented on the acoustic similarity of these two classes of
sounds. Winitz et al. (1972), studying listeners' identifications of
CV syllables (formed from the set C = [p t k], V = [i a u]), heard
under a variety of conditions, found that confusions between the
syllables [ku] and [pu] (where one can assume that the [k] was
phonetically labialized before the rounded [u]) were among the
highest of any of the CVs included.

2.2.2.3   Vowel quality shifts under nasalization
Although there are some complexities and puzzles still to be
solved in the case of the phonetic and perceptual consequences of

adding nasalization to vowels, it is fairly well established that distinctively (i.e. non-contextually) nasalized vowels tend to be lower than their corresponding oral counterparts or the oral vowels from which they sprang (Beddor 1983). French presents an extreme case of this as evidenced by the cognate pairs in (4).[3]

(4) Oral   Nasal
     linoleum [linoleym] 'linoleum'   lin [lɛ̃] 'flax'
     brune [bʁyn] 'brunette'   brun [bʁœ̃] 'brown'

Paralleling this is the finding by House and Stevens (1956) (with an important qualification added by House 1957) and supported by data presented by Fujimura and Lindqvist (1971) and Beddor et al. (1986)) that coupling the oral and nasal resonators leads to an elevation of the first formant [F1] in non-low vowels (which means a lowering of perceived vowel height). Wright (1986) and Beddor et al. (1986) confirmed that perceptually non-contextually nasalized vowels sound lower than their articulatorily equivalent oral counterparts.

3 The implications of parallels between variation in the synchronic phonetic and the diachronic domains

3.1 Synchronic variation = sound change?
I reviewed above just a few examples out of many possible[4] that demonstrate the parallels to be found between sound change, on the one hand, and synchronic phonetic variation, both in the production and in the acoustic-auditory domains, on the other. Does this mean that the phonetic variation is sound change? The answer to this question is somewhat complex.

3.1.1 Variation in perception may equal 'mini' sound change
In the case of the variation in perception, caused by the confusion of acoustically similar (but sometimes articulatorily different) speech sounds, such variation is potentially sound change. At least, we could refer to this as a 'mini sound change' – one that takes place in the interaction between a single speaker and a single hearer. All that would be necessary for such mini sound changes to become the 'maxi' sound changes that get recorded in the historical grammars of languages would be that some of the subjects in the Miller and Nicely (1955) or the Winitz et al. (1972) studies leave the laboratory and to start pronouncing the name of the thing that had been presented to them in the laboratory as [θa] or [ku] as [fa] and [pu], respectively, and then for other speakers to copy their pronunciation. Anecdotal

evidence suggests that the kind of misperceptions that these researchers found in the laboratory setting go on all the time in ordinary exchanges between speakers and hearers. What keeps the vast majority of these from leading to maxi sound changes are factors such as the following:

a) Pronunciation norms are redundantly represented in all speakers in the given language community. A listener who misapprehends a word spoken by one speaker has many opportunities to hear the word spoken by others and presumably would not be likely to mishear in all cases. In addition, others' puzzled reactions or amusement can alert a speaker to his odd pronunciation. In some cultures, orthography provides yet another guide to pronunciation.

b) It is probably a rare thing for one speaker's innovative pronunciation to spread via imitation to sizable numbers of other speakers such that it becomes a persistent and characteristic feature of a well-defined dialect community.

Nevertheless, some small fraction of misapprehensions of pronunciation can and do go uncorrected and can spread to other speakers and thus give rise to maxi sound changes. The essential aspect of misperceptions which make them equivalent to sound changes is that they constitute a *change of norms*: the listener forms a phonological norm that differs from that intended by the speaker.

3.1.2 Variation in production does not automatically equal sound change

As for variation in speech production, e.g. the FO differences on vowels after voiced and voiceless consonants, these do *not* by themselves constitute sound change precisely because they do not necessarily involve a change in pronunciation norm. There are several reasons for asserting this.

First, it is not clear that speakers intend primarily to produce these effects; rather they are consequences of other effects which the speaker intends. Of course, it is difficult to get an accurate picture of the speaker's intentions in speech production and, accordingly, opinions differ on this point (cf. Stevens et al. 1986; Stevens and Keyser 1989) but there is some evidence that at least some of the variation seen in the speech signal can occur without involving a corresponding modification in the speaker's underlying pronunciation target (Ohala 1981; Browman and Goldstein 1990).

Secondly, most of the types of variation have been found to

occur widely in virtually all languages studied instrumentally. Phonetic features that are universal are likely to be physically caused and not maintained by culturally established templates.

Thirdly, in many of these cases it is possible to explain the occurrence of such variations by reference to physical phonetic theories. For example, Zue (1976) found that the centre frequency and the amplitude of noise at stop burst for [g] tends to be higher for front vowels than back vowels. This is explicable from basic acoustic and aerodynamic principles (Fant 1960; Stevens 1971). Other examples could be given, for example, the tendency for velars to devoice (Ohala 1983b, 1991).

Fourthly, and perhaps most importantly, there is evidence that listeners can normalize predictable variation: one of the principal acoustic differences between /s/ and /ʃ/ is the lower centre frequency of the latter. But the centre frequency can also vary due to contextual influences, for example, anticipatory assimilation of lip-rounding from a following rounded vowel (which serves to lower the frequency). Mann and Repp (1980) found that a synthetic fricative that would be identified as /ʃ/ before a following /ɑ/ is identified as [s] when the following vowel is [u]. Listeners presumably expect the lowering of the centre frequency of an /s/ before rounded vowels like /u/ due to anticipatory assimilation. Thus, when the sibilant has a lower centre frequency and the following vowel is heard as round, they apparently factor out the expected low frequency and 'reconstruct' a higher centre frequency characteristic of /s/. Similarly, Kawasaki (1986) presented evidence that listeners can factor out some of the nasalization on vowels when there is a nasal consonant nearby. Beddor et al. (1986) demonstrated that listeners can factor out the predictable lowering effects of nasalization on vowel quality when a nasal consonant is immediately adjacent to the vowel. Another way of describing such behaviour is to say that listeners *normalize* or *correct* the speech signal in order to arrive at the pronunciation intended by the speaker minus any added contextual perturbations. In the following discussion I will use the term 'correction' to describe this process of perceptual normalization.

Such perceptual correction of the speech signal by listeners serves to *prevent* sound change, that is, to prevent the change of pronunciation norms between speaker and listener even though the speech signal exhibits an incredible amount of variation. Thus, finding variation in speech production that parallels diachronic variation does not permit us to say that such synchronic variation *is* sound change.

3.2 The ubiquity of perceptual correction

Perceptual correction of a distorted, variable stimulus is not unique to speech and, in fact, is well known in other sensory modalities. Under the topic of 'perceptual constancies' it has been posited and studied extensively in the visual domain (Rock 1983). How is it that we are able to extract a constant percept of scenes that we view in spite of their showing variations in size, colour, shape, and so on, depending on the conditions under which they are seen? A person seen from a distance subtends a small angle in the visual field for simple physical reasons that are easily explained by geometry. Thus a person seen from a distance might appear physically to be as large as one's thumb. But the true size of the person can be reconstructed if the viewer can exploit any of a number of cues that the person is far away, e.g., parallax cues, interposition of other closer objects, perspective (convergence of the parallel lines), the texture of the scene (the degree of detail visible), etc.

In fact, as regards correction of the speech signal, there is evidence that listeners are able to do it in the case of distortions imposed by the channel over which it is transmitted, for example, with certain frequency bands filtered out or with noise super-imposed (Ohala and Shriberg 1990; Shriberg and Ohala 1991; these are discussed below). Much the same ability must underlie how we learn to understand different dialects or foreign accents of languages we know.

3.3 How variation in production can lead to sound change: hypo-correction

If the variation observed in the speech production domain does not constitute sound change, then what are we to make of the parallels between such variation and the diachronic variation? The answer is simple: if the listener fails to correct the perturbations in the speech signal, then they will be taken at face value and will form part of his conception of its pronunciation. Via such 'hypo-correction', as I call it, the phonetic perturba-tions, originally just fortuitous results of the speech production process, become part of the pronunciation norm. This, presum-ably, is what is meant by the term 'phonologization'.

Why would a listener fail to correct a perturbed speech signal? First, it must be emphasized again that such failure represents a very small fraction of all the interactions between speaker and listener. That said, it is possible to speculate about several possible situations where it might happen. First, the listener may not have the experience to enable him to do such correction.

Children in the process of acquiring the phonology of their language are in this position as are adult second-language learners. A propos of this, it is interesting to note that in linguists' phonological descriptions of languages, one frequently finds longer lists of allophones of phonemes when the linguist is *not* a native speaker of the language as opposed to when he is. Could it be that the non-native speaker linguist notices more variation because he lacks the experience the native speaker has which allows the perceptual factoring out of predictable variation?

A second reason for hypo-correction is that a listener may, for various reasons, fail to perceive or to attend to the phonological environment which causes, or as phonologists usually put it, 'conditions' the variation. Thus it is frequently the case that sound changes which are the result of assimilations and other effects assignable to the domain of speech production take place with the simultaneous loss of the conditioning environment, as in (1), where the tonal development was accompanied by loss of the voicing distinction. Many (but certainly not all) of the most common sound changes have this feature, e.g. the development of distinctive nasal vowels is generally correlated with the loss of the nasal consonant which conditioned the change from oral to nasal in the vowel. This is an important aspect of many hypo-corrective sound changes and more will be made of this.

We may also speculate that the farther away the conditioning environment is from the conditioned change – that is, the greater the temporal gap between cause and effect – the more difficult will it be for the listener to be able to establish the causal link between the two and use this link as the basis for correction.

3.4 Shorthand notation of sound changes

It may be helpful to summarize some of the essential points of sound change by hypo-correction using the kind of informal shorthand representations phonologists have become used to. The development of distinctively nasal vowels from loss of a post-vocalic nasal consonant has usually been represented as in (5).

(5) $VN > \tilde{V}$

Alternatively, this has sometimes been broken down into two stages, as in (6).

(6.a) $V > \tilde{V} \, / \,$ ___ N

(6.b) $N > \emptyset \, / \,$ ___ $\tilde{V}$

But stage (6.b) is frequently unattested and is assumed simply because the process in (6.a) failed to dispose of the N.

According to the mechanism I propose this should be represented as in (7).

(7)   Time 1   Time 2

(7.a)   /VN/ > [ṼN]   (7.c)   /VN/ > [Ṽ(N)]

(7.b)   [ṼN] > /VN/   (7.d)   [Ṽ] > /Ṽ/

Here, as usual, forms between slashes represent the intended pronunciation; those between square brackets, the phonetic form. At Time 1 before any change has occurred, according to (7.a), an intended sequence of a /VN/ is produced with the vowel phonetically nasalized. This is not a rule of grammar; it is a constant, timeless process that owes its existence to the physical constraints of the vocal tract. At this time, according to (7.b), listeners are able to take the [ṼN] sequence and reconstruct the intended /VN/ sequence. (7.b) is a rule of grammar; it is what I have been calling 'correction'. At Time 2, which represents the change itself, the process in (7.a) also occurs as (7.c) with the modification that the final N is weakly implemented such that it is difficult to detect or to associate with the preceding [Ṽ] (here the conventional notations do not serve us well). Like (7.a), (7.c) is also not a rule of grammar. (7.d) represents the action of the listener who detects only [Ṽ] and thus can only reconstruct /Ṽ/ as the intended pronunciation.

3.5   Advantages of viewing certain sound changes as hypo-correction

An advantage of (7) is that it indicates that the end product, the Ṽ, was present phonetically before the change. In fact, for all sound changes of the type called hypo-correction it is the case that the 'after' state is present in an incipient form in the 'before' state and can be studied in any present-day human language having the appropriate structure.[5] The only difference is that in the before state listeners effectively discount the predictable variations of sounds. Nevertheless, (7) is still no proper substitute for the full story which must derive (7.a,c) from first principles and demonstrate (7.b,d) via perception tests. The above-cited work by Kawasaki and by Beddor et al. (1986) constitute the required perceptual demonstration.

According to generative phonology sound change occurs because of a change in the grammar. In contrast, in the account I give, the only type of grammatical rule that changes anything, e.g. (7.b), has the function of preserving a pronunciation norm, not changing it. The change itself is the result of an unintended failure of the perceptual process.

One of the most important aspects of this account of sound changes due to hypo-correction is that it explains in a very simple way why these 'natural' sound changes parallel the kind of variation found in ordinary speech production. The parallels can be found in the segments affected, the conditioning environments, and the direction of the variation. Even so it does not equate sound change with synchronic variation; a mini sound change emerges from them only when a listener fails to normalize or correct the variation.

But there is an important class of sound changes that is not 'natural': changes in this class may involve similar segments and conditioning environments to those discussed above but the direction of change is the reverse. These are dissimilative sound changes, and are discussed in the next section.

4 Dissimilation

4.1 Dissimilation is 'correction' erroneously implemented

Dissimilation is defined as the loss or change of one or more features, including whole segments, when the same feature is distinctive at another site within a word. It can be manifested in several ways: as dissimilation on adjacent segments (called 'contact dissimilation' here), dissimilation involving non-adjacent segments (called 'distant dissimilation'), the prevention of an otherwise regular sound change that would have resulted in a sequence of sounds subject to dissimilation ('preventative dissimilation'), and as a constraint against the co-occurrence of similar segments. Examples of dissimilation are given in (8).

(8.a) *Proto-Indo-European* > *Sanskrit*
    bend̤   band̤   'blind'
    Proto-Quichean > *Tzutujil*
    k'aq   k'ʲaq   'flea'
    Ancient Chinese > *Cantonese*
    pjam   pin   'diminish'
    Proto-Quechumaran > *Quechua*
    t'ant'a   t'anta   'bread'

(8.b) *Slavic*
    stoj + ā   > stojā   'stand'

(8.c) *Sanskrit*
    sarsrāṇa (for expected *sarṣrāṇa)

(8.d) *Yao*
    *C^w V   C
           [lab]

    English
    * #C w − ;   * #C   l −
    [lab]   [stop]
                                      [apical]

    Arabic
    * C   V C
    [phar]   [phar]

These are 'unnatural' sound changes in the sense that, first, we are unable to invoke any principles of speech production that would predict changes in this direction. In fact, in the case of the backing of front [a] to back [ɑ] in (8.b) above, we would predict the opposite. Even if we move further 'upstream' and attempt to invoke putative cognitive principles of speech production, we are unable to make a good case (see below and Ohala 1991). Meringer and Mayer (1895) conducted their classic study of speech errors in order to determine whether they were the cause of dissimilative sound changes (Cutler 1982). They concluded that the types of variation were too different to be related to each other.

Secondly, this is not what we find in ordinary speech production. Broad and Fertig (1970) found the interactions between initial and final consonants in a CiC syllable to be small and what interactions there were, were positive, not negative or inhibitory (however, see Weismer 1979).

How can we account for sound changes which go in a direction that is the reverse of the 'natural' direction, that is, from what would be expected given speech production constraints? In fact, we have already discussed such a mechanism earlier: the listener's ability to undo or reverse the predictable perturbations found in speech. I propose that dissimilation arises due to the listener's mis-application of these corrective processes. I call this 'hyper-correction'.

For example, considering the case of Latin /kwiŋkwē/ > */kiŋkwē/ (and subsequently to Italian /tʃiŋkwe/, etc.) where initially lip rounding existed distinctively at two sites in the word. In addition, the lip rounding no doubt was evident on the intervening vowel given that it was flanked by lip-rounded segments; in fact, non-distinctive lip rounding was probably often present even on vowels just followed by /kw/ (according the Latin grammarians; see Devine and Stephens 1977: 37–42). A listener then, could have been confused as to whether the lip rounding detected at the beginning of this word was distinctive or a non-distinctive perturbation caused by the lip rounding on the second syllable. Some listeners apparently guessed wrong.

Perceptual confusions such as those posited as the basis of dissimilation are not unique to speech. This is, in essence, the same mechanism underlying camouflage, that is, hiding some-thing by making it similar to its surroundings. The white arctic hare surrounded by white snow is 'hidden' from predators by being visually indistinguishable from the snow. The distinctive labialization on the initial stop of /kwiŋkwē/ is 'hidden' by being adjacent to and thus equated with labialization attributable to the second stop. In both cases the camouflaged thing can be *physically* detected by viewers/hearers but the percept – the *cognitive representation* of the scene/word formed by them – lacks the hidden element.

4.2 Supporting evidence for analysis of dissimilation as hyper-correction

4.2.1 *Which features do and do not dissimilate*

(a)   Dissimilation restricted to 'stretched out' features

A logical consequence of this account of dissimilation is that it should only involve features which manifest themselves over fairly long temporal intervals, that is, which can encroach on adjacent segments and thus create an ambiguity as to where the feature is distinctive and where fortuitous. Examples of such 'stretched out' features are labialization, aspiration, retroflexion, pharyngealization, the voice quality called 'glottalization',[6] and place of articulation. It would not involve features such as 'stop', 'affricate' which do not stretch over long temporal intervals. In general, this prediction is borne out.

This prediction regarding the features that should and the features that should not be subject to dissimilation needs further refinement as to what is meant by the term 'feature'. This word is sometimes used to mean 'classificatory label', in which case the term may be completely devoid of phonetic substance, e.g. FORTIS, LENIS, or partially lacking in phonetic substance, as is the case sometimes with the feature VOICE. 'Feature' is also used variously to refer to articulatory events, e.g. NASAL, LATERAL, or to acoustic properties, e.g. STRIDENT, GRAVE. What matters in the present case are the *acoustic-auditory cues* which serve to differentiate linguistic signals. There are typically multiple cues differentiating what are called 'features'. For example, the cues to the feature NASAL (in the case of consonants) include the abrupt discontinuity in amplitude

and spectrum with respect to adjacent vowels or other sonorants
and the increased bandwidth of the formants of adjacent vowels
(i.e. vowel nasalization). The first of these cues manifests itself
rapidly, within some 20 to 30 msec.; the second cue manifests
itself over at least 50 msec, sometimes longer. The major cues to
features like LABIALIZED (lowered resonances and overall
amplitude) occur over a time-span that may be 100 msec or more.
Cues then may be characterized according to the time window
which they require to be heard. This, in turn, determines the
extent to which they overlap with cues for adjacent segments. In
general, manner of articulation, e.g. stop vs. fricative vs. nasal
(consonant), tend to be conveyed primarily by fast cues whereas
so-called secondary articulations and modifications, e.g. labialization, retroflexion, velarization, pharyngealization, glottalization,
aspiration, tend to be cued by slow cues. Some of the place of
articulation cues are intermediate on this continuum: the formant
transitions cuing place may range from 30 to 80 msec or more
(Lehiste and Peterson 1961; Kewley-Port 1982). The modified
prediction regarding the phonetic elements subject to dissimilation is, then: features requiring a long time window for their
perception are more likely to be subject to dissimilation than are
those requiring short time windows. In the case of segments like
nasal consonants which have some rapid cues and some slow
cues, it will depend on which of these cues dominate the percept.
(See Massaro and Oden 1980 and Abramson and Lisker 1985 for
studies which attempt to explore the interaction of various cues.)
In addition, the relative salience of various cues may differ from
one language to the next. How various cues function in speech is
ultimately an empirical question but since few studies on this
topic have been carried out, the best I can do at present is to
argue for the plausibility of my claims.

It seems clear that at the two extremes of the time-window
continuum, stops and affricates seem not to be subject to
dissimilation whereas secondary articulations like labialization
and retroflexion are. But there are interesting apparent counter-
examples.

(b) Dissimilation of laterals
According to phonetic arguments given above, laterals would
seem to be segments that should not dissimilate since laterality
cannot easily spread to adjacent segments; nevertheless, [l]s are
subject to dissimilation in Latin as in (9).

(9) Latin dissimilation of /l/ in stems containing /l/

liber-alis   BUT   famili-aris

mort-alis   BUT   popul-aris

But laterals do have very long transitions of Formants 2 and 3 (Lehiste 1964; ch. 2; Javkin 1979: 38ff.) and these are probably prominent cues. In fact, there are well-known sound changes where /l/'s become just glides, palatal or labial velar, depending on whether the laterals themselves were originally palatalized or velarized (von Essen 1964); see (10).

(10)   Examples of laterals changing to glides.

Late Latin pleno-   >   Italian   pjeno

Late Latin alterum >   French   autre

Furthermore, O'Connor et al. (1957) (and several studies since) demonstrated that /l/'s and the North American English /r/ can be synthesized as endpoints of a continuum which involves only variations of Formant 3, the lateral having high F3 and /r/, low. Thus it seems that laterals do have cues that require a long time-window for their perception and so their involvement in dissimilation is not puzzling. In addition, the study of O'Connor et al. (1957) suggests why /l/ generally dissimilates to /r/ rather than some other segment.

(c)   Dissimilation of voicing?

The feature [voice] would seem to be a prime candidate for dissimilation since it has some reputation as a feature that spreads to adjacent segments (especially intervocalically) and there are a number of cases reported as voicing dissimilation: the dissimilation of the voicing of intervocalic fricatives in Gothic (Thurneysen's Law), the dissimilation of voicing in stops in Sakuma (Bantu), and the well-known co-occurrence constraint against successive voiced stops in Proto-Indo-European roots. However all these cases have been reanalysed – in some cases not without controversy – in a way which casts them as other than voicing dissimilation (Flickinger 1981; Bennett 1967; Hopper 1973; Gamkrelidze and Ivanov 1973). Furthermore, based on my understanding of the principal cues for voicing, I would predict that [voice] should not be subject to dissimilation. Although one might conclude that there are 'prosodic' or long time-window cues to voicing from such often-encountered claims of the sort 'preceding vowel duration is a cue to consonant voicing', in fact there is no evidence supporting such claims. What one has instead is evidence that vowel duration is sufficient to cue

THE PHONETICS OF SOUND CHANGE

contrasts that may *also* be cued (or were *once* cued) by consonantal voicing. There is no evidence that a listener judges a voiceless consonant as physically voiced after a long vowel.[7] Rather, the primary cue to a segment being voiced is the generally robust cue of periodic pulsation in the lower frequencies. This cue operates in a relatively short time-window and does not manifest itself by colouration of adjacent segments; therefore it should not be susceptible to dissimilation. This matter is hardly settled but I would predict that the eventual resolution of the putative cases of voicing dissimilation cited above would show that [VOICE] was not involved.

(d)   Robust vs. non-robust cues in creating languages' segment
      inventories
The characterization of cues by the amount of time needed to perceive them was inspired by Stevens' (1980) differentiation of features into robust, short ones and less robust, long ones. (The only modification I have made is to focus not on phonological features per se but the acoustic-auditory cues which signal them.) He pointed out that when constructing their segment inventory, languages generally use up the robust features first before exploiting the less robust ones. Thus only languages with very large consonant inventories make use of labialization, retroflexion, pharyngealization, glottalization, etc., and only languages with a relatively large vowel inventory make use of nasalization or front-rounding and back-unrounding. It seems evident that those sound types which appear only in large segment inventories are approximately the same ones which are most subject to dissimilation. Furthermore, a dissimilated segment, that is, the result of dissimilation, is generally one from the 'robust' class rather than the original less robust set. The link between the phenomena of segment inventory constraints and those of dissimilation is the long time interval needed for the perception of the acoustic modulations which cue certain features: this makes them auditorily less salient and makes them 'run into each other' when they appear on nearby segments thus leading to camouflage.

   Having made the prediction in 4.2.1.1 above, I have tried to marshal some of the available evidence in support of it and to account for apparent counterexamples. Of course, other counter-examples exist (Ohala 1981). It is apparent that these (as well as the cases which are apparently consistent with the prediction) have to be examined carefully. Nothing should be accepted at face value. The outcome of conflict between the prediction and the counter-examples will be one of the following:

(a) the prediction will be abandoned or modified:
  (i) the prediction has so many counter-examples that it has to be abandoned;
  (ii) the general prediction is correct but the specifics as to which cues make a segment subject to dissimilation requires modification;
  (iii) dissimilation arises due to different mechanisms; the prediction only covers one of these.
(b) the counterexamples can be reanalysed in a way that eliminates their conflict with the prediction.
  (i) they may not be cases of dissimilation;
  (ii) they may not involve the feature originally proposed.

4.2.2 Hyper- and hypo-correction have different constraints on conditioning environment

As was discussed above, a common although not invariable characteristic of sound changes due to hypo-correction is that the conditioning environment is lost at the same time as the conditioned change occurs. In fact, failure to detect the conditioning environment is a direct cause of the listener failing to implement correction of a contextually caused perturbation and therefore taking it at face value. In contrast, from the account just given it would be predicted that in sound changes due to hyper-correction the conditioning environment may *not* be lost at the same time as the conditioned change. Hyper-correction involves the listener blaming (so to speak) the conditioning environment for an imagined perturbation; obviously, then, the conditioning environment must be detected. (11) gives examples of a hypothetical version of Grassmann's Law in Sanskrit that should not occur.

(11) bhandh > ban (where the 'dh' drops just when the 'bh' is dissimilated)

I am unaware of any exceptions to this prediction.

4.2.3 Hyper-corrective sound changes do not result in 'new' segments

Although sound changes due to hypo-correction may often result in the introduction of new segments, for example nasalized vowels from loss of a post-vocalic nasal consonant, sound changes caused by hyper-correction apparently do not. The end product of dissimilation seems to be a segment drawn from the same set

that the language had before the sound change. This behaviour
follows from dissimilation being the result of the listener applying
normalization processes to the speech signal: normalization
involves recovering a (presumed) standard sound from a signal
that differs in some way from the standard.

4.2.4 Dissimilation-at-a-distance blocked in certain environments
In Tzutujil the dissimilation of back velars fails to occur if the
intervening vowel is [o]; see (12, from Campbell 1977).

(12)	Proto-Quichean	Tzutujil	Translation
	ke:x	kʲe:x	'horse'
	k'aq	k'ʲaq	'flea'
	BUT:		
	koxl	kox	'cougar'
	k'ox	k'o:x	'mask'

This otherwise puzzling behaviour makes sense if we take into
account the phonetic manifestation of the back velar perturbation
on vowels and the inherent properties of back rounded vowels
like [o]. Back velars cause a lowering of the F_2 of adjacent
vowels (Klatt and Stevens 1969; Ghazeli 1977). Back rounded
vowels, especially [o] and [ɔ] have the lowest possible F_2 of all
vowels. Apparently, then, dissimilation-at-a-distance is blocked if
the intervening segments are *saturated* in the acoustic property
(in this case low F_2) that would otherwise manifest the
consonantal perturbation. Not being able to detect any consonantal colouring of the vowel, the listener has no basis to imagine
that such a perturbation migrated to distant sites in the word.
(This account assumes, of course, that there are other cues to the
feature BACK-VELAR than the lowered F_2 transitions, otherwise the [o] itself might cause dissimilation of these segments.
Presumably the spectrum of the stop burst would be sufficient to
cue the BACK-VELAR feature even in the absence of distinctive
modulations of the F_2 transitions.)
   I am unable to say how generally this 'saturation' phenomenon
blocks dissimilation-at-a-distance but if found more widely it
offers support to the account of dissimilation offered here.

*4.2.5 Experimental evidence of the perceptual basis for hypo-
        correction and hyper-correction*
Perhaps the most persuasive support that can be given for the
above account of sound change in terms of hypo- and hyper-
correction is experimental results. I cited above experimental
evidence for listeners' ability to 'correct' the speech signal. Many

of the same experiments implicitly duplicate the phenomenon of hypo-correction, for example Kawasaski's result that listeners judge a vowel from a syllable like [mɪm] to be more nasal when the flanking nasal consonants are removed (than when they are present) and Beddor et al.'s (1986) result that listeners hear more [æ] vowels on a [ɛ]–[æ] continuum when they are nasalized than when they are either oral or when the nasal vowels are followed immediately by a nasal consonant. But this latter study also found evidence for hyper-correction: the nasal vowels that were successfully normalized or corrected back to their equivalent oral quality when followed by a nasal consonant were over corrected, i.e., hyper-corrected, when the degree of nasalization was slight.

Ohala and Shriberg (1990) demonstrated hyper-correction in a vowel confusion study. As revealed in the traditional vowel chart where height correlates inversely with F1 and frontness with F2, front and back vowels of equivalent height have similar F1 values but are differentiated by F2. When short context-independent vowels are low-pass filtered in a way to eliminate F2, listeners naturally make many errors where front vowels are confused with back vowels, whereas the reverse confusion is rare. However, when these filtered vowels are embedded in a sentence context which has also been subjected to the same filtering, two things result: first, the overall level of errors decreases significantly (meaning that 'correction' takes place) and, secondly, there is a disproportionate increase in the number of back vowels confused with front (indicating hyper-correction). Taking their cue from the filtered sentence which was obviously missing acoustic energy at the higher frequencies, the listeners in effect 'added' high frequency energy to a few tokens of the back vowels and thus made front vowels of them. Although the particular pattern of perceptual errors studied in this case does not show close parallels to any known sound change (since low-pass filtering is not a common distortion of speech under normal conditions), it does show that listeners may hyper-correct the speech signal.

5 Overview

5.1 What can happen between a speaker and hearer: a basic taxonomy

To sum up the preceding two sections (3 and 4), there are four outcomes from an exchange between speaker and listener where the signal may be potentially ambiguous regarding the speaker's intended pronunciation.

A. Correction
B. Confusion of Acoustically Similar Sounds
C. Hypo-correction
D. Hyper-correction

In A there is no sound change; the listener successfully recovers the speaker's intended pronunciation from the less-than-perfect signal. B, C, and D all result in sound change – B and C due to failure to correct an ambiguous signal and D due to 'correcting' a signal that didn't require it. B could be included under C; the only basis for differentiating B from C is whether the disambiguating cues that could have been used by the listener (but were not) are temporally co-terminous with the ambiguous part or whether they are not, respectively. For example, at least one of the cues differentiating the stops in the syllables /gi/ and /di/ is a sharp peak in burst spectrum around 3 KHz; in other respects the spectra are quite similar (Ohala 1985b). On the other hand, in the case of the confusion of high vowels with lower vowels when nasalized, one disambiguating cue is the presence of an adjacent nasal consonant. Many, perhaps most, sound contrasts have both temporally simultaneous and temporally sequential cues which differentiate them from other sounds. Collapsing B and C yields the three categories

A'. Correction
B'. Hypo-correction
C'. Hyper-correction

5.2 Constraints on the explanation of the mechanism of sound changes

I have attempted to present a general paradigm for explaining how certain sound changes start. But a casual reading of this presentation may give the impression that it is unconstrained, that hypo-correction and hyper-correction can be played like 'wild cards' whenever needed: finding a sound change where A > B one labels it hypo-correction whereas given another where B > A, one simply labels it hyper-correction. If this were true the paradigm would offer no advance over the kind of explanation for sound changes where paradigmatic pressures, syntagmatic pressures, symmetry, asymmetry, simplicity, etc. – and these from any level: phonological, morphological, lexical, syntactic, and semantic, socio-pragmatic – can all be invoked with little or no independent justification.

It is inevitably true that the passage of time does result in loss of information – a rise in entropy – that makes reconstruction of past events ambiguous. Detective stories often feature events with an ambiguous history: the single shoe print in the sandy beach – did it happen due to someone stepping there or was the shoe in place for a long time while the surf caused the sand to rise around it and then the shoe removed? But after acknowledging the existence of ambiguities in reconstructing the past, there are still cases where some of the ambiguities can be resolved and it is these constraints on invoking hypo- and hyper-correction as a source of sound change that I review now.

5.2.1 Constraints on using hypo- and hyper-correction in historical reconstruction

First, one of the overriding constraints is that sound changes due to hypo-correction are those which are consistent with known properties of the speech production mechanism. That is, in an ideal case one would have empirically-based theories or models of speech production, for example anatomical (Harshman et al. 1977), aerodynamic (Rothenberg 1968; Stevens 1971; Ohala 1976; Muller and Brown 1980), the mapping from vocal tract shape to sound (Fant 1960; Carré and Mrayati 1990), and one could refer to these to see how the speech output is constrained. For example, an aerodynamic model would indicate that the maintenance of voicing on back-articulated stops like velars and uvulars would require special gestures; maintaining voicing on *any* stop longer than some 65 msec would require special gestures. Lacking these special gestures, devoicing is likely to occur (Ohala 1976, 1983b; Ohala and Riordan 1979; Westbury 1979). Even in the absence of a comprehensive model of speech production, we may obtain generally reliable information on natural tendencies of speech production by inductive means, that is, by surveying phonetic behaviour in several diverse languages. For example, cross-language studies suggest that vowels are generally longer before fricatives than corresponding stops (Peterson and Lehiste 1960; Delattre 1962) but to my knowledge this pattern has not yet been explained by reference to known properties of the speech production mechanism. Sound changes attributed to hypo-correction, then, would involve listeners copying at face value those details of speech that originally owe their existence to the influence of physical phonetic properties of the speech production system. It must be allowed, however, that after a sound change has occurred – that is, the listener mis-interprets the function of these phonetic details – the shape of these phonetic events and features may be different, perhaps exaggerated *vis-à-vis* their original state. Thus, for example, distinctive vowel nasalization on vowels that used to stand next to nasal consonants may be considerably greater in amplitude and temporal extent than it was when the nasalization was a predictable phonetic feature (Solé and Ohala 1991).

Sound changes due to hyper-correction do not conform to known constraints of speech production. I will consider in detail one proposed counter-example to this principle.

5.2.2 Dissimilation of aspiration: a counter-example?

There has been speculation that Grassmann's Law in Sanskrit and Greek occurred due to the greater 'effort' required to make two aspirates in a row:

> An aspirate requires great effort . . . beginning from the abdominal muscles and ending in the muscles that open the glottis to its widest extent. It was in order to economize this muscular energy that the tenuis was substituted for the aspirate (Müller 1864: 179–80).

> Aspirated consonants are . . . costly in that they use considerable respiratory energy. A word with two such sounds is very costly, and an obvious candidate for pruning in any attempt to reduce the overall effort required for an utterance (Ladefoged 1984).

In fact, however, although 'ease of articulation' is often appealed to as a cause of sound change, no one has found a way to measure total energy expenditure in speech in order to establish convincingly its relevance. However, the amount of air under pressure in the lungs can easily be measured but it is not clear that aspirated consonants in speech push the respiratory system to its limits (Ohala 1990b). In general, speakers have a considerable respiratory reserve at their command and seldom exhaust it. Moreover, there are inherent aspects of the operation of Grassmann's Law (and similar processes in other languages; see de Reuse 1981; Turner 1923–5; Grammont 1933: 316; Jhā 1958: 142; Allen 1957) which are inconsistent with the hypothesis which invokes 'economy of articulatory energy': Energy cost is presumably cumulative from beginning to end of utterances and one would suppose that the urgency to reduce energy expenditure would be greater later in the utterance rather than earlier. Yet it is generally the first aspirate of two which is de-aspirated, not the second. Furthermore, if the energy expenditure mattered one would suppose that dissimilation of aspirates would occur any time two or more of them followed each other in speech not just when the two were found within the boundaries of a single word, as seems generally to be the case. (See pp. 263–4 for an account of why sound change generally takes place within word boundaries.) Finally, if articulatory energy figured in dissimilation it should not matter whether the two sounds involved are similar or not; any two energy-costly sounds, even those very different from each other would be likely to dissimilate. But again, this seems not to be what is found. There is therefore no evidence that Grassmann's Law is initiated by the speaker trying to conserve articulatory energy.

5.2.3 Further differences between hypo- and hyper-correction
As argued above, hypo- and hyper-correction can also be differentiated by the criteria in (13).

(13)

Criterion	Hypo-correction	Hyper-correction
Loss of conditioning environment?	Possible	No
Results in new segments?	Possible	No
Change from robust segment to less robust (by Stevens' criteria, Stevens et al. 1986)?	Possible	Usually no

5.2.4 The ultimate check: duplicating sound change in the lab
Perhaps the ultimate check on any hypothesis about the cause of a particular sound change is to test the hypothesis in the laboratory. If particular sound changes are posited to have a phonetic basis then one should be able to duplicate the conditions under which they occurred historically and find experimental subjects producing 'mini' sound changes that parallel them. It is because of the posited phonetic character of sound change that a laboratory study is possible: were the initiation caused by grammatical and cultural factors, this would be more difficult or perhaps impossible. I have referred above to several studies which, in effect, simulate sound change in the laboratory: some, like Kawasaki (1986) and Wright (1986) were designed with diachronic questions in mind, others, like Winitz et al. (1972) and Mann and Repp (1980), are relevant to diachronic issues even though that was not their original purpose.

6 Discussion

I have presented a general plan to explain the initiation of sound changes found in similar form in diverse languages. Certain

specific sound changes were discussed in detail and for some of
these experimental evidence was cited in support of the
hypothesized explanation. Obviously, much more research is
needed to flesh out this plan; however, I hope the outline given
here in addition to the experimental papers cited lend it
plausibility. This plan has the following potentially important
characteristics which differentiate it from other accounts of sound
change.

6.1   Sound change is non-teleological

There is a long tradition of teleological accounts of sound change
where speakers are claimed to choose (no doubt unconsciously) a
novel pronunication in order to optimize some aspect of
communication: to make speech easier to pronounce, easier for
the listener to hear, or easier to process by making the grammar
simpler (Müller 1864: 176ff.; Whitney 1867: 69ff.; King 1969: ch.
4). But the mechanism of sound change I propose above is non-
teleological: there is no intention by either the speaker or the
listener to change pronunciation. Indeed, the whole purpose of
the listener's interpretive activity is to attempt to deduce the
pronunciation intended by the speaker, i.e. to *preserve, not to
change*, the pronunciation norm. It is when the listener makes
mistakes in this interpretation that sound change can start.

As a corollary of this it must be emphasized that pronunciation
change itself is not included in the cognitive processes of either
speaker or hearer. That is, although distinctive vowels arose in
French from sequences of VN, the rule in (14) was not part of
either the speaker's or listener's grammar.

$$(14)\quad VN > \tilde{V}$$

Using the terms of the communication engineer, change occurs
not in the message source (the speaker's brain) nor the message
destination (the listener's brain) but in the transmission channel
between them. This includes the speech production system and
the listener's decoding system.

Sound change is thus like change in other domains: many of
the errors made by scribes copying manuscripts, errors students
make when taking notes on professors' lectures, errors in the
transcription of codons in DNA – all are unintended and the
change itself is not part of any rule set guiding or characterizing
the behaviour of the thing doing the copying.

In disposing of teleology from the domain of sound change we
free the study of diachronic phonology from many logical and
strategic impediments. For example, Lightner (1970) proposed,

in essence, that vowels become nasalized after loss of a post-vocalic nasal in order to preserve lexical distinctions. This is not an atypical claim. But there are profound logical inconsistencies in such a claim. First, lexical distinctions *are* commonly lost even though vowel nasalization occurs, for example French [blɑ̃] for both *blond* and *blanc*. Languages teem with homonymy and polysemy without suffering any apparent distress. Preservation of contrast, then, might as effectively be attributed to chance than to the speaker. Secondly, if speakers have such control over their pronunciation as to worry about maintaining the phonetic distinctions between words, then why did they allow the final nasal in such words to disappear in the first place? Why are they helpless in the face of one phonological change but masters of the situation in another?

Furthermore, reliance on teleological accounts of sound change is poor scientific strategy. For the same reason that the mature sciences such as physics and chemistry do not explain their phenomena (any more) by saying 'the gods willed it', linguists would be advised not to have the 'speaker's will' as the first explanation for language change. Not that the will of the gods and the will of speakers may not be the ultimate answer in both cases, but one should explore the less extravagant hypotheses before the more extravagant ones. This strategy has had a splendid payoff in every science that has embraced it. Explanation is, after all, reducing the unknown to the known, not to further unknown, uncertain, or unprovable entities.

None of this is meant to deny the role of teleology in other aspects of language change, especially its spread. I just deny the necessity of teleology in accounting for the pre-conditions or initiation of sound change.

6.2 Sound change is phonetic

This account of sound change also locates the mechanism centrally in the phonetic domain and primarily within the listener. The speaker is responsible for much variation in speech but normally most of this is discounted by the listener and so does not lead to sound change. It is only when the listener fails to normalize the variations in the speech signal or 'corrects' details that did not require correcting that sound change may take place. Thus the inescapable parallelism between diachronic and synchronic variation is accounted for.

Much of sound change can be viewed as a kind of parsing error by the listener (for the use of 'parsing' as it applies to speech perception, see Fowler 1986). In hypo-correction the listener fails to parse or associate a given perturbation or variation in the speech signal with the conditioning environment. In hyper-correction the listener erroneously parses a given event with another event.

Related to this is the fact that in the stream of speech the domain of change is overwhelmingly the word or possibly phrases which occur so often that they could also be said to be lexicalized. Why should this be so? Consider that if sound change were simply a matter of the speaker trying to make pronunciation easier there is no reason to limit change to the domain of the word. It could have been the case, as alluded to above, that in some language no more than one aspirated consonant could be produced per breath group such that the second and subsequent aspirated stops in an utterance would be de-aspirated. But generally this is not what is found. To be sure there are phonological changes that occur across word boundaries, for example French liaison, the palatalization of alveolars in English before a following palatal segment: *gas shortage* > [gæʃ·ɔɹɾəʤ], but even in the latter case there is evidence that such changes occur only with certain lexical items in certain collocations, not across-the-board (Solé and Ohala 1990). The dominance here of lexical units or lexicalized phrases is thus not contradicted. The principal role of the word in sound change follows from sound change being essentially a parsing error on the part of the listener. Accurate parsing of the different phonetic events in a word requires that the parts be separately identifiable. The optimal conditions for this occur when the parts are freely combinable and permutable, that is, when they appear inde-pendently of each other. A word is in essence a string of phonetic events frozen in a fixed order. It thus presents the maximum ambiguity to the listener of the separate parts (i.e. as intended by the speaker). This then is the domain where the listener is likely to make the most parsing errors.

Structuralist accounts of sound change (Jakobson 1978 [1931]) provide teleological scenarios that emphasize how a given change was motivated or shaped by its function within the whole system or structure of the language. I have given my views on teleology in sound change above. What about the influence of language structure on sound change? At best, I think this has been seriously exaggerated. While not denying the role of a given language's structure on sound change, especially in the spread of a given type of change to all structurally similar sounds, for example Grimm's Law where all the Indo-European voiceless stops became homorganic voiceless fricatives (but cf. Japanese where just the earlier /p/ changed to a fricative), I think a more readily apparent influence on sound change is the physical phonetic character of the sound involved. In Ohala (1979) I demonstrated how labial velar sounds, e.g. [k͡p, g͡b, w], show substantially similar phonological behaviour even though the languages involved have widely different phonological structure. Labial velars are by no means unique in this respect: similar demonstrations could be made for the behaviour of nasal consonants, nasal vowels, the interaction between voice and obstruents, segments designated [+flat] (Ohala 1975, 1983b, 1985a). A fundamental problem with structuralist accounts of sound change is that they are largely unconstrained: given a certain change, there are a great variety of structural 'pressures' that can be invoked to explain it, after the fact. One can appeal to (a) the language's segment inventory which itself has several degrees of freedom, place and manner contrasts, symmetry or asymmetry in certain contrasts, its size and relative 'density', (b) phonotactics, (c) the lexical or grammatical function of the contrasts, (d) the frequency of occurrence or functional load of the contrast, and so on. There are few rigorous attempts to show via broad cross-language surveys that in a significant number of cases languages showing a given structural trait undergo a sound change claimed to be a response to that trait. The accounts of sound change based on phonetics do not share this weakness.

6.3   Natural and 'unnatural' sound changes

The account given here provides a consistent, integrated account of sound changes generally regarded as opposite in character, 'natural' vs. 'unnatural', assimilative vs. dissimilative.[8] Central to this is the distinction between hypo-correction where the listener copies at face value the naturally occurring perturbations in the speech signal, thus producing natural, assimilative changes, vs. hyper-correction where the listener unnecessarily corrects the speech signal, thus giving rise to unnatural, dissimilative changes. (The terms 'natural' vs. 'unnatural' are perhaps unfortunate because, as I have tried to argue, dissimilation is natural in the sense that it can be understood by reference to universal perceptual strategies.)

6.4   Sound change in the laboratory

Studying sound change in the laboratory, as in work cited here, is not a novel undertaking. It has at least a century-old tradition (Rousselot 1891; Verner 1913; Stetson 1928; Grammont 1933; Haden 1938; Janson 1986). However, it has never been a 'mainstream' concern in historical phonology for a variety of reasons, not the least being the structuralist de-emphasis of the relevance of phonetic substance. The growing body of experimental literature addressing issues of phonetic and phonological universals and sound change should attract the attention it deserves based on its own merits, that is, what it can do for the historical linguist.

Language history, like history of any sort, and like astrophysics and much of geology deals with a subject matter that is inherently inaccessible to direct study. But conceptual breakthroughs for these latter two disciplines were achieved by adopting the so-called uniformitarian assumption, that is, that the composition of the stars and the earth and the forces and processes which shaped them throughout their remote history are in essence the same elements and forces that are present and detectable now. Studying sound change in the laboratory is also based on an assumption of uniformitarianism: variation in speech studied today parallels variation in centuries past. *In vitro* study of this variation substitutes for the physically impossible *in situ* diachronic study. However, laboratory study does not replace the detective work of the comparative method, it supplements and strengthens it by allowing a more rational choice of sound changes to be posited to convert reconstructed into attested forms.

6.5   Sound change is phonetically abrupt

Almost everyone speculating about sound change allows that it must be going on now as it always has and yet finds it difficult to detect. There is no report in history 'Today, everyone started to pronounce "meat" with an [i] vowel.' From this it follows that sound change must be gradual and taking place at a rate too slow to detect. This led to the supposition that the phonetic shift from one sound to another was progressing in steps too small for the ear to detect. An inherent aspect of the account presented here is that sound change is phonetically abrupt: the shift from one pronunciation to another is large enough to be detected. In most cases the 'before' and 'after' states could be contrasting sounds or sound sequences in some human language (though not necessarily in the language in which the change occurred). Gradualness, then, must lie in other domains: its spread from one speaker to another, from one speaking style to another, from one word to another, etc. There is substantial evidence that such gradual spread does occur (Wang 1977).

6.6 There will never be a 'complete' explanation of sound change

Lass (1980) finds that no account of sound change, including those based on phonetics, permits one to predict (or post-dict) its course by appeal to laws derived from first principles. Historical linguistics thus fails to be a *deductive nomological* discipline, which, according to him, is the goal of all mature scientific disciplines such as physics and chemistry. (See similar remarks by Dinnsen 1980.) The account of sound change given here also is not capable of predicting why a particular sound change takes place in a given language at a particular time and so, by Lass's criteria, this is not a scientific work. But, as outlined in detail in Ohala (1987), there is a fundamental error in Lass's reasoning.

Deductive nomological disciplines do not exist (with the possible exception of mathematics which deals with an artificial universe, not the real one). The problem is with the term 'nomological' or law-based. It implies perfect knowledge of the universe – something which is unattainable. However absolutely scientists may state their beliefs, the actual data on which they are based invariably shows some quantifiable discrepancies which are regarded as negligible. But the history of science suggests that what one age neglects the next uses to overthrow the 'laws' of the previous one. What we are left with in science is *deductive probabilistic* explanations of phenomena and this applies as well to physics and the account of sound change given here. Physics, the more mature science and with more control over the factors influencing events in its domain, makes more accurate probabilistic accounts than anything linguistics is capable of, but there is no qualitative difference between them.

The study of the phonetic bases of sound change is at the very threshold of being able to make deductive probabilistic predictions. Although there will always be more to learn, there is a good understanding in phonetics of the mechanisms for turning gestures and postures of the vocal organs into sound (Fant 1960; Lindblom and Sundberg 1971; Maeda 1990; Carré and Mrayati 1990). There is also some understanding of how physical constraints of this mechanism can give rise to variation (Ohala 1976, 1983b; Goldstein 1983; Westbury and Keating 1985). We have the beginnings of models which can predict auditory response, including rate of confusions, to stimuli based on their acoustic properties (Klein et al. 1970; Wright 1986; Bladon and Lindblom 1981; Lindblom 1986; Stevens 1989) – indeed, this latter measure is inherent in all template-based automatic speech recognition systems (Waibel and Lee 1990).

We are thus almost in a position to give probability estimates of which sounds will be confused based on deductions from first principles. We can already do this inductively (e.g. based on confusion matrices such as those published by Winitz et al. 1972). Thus we can predict that confusions of the sort [gi] > [di] will be more common than [gu] > [bu]. In the laboratory these predictions apply to the population of listeners hearing speech under specified conditions (usually with no higher-order linguistic redundancies present to influence their judgements). The predictions do not apply to individual listeners. No one can say why listener A identified the stimulus as X, not Y, but listener B identified Y correctly. Likewise, when extrapolating these predictions to languages, it will not be possible to say anything about individual languages or specific time periods in their history, simply that considering a large and representative sample of human languages, such-and-such confusion or change is more likely than another. But equally, it may be no more interesting or fruitful to try to identify the factors which initiated a change in a specific language at a specific time in history than it is to enquire further into why listener A responded differently from listener B in laboratory-based speech perception experiments. As in public health and epidemiological science, it should be sufficient to be able to make useful predictions about influence on the large mass of the population without being able to say anything certain about what will happen to individuals.

What should one make of the many attempts in the historical phonology literature to explain sound changes in a specific language at specific times by referring to contemporary cultural and psychological forces? At their best, they are accounts of why these sound changes *spread* – because at any given time all languages are probably flooded by all applicable mini-sound changes. Maxi-sound changes arise due to some of these mini-sound changes spreading selectively whereas others fail to spread; cultural and psychological factors undoubtedly play a role in this. At their worst, they are Kiplingesque 'Just So' stories: *ad hoc* hypotheses never subjected to empirical test and stated in terms of explanatory principles that themselves require explaining. Historical phonology would do well to wean itself away from this latter genre of explanation; they are neither helpful nor necessary to a larger understanding of sound change.

6.7   Relevance of historical phonology to practical domains
The relevance of phonetic research in practical domains such as communication disorders and speech technology has never been questioned (for the most part). I have attempted here to show

the relevance of phonetic research to an understanding of the mechanism of sound change initiation. If this is accepted then it implies that basic research on speech production and perception as done in phonetics, the study of sound change, and applied research on speech all have a common scientific core. The flow of useful information and hints could be from any of these domains to the others, including from historical phonology to speech technology. Whether in speech synthesis or automatic speech recognition a knowledge of all the multiple cues used to differentiate words is useful; hints on these multiple cues for a given sound can be obtained by seeing what sorts of changes it induces in neighbouring sounds. For example, Lea (1973) proposed that the perturbations of FO on vowels following consonants with distinctive voicing contrasts – which diachronically led to the development of tones – could be used in a speech recognition task. Many other examples could be provided (Ohala 1975, 1985b, 1986). It would benefit all researchers studying the behaviour of speech, including the historical linguist and the communication engineer, to integrate their data, methods, and theories; let us not repeat the folly of the blind men each describing a separate part of an elephant.

Notes

1. But also in other languages, e.g. Punjabi (Gill and Gleason 1969: 33), and Nama (Beach 1938: 247–53).
2. Hombert et al. (1979) cautiously endorsed the hypothesis that the consonantally induced perturbation of FO on vowels was caused by a difference in larynx height which in turn created a difference in vocal cord tension. They reviewed but offered counterarguments to the hypothesis of Halle and Stevens (1971) that differences in vocal cord stiffness were responsible. However, given the study by Löfqvist et al. (1989) and the work by Riordan (1980) and Kingston (1985) casting doubt on the larynx height hypothesis, it seems the Halle and Stevens hypothesis has the most empirical support.
3. The historical processes leading up to alternations such as those in (4) are somewhat complex. From this data it is safe only to conclude that when nasalization affects vowel quality it can cause reduction in height distinctions and tends to lower non-low vowels.
4. See Ohala 1974a,b, 1975, 1978a, 1981, 1983a,b, 1985a, 1986, 1990a; Ohala and Lorentz 1977; Ohala and Ohala in press.
5. The qualification 'appropriate structure' is added here to eliminate trivial exceptions to this generalization, e.g. one could not very well find out how vowels are treated before nasal consonants in a language that either did not have nasals or did not have syllables closed by nasals. Similarly, one could only study the influence of consonant

voicing on following vowels if a language had consonants contrasting in voicing.
6. The voice quality called 'glottalization' is often found on voiced sonorants flanking 'glottalized' consonants, e.g. ejectives and implosives.
7. Taking vowel duration as a cue to 'voicing' is a prime example of confusing the classificatory (not necessarily phonetic) feature [+VOICE] with the physical entity 'voice'.
8. Also certain cases of syncope vs. epenthesis; see Ohala 1991.

References

ABRAMSON, ARTHUR and LISKER, LEIGH (1985) 'Relative power of cues: FO shift versus voice timing.' In FROMKIN, VICTORIA A. (ed.) *Linguistic Phonetics*. New York: Academic Press.
ALLEN, W. SYDNEY (1957) 'Aspiration in the Hāṛautī nominal.' *Studies in Linguistics Analysis* (Special Volume of the Philological Society of London). Oxford: Blackwell, pp. 68–86.
AMMAN, JOHANN CONRAD (1700) *Dissertation de Loquela*. Amsterdam: Wolters.
BEACH, DOUGLAS M. (1938) *The Phonetics of the Hottentot Language*. Cambridge: W. Heffer.
BEDDOR, PATRICE SPEETER (1983) *Phonological and phonetic effects of nasalization on vowel height*. Bloomington, IN: Indiana University Linguistics Club.
BEDDOR, PATRICE S., KRAKOW, RENA A. and GOLDSTEIN, LOUIS M. (1986) 'Perceptual constraints and phonological change: A study of nasal vowel height', *Phonology Yearbook* 3: 197–217.
BENNETT, PATRICK R. (1967) 'Dahl's Law and Thagicu.' *African Language Studies* 8: 127–59.
BLADON, R., ANTHONY, W. and LINDBLOM, BJÖRN (1981) 'Modeling the judgment of vowel quality differences.' *Journal of the Acoustical Society of America* 69: 1414–422.
BLOCH, JULES (1920) *La Formation de la Langue Marathe*. Paris, E. Champion.
BLOCH, JULES (1965) *Indo-Aryan: From the Vedas to Modern Times*. Paris: Librairie d'Amerique et d'Orient Adrien-Maisonneuve.
BLOOMFIELD, LEONARD (1914) *An Introduction to the Study of Language*. New York: Henry Holt.
BROAD, DAVID J. and FERTIG, RALPH H. (1970) 'Formant-frequency trajectories in selected CVC-syllable nuclei', *Journal of the Acoustical Society of America*, 47: 1572–82.
DE BROSSES, CHARLES (1765) *Traité de la Formation Méchanique des langues, et de Principes Physiques de l'Étymologie*. Paris: Chez Saillant, Vincent, Desaint.
BROWMAN, CATHERINE P. and GOLDSTEIN, LOUIS (1990) 'Tiers in articulatory phonology, with some implications for casual speech.' In KINGSTON, J. and BECKMAN, M. (eds) *Papers in Laboratory Phonology I: Between the*

Grammar and the Physics of Speech. Cambridge: Cambridge University Press, pp. 341–76.

CAMPBELL, LYLE (1977) *Quichean Linguistic Prehistory*. University of California Publications in Linguistics, No. 81. Berkeley: University of California Press.

CARRÉ, RENÉ and MRAYATI, MOHAMMED (1990) 'Articulatory-acoustic-phonetic relations and modelling, regions and modes.' In HARDCASTLE, WILLIAM J. and MARCHAL, ALAIN (eds) *Speech Production and Speech Modelling*. Dordrecht: Kluwer Academic, pp. 211–40.

CUTLER, ANNE (ed.) (1982) *Slips of the Tongue and Language Production*. The Hague: Mouton.

DARDEN, BILL J. (1970) 'The fronting of vowels after palatals in Slavic.' *Proceedings of the Regional Meeting, Chicago Linguistic Society*, Vol. 6, pp. 459–70.

DELATTRE, PIERRE (1962) 'Some factors of vowel duration and their cross-linguistic validity', *Journal of Acoustical Society of America* **34**: 1141–2.

DEVINE, ANDREW M. and STEPHENS, LAWRENCE D. (1977) *Two Studies in Latin Phonology*. Saratoga: Anma Libri.

DINNSEN, DANIEL A. (1980) 'Phonological rules and phonetic explanation', *Journal of Linguistics*, **16**: 171–91.

DURAND, MARGUERITE (1955) 'Du rôle de l'auditeur dans la formation des sons du langage', *Journal de Psychologie Normale et Pathologique* **52**: 347–55.

EDKINS, JOSEPH (1864) *A Grammar of the Chinese Colloquial Language Commonly Called the Mandarin Dialect*. Shanghai: Presbyterian Mission Press.

ELLIS, ALEXANDER J. (1889) *On Early English Pronunciation*, Part V. London: Trübner.

VON ESSEN, OTTO (1964) 'An acoustic explanation of the sound shift [ł] > [u] and [l] > [i].' In ABERCROMBIE, DAVID, FRY, D. B., MACCARTHY, P. A. D., SCOTT, N. C. and TRIM, J. L. M. (eds) *In Honour of Daniel Jones*. London; Longmans, pp. 53–8.

FANT, GUNNAR (1960) *Acoustic Theory of Speech Production*. The Hague: Mouton.

FLICKINGER, DAN P. (1981) 'Dissimilation in Gothic without Thurneysen's Law', *Proceedings of the Annual Meeting, Chicago Linguistic Society*. Vol. 17, pp. 67–75.

FOWLER, CAROL A. (1986) 'An event approach to the study of speech perception from a direct realist perspective', *Journal of Phonetics* **14**: 3–28.

FUJIMURA, OSAMU and LINDQVIST, JAN (1971) 'Sweep-tone measurements of vocal-tract characteristics', *Journal of the Acoustical Society of America* **49**: 541–58.

GAMKRELIDZE, TAMAS V. and IVANOV, VIACHESLAV V. (1973) 'Sprachtypologie und die Rekonstruktion der gemeinindogermanischen Verschlüsse', *Phonetica* **27**: 150–6.

GHAZELI, SALEM (1977) 'Back consonants and backing coarticulation in

Arabic'. Unpub. Ph.D. Dissertation, University of Texas, Austin.

GILL, HARJEET SINGH and GLEASON, HENRY A. JR (1969) *A Reference Grammar of Punjabi*. Patiala: Punjabi University.

GOLDSTEIN, LOUIS (1983) 'Vowel shifts and articulatory-acoustic relations.' In COHEN, A. and BROECKE, M. P. R. (eds) *Abstracts of the Tenth International Congress of Phonetic Sciences*. Dordrecht: Foris, pp. 267–73.

GRAMMONT, MAURICE (1933) *Traité de Phonétique*. Paris: Librairie Delagrave.

GRIERSON, GEORGE (1922) 'Spontaneous Nasalization in the Indo-Aryan languages', *Journal of the Royal Asiatic Society of Great Britain*, July: 381–8.

HADEN, ERNEST F. (1938) 'The physiology of French consonant changes.' *Language Dissertations* No. 26.

HALLE, MORRIS and STEVENS, KENNETH N. (1971) 'A note on laryngeal features.' *Quarterly Progress Report* (Research Laboratory of Electronics, MIT). Vol. 101, pp. 198–213.

HARSHMAN, RICHARD, LADEFOGED, PETER and GOLDSTEIN, LOUIS (1977) 'Factor analysis of tongue shapes', *Journal of the Acoustical Society of America* 62: 693–707.

HOMBERT, JEAN-MARIE (1978) 'Consonant types, vowel quality, and tone.' In FROMKIN, V. A. (ed.) *Tone: a Linguistic Survey*. New York: Academic Press, pp. 77–111.

HOMBERT, JEAN-MARIE, OHALA, JOHN J. and EWAN, WILLIAM G. (1979) 'Phonetic explanations for the development of tones', *Language* 55: 37–58.

HOPPER, PAUL J. (1973) 'Glottalized and murmured occlusives in Indo-European'. *Glossa* 7: 141–66.

HOUSE, ARTHUR S. (1957) 'Analog studies of nasal consonants.' *Journal Speech and Hearing Disorders* 22: 190–204.

HOUSE, ARTHUR S. and STEVENS, KENNETH N. (1956) 'Analog studies of the nasalization of vowels', *Journal Speech and Hearing Disorders* 21: 218–32.

JAKOBSON, ROMAN (1978) 'Principles of historical phonology.' In BALDI, PHILIP and WERTH, RONALD N. (eds) *Readings in Historical Phonology*. University Park, PA: Pennsylvania State University Press, pp. 253–60.

JANSON, TORE (1986) 'Sound change in perception: an experiment.' OHALA, JOHN J. and JAEGER, JERI J. (eds) *Experimental Phonology*. Orlando, FL: Academic Press, pp. 253–60.

JAVKIN, HECTOR R. (1979) *Phonetic Universals and Phonological Change*. Report of the Phonology Laboratory. No. 4. University of California, Berkeley.

JHĀ, SUBHADRA (1958) *The Formation of the Maithilī Language*. London: Luzac.

KAWASAKI, HARUKO (1986) 'Phonetic explanation for phonological universals: the case of distinctive vowel nasalization.' In OHALA, JOHN J. and JAEGER, JERI J. (eds) *Experimental Phonology*. Orlando, FL: Academic Press, pp. 81–103.

KENT, ROLAND (1936) 'Assimilation and dissimilation', *Language* **12**: 245–58.

KEWLEY-PORT, DIANE (1982) 'Measurement of formant transitions in naturally produced stop consonant-vowel syllables', *Journal of the Acoustical Society of America* **72**: 379–89.

KEY, T. HEWITT (1855) 'On vowel-assimilations, especially in relation to Professor Willis's experiment on vowel-sounds.' *Transactions of the Philological Society*, Vol. 5, pp. 191–204.

KING, ROBERT D. (1969) *Historical Linguistics and Generative Grammar*, Englewood Cliffs, NJ: Prentice-Hall.

KINGSTON, JOHN C. (1985) 'The phonetics and phonology of the timing of oral and glottal events.' Unpublished PhD Dissertation. University of California, Berkeley.

KLATT, DENNIS H. and STEVENS, KENNETH N. (1969) 'Pharyngeal Consonants', *Quarterly Progress Report, Research Laboratory of Electronics (MIT)* **93**: 207–16.

KLEIN, W., PLOMP, REINIER and POLS, LOUIS C. W. (1970) 'Vowel spectra, vowel spaces, and vowel identification', *Journal of Acoustical Society of America (JASA)* **48**: 999–1009.

LADEFOGED, PETER (1984) '"Out of chaos comes order"; Physical, biological, and structural patterns in phonetics.' In VAN DEN BROECKE, MARCEL P. R. and COHEN, ANTONIE (eds) *Proceedings of the Tenth International Congress of Phonetic Sciences*. Dordrecht: Foris, pp. 83–95.

LASS, ROGER (1980) *On Explaining Language Change*. Cambridge: Cambridge Univeristy Press.

LEA, WAYNE A. (1973) 'Segmental and suprasegmental influences on fundamental frequency contours.' In HYMAN, L. M. (ed.) *Consonant Types and Tone*, Southern California Occasional Papers in Linguistics, No. 1. Los Angeles: University of Southern California, pp. 15–70.

LEHISTE, ILSE (1964) *Acoustical Characteristics of Selected English Consonants*. International Journal of American Linguistics (IJAL) Publication **34**.

LEHISTE, ILSE and PETERSON, GORDON E. (1961) 'Transitions, glides, and diphthongs', *Journal of the Acoustical Society of America* **33**: 268–77.

LIGHTNER, THEODORE M. (1970) 'Why and how does vowel nasalization take place?' *Papers in Linguistics* **2**: 179–226.

LINDBLOM, BJÖRN (1963) 'Spectrographic study of vowel reduction', *Journal of the Acoustical Society of America* **35**: 1773–81.

LINDBLOM, BJÖRN (1986) 'Phonetic universals in vowel systems.' In OHALA, JOHN J. and JAEGER, JERI J. (eds) *Experimental Phonology*. Orlando, FL: Academic Press, pp. 13–44.

LINDBLOM, BJÖRN and SUNDBERG, JOHAN (1971) 'Acoustical consequences of lip, tongue, jaw, and larnyx movement', *Journal of the Acoustical Society of America* **50**: 1166–79.

LÖFQVIST, ANDERS, BAER, THOMAS, MCGARR, NANCY S., and SEIDER STORY, ROBIN (1989) 'The cricothyroid muscle in voicing control', *Journal of the Acoustical Society of America* **85**: 1314–21.

MAEDA, SHINJI (1990) 'Compensatory articulation during speech: evidence from the analysis and synthesis of vocal-tract shapes using an articulatory model.' In HARDCASTLE, WILLIAM J. and MARCHAL, ALAIN (eds) *Speech production and speech modelling.* Dordrecht: Kluwer, pp. 131–49.

MANN, VIRGINIA A. and REPP, BRUNO H. (1980) 'Influence of vocalic context on perception of the [š] vs [s] distinction', *Perception and Psychophysics* **28**: 213–28.

MASPÉRO, HENRI (1912) 'Études sur la phonétique historique de la langue annamite: les initiales', *Bulletin de l'École Française d'Extrême Orient* **12**: 114–16.

MASSARO, DOMINIC W. and ODEN, GEORGE C. (1980) 'Evaluation and integration of acoustic features in speech perception', *Journal of the Acoustical Society of America* **67**: 996–1013.

MATISOFF, JAMES A. (1975) 'Rhinoglottophilia: the mysterious connection between nasality and glottality.' In FERGUSON, CHARLES A., HYMAN, LARRY M. and OHALA, JOHN J. (eds) *Nasálfest: Papers from a Symposium on Nasals and Nasalization.* Stanford: Language Universals Project, pp. 265–87.

MEILLET, ANTOINE (1964) 'Introduction à l'étude comparative des langues indo-européennes.' (Reprint of 8th edn, 1937). University, Alabama: Univeristy of Alabama Press.

MERINGER, RUDOLF and MAYER, KARL (1895) *Versprechen und Verlesen: Eine Psychologisch-Linguistische Studie.* Stuttgart: Göschensche Verlagsbuchhandlung.

MILLER, GEORGE A. and NICELY, PATRICIA E. (1955) 'Analysis of perceptual confusions among some English consonants', *Journal of the Acoustical Society of America* **27**: 338–53.

MULLER, ERIC M. and BROWN, WILLIAM S., JR (1980) 'Variations in the supraglottal air pressure waveform and their articulatory interpretations.' In LASS, N. J. (ed.) *Speech and Language: Advances in Basic Research and Practice.* Vol. 4. New York: Academic Press, pp. 317–89.

MÜLLER, F. MAX. (1864) *Lectures on the Science of Language* (second series). London: Longman, Green, Longman, Roberts and Green.

O'CONNOR, J. D., GERSTMAN, LOUIS, LIBERMAN, ALVIN M., DELATTRE, PIERRE and COOPER, FRANK S. (1957) 'Acoustic cues for the perception of initial /w, j, r, l/ in English', *Word* **13**: 24–43.

OHALA, JOHN J. (1974a) 'Experimental historical phonology.' In ANDERSON, JOHN M. and JONES, CHARLES (eds) *Historical linguistics*, Vol. II, *Theory and Description in Phonology* (Proceedings of the 1st International Conference on Historical Linguistics. Edinburgh, 2–7 September 1973.) Amsterdam: North Holland, 353–89.

OHALA, JOHN J. (1974b) 'Phonetic explanation in phonology.' In BRUCK, ANTHONY, FOX, ROBERT A. and LAGALY, MICHAEL W. (eds) *Papers from the Parasession on Natural Phonology.* Chicago: Chicago Linguistic Society, pp. 251–74.

OHALA, JOHN J. (1975) 'Phonetic explanations for nasal sound patterns.' In FERGUSON, CHARLES A., HYMAN, LARRY M. and OHALA, JOHN J. (eds) *Nasálfest: Papers from a Symposium on Nasals and Nasalization.*

Stanford: Language Universals Project, 289–316.

OHALA, JOHN J. (1976) 'A model of speech aerodynamics.' *Report of the Phonology Laboratory*, University of California, Berkeley. Vol. 1, pp. 93–107.

OHALA, JOHN J. (1978a) 'Southern Bantu vs. the world: the case of palatalization of labials.' *Berkeley Linguistic Society, Proceedings, Annual Meeting*, University of California, Berkeley. Vol. 4, pp. 370–86.

OHALA, JOHN J. (1978b) 'Phonological notations as models.' In DRESSLER, WOLFGANG U. and MEID, W. (eds), *Proceedings of the 12th International Congress of Linguists, Vienna, 28 August–2 September 1977*. Innsbruck: Innsbrucker Beitrage zur Sprachwissenschaft, pp. 811–16.

OHALA, JOHN J. (1979) 'Universals of labial velars and de Saussure's chess analogy.' *Proceedings of the 9th International Congress of Phonetic Sciences*, Vol. 2. Copenhagen: Institute of Phonetics, pp. 41–7.

OHALA, JOHN J. (1981) 'The listener as a source of sound change.' In MASEK, CARRIES, HENDRICK, ROBERTA A. and MILLER, MARY FRANCES (eds) *Papers from the Parasession on Language and Behavior*. Chicago: Chicago Linguistic Society, pp. 178–203.

OHALA, JOHN J. (1983a) 'The phonological end justifies any means.' In HATTORI, SHIRÔ and INOUE, KAZUKO (eds) *Proceedings of the XIIIth International Congress of Linguists, Tokyo, 29 August–4 September 1982*. Tokyo: Sanseido Shoten, pp. 232–43.

OHALA, JOHN J. (1983b) 'The origin of sound patterns in vocal tract constraints.' In MACNEILAGE, PETER F. (ed.) *The Production of Speech*. New York: Springer-Verlag, pp. 189–216.

OHALA, JOHN J. (1985a) 'Around *flat*.' In FROMKIN, VICTORIA A. (ed.) *Phonetic Linguistics. Essays in Honor of Peter Ladefoged*. Orlando, FL: Academic Press, pp. 223–41.

OHALA, JOHN J. (1985b) 'Linguistics and automatic speech processing.' In DE MORI, RENATO and SUEN, C.-Y. (eds) *New Systems and Architectures for Automatic Speech Recognition and Synthesis*. NATO ASI Series, Series F: Computer and System Sciences, Vol. 16. Berlin: Springer-Verlag, pp. 447–75.

OHALA, JOHN J. (1986) 'Phonological evidence for top-down processing in speech perception.' In PERKELL, JOSEPH S. and KLATT, DENNIS H. (eds) *Invariance and Variability in Speech Processes*. Hillsdale, NJ: Lawrence Erlbaum, pp. 386–97.

OHALA, JOHN J. (1987) 'Explanation in phonology: Opinions and examples.' In DRESSLER, WOLFGANG U., LUSCHÜTZKY, HANS C., PFEIFFER, OSKAR E. and RENNISON, JOHN R. (eds) *Phonologica 1984*. Cambridge: Cambridge University Press, pp. 215–25.

OHALA, JOHN J. (1990a) 'The phonetics and phonology of aspects of assimilation.' In KINGSTON, JOHN and BECKMAN, MARY (eds) *Papers in Laboratory Phonology*, Vol. I, *Between the Grammar and the Physics of Speech*. Cambridge: Cambridge University Press, pp. 258–75.

OHALA, JOHN J. (1990b) 'Respiratory activity in speech.' In HARDCASTLE, WILLIAM J. and MARCHAL, ALAIN (eds) *Speech Production and Speech*

Modelling. Dordrecht: Kluwer, pp. 23–53.

OHALA, JOHN J. (1991) 'What's cognitive, what's not, in sound change.' Paper A297. Linguistic Agency of the University of Duisburg, (LAUD) Universität Duisburg Gesamthochschule.

OHALA, JOHN J. (1992) 'The segment: Primitive or derived?' In DOCHERTY, G. J. and LADD, D. R (eds), *Papers in Laboratory Phonology: Gesture, segment, prosody*. Cambridge: Cambridge University Press, pp. 166–83.

OHALA, JOHN J. and AMADOR, MARISCELA (1981) 'Spontaneous nasalization', *Journal of the Acoustical Society of America* 68: S54–S55 (Abstract).

OHALA, JOHN J. and RIODAN, CAROL J. (1979) 'Passive vocal tract enlargement during voiced stops.' In WOLF, JARED J. and KLATT, DENNIS H. (eds) *Speech Communication Papers*. New York: Acoustical Society of America pp. 89–92.

OHALA, JOHN J. and LORENTZ, JAMES (1977) 'The story of [w]: an exercise in the phonetic explanation for sound patterns.' *Berkeley Linguistic Society, Proceedings, Annual Meeting*, University of California, Berkeley. Vol. 3, pp. 577–99.

OHALA, JOHN J. and SHRIBERG, ELIZABETH E. (1990) 'Hyper-correction in speech perception.' *Proceedings, ICSLP 90* (International Conference on Spoken Language Processing, Kobe 18–22 November 1990), Vol. 1, pp. 405–8.

OHALA, MANJARI (1983) *Aspects of Hindi Phonology*. Delhi: Motilal Banarsidass.

OHALA, MANJARI and OHALA, JOHN J. (1991) 'Nasal epenthesis in Hindi', *Phonetica* 48: 207–20.

OSTHOFF, HERMAN and BRUGMANN, KARL ([1878] 1967) Preface to *Morphological Investigations in the Sphere of the Indo-European Languages I*. In LEHMANN, WINFRED P. (ed. and trans.) *A reader in Nineteenth-Century Historical Indo-European linguistics*. Bloomington: Indiana University Press, pp. 197–209. (Originally published as Preface. *Morphologische Untersuchungen auf dem Gebiete der indogermanischen Sprachen I*. iii–xx, Leipzig: S. Hirzel, 1878.)

PERKELL, JOSEPH S. and COHEN, MICHAEL H. (1989) 'An indirect test of the quantal nature of speech in the production of the vowels [i], [a] and [u]', *Journal of Phonetics* 17: 123–33.

PETERSON, GORDON E. and LEHISTE, ILSE (1960) 'Duration of syllable nuclei in English.' *Journal of the Acoustical Society of America* 32: 693–703.

VON RAUMER, RUDOLF (1863) *Gesammelte Sprachwissenschaftliche Schriften*. Frankfurt: Heyder & Zimmer.

DE REUSE, WILLEM J. (1981) 'Grassmann's Law in Ofo', *International Journal of American Linguistics* 47: 243–4.

RIORDAN, CAROL J. (1980) 'Larynx height during English stop consonants', *Journal of Phonetics* 8: 353–60.

ROCK, IRVIN (1983) *The Logic of Perception*. Cambridge, MA: MIT Press.

ROTHENBERG, MARTIN (1968) 'The breath-stream dynamics of simple-released-plosive production', *Bibliotheca Phonetica* 6.

ROUSSELOT, L'ABBÉ PIERRE-JEAN (1891) *Les Modifications Phonétiques du Langage, Étudiées dans le Patois d'une Famille de Cellefrouin (Charente)*. Paris: H. Welter.

SATO, T. (1950) 'On the differences in time structure of voiced and unvoiced stop consonants', in Japanese, *Journal of the Acoustical Society of Japan* 14: 117–22.

SHRIBERG, ELIZABETH E. and OHALA, JOHN J. (1991) '"Correction" in the perception of filtered vowels.' Paper presented at 121st Meeting of the Acoustical Society of America, Baltimore, 29 April–3 May 1991.

SOLÉ, MARIA JOSEP and OHALA, JOHN J. (1990) 'Cognitive representation and the varying pronunciation of frequently occurring expressions.' Paper presented at International Pragmatics Conference. Universitat de Barcelona, 9–13 July.

SOLÉ, MARIA JOSEP and OHALA, JOHN J. (1991) 'Differentiating between phonetic and phonological processes: the case of nasalization.' In *Proceedings of the 12th International Congress of Phonetic Sciences, Aix-en-Provence, 19–24 August, 1991*. Aix-en-Provence: Institut de Phonétique. Vol. 2, pp. 110–13.

STETSON, RAYMOND H. (1928) *Motor Phonetics*. La Haye: Martinus Nijhoff.

STEVENS, KENNETH N. (1971) 'Airflow and turbulence noise for fricative and stop consonants: static considerations', *Journal of the Acoustical Society of America* 50: 1180–92.

STEVENS, KENNETH N. (1980) 'Discussion.' *Proceedings, Ninth International Congress of Phonetic Sciences*, Vol. 3. Copenhagen: Institute of Phonetics, University of Copenhagen, pp. 185–6.

STEVENS, KENNETH N. (1989) 'On the quantal nature of speech', *Journal of Phonetics* 17: 3–45.

STEVENS, KENNETH N. and KEYSER, SAMUEL JAY (1989) 'Primary features and their enhancement in consonants', *Language* 65: 81–106.

STEVENS, KENNETH N., KEYSER, SAMUEL JAY and KAWASAKI, HARUKO (1986) 'Toward a phonetic and phonological theory of redundant features.' In PERKELL, JOSEPH R. and KLATT, DENNIS H. (eds) *Invariance and variability in speech processes*. Hillsdale, NJ: Erlbaum, pp. 426–49.

SVANTESSON, JAN-OLOF (1983) *Kammu phonology and morphology* (Travaux de l'institut de linguistique de Lund 18). Lund: Gleerup.

SWEET, HENRY (1874) *History of English sounds*. London: Trübner.

SWEET, HENRY (1877) *A Handbook of Phonetics*. Oxford: Clarendon Press.

TRAUNMÜLLER, HARMUT (1981) 'Perceptual dimension of openness in vowels', *Journal of the Acoustical Society of America* 69: 1465–75.

TURNER, SIR RALPH L. (1921) 'Gujarati phonology', *Journal of the Royal Asiatic Society* pts 3–4.

TURNER, SIR RALPH L. (1923–25) 'The Sindhi recursives or voiced stops preceded by glottal stop', *Bulletin of the School of Oriental Studies* 3: 301–15.

VERNER, KARL (1913) (Letters to Hugo Pipping). *Oversigt over det kongelige Danske Videnskabernes Selskabs Forhandlinger*. No. 3. 161–211. Copenhagen.

WAIBEL, ALEX and LEE, KAI-FU (eds) (1990) *Readings in Speech Recognition*. San Mateo, CA: Morgan Kaufmann.

WANG, WILLIAM S.-Y. (ed.) (1977) *The Lexicon in Phonological Change*. The Hague: Mouton.

WEISMER, GARY (1979) 'Sensitivity of voice-onset-time (VOT) measures to certain segmental features in speech production', *Journal of Phonetics* 7: 197–204.

WESTBURY, JOHN R. (1979) 'Aspects of the temporal control of voicing in consonant clusters in English.' PhD Dissertation, University of Texas.

WESTBURY, JOHN R. and KEATING, PATRICIA A. (1985) 'On the naturalness of stop consonant voicing.' *Working Papers in Phonetics* (UCLA) Vol. 60, pp. 1–19.

WHITNEY, WILLIAM DWIGHT (1867) *Language and the Study of Language*. New York: Charles Scribners.

WINITZ, HARRIS, SCHEIB, M. E. and REEDS, J. A. (1972) 'Identification of stops and vowels for the burst portion of /p, t, k/ isolated from conversational speech', *Journal of the Acoustical Society of America* 51: 1309–17.

WRIGHT, JAMES T. (1986) 'The behavior of nasalized vowels in the perceptual vowel space.' In OHALA, JOHN J. and JAEGER, JERI J. (eds) *Experimental phonology*. Orlando, Florida: Academic Press, pp. 45–67.

YOUNG, THOMAS (1819) 'Remarks on the probabilities of error in physical observations and on the density of the earth considered especially with regard to the reduction of experiments on the pendulum.' *Transactions of the Philosophical Society*, Cambridge, pp. 70–95.

ZUE, VICTOR W. (1976) *Acoustic Characteristics of Stop Consonants: a Controlled Study*. Bloomington, IN: Indiana University of Linguistics Club.

Chapter 10

Nicaraguan English in history

Wayne O'Neil

1 Introduction

In the sections that follow the focus of attention is on the grammar of a creole and the history of that creole, insofar as it is possible to explicate the latter. Because of their peculiar ontogeny, creoles are supposed to shed extraordinary light on language and its growth in the individual and in society. In fact, this must certainly be the justification for the great deal of time and energy expended on them in modern linguistics. I take a somewhat less apocalyptic point of view in the course of a close examination of the idiosyncrasies of a language that I take simply to be a variety of English, Nicaraguan English: the point of studying it being to understand what it is and how it got to be whatever it is.

2 Nicaraguan English

Nicaraguan English (also known in the creole literature as Miskitu Coast Creole English) is the term used in the following pages to refer to the variety of English spoken natively on the Atlantic side of Nicaragua by 30,000 or so people (Hale and Gordon 1987), the small city of Bluefields in the South Atlantic Autonomous Region being their commercial and cultural capital. For the most part, they are African-Americans, descendants of slaves who escaped to the Miskitu Coast or were held in captivity there, brought from other parts of the Caribbean by British entrepreneurs as early as the mid-seventeenth century, or who migrated to the Coast from other British Caribbean colonies following their mid-nineteenth century release from slavery by the British (Holm 1986). Nicaraguan English also includes among its 30,000 speakers some two thousand or so Black Caribs and Rama Indians, both of these small groups having largely lost their original languages. Some few Ramas, however, still speak their native language (Craig 1990: 12–14) while the Caribs – exiled from their native St Vincent's Island by the British to the Caribbean coast of Central America late in the eighteenth century – strongly maintain their native *garífuna* in Honduras, Guatemala, and Belize. An indeterminate but significant number of Nicaragua's nearly 70,000 Miskitu Indians also have Nicaraguan English as their native language, others of them speaking it as a second language as well.

Note that in what follows, as in what has already preceded, I vary between referring to Nicaraguan English as a separate language or as a variety of English, in accordance with the intended emphasis of the moment. There is nothing linguistically serious at stake in this variation in usage. For whether we choose to call Nicaraguan English a separate language distinct from any of the other Englishes of the world, as I believe we should, is a matter of politics and not of linguistic theory (see Baldwin 1979).

3 General comments on the state of the language and sources for its study

Nicaraguan English is a language without a school system, or more accurately: although its speakers control a school system, they have chosen to try to conduct business there in International English, and in Spanish, without paying serious attention to the English that they actually speak and know. Moreover, since there is next to nothing written in the language, there are few prescriptive restraints on its use. As a consequence, the variation among and within speakers of the language and their speech communities is said by its speakers, and by some outside observers as well, to be great – in a relative sense, varying more noticeably from neighbourhood to neighbourhood in Bluefields, from community to community in the South Atlantic Autonomous Region of Nicaragua than is thought to be usual for the languages of the world. There is, however, no documentation of this belief. And when, in fact, the language is steadily viewed from the outside, variation from one community to another is not very noticeable – a not surprising difference in point of view.

In the context of the other, indigenous languages of Nicaragua, Nicaraguan English stands out, like Spanish, as a transplanted European language, though clearly one of far less importance than Spanish in Nicaragua, as in the rest of Central America except in Belize. It is, further, a variety of Central American English (found all along the Atlantic side of the Central American isthmus – formerly the westernmost edge of the British Caribbean empire, from Belize to Panama and on to Colombia with its English-speaking island possessions, Providencia and San Andrés, and finally to the northern coast of South America), itself a part of the larger Caribbean English-speaking community.

These languages, or language varieties, are creoles and therefore they have connections that from the linguistic point of view extend, through their supposed Africanness, beyond their Englishness to the larger Caribbean and West African, i.e. Atlantic (even, depending on your creolistic orientation, to the world) creole community.

The word *creole* is supposed to indicate that these languages are somehow special among the languages of the world. Originally used to label the descendants of Europeans born in the New World, *creole* was taken over to label the descendants of European languages born in the New World as well. The specialness attributed to creole languages depends on one's theoretical persuasion on these matters: either the languages are special because they are hybrid languages, fashioned out of the vocabulary of a European language (the superstrate) and the syntax of, in the case of the Atlantic creoles, certain or all West African languages (the substrate). Or they are special because they were born under such straitened conditions that they very clearly reveal universal characteristics of language, perhaps even the original 'hand' at work in the fashioning of human language itself. My own view is that these positions on the specialness of the so-called creole languages are prematurely taken, that the linguistic theoretic task is simply to figure out how these languages work, and what contribution their study can make to our understanding of universal grammar and, perhaps, of language change, as we would hope to do with any one of the other languages of the world.

Considering the isolated location and relative obscurity of the language, the sources for studying Nicaraguan English, beyond simply engaging in fieldwork with the large number of native speakers living in Nicaragua, are rather great in number. There is, first of all, a very ambitious doctoral dissertation on the language by John Holm: *The Creole English of Nicaragua's Miskito Coast: Its Sociolinguistic History and a Comparative Study of its Lexicon and Syntax* (1978 – epitomized in Holm 1983: chs 1 and 4; see also Holm 1989: sections 10.4.3–4). Holm 1978 provides a great deal of political and linguistic historical background, a fifty-three-page word list, seventy pages of text (transcriptions of some of his 1976 field recordings), and a great deal of lexical and some descriptive grammatical analysis. There is also available a tape of the three texts from Holm 1978 that are included in Holm 1983, an adjunct to the latter volume. Many of the examples given below are, indeed, taken – with their spelling modified to that of International English – directly from Holm 1978; 1983. His work has also been a rich source of material for me to use as probes in my own fieldwork.

I have supplemented the material from Holm through ongoing fieldwork during several recent trips to Nicaragua and to the Atlantic coast: in January 1986, 1987, 1988, and 1990 and in July–August 1985, 1986, 1987, 1988, 1989, and 1990 – trips which, in the context of the work of Linguists for Nicaragua with Nicaraguan bilingual education, appear destined to continue on some similarly regular schedule. This fieldwork has been largely done collectively with native speakers in classroom settings, augmented by some one-on-one informant work during January workshops with the Nicaraguan Bilingual-Bicultural Education Program (PEBB) for teachers and technical staff in Bluefields; in Managua, during the July–August course in linguistics, devoted partly to the languages of Nicaragua, that Linguists for Nicaragua ran in 1986, 1987, and 1988 at the Universidad Centroamericana/ Managua; and in various other settings in Managua and on the Coast. Some interim results of this work have been reported on at various conferences, in colloquia, in an MIT seminar, and in, for example, O'Neil and Honda 1987, O'Neil et al. 1987.

Other sources include records and tapes of popular music from the Coast; the now defunct bilingual (English-Spanish) newspaper *Sunrise* published in Bluefields following the Triumph of the Revolution in 1979 until the devastating Bluefields hurricane of October 1988 and Nicaraguan elections of 1990; and letters, notes, and other written and recorded texts that have come my way during the past six years. And casual conversations and eavesdropping, at home and in Nicaragua – for I happen to live in a Boston neighbourhood (Dorchester) in which there is a good deal of Caribbean English spoken. What I hear on the streets of Dorchester can and does easily inspire lines of inquiry in Nicaragua.

I should add that the aim of our work in Nicaragua and on English and its other languages (see Linguists for Nicaragua 1989) is rather different from the descriptive, socio-historical, and polemical (with respect to the genesis of creole languages) work of Holm: for here I try to begin to explicate the grammar of

Nicaraguan English from the native speaker's point of view, that is, to lay bare the knowledge of his/her language that a speaker of Nicaraguan English has, according to a particular theoretical framework; to understand something of the history of the language; to train native-speakers of the language to carry the work on to some satisfactory level of completion; and to contribute to the English curriculum of the PEBB, insofar as linguistics can be of use, in the form of classroom activities with language, storybooks, and so on.

There is, then, a considerable amount of immediately accessible data for linguistic work on Nicaraguan English, and an unlimited amount readily available in the field. There are as yet, however, no native speakers trained as linguists, though a number of teachers and technical staff have received minimal training from the Linguists for Nicaragua workshops in Bluefields and somewhat more has been offered in Managua for a much smaller number. But the fact remains that there are no native speakers of Nicaraguan English willing and able to carry forward the work reported on here. And given the economic conditions that prevail in the area and the continued emigration of those most qualified to carry out the work, there is little prospect at the moment of our training even one native-speaker linguist. Indeed, in the present situation, there is the distinct danger that the Nicaraguan creole community and its culture will disappear entirely unless the economy and political and social conditions of Nicaragua improve dramatically and quickly.

4 Nicaraguan English grammar: structure and history

Given our work and that of others (chiefly Holm), how do we answer the question: what is the language like? And what can we say about how it got to be whatever it is? In its word order, vocabulary, sentence structure, etc., it is very much like the more familiar varieties of English. I say this now because as we proceed we will understandably concentrate on ways in which Nicaraguan English differs from the more familiar International English varieties and thus differently illuminates the theory of grammar and of language change. For the language is – from another, more narrow perspective – strikingly different from International English: in its phonology, and in morphology and syntax as well, as we shall see soon enough. Yet at the outset, it is important to emphasize its similarity to the more familiar varieties of English, and not to be deluded by the points of difference into believing – like many creolists – that we are looking at something quite unrelated to English, so different as to be a language of a separate and quite different kind typologically.

In its vocabulary and grammar, Nicaraguan English got to be what it is through its contact with the languages and peoples about it, including the largely West African languages that the Africans came into their slavery with. Nicaraguan English also got to be what it is simply because it changed over time as any language will. There is no necessary external explanation for this latter sort of change, Sapir's notion 'drift' being as good as any other (1921); for as far as we know change simply takes place within the constraints imposed by Universal Grammar and learnability, whatever these limits are – the principles of language change being on this view indistinguishable from the principles determining the growth or development of a particular grammar in the individual.

I turn now to some particulars about Nicaraguan English grammar, presented – as I mentioned above – in a theoretical framework whose relevant details will emerge in the course of the presentation, the principles and parameters framework of Chomsky (1988, e.g.) and others. Keep in mind that the ultimate goal here is to illuminate the relationship between Universal Grammar, a part of our human intellectual endowment, and the grammar of a particular language, as mediated through the child's experience in language. It is a relationship that we assume without question, but which, despite its ordinariness, provides the substance of normal scientific inquiry. Thus one of Holm's informants – a seventy-five year-old Garífuna – when asked how she acquired Nicaraguan English (or as she quite sensibly takes Holm's question, how one acquires a language) and about the loss of *garífuna*, answers him straightforwardly as follows (Holm 1978: Appendix PZ12):

(1) JH: Well, how did you learn creole?
     PZ: What he say?
     EZ: How you learn creole, how you . . .
     PZ: By . . ., by . . . them is here. The children-dem when you small will learn it . . .

[Moving on to a discussion of the loss of *garífuna*:]

     EZ: The sin wouldn't fall on we. It would be our parents because they don't talk it with us . . .
     PZ: Yeah, them [children] learn it quick, you know. Before you can say 'one and a blow', they learn it.

Indeed, the basic stuff of cognitive science, of science in

general, lies in working out in some detail the answers to questions whose answers appear self-evident to people who do not labour under the negative benefits of an empiricist-based education.

5 Nicaraguan English phonology

5.1 Writing the language down

In order to provide a written representation of Nicaraguan English, I use – as we would for any variety of English – ordinary English orthography. When there is need to represent some form special or unique to Nicaraguan English or when the focus is on particular details of Nicaraguan English phonology – as in these sections of the present chapter – I employ a broad phonetic (i.e., phonemic) transcription based, with some slight modifications adopted in order to better represent Nicaraguan English pronunciation, on that generally used in Caribbean English creole studies (see, e.g., Holm 1983: 23–6). Insofar as the phonemic values of the symbols used are not self-evident, they will be clarified below at the time of their use.

As with any variety of English, it is then necessary to explain how to interpret the International English orthography phonetically. The main outlines of this explanation follow.

5.2 Segmental phonology

5.2.1 Consonants

In Nicaraguan English, there are overall no startling or unusual consonantal differences to attend to; however, it should be noted that in Nicaraguan English, *th-* spellings represent the pronunciations /d/ or /t/: /d/ if the word is pronounced with the voiced sound represented with *th* in International English (as in *the*, *them*, etc.). Otherwise a *th* represents /t/ (as in *throw*, *anything*, etc.).

Another striking characteristic of Nicaraguan English is the fact that /zh/ (a marginal International English phoneme, represented a number of different ways in its spelling, as in *garage* and *azure*, and derivationally in *decision*, for example) is pronounced /j/ in Nicaraguan English, as in the first and last segments of *judge*. The loss of /zh/ – and of /θ/, /ð/ – in varieties of English protected from an educational system is a quite general historical development or state (see, e.g., Cassidy 1985: liii), their loss being arguably a function of their phonological markedness and relatively marginal status.

In addition, Nicaraguan English is in part an /r/-less dialect.

What this means for this language is that in cases where an ɾ appears in International English spelling syllable-finally, there is no /r/ in pronunciation. For example, *fisherman* is pronounced without an /r/ in this variety of English. However, in words such as *reward* and *cutboard*, where the *r* is the first part of a complex syllable coda, it generally reflects an /r/.

Then there is the theoretically interesting fact that the velar stops /k/ and /g/ are palatalized to /ky/ and /gy/ (as in /kyat/, *cat*; /gyal/, *gal*, *girl*; etc.) when the vowel following the /k/ or /g/ was *historically* /æ/. In parallel fashion, the peripheral stops /b/, /p/, /g/, and /k/ are labialized to /bw/, /pw/, /gw/ and /kw/ when followed by the Nicaraguan English /ay/ deriving historically from /oy/, as in /bway/ *boy*; /di pwayn/ *The Point – Pointeen*, a Bluefields neighbourhood; /gwayn/ *going*; /kwayn/ *coin*; cf., however, /payn/ *pine*, /kayn/ *kind*, and so on. Given evidence of this sort, we then naturally assume that Nicaraguan English has phonological /æ/ and /oy/ underlyingly (accounting for the assimilatory – palatalization and rounding – effects noted above) and that the differences between underlying /æ/~/a/ and /oy/~/ay/ are neutralized in favour of the latter phoneme of each pair by some rule late in the phonological component of the grammar of Nicaraguan English.

In Nicaraguan English, most consonant clusters are simplified at the ends of words, as in *The Point* above. Thus, in words like *kind*, *servant*, *want*, *fourth*, *wasp*, etc., the final /d/, /t/, /p/, etc. will not generally be heard in speech, informal or otherwise. Furthermore, final /sk/ is reduced to /s/ or metathesized to /ks/: thus, /dwon as~ask mi/ for *don't ask me*.

There is also some variation in the nature of consonant clusters at the beginning of words. One example of this is revealed in the pronunciation indicated in such a spelling as *scrumbs* for *crumbs* (see section 5.4. (4) below). There is evidence that speakers of Nicaraguan English freely vary between initial /skr/ and /kr/ in the pronunciation of words that are distinctly spelled (and pronounced) in International English with *cr-* and *scr-*, perhaps through hyper-correction. Thus, the Nicaraguan English pronunciations for International English *crumbs* could be spelt *scrumbs* or *crumbs* and for International English *scratch* as *scratch* or *cratch*. Since there is sporadic evidence of more extensive simplification of /s/-initial three-segment clusters (/pwayl/~/spwayl/ *spoil*), more investigation is needed in order to describe this phenomenon fully.

It should be noted that all these features of Nicaraguan English consonants, including the last, are unexceptional and common to other varieties of English in the British Isles, in the United States, as well as in other places, in which general characteristics of the standard varieties of English are simply further generalized. (See, e.g., Cassidy 1985: xli–lxi.)

5.2.2 Vowels

There are several quite striking features of the Nicaraguan English vowel system, some being of historical interest. The first is that the [-low] short vowels are a good deal closer in pronunciation than their North American International English counterparts. Thus the sounds of words like *sick* and *beg* are [i] and [e], respectively; not [ɪ] and [ɛ], with the vowels of *sick* and *seek*, for example, differing not by any noticeable vowel height but by the fact that the latter is diphthongal. This may simply be an areal phenomenon.

In addition, the low short vowel [a] is the single articulation for three possible International English short vowels, [æ], [a], and [ɔ]: thus Nicaraguan English *battle* and *bottle*, for example, are pronounced alike as /batl/. However, as noted above in connection with the palatalization and labialization of certain stop consonants, there are consonantal effects, residue of the earlier differences between and among vowels in the language and thus strong evidence for a larger set of underlying vowels in Nicaraguan English than the surface phonemics or broad phonetics reveals.

But the most striking feature of the vowel sounds in Nicaraguan English (to non-Nicaraguan English ears) is the pronunciation of several of the 'long' (i.e., diphthongal) vowels. For example, *out* is pronounced with the vowel [ow] of North American *boat*; *sane* is pronounced as if it were spelled (phonetically) /syen/ – much like the pronunciation of the Spanish word *cien*; and *go*, as if it were spelled (phonetically) /gwo/. Moreover, the vowel of *oil* is pronounced with the vowel [ay] of North American *aisle* – with, however, the differing effects of underlying /oy/ and /ay/ on preceding peripheral consonants noted above.

5.2.3 Nicaraguan English vowel shift

To understand the structure of the Nicaraguan English 'long' vowels and diphthongs and their history, let us compare the development of the earlier English diphthongal vowels in, say, the variety of International English (InE) examined by Chomsky and Halle (1968: ch. 6) and their development in Nicaraguan English (NcE):

(2) *Early Modern English*   *InE*   *as in*:   *NcE*
     /oy/ (< OF /oy/)   /oy/   boil   /ay/
     /ey/ (< OE /ii/)   /ay/   rice   /ay/
     /iy/ (< OE /ee/)   /iy/   feed   /iy/
     /æy/ (< OE /ææ/)   /ey/   sane   /ye/
     /ow/ (< OE /uu/)   /a~æw/   town   /ow/
     /uw/ (< OE /oo/)   /uw/   fool   /uw/
     /ɔw/ (< OE /aa/)   /ow/   go   /wo/

From (2), we see that the long vowel/diphthong-shift of
Nicaraguan English has followed along a differently symmetrical
path from that of the variety of International English discussed in
Chomsky and Halle 1968. In particular, the originally (in Old
English) [+low, +long – i.e. geminate] vowels developed
harmonized on-glides with their peaks then shifting to [−high,
−low]; the originally [+high, +back] long vowel has retained its
[+round] character while shifting to [−high]; and /oy/ and /ay/, as
noted above, has fallen together at /ay/. Pieces of this particular
outcome of English Vowel Shift are familiar from descriptions of
a number of British and American English dialects; see, for
example, Orton 1933; Wells 1983; Cassidy 1985.

5.3 Stress accent
From the point of view of its stress accent, Nicaraguan English
seems very much like International English except in one very
clear respect: simple compound-nominal stress. As first noted in
McLean and Past 1976, simple compounds in Nicaraguan English
have the heaviest stress accent on their second part – on the
head, rather than on the first as in International English, for
example:

(3.a) head-áche

(3.b) type-wríter

(3.c) baby-sítter

(3.d) one-mínded (i.e. 'single-minded')

(3.e) test-glásses (i.e. 'prescription glasses')

(3.f) fisher-mán

Nicaraguan English stress accent has not yet been further
investigated; it would, therefore, be interesting to inquire more
deeply into the characteristics of this aspect of Nicaraguan
English phonology. For example, are there further consequences,
as one might expect, of this feature of compound stress in the

phonology of more intricate compounds? How are word (including compound) stresses adjusted one to the other at the level of phrase structure?

Other aspects of phrasal phonology await investigation as well. For example, it has long been obvious to people working with these languages that the intonation of the Atlantic creoles, generally attributed to West African influence, is very different from that of their European bases. Yet the nature of this difference is not well-described, much less explained for Nicaraguan English or for any other Caribbean creole. For some discussion and references, see Holm 1988: 137–43.

5.4

There follows a Nicaraguan English text in International English spelling and in a phonemic transcription broadly representative of Nicaraguan English pronunciation. The text, grammatically quite close to familiar varieties of International English, is taken from Holm (1983: 112); however, given the number of errors in transcription there, it has been retranscribed (by Tim Shopen) from the tape accompanying Holm's 1983 volume. In this text, in which simple /o/ represents [ɔ] and /ah/ = [aa], the full range of phonological characteristics discussed above is illustrated.

(4)   *The Golden Fish*
                        /Di Gwoldin Fish/
        It was a ragged fisherman. He used to like the fishing and every day
        /it waz a ragid fishamán. i yuwsa layk di fishin an evar dye
    he goes out fishining and catch fish and bring it and sell. So one day he
    /hi gwoz out fishinin an kech fish an bring it an sel. swo wan dye hi
        went out fishing and he didn't catch anything. Five day we fight there
        /wen owt tu fishin an he din kech eniting. fayv dye wiy fayt de
    til he catch a golden fish. And the fish says to him, he says, 'Throw me
    /til hi kech a gwoldin fish. an di fish sez tu him, i sez, 'trwo mi
        back into the sea,' he said, 'I'll give you a reward!'
        /bak intu di siy,' i sed, 'ayil giv yu a riwahrd!'
    So the old man take the fish and he throw him back into the sea. So
    /swo di wol man tyek di fish an i trwo im bak intu di siy. swo
    when he went home, his wife says to him, he says, 'What you catch?'
    /wen i wen hwom, hiz wayf sez tu him, i sez, 'wat yuw kech?'
        He says, 'Old lady,' he says, 'I's only catch a golden fish.'
        /i sez, 'wol lyedi,' i sez, 'ayz wonli kech a gwoldin fish.'
                'Then what you done with it?'
                /'den wat yuw don wid it?'
    He say, 'Fish told me to throw him back in the sea and he will give me
    /he sye, 'fish twol mi tu trwo im bak in di siy an hi wil giv mi
                a reward.'
                /a riwahrd.'

    'Hmm,' he says, 'and what you ask for a reward?'
    /'hmm,' hi sez, 'an wat yuw aks for a riwahrd?'
    He says, 'Nothing.'
    /i sez, 'noting.'
Now they says to him, he says, 'You know that our cutboard are empty.
    /now dye sez tu him, i sez, 'yuw nwo dat owr cotbword ar empti.
We don't have a scrumbs of cheese nor a piece of bread to eat. Go back and
    /wiy dwon hav a scromz av chiyz nar a piys av bred tu iyt. gwo bak an
    tell the fish that we don't want our cutboard are empty.' . . .
    /tel di fish dat wiy dwon wan owr cotbword ar empti.'/. . .

6 Nicaraguan English morphology

The words and forms of Nicaraguan English fall into the universal categories: nouns, adjectives, verbs, and prepositions – cross-classified with the universal lexical features $[\pm N]$, $[\pm V]$, according to which nouns are $[+N, -V]$, i.e. purely nominal; verbs, $[-N, +V]$, i.e. purely verbal; adjectives, $[+N, +V]$, i.e. partake of characteristics both nominal and verbal; and prepositions, $[-N, -V]$, i.e. lie outside the categories 'nominal' and 'verbal'. Under this analysis, $[+V]$ categories (verbs and adjectives) constitute the set of predicatives; $[+N]$ categories (nouns and adjectives), the set of substantives. In addition to these universal lexical categories, the language has a full array of functional categories as well: an extra-propositional position (COMP), verbal inflections and English-type modal verbs (INFL), and determiners.

There is much discussion in the creole literature in which it is argued that under the influence of the grammar of certain West African languages, the adjectives of creole languages generally, and thus of Nicaraguan English specifically, have come to constitute a class of stative verbs (e.g. Holm 1988: 176–7). The motivation for this analysis is the descriptive fact that Nicaraguan English adjectives, e.g., surface as the sole, even tense-marked predicate in a sentence (e.g. *everything (did) cheap, but now everything (did) dear)*, as in many languages of the world. But the case for this analysis of Nicaraguan English adjectives is quite weak. For one thing, these 'adjectival' verbs, quite unlike the ordinary verbs, have the distinct property of being able to precede nouns and modify them in NPs (e.g. *the young coconut, the little boy*, and so on). They are, moreover, uniquely involved in comparative constructions of a certain type (e.g. *now he more happier than me*). And finally, as predicative adjectives, they must always be preceded by either an expressed or null copular verb, the presence of the latter of which can be deduced from certain syntactic regularities discussed below. Thus adjectives do not, as lexical verbs do, grammatically head the predicative phrases in which they are located.

This matter aside, in the sections that follow we examine some of the characteristics of Nicaraguan English morphology that have been discussed in the literature and/or have emerged during the course of our work on the language. The general observation here is that though there is very little inflectional morphology in English generally, in Nicaraguan English there is even less – compared, say, to earlier English.

We have nothing to say at this stage of our work about the derivational morphology of the language, except that it appears to be quite restricted *vis-à-vis* that of International English, or about the reduplicatory morphology of Nicaraguan English, as in *that's the best-best thing; they have the bad-bad one; I going to tell the policeman right-right now*; and so on. These matters await further work and further developments in the theory of morphology.

6.1 Nouns

There is little to discuss here except the general absence of inflectional morphology and little of interest except the formation of plurals NP's. For example, the various thematic and semantic relationships indicated in International English with the genitive inflectional /S/ (realized variously as [s], [z], or [iz]) are left unmarked in Nicaraguan English whether the modifier is a noun or pronoun; the head noun is animate or inanimate; the relationship alienable or inalienable; and so on. For example:

(5)   *ø-genitive*

(5.a)   the lagoon edge

(5.b)   the woman baby

(5.c)   that little boy name

(5.d)   you baby

(5.e)   live you life!

(5.f)   that me brother son

More interesting for both structural and historical reasons is the fact that Nicaraguan English noun pluralization is indicated by *-dem*-suffixation (this suffix deriving historically from earlier English pronominal *them*). Note the following examples, with some International English plural forms reanalysed as singular in Nicaraguan English:

(6)   -dem-*suffixation*

(6.a)   the boat-dem *de* in the river, 'the boats are in the river'

(6.b)   I did see Ronald book-dem, 'I saw Ronald's books'

(6.c)   the people-dem want food, 'the people want food'

(6.d)   Manuel children-dem happy, 'Manuel's children are happy'

In its distributional details, however, the Nicaraguan English noun plural suffix *-dem* is only very roughly equivalent to the International English plural suffix /S/ (realized variously as [s], [z], and [iz] for regular nouns, depending on the character of the final sound of the noun stem). Thus although we expect and do find the following equivalences:

(7) *NcE*   *InE*
     the book-dem   the book[s]
     the dog-dem   the dog[z]
     the dress-dem   the dress[iz]

the picture is a great deal more complicated than would be allowed by the simple statement 'let Nicaraguan English *-dem* = International English /S/ everywhere'. In other words, the rule for making plural NPs in Nicaraguan English is something more than just 'add *-dem* to the singular form of the noun to get its Nicaraguan English plural form.' We now explore the nature of this complication, a piece of it at a time.

A popular Bluefields musical group, Dimensión Costeña/Coast Dimension, has recorded a number of traditional British Christmas songs, including 'The Twelve Days of Christmas', in an album entitled *Navidad con Dimensión Costeña*. Their idiosyncratic version of the song consists entirely of this verse, twice repeated:

(8)   On the first days of Christmas, my true love send to me two turtledove, four callingbird, five golden ring, four callingbird, three Frenchhen and a partridge in a pear tree

In particular, the lyrics would be ill-formed in Nicaraguan English if they took the following form (in which the asterisk indicates that a form or structure does not follow from the grammar of the language under discussion):

(9) On the first days of Christmas my true love send to me two *turtledove-dem, four *callingbird-dem, five golden *ring-dem, four *callingbird-dem, three *Frenchhen-dem, and a partridge in a pear tree . . .

In the light of these data, we must revise the rule ('add -*dem* to the singular form of the noun to get its Nicaraguan English plural form') for forming plural NPs in Nicaraguan English to something like: no -*dem*-pluralization in NP's with expressed cardinality.[1]

Furthermore, in Nicaraguan English, constructions of the following sort are typical, in which, in fact, -*dem* plurals are ungrammatical:

(10) all (of) the dog did bark ~ all (of) the *dog-dem did bark

(11) some dog did bark loud ~ some *dog-dem did bark loud

(12) is [= InE 'there are'] many dog in Bluefields ~ is many *dog-dem in Bluefields

On the basis of these data we can further reformulate the rule to account for the fact that -*dem*-less plural forms are required in unambiguously quantified NP's, predicting, e.g., the ungrammaticality of (13) and the grammaticality of (14):

(13) *several dog-dem did bark last night

(14) these dog *de* [= are] in the street

Continuing this line of inquiry, we note that in Bluefields, a well-known English nursery rhyme is typically recited as follows:

(15) What are little boy made of? What are little boy made of? Little boy made of . . . What are little girl made of? Little girl made of sugar and spice and everything nice. That what little girl made of.

And definitely *not* the following:

(16) What are little *boy-dem made of? What are little *boy-dem made of? Little *boy-dem made of . . . What are little *girl-dem made of? Little *girl-dem made of sugar and spice and everything nice. That what little *girl-dem made of.

Thus we see that -*dem* is not used in generic nominal expressions.

The proper generalization needed to account for the grammar

of -*dem* in pluralization then appears to be the following: -*dem* pluralization is employed only in definite NP's, *the* being the only quantifier that does not itself reveal the notion 'plural'. The redundancy involved historically in English NP pluralization is thus reduced in Nicaraguan English, as in many varieties of spoken English.

As a final complication in Nicaraguan NP pluralization, note the grammaticality judgements for the following types of constructions:

(17) he want seven case of beer

(18) he want only one case of beer

(19) he did see the *case-dem of beer ~ case of beer-dem [= InE 'the cases of beer'] on the Bluefields Express

(20) she did own the team of horse-dem [= 'the teams of horses']

(21) she did own the team of horse [= 'the team of horses']

(22) she did see one sack of rice in the store

(23) she did see the sack of rice-dem ~ *sack-dem of rice [= InE 'the sacks of rice'] in the store

(24) she did see one boy in the dark

(25) she did see the boy-dem in the dark ~ boy in the *dark-dem [= InE 'the boys in the dark']

In constructions of the sort illustrated in (17) through (23), as distinct from those in (24)–(25), words such as *case* and *sack* appear to be taken as classifiers (part of the determiner phrase?) and the NP plural marker -*dem* then ends up on the head noun despite the fact that it is the classifier that it enumerated, whether the head noun is a mass or count noun.

6.2 -*dem*-pluralization

-*dem*-pluralization is, of course, unparalleled in the history of English, posing something of a problem for historical analysis. One possible account derives from the tendency in spoken English for people to mark the position of a left-dislocated/topicalized NP with a resumptive pronoun, as in *my friends, I really like them*; *my friends, they really like me*; etc. The model for forming the -*dem* plural forms would then be understood to arise and extend from the structures available for the left-dislocation of subjects, structures in which *them* has become the subject pronoun form (*my friends, them really like me*). However, this line of argument is not accompanied by any evidence and thus is in need of a great deal more empirical work.

Attempts to relate the -*dem*-plural forms to grammatical features of, say, Yoruba (held 'to be one of those undisputed cases in which West African influence is generally recognized' (Holm 1988: 193, quoting Boretsky 1983: 91) are also unconvincing, being based entirely on quite superficial characteristics of the substrate languages putatively involved: the supposedly parallel use of the third-person plural pronoun to mark the plural of nouns in some West African languages – *àwon* in Yoruba, for example. For further discussion see also Holm 1978: 278ff., Singler 1988, among others, and O'Neil et al. 1987, citing Bamgbose 1966. The history of this Nicaraguan and general Caribbean English structure remains a mystery, I believe.

There is, nevertheless, a simpler, more direct way of deriving the -*dem*-plural construction; for quite general to English is the construction *Mary and them*, meaning 'Mary and whoever she is normally accompanied by' – see Cassidy 1985: s.v. *and them*. A step in the generalization of this construction can then be seen in Bahamian English (Holm with Shilling 1982: s.v. *them*), where it is said that *them* pluralizes only animate NP's. In Nicaraguan English there is a further generalization such that all [+definite, +plural] NP's show -*dem*-suffixation.

6.3 Verbs

What is most interesting here, both from a structural and from an historical point of view, is tense formation in Nicaraguan English. In this section, we look at some of the morphophonological aspects of Nicaraguan English tense formation, returning in section 7 to consider some of its large syntactic connections.

For International English, the structure and history of regular past-tense formation is well understood (see Keyser and O'Neil 1985: ch. 4): structurally, a phonologically underspecified morpheme /T/ is suffixed to the verb stem. This /T/, an underspecified segment, is characterized by just the phonological features and their values that /t/ and /d/ have in common. If the verb stem ends in a segment with this same set of feature-values, then the unmarked vowel (for English, specified before reduction as /ɪ/, i.e. [+high, −back, −round, −tense]) is epenthesized (i.e., inserted) between the stem-final consonant and the /T/ suffix, thus syllabifying the inflection. Voicing is then spread rightward to /T/, specifying it as /t/, i.e. voiceless, if the segment preceding it is [-voice]; as /d/, i.e.

voiced, if the preceding segment, including how the epenthetic /ɪ/, is [+voice]. These two rules – applied in the order given above – then account for the full range of forms, for example:

(26)   (*1. Epenthesis*)   (*2. Voicing assimilation*)

(26.a) /weytT/ -1- > /weytɪT/ -2- > /weytɪd/   *waited*

(26.b) /beykT/ n.a.   -2- > /beykt/   *baked*

(26.c) /fænT/   n.a.   -2- > /fænd/   *fanned*

This system of rules – which, suitably revised, accounts for the forms involving inflectional /S/ (including present-tense, singular verb forms) and /d/ and /z/, the result of contraction, as well – was fully in place by the beginning of the eighteenth century (Keyser and O'Neil 1985: ch. 4).

Consider now tense formation in Nicaraguan English, that is, tense formation for regular verbs (nearly all the verbs) in this language: it is accomplished simply and pro-clitically with what are historically forms of *do*, essentially just *do* /duw/ and, for the past tense, *did* /di(d)/; for example:

(27.a) so now when he do come off to anything

(27.b) so do try keep you eye open

(27.c) that child don't care where the mother do go

(27.d) she did feel like she was breeding 'she felt as if she were pregnant'

(27.e) they did hate we

(27.f) I did go one year

(27.g) I did used to stay at him house

Here *do* and *did* have none of the emphatic stress or sense associated with them in the analogous International English structures.[2]

Moreover, as in many varieties of spoken English not under the control of educational and/or editorial authority, tense is often unexpressed morphologically in Nicaraguan English, the fixing of an event in time (a quite different thing from morphological tense-marking) then being in any case interpretable from adverbial adjuncts, context, and so on. Thus in addition to the tense morpheme of INFL taking the values [±past] in Nicaraguan English, INFL can simply be null or missing.

In Nicaraguan English, *do* and *did* (and their negative forms *don't*

/dwon/ and *didn't* /di(d)n/) are pure expressions of tense: this can be seen from their ability to mark present and past tense in adjectival predicates (though the evidence is clearer in the past tense) and on present participles:

(28.a)   I don't sure

(28.b)   everything did cheap

(28.c)   the prof get hate me like I did bad inside

(28.d)   but them did dead . . . them did die

(28.e)   I did tired and never come

(28.f)   I buy it from one boy we did cripple we did name Silly
                              'who'   'who'

(28.g)   the ship did loaded

(28.h)   they got a warning that this person did going to die

There is much to say about the grammar and origin of the proclitic, tense-marking forms of *do*: presumably they arise as a result of the rule of *do*-support, according to which syntactically stranded instances of [±past] are linked up with the (inserted?) empty verb *do* in the phonological component of the grammar. That is the rule of *do*-support has a wider range of application in Nicaraguan English than in, say, International English. This is because Nicaraguan English has lost the rule of INFL(ection)-lowering that – in many varieties of English – lowers the INFL of a tensed clause to the main verb, the analog in current theory to the rule of affix-hopping in earlier theory (see Emonds 1978, and more recently: Chomsky 1989; Pollock 1989). In many varieties of English, it is this rule that links the tense morpheme with the main verb. Without the rule of INFL-lowering – as in Nicaraguan English, the tense morpheme is left stranded, requiring *do*-support – perhaps lexicalizing it.

Furthermore, we know that in earlier English – of the sixteenth, seventeenth, and eighteenth centuries – the various forms of *do* participated in the marking of tense, appearing in contrast to dialects with the now standard inflectional endings /T/ and /S/, in the verb paradigms. (For the details and incidence of forms of this sort in the period of earlier English in question, see Visser 1978: sections 1419–21; for theoretical discussion, see Pollock 1989.) That is, in this earlier period in some varieties of the language, the rule of INFL-lowering (to V) was already lost, or perhaps never developed, tense-marking being fully lexicalized. The difference, then, between Nicaraguan English and International English in this respect is that the rule of INFL-lowering disappeared entirely from the grammar of the former while becoming obligatory in the latter. Note, in passing, that Nicaraguan English has lost overt expression of the AGR(eement) morpheme as well.

Following up on a suggestion of J. Mascaró (personal communication), we gain some insight into what may have triggered the use of these proclitic, unlowered tense structures in Nicaraguan English, leading to the wider application/lexicalization of *do*-support in the grammar of this language. For note another characteristic of the language, referred to above in section 5.2.2: the fact that syllable-final consonant clusters in Nicaraguan English are simplified in contrast with the better known varieties of International English. Thus in Nicaraguan English, there are, in particular, no syllable-final clusters that end in a stop, so that we find, for example /askyér/ for *ascared*; /bil/ for *build*; /grown/ for *ground*; /syev/ for *saved*; /byek/ for *baked*; /dwon/ for *don't*; /hays/ for *hoist*; /entatyénmen/ for *entertainment*; /ans/ for *ants*; /biys/ for *beast*; /was/ for *wasp*; and so on. As mentioned earlier, final /sk/ is either metathesized to /ks/ or reduced to /s/: /deks/~/des/ for *desk*; and so on. Consequently, then, we find *inter alia* /T/-less verb and deverbal forms:

(29)   /T/-*less verb forms*

(29.a)   you have this thing in you pocket name garlic

(29.b)   the teacher get vex with me

(29.c)   I buy it from one boy we did cripple . . .

(29.d)   the shrimps net is fill with shrimps

(29.e)   put the label parts in alphabetical order

(29.f)   what the best method that could be use in teaching . . .?

(29.g)   that make us feel so discourage

(29.h)   them must be shame but we not shame

Reverse evidence, provided by frequently hyper-corrected spoken as well as written examples (for example, the form of the infinitive in 'it will also get the children to asked the teacher question') gives us insight into this phenomenon as well.

Now it is obvious that one effect of cluster reduction is to greatly reduce the number of regular verbs with distinct past-tense (and past-participial) forms of the type with inflectional /T/.

Cluster reduction would not, however, do away with this inflectional consonant if it were not part of a syllable-final consonant cluster; for here it was preserved, as, for example, in the syllabic and post-vocalic forms of the participial ending: /wan+máyndid/, i.e., 'single-minded'; /lyetid/, i.e., 'belated'; /drowndid/ for *drowned*; /tayad/ for *tired*; and so on. Thus Mascaró's suggestion carries us only part of the way to an account of tense-marking in Nicaraguan English. For we must still explain the loss of the /T/ in verbs that end in /t/, /d/, or with a vowel.

In Nicaraguan English, however, such deverbal forms seem to appear only sporadically as adjectives, never as past-tense or participial forms, the uninflected forms having been adopted throughout the verb paradigms. Except now and then as adjectival passives, distinctly marked past and passive participles have disappeared from the language: for Nicaraguan English appears, for example, to have neither syntactic passive nor perfective constructions – but see below, (99)–(105), and discussion there.

However, as indicated above, the past tense takes the form of *did* + V; the present tense – perhaps, of *do* + V, insofar as inflections are at all involved in verbal paradigms. In Nicaraguan English, when the syllable-final consonant clusters were reduced, a way remaining to form the past tense of verbs was for all regular verbs to adopt the readily available proclitic forms with the forms of *do*, i.e. for the rule of INFL-lowering to be dropped from the grammar. We return below to further discussion of tense formation in the context of the structure of Nicaraguan English INFL.

As we have seen above (section 6.1), there is another, quite similar development in Nicaraguan English: the form that NP pluralization has assumed in the language. As noted above, the situation is this: under certain, well-defined conditions *-dem* is suffixed to a noun in order to indicate that an NP is plural. Thus we find the relationship, (7) repeated as (30), between Nicaraguan and International English forms:

(30) *NcE*   *InE*
      the book-dem   the book[s]
      the dog-dem   the dog[z]
      the dress-dem   the dress[iz]

By analogy with the discussion of the origins of the past-tense forms, we might then expect the NP plural forms to have arisen through the loss of post-consonantal, syllable-final /S/, which was then replaced by an alternating form in the language that employed something like -*dem*.

Though, as we have seen above, there was a possibly generalizable *dem*-like alternative to /S/-pluralization, there is still a fatal objection to such a phonological trigger for such a change: syllable-final consonant clusters ending in /s/ or /z/ did not simplify in Nicaraguan English. There are, for example, many examples of words like *fence*, *else*, *horse*, *dance*, *Charles*, /deks/ (= *desk*), etc. that survive unreduced in their final /S/-clusters. Moreover, as noted above, many /S/ plurals show up as well, especially with words that generally, in some intuitive sense, appear in the plural: e.g. *ants*, *bangles*, *worms*, etc. In fact, these plural forms are generally, as indicated above, reanalysed as singulars in Nicaraguan English and from there they take on a singular life of their own, a characteristic common to many varieties of English. Thus we find such words entering into pluralization with -*dem* (*the ants-dem*, *the bees-dem*, etc.) and into compound structures as well (e.g. *flowers-pot*, *shoes-maker*) reinterpreted as singulars and generics, respectively.

Thus there is no account of the history of -*dem*-pluralization, parallel to past-tense formation with *did*, to be found in the structure of earlier English.

Returning now to the changes in the grammar of English that led to the Nicaraguan variety: here we seem able to say that the simplification of some types of syllable-final consonant clusters in the language was, perhaps, a necessary pre-condition for the grammatical change in tense-formation, but it is, of course, not a sufficient condition. For cluster simplication does not account for the loss of inflectional /T/ from verbs whose stems terminated in /t/ or /d/ or a vowel. It is here that the notion of rule loss or narrowing (specifically the loss or narrowing of the rule of INFL-lowering) assumes its importance as an explanation of the difference between Nicaraguan English and earlier English, on the other hand, and it and International English on the other.

7 Syntax

The main characteristics of Nicaraguan English syntax, obvious from the examples already given above, are familiar enough to speakers of all varieties of English: a prevailingly subject-verb-complement ordering of major sentence elements; left-headed phrase constructions – that is, complements following rather than preceding their heads; movement of *wh*-phrases to a (COMP) position at the beginning of the clause; and so on. There are, however, some interesting, specifically historically interesting, characteristics of Nicaraguan English syntax that have emerged in the course of our work on the language and from the work of Holm. In the materials that follow we will look briefly at question-formation in Nicaraguan English; then more thoroughly at the syntax of the copular verbs of Nicaraguan English and at a variety of constructions in which NPs are unexpressed phonologically in the language.

7.1 Question formation

There is no subject-auxiliary inversion in Nicaraguan English questions; that is there is no distinction in word order between direct and indirect questions, as there is in International English. Thus the following are typical for Nicaraguan English, in which the *wh*-word (or question-word) raised to the beginning of the clause is interpreted in the position marked *t* in the examples given. What we mean by this is that in answers to the questions, the new material appears in the position marked by *t* (the *trace* of the position from which the question word is presumed to have been moved in syntax, or to which it is referentially related); for example (for (31.c, d)): *it cost five córdoba*; *bilingual does pay the salary so small because . . .*; and so on:

(31.a) why it is that . . . *t*?

(31.b) and why we don't receive materials *t*?

(31.c) what it cost *t*?

(31.d) why bilingual does pay the salary so small *t*?

(31.e) he did ask what it cost *t*

Once again the difference between Nicaraguan English and International English is captured by a rule difference between the grammars of the two languages: for in International English subject-auxiliary inversion comes about through the raising of constituents in INFL (F: [±past], modal, and the forms of the auxiliary verbs *be* and *have*) to the head of COMP – one of the positions preceding and higher than the main elements of a clause, the subject of the sentence remaining in its underlying position. The grammar of Nicaraguan English is, however, characterized by the loss of INFL-raising from the grammar, another instance of the loss of a raising rule – accounting, thus, for just the right array of facts.

Note that the grammars of both languages contain the rule of *wh*-movement, whereby the various *wh*-phrases are raised to a position in COMP, specifically to Spec of COMP. The tree (32) summarizes and locates the several movement and raising rules referred to thus far:

(32)

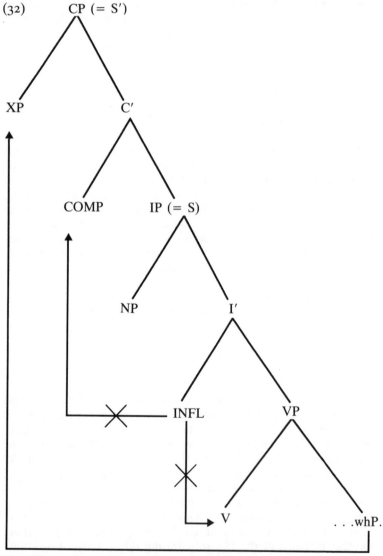

(An 'X' through the line that indicates a movement rule or relationship is meant to show that the movement, though possible in International English, is not possible in Nicaraguan English.)

7.2   Further remarks on Nicaraguan English copular verbs and the structure of INFL

A problem for verb morphology is to give an account of the order of elements in the sentence; for example, in French and English, for the differing order of the verb and VP adverbials:

(33)   Berkman completely lost his mind

(34)   Berkman perdit complètement la tête

But note the following, in which English *be* and auxiliary *have* behave like lexical verbs in French:

(35)   Berkman has completely lost his mind

(36)   Berkman is often completely out of control

(37)   Berkman is closely watched by the prison guards

And simple negation, in which *neg* blocks lowering in English, but not raising in French:

(38)   Goldman (n')aime pas Berkman

(39)   Goldman doesn't love Berkman ~ *Goldman loves not Berkman

(40)   Goldman hasn't seen Berkman lately

Thus, given these facts, we assume the following structure for IP (= S), somewhat simplified:

(41) $[_{IP}$ NP $[_{I'}$ AGR $[_{FP}$ F $[_{(negP)}$ neg $[_{VP}$ (ADV) $[_{VP}$ V . . .]]]]]], where AGR = subject-verb agreement; F = [±finite] (with [+finite] further specified for tense); ADV = VP-adjoined adverbial elements.

In tensed-clauses in French, V raises over ADV and neg to F to AGR; in English, AGR lowers to F to V, with – however – *be* and auxiliary *have* (and in some varieties lexical *have* as well) raising as in French generally. In English, neg (i.e. *not*) blocks lowering (but not *be-*, *have-* raising), thus forcing *do*-support.

7.2.1   Sentence negation in Nicaraguan English

As discussed in section 6.3 and immediately above, tense is either absent or lexicalized in Nicaraguan English, e.g.:

(42)   she (do) know the answer [marginal, and perhaps not systematic, but cf. *is ~ e*]

(43)   she did know the answer [[+past] grammatically]

Simple negation is expressed as follows:

(44)   he don't/no know the answer

(45)   he didn't know the answer

With modals and negation interacting as follows:

(46)   he wouldn't know the answer

(47)   she can't ([kyaan]) . . . can ([kan]) not go

(48)   he wouldn't have ([wudna]) say nothing

In Nicaraguan English, as we argued above, there is no AGR/F-lowering to V in finite constructions: in [+past] clauses without modals or *be*, there is always *do*-support (cf. 43), as well as in negative constructions (44), (45). [±past] is 'weakened' to the point of being (partially, perhaps fully) lexicalized: not being stranded, tense cannot lower; thus it does not lower. As we see below, finite forms of Nicaraguan English *be*, perhaps *have*, raise, as in more familiar varieties of English.

Turning to Nicaraguan English copular constructions, as noted above, there appear to be two copular verbs in this language: *is* and *de*. Some of their privileges of occurrence are suggested in (49)–(58), and by the ungrammaticality of (59)–(62):

(49)   I *de* upon Caesar right now 'I'm after Caesar right now'

(50)   the girl-dem, all *de* upon the veranda
              'are'

(51)   Olga *de* by her
              'is'

(52)   but now no kind of work *de* here
                            'is'

(53)   this one *de* with leaf 'this one [house] is thatched'

(54)   she is the boss

(55)   him is the captain and I is the striker
                                'harpooner'

(56)   I is the oldtime riding horse

(57)   you is a rich man

(58)   Alicia husband is a shrimps-man

(59)   *he *de* the oldtime riding horse

(60) *A. husband *de* a rich man

(61) *the girl-dem, all is upon the veranda

(62) *Olga is by her

Note, also, the presence of null-copular constructions in Nicaraguan English, as in the following – where the position in which the copula would occur is marked *e*:

(63) I no know if it *e* in the bible

(64) right now he *e* up hospital

(65) he farm *e* here in this place
      'his'

(66) and I *e* the boss

(67) Ronald brother *e* a fisherman

In each case, there is but one way to fill the empty position: *de* for (63)–(65); *is* for (66)–(67).[3]

It is furthermore the case that the following grammaticality judgements hold for Nicaraguan English:

(68) she *de* sick ~ *she is sick

(69) if you *de* safe, you . . .

(70) she *e* sick

(71) she *e* ~ *de* kind of weak

(72) ah, they talk *se* the language *e* bad

(73) ah, they talk *se* the language *de* bad ~ . . . is bad

(74) if you would *e* safe, you would run

The privileges of occurrence appear to parallel those of Spanish, which also has two copular verbs, *estar* and *ser*. The usual way of talking about their distribution goes as follows (*The American Heritage Larousse Spanish Dictionary* 1986: x):

(75) G13 Ser and Estar
      Ser is used to express a quality or characteristic of the subject . . ., the origin of the subject . . ., and in expressing time and dates . . . Impersonal expressions are also formed with the verb *ser* . . . The passive voice is formed with *ser* and the past participle . . .
      Estar is used to indicate a state or condition of the

subject . . . It is also used to express location or position
. . . The progressive tenses are formed with *estar* and the
present participle . . .

Some adjectives may be used with either *ser* or *estar*.
In those cases, use of *estar* indicates a personal reaction
to something whereas *ser* refers to what is considered
characteristic of the subject by relatively objective
standards . . .

The point here is not that Nicaraguan English has been
influenced by Spanish with respect to its copular verbs, but that
the distinction exhibited in the grammar of Spanish is available in
Universal Grammar to a child developing a language, and that
Nicaraguan English appears to have developed a copular verb
system shared by many languages of the world. These parallels
are born out by the following:

(76) Alicia husband is from Bluefields

(77) *Alicia husband *de* from Bluefields

(78) Alicia husband *e* from Bluefields

(79) they no *de* like we

(80) if you *de* safe, you *de* run [cf. if you would *e* safe, you
would *e* run]

(81) but anyhow I *de* try to soap out me clothes

(82) the gal no *de* breed, man

7.2.2 *Further comment on* de *constructions*
Yet there is reason to suspect that *de*, rather than being a locative
copula (behaving more or less like Sp. *estar*), is a quasi-auxiliary
verb at best, and perhaps not a verb at all. Compare, for
example, the following data and the constructions with *de* and
those with the manifestly copular verb, *be* and its forms:

(83) Miss Angelica (*de*) at home

(84) Ronald (*de*) here

(85) he (no) (*de*) sick

(86) he (no) *de* rest ~ he (not) resting

(87) she did (*de*) at home yesterday

(88) he didn't (*de*) at home today

(89)   she ?don't/no (*de*) there right now

(90)   where it *?(*de*)?

(91)   he (is)/was old

(92)   he (is)/was a shrimps-man

(93)   he (is)/was from Bluefields

(94)   he (is) not old ~ *he (is) no old (isn't = [ent])

(95)   he (is) not a old man ~ *he (is) no a old man

(96)   who he *(is)?

Clearly, *de* behaves quite differently from the tensed forms of copular *be*: it does not (as *is* does) raise in finite constructions, thus its tense is marked by the forms of *do*; it is (unlike *is*) negated by a preceding *no* or negative forms of *do*; and unlike *is*, it can apparently be deleted before a trace or gap. Moreover, it does not show up in non-finite constructions, e.g.:

(97)   *he want (to) *de* at home

(98)   he want (*?to) be at home

For these reasons, *de*'s status as a copular verb is in doubt. It thus seems more reasonable to argue that the grammar of Nicaraguan English simply has a rule which requires the deletion of *is* and its forms when they immediately precede *de*, another way of realizing the descriptive facts noted above for *de*.

There is another Nicaraguan English form, *mi*, for which auxiliary verb status has been claimed. Some examples of the *mi*-construction follow (*mi* < *been*, by Voltaire's principle):

(99)   why you no *mi* want come visit Miss Betty?

(100)   Miss Angélica *mi* sick

(101)   he no *mi* (*de*) by Miss Betty house

(102)   we *mi* de look for you

(103)   the man [*we* (=who) *mi* in Managua] *de* here

(104)   she *mi* gone to Lagoon

(105)   where he *mi* lost?

Holm (1978: 251–4) argues that *mi* is a past-tense (anterior) marker, but if so, *mi* would stand out in its quite different behaviour from the forms of *do* and *be*, for example. It is negated by *no* rather than by *not*; and like *de*, it is located below (i.e. to the right of) *no*. *Mi* appears, moreover, to force a perfective interpretation generally, which – given the slim presence of perfective *have* in Nicaraguan English (but see (48)) – fills a gap in the verb paradigm. Its supposed historical derivation from *been* lends some support to this way of viewing *mi*. In fact, insofar as perfective *have* does show up in Nicaraguan English, it is in complementary distribution with *mi*. For example:

(106)   Ronald have try to go to Bluff

(107)   Ronald *mi* try to go to Bluff ≠ Ronald did try to go to Bluff

(108)   *Ronald *mi* have try to go to Bluff

(109)   *Ronald have *mi* try to go to Bluff

7.2.3   *Copular verbs in questions*
In International English, contractible verbs (e.g., the finite forms of *be*, *have*, *will*, etc.) cannot be contracted if they cannot be de-stressed, and they cannot be de-stressed if they immediately precede a null element – a 'gap', one created by movement or by deletion. Thus, consider the following International English sentences (in which *t* marks the position from which something has been moved and/or deleted) and their grammaticality judgements:

(110.a) I wonder where *Emma's *t* today

(110.b) I wonder when Emma's at home *t*

(111.a) Emma's generous and *Peter's *t* too [cf. . . . and so's Peter *t*]

(111.b) Emma's generous and Peter is *t* too

(112)   Alex'll go to jail, and *I'll *t* too

In the light of these data, consider further the following grammaticality judgements in Nicaraguan English, in which the presence of the copular verbs or their absence (noted with *e*) should be the focus of attention:

(113)   ?how she *e* *t*?

(114)   how she *de* *t*?

(115)   where he *de* *t*?

(116)   ?where he *e* *t*?

(117)   he know where Shirley *de t*

(118)   ?he know where Shirley *e t*

(119)   like how he *de t* right now?

(120)   ?like how he *e t* right now?

(121)   what Alicia husband is *t*?

(122)   *what Alicia husband *e t*?

Clearly, the copular verb *is* cannot be deleted (which in this variety of English is equivalent to contraction) before a gap. The deletion of the putatively copular *de*, while not perfect, is, however, acceptable, thus casting further doubt on the status of *de* as a copular verb.

There is more to understand about the copular constructions of Nicaraguan English; for example, consider the following:

(123)   *e* is a balance of things what go there

(124)   it is a woman outside

(125)   *e* is easy for do that

(126)   you know *e* is really true for say that

(127)   and in the night when *e* is time for eat

(128)   well, *e* is better you pass the day here with me

Here, there is no alternative to these sentences with the null copular verb. It appears, then, that it is not possible to delete *is* after an empty element, nor following an empty element phonetically realized at some point in the derivation of the sentences as *it*. (129) and (130) seem to contradict this generalization:

(129)   *e* is what the trouble, *e* is why *unu* running so for?
                           2nd p. pl

(130)   *e* is asthma he got

since there are perfectly well-formed sentences like (131), (132):

(131)   what the trouble, why *unu* running so for?

(132)   asthma, he got

But the contradiction is only an apparent one; for it can be shown that (131), (132) are formed in a different way from their apparent analogs (129), (130) – see section 7.3.2.

7.3   Null NPs

In the more familiar varieties of English, there is little tolerance
for unfilled or implicitly filled NP positions in most untransform-
ed constructions. In fact, generally the only unfilled NP subject-
positions allowed in International English involve implicit
arguments and so-called control-Pro; that is, constructions of the
following sort, in which Pro (a phonetically null pronominal) is a
syntactically and computationally present element, *e* marking the
location of null objects (reflexive or otherwise):

(133)   *Constructions with controlled subject-*Pro *and/or implicit
        objects*

(133.a)   Emma persuaded Alex [Pro to change his plans]

(133.b)   Emma promised Alex [Pro to change her plans]

(133.c)   Alex is too stubborn [Pro to talk to *e*]

(133.d)   Emma is reading *e*

(133.e)   Alex is shaving *e*

In (133.a) Pro is construed as *Alex*; in (133.b) it is coreferential
with *Emma*; in (133.c) the Pro is arbitrary, that is, roughly
equivalent to 'for anyone' and *e* is coreferential with *Alex*; in
(133.d) *e* stipulates anything/something so long as it is readable;
and in (133.e) *e* is reflexive of *Alex*.

In Nicaraguan English, there is, in addition to those just
mentioned, a wider range of lexically unfilled NP positions, some
of which are construed from the larger (discourse) context and
others that are arbitrary in construal, but all of which would be
ill-formed in International English. For example, consider the
following sentence, found early in the transcribed passage above
(section 5.4), where *e* again marks the phonetically unfilled
position:

(134)   he catch fish and bring it and sell *e*

In (134), the object NP of *sell* is left unexpressed, but it is
recovered as co-referential with *fish*. Note that the directional
prepositional phrase following *bring* is implicit as well.

Sentences in which the phonetically null element receives
arbitrary interpretation also appear in Nicaraguan English:

(135.a)   you should send *e* to him that way

(135.b)   because you just send *e* to we the Carib people

Here *e* is interpreted as 'something/-one sendable'.

7.3.1   Null NPs and serial verbs
This topic is properly a part of syntax, I believe, as will be argued
below – at least for Nicaraguan English. However, others would
maintain that serial verbs lie in the domain of morphology.

First let us define what we mean by a 'serial verb': a serial verb
construction is a sequence, arbitrary in length, of (non-auxiliary)
verbs unseparated by phonetically represented nominal and/or
inflectional elements; that is, the difference between (136.a, b)
and (136.c), in the last of which the verbs in sequence are broken
up by the INFL element *to*:

(136.a) he send call the husband again
        's/he sent someone to call the husband again'

(136.b) Zion, send come call me
        'Zion, send someone to come call me'

(136.c) I just decide to send *e* to call you
        'I just decided to send someone to call you'

The verbs in sequence need not have the same unexpressed
subjects, as in (136), where the sender is not the caller; however,
the unexpressed subjects of the verbs in sequence are often the
same, as in *come call* and *decide to send* in (136.b, c) and in (137):

(137.a) you no want go look after you baby

(137.b) and he begin shout

(137.c) I bathe the horse-dem in the morning soon and carry
        them go eat grass
        'I bathe the horses early in the morning and carry
        them to go eat grass'

(137.d) him no remember for go see the children-dem
        'he didn't remember to go to see the children'

The deeper question about verb sequences of this sort is
whether or not they are broken up by phonetically null nominal
and/or inflectional elements. (We know that the latter option
exists in this language in tensed clauses, where it is not necessary
to fill the tense position INFL with F (= [±past]) and where
there is, thus, no *do*-support.)

The answer to this question appears necessarily to be yes: if we
wish to maintain, as I believe we do, that the lexical properties
are satisfied by the individual parts of the serial verb, just as they
would be by the verbs in isolation. By this principle the structure
of, say, (136.a) would be, at least (138), in which Pro and *e* are co-

referential as some arbitrary person(s), indicated by the co-indexing; that is, elements indexed '$_i$' co-refer with other elements so indexed, but not with those indexed '$_j$'.

(138)   he sent e_i [PRO$_i$ INFL call the husband again]

Thus (136.a, b) and (136.c), although quite different in their surface syntax, are very much alike in their underlying syntax, (139), (140) = (136.b, c), respectively their difference residing in whether INFL is phonetically realized as *to* or not:

(139)   Zion$_i$, [e_i send e_j [PRO$_j$ INFL come [PRO$_j$ INFL call me]]]

(140)   I$_i$ just decide [PRO$_i$ to$_{INFL}$ send e_j [PRO$_j$ to call you]]

in which the coreferentially of the various NPs is again indicated by co-indexing.

7.3.2 Null NPs in other constructions: expletives and pleonastics

Continuing the discussion begun above (see (123)–(132)), we note that there are two other constructions in which we find full NPs in Nicaraguan English:

(141.a) *e* was a little boy name Jack

(141.b) once *e* was a king

(141.c) well, the ship have the motor, and *e* is a balance of things what go there

In International English, we expect expletive *there* in such constructions, but in Nicaraguan English these constructions appear with no phonologically expressed element, as in (141), above, or with an expletive *it*, as in (142):

(142.a) it was a ragid fisherman

(142.b) it is a woman outside

What then about the pleonastic *it* (distinct from the referential *it*) of International English? From such sentences as those in (143), it appears that in Nicaraguan English the pleonastic subject is never realized phonologically:

(143.a) *e* is easy for do that

(143.b) you know *e* is really true for say that

(143.c) *e* seem they never happy 'they seem never happy'

(143.d) and in the night when *e* is time for eat

(143.e) well, *e* is better you pass the day here with me

(143.f) *e* look like they have blood 'they appear to be alive'

(143.g) *e* always *de* rain in Bluefields, *e* never *de* snow
         'it always rains in Bluefields; it never snows'

This is the case for topicalized, clefted constructions as well:

(144.a) *e* is what the trouble, *e* is why *unu* running so for?
                                               2nd p. pl

(144.b) *e* is asthma he got

Topicalization does not, however, require the presence of *is*:

(145) several complaint, they does go with

Nor, as we have seen above (section 7.2.3), does question-formation. Nicaraguan English is thus a language with null expletive and null pleonastic NPs.

There are other idiosyncracies of Nicaraguan English syntax, but at the moment, it is not clear what their interest, either for the theory of grammar or linguistic change is.[4]

7.4 Summary remarks on syntax

There is much more to say about Nicaraguan English syntax, of course: for example, (143.c, f) suggest that there are no raising verbs in the language, that is, verbs which require NP movement of the subject of the lower, untensed clause into the subject position of the higher clause, as in the International English gloss of (143.c). Moreover, there appear to be no other raising predicates. This observation, coupled with the fact that Nicaraguan English appears not to have syntactic passive constructions, further suggests that the grammar of the language does not contain NP movement. In summary, then, we can tentatively capture some important differences among earlier English, Nicaraguan English, and International English in the tabular form given in (146), where '+' indicates that the grammar of the language contains the rule in question; '−' indicates that it does not; and '+/−' indicates that there were two varieties of earlier English with respect to the rule or construction in question:

(146)		*EarlierE*	*NcE*	*InE*
1.	INFL-lowering (to V)	+/−	−[5]	+
2.	INFL-raising (to COMP)	+	−	+
3.	*do*-support (of stranded F)	+	+[6]	+
4.	NP-movement (to NP)	+	−	+
5.	*wh*-movement (so Spec of COMP)	+	+	+

8 Conclusion

The preceding sketch of Nicaraguan English grammar is, of course, incomplete and some of the historical connections between it and the grammar of earlier English are only tentatively understood as well, or not understood at all. There is, for example, nothing to say about the tolerance that Nicaraguan English shows for empty NP's. Perhaps it is simply the sort of thing typical of languages that we know from conversation rather than from books.

Other historical connections and explanations for peculiarities of Nicaraguan English grammar are however stronger: its loss of the rule of INFL-raising to the head of COMP resulting in the disappearance of the subject-aux-inversion effect; its tense-marking system involving the loss of INFL-lowering and, perhaps, the lexicalization of F: [±past]); its NP-pluralization system with its generalization of 'and them'; its copular constructions; its working out differently the Vowel Shift characteristic of all varieties of English.

Nicaraguan English is in any case not remarkably different from the other Englishes of the world.

Acknowledgements

Thanks are due to Ken Hale and Maya Honda for their helpful comments on this chapter in one or another of its earlier incarnations. Chief among my native-speaker informants, linguistic collaborators, and friends are: Ronald Brooks, Miss Azalie Hodgson, Miss Dora Joiner, Guillermo McLean, Alicia Slate, Miss Shirley Taylor, and many of the teachers and *técnicas* in the Bilingual-Bicultural Education Program of the South Atlantic Autonomous Region of Nicaragua.

Notes

1. Note, in passing, that *days* in Nicaraguan English is not a plural form; for a good number of International English plural noun forms (words that often, in some intuitive sense, appear in the plural) have been taken over into Nicaraguan English as singulars, to which *-dem* is then suffixed in order to indicate plurality. Thus, e.g. Nicaraguan English *ants* = International English *ant* and *ants-dem* = *ants*; *children* = *child*

and *children-dem* = *children*; etc.

2. The form *does* appears in the language as well, apparently in the language of people with relatively advanced education and/or perhaps with an interpretation 'habitual' – uncontrolled, however, by number agreement; thus:

   (a) why bilingual [education] does pay the salary so small?
   (b) two time in the year he does work . . . the first of the year he does work . . . two time in the year he does serve . . . and when he working several people does go . . . and he does try his best
   (c) but first the people does go and tell him about this
   (d) several complaint, they does go with

3. The null-copula is, for some reason, relatively restricted in the environment preceding a predicate nominal NP, a matter characteristic of such languages and thus one that deserves further attention, attention which we are unable to give it in our present state of knowledge.

4. In Nicaraguan English, for example, relative clauses are generally formed with an all-purpose relativizer *we* (historically derived from International English *where* and *who*(?)), with the *we* related to the positions marked with a *t* in the examples given, according to a principle similar to that mentioned in section 7.1:

   (a) you got some people *we t* know something to do
   (b) and bring him from *we* he take him *t*
   (c) I know one *we* I like *t*
   (d) I going find one *we* we used to sing *t* when we go Lagoon
   (e) and the one *we* they sing *t* when they going do the Wallagallo

Note also the *se*-type complement clauses. *se* (historically derived from the English verb *say*) is used to introduce both direct and indirect discourse, as in the following:

   (a) him believe *se* I no coming back
   (b) she said to me *se* you know I like to hear some Nancy story
        [i.e., (West African) Anansi stories]
   (c) if I never . . ., I wouldn't know *se* Elba get the children-dem sick again
   (d) ah, they talk *se* (that) the language bad
        'ah, they say that the language is bad'

But the example of (d), with *se* and *that*, suggests a different analysis.

5. English does, however, have V-raising of *be* and auxiliary *have*.

6. Perhaps, as suggested repeatedly above, better conceived of as the lexicalization of F.

316   NICARAGUAN ENGLISH IN HISTORY

References and suggestions for further reading

The American Heritage-Larousse Spanish Dictionary (1986) Boston: Houghton Mifflin & Libraire Larousse.

BAILEY, B. L. (1966) *Jamaican Creole Syntax: A Transformational Approach*. Cambridge: Cambridge University Press.

BALDWIN, J. (1979) 'If Black English isn't a language, then tell me, what is?' *New York Times: Op-ed*: 29 July. Reprinted in BALDWIN, J. (1985) *The Price of the Ticket: Collected Nonfiction 1948–1985*. New York: St Martin's Press.

BAMGBOSE, A. (1966) *A Grammar of Yoruba (West African Language Monograph No. 5)*. Cambridge: Cambridge University Press.

BICKERTON, D. (1988) 'Creole languages and the bioprogram.' In NEWMEYER, F. J. (ed.) (1988).

BICKERTON, D. and MUYSKEN, P. (1988) 'A dialog concerning the linguistic status of creole languages.' In NEWMEYER, F. J. (ed.) (1988).

BORETSKY, N. (1983) *Kreolsprachen, Substrate, und Sprachwandel*. Wiesbaden: Harrassowitz.

CASSIDY, F. G. (ed.) (1985) *Dictionary of American Regional English. Vol. I, Introduction and A–C*. Cambridge: Harvard University Press.

CHOMSKY, N. (1988) *Language and Problems of Knowledge: the Managua Lectures*. Cambridge, MA: MIT Press.

CHOMSKY, N. (1989) 'Some notes on economy of derivation and representation.' *MIT Working Papers in Linguistics: Functional Heads and Clause Structure* 10: 43–74.

CHOMSKY, N. and HALLE, M. (1968) *The Sound Pattern of English*. New York: Harper & Row.

CRAIG, C., et al. (1990) *Rama Kuup/Gramática Rama*. Managua: CIDCA.

DISKIN, M., BOSSERT, T., NAHMAD, S. and VARESE, S. (1986) *Peace and Autonomy on the Atlantic Coast of Nicaragua. A Report of the LASA Task Force on Human Rights and Academic Freedom*. Pittsburgh: Latin American Studies Association.

EMONDS, J. (1978) 'The verbal complex V'-V in french', *Linguistic Inquiry* 9: 151–75.

FREELAND, J. (1988) *A Special Place in History: The Atlantic Coast in the Nicaraguan Revolution*. London: Nicaraguan Solidarity Campaign.

HALE, C. R. and GORDON, E. T. (1987) 'Costeño demography: Historical and contemporary demography of Nicaragua's Atlantic coast.' In CIDCA and Development Study Unit (eds) *Ethnic Groups and the Nation State: The Case of the Atlantic Coast in Nicaragua*. Stockholm: Akademitryck AB.

HALE, K., HONDA, M., LAUGHREN, M. and O'NEIL, W. (1986) 'Bilingual-bicultural education in Nicaragua.' In *Proceedings of the Sixth Annual International Native American Language Issues Institute*. Choctaw OK: NALI Planning Committee.

HOLM, J. (1978) *The English Creole of Nicaragua's Miskito Coast: its sociolinguistic history and a comparative study of its lexicon and syntax*. Doctoral dissertation. University of London.

HOLM, J. (ed.) (1983) *Central American English*. Heidelberg: Julius Groos Verlag.

HOLM, J. (1986) 'The spread of English in the Caribbean area.' In GÖRTACH, M. and HOLM, J. A. (eds) *Focus on the Caribbean*. Amsterdam: John Benjamins.

HOLM, J. (1988) *Pidgins and Creoles, Vol. I: Theory and Structure*. Cambridge: Cambridge University Press.

HOLM, J. (1989) *Pidgins and Creoles, Vol. II: Reference Survey*. Cambridge: Cambridge University Press.

HOLM, J. with SHILLING, A. W. (1982) *Dictionary of Bahamian English*. Cold Spring, NY: Lexik House.

HURTUBISE, J. (1990) *Bi-lingual Education in Nicaragua: Teaching Standard English to Creole Speakers*. Dissertation (Dip. Ed.) University of Auckland, New Zealand.

KAYNE, R. S. (1989) 'Notes on English agreement' (ms). Graduate Center, CUNY.

KEPHART, R. F. (1985) *'It Have More Soft Words': a Study of the Creole English and Reading in Carriacou*, Grenada. Doctoral dissertation. Gainesville: University of Florida.

KEYSER, S. J. and O'NEIL, W. (1985) *Rule Generalization and Optionality in Language Change*. Dordrecht: Foris.

LINGUISTS FOR NICARAGUA (1989) 'Language rights on the Nicaraguan Atlantic coast', *Cultural Survival Quarterly: Central America and the Caribbean* 13: 3: 7–10.

MCLEAN, G. and PAST, R. (1976) 'Some characteristics of Bluefields English.' In DIPIETRO, R. and BLANSITT, E. (eds) *The Third LACUS Forum*. Columbia, South Carolina: Hornbeam Press.

MUYSKEN, P. (1988) 'Are creoles a special type of language?' In NEWMEYER, F. J. (ed.) (1988).

MUYSKEN, P. and SMITH, N. (eds) (1986) *Substrata versus Universals in Creole Genesis: Papers from the Amsterdam Creole Workshop, April 1985*. Amsterdam: John Benjamins.

NEWMEYER, F. J. (ed.) (1988) *Linguistics: the Cambridge Survey, Vol. II, Linguistic Theory: Extensions and Implications*. Cambridge: Cambridge University Press.

O'NEIL, W. and HONDA, M. (1987) 'Nicaraguan English/El inglés nicargüense', *Wani: Revista Sobre la Costa Atlántica* 6: 49–60 (October–December).

O'NEIL, W., JOINER, D. and TAYLOR, S. (1987) 'Notes on NP pluralization in Nicaraguan English.' In NAKAO, T. (ed.) *Historical Studies in Honour of Taizo Hirose*. Tokyo: Kenkyusha.

ORTON, H. (1933) *The Phonology of a South Durham Dialect: Descriptive, Historical, and Comparative*. London: Kegan Paul.

POLLOCK, J.-Y. (1989) 'Verb Movement, Universal Grammar, and the Structure of IP', *Linguistic Inquiry* 20: 365–424.

RICKFORD, J. R. (1987) *Dimensions of a Creole Continuum: History, Texts and Linguistic Analysis of Guyanese Creole*. Stanford: Stanford

University Press.

ROMAINE, S. (1988) *Pidgin and Creole Languages*. London: Longman.

SAPIR, E. (1921) *Language*. New York: Harcourt.

SINGLER, J. V. (1988) 'The homogeneity of the substrate as a factor in pidgin/creole genesis', *Language* **64**: 27–51.

VILLAS, M. C. (1989) *State, Class, and Ethnicity in Nicaragua: Capitalist Modernization and Revolutionary Change on the Atlantic Coast*. Boulder, CO: Lynne Rienner.

VAUGHAN, W. A. I. (1959) *Diccionario Trilingüe: Miskito-Español-Inglés. Español-Miskito. Inglés-Miskito*. Waspam, Río Coco, Nicaragua: La Misión Católica.

VISSER, F. TH. (1978) *An Historical Syntax of the English Language. Part III*. Leiden: E. J. Brill.

WELLS, J. C. (1983) *Accents of English* (3 vols). Cambridge: Cambridge University Press.

Chapter 11

Language change as language improvement

Theo Vennemann

In the scientific study of the causes of language change one can find two polar positions. One says that language change is caused in the same way as change in other domains of human social behaviour, namely as a matter of fashion. This position has been advocated most explicitly by Postal (1968: 283) who says: 'There is no more reason for languages to change than there is for automobiles to add fins one year and remove them the next, for jackets to have three buttons one year and two the next, etc. . . . The "causes" of sound change without language contact lie in the general tendency of human cultural products to undergo "nonfunctional" stylistic change.' The other position says that language change is functional. This position has been defended in a careful, balanced analysis by Anna Giacalone Ramat (1985) who also discusses much recent work on explaining language change by Lyle Campbell, Martin Harris, Esa Itkonen, Roger Lass, Helmut Lüdtke, Willi Mayerthaler, and others. The polar opposition is thus fashion versus function. There are, as always, positions between the two polar ones, saying that language change is sometimes a matter of fashion, sometimes a matter of function, or that certain types of language change are a matter of fashion, others a matter of function. Of course, there are also those who take the position – which I consider uninteresting – that language change cannot be explained at all.

This fashion-versus-function approach to the causes of language change has always troubled me. I can see, of course, that there may be many and heterogeneous causes of language change, such as causes rooted in the physical or mental make-up of human beings, in the physical structure of language signals and the media carrying them, and in the social organization of the speakers of languages and their communicative needs. But it strikes me as improbable that there should be either exactly one motivation for language change, namely either fashion or function, or exactly two motivations, namely fashion and function (or, for that matter, no motivation at all). What I consider most likely on *a priori* grounds is that there are many motivations for language change, but only a single teleology for all of them.

There is also something logically inconsistent about the concepts of fashion and function as polar opposites: they overlap, and together they do not exhaust their domain.

First, fashion and function overlap. As a matter of fact, it is easy to see that all changes in fashion, whether of language or of other kinds of patterned behaviour, have a function, namely a social function. People creating a fashion, or borrowing it in order to carry it into their own group, gain the advantage of being seen as trendsetters; people adopting a fashion gain the advantage of being seen as part of the trend. Both kinds of behaviour have important social functions. They act together to change the behaviour patterns of a group either for a short time or for good, depending on the degree of currency a new pattern acquires. It will not do to counter this argument by saying that function refers to the communicative aspect of structural elements of language. In the first place this would be an illegitimate, idiosyncratic, narrowing of the meaning of the functions of language. And in the second place, it is sometimes hard to distinguish between the two domains. For example, a linguist was heard at a recent conference to say, 'Phonology is cognitive'. Considering the special meaning the word *cognitive* has recently acquired in linguistics, that person was undoubtedly trying to say something. But he was, at the same time, being trendy. Apparently the adoption of the word *cognitive* by linguists into their linguistic jargon is a matter of both fashion and function.

Second, the concepts of fashion and function together do not exhaust their domain. Many changes occur in languages that are neither a matter of fashion nor of function. This is true, for example, of most sound changes, specifically those which remain below the level of social awareness. Since the language group is not aware of them, no social valuation can be associated with them; neither the inception nor the spread of the change can be a matter of fashion. That leaves us with function. But what does it mean to say that the cause of a sound change is function, or that sound change – one that is not a matter of fashion – is functional?

It means nothing. I would not even know what such a manner of speaking would make reference to. Would it refer to the change itself? Surely that makes no sense. The change may have a cause, and it does have an effect, namely a modification in the behaviour of speakers. But a function it cannot have. Does the concept of function refer to the phonological patterns the change brings into being? That cannot be true either. I have shown in an article specifically directed at the question of function in phonology that there is no way of speaking coherently of function with reference to phonology (Vennemann 1981). For example, it is appropriate to say that certain words differ by their phonological forms, but it is incorrect to say that it is the function of those phonological forms to differentiate those two words. The arguments presented there still seem valid to me, despite Vachek's (1981) reply which merely reasserts the Praguean position and refers to certain marginal uses of phonological patterns as signals of emotion. For changes at levels of linguistic organization that involve meaning it may be reasonable to say that certain patterns have a certain function. But even there I would doubt that the same could be said of a change creating such a pattern: it would be the effect of the change to introduce a certain functional element into the language system but certainly not its function. So very likely it is inappropriate to call any kind of language change functional.

I would like to suggest that we abandon talk of fashion and function in our discussion of the causes of language change and look for a unified principle which accommodates both the conscious and the subconscious and both the socially and the structurally motivated changes, as well as those motivated by the needs of communication, which straddle the gap between the structural and the social – a principle that would at the same time not be limited to language change but apply to all human behaviour. I think there is such a principle; it is the principle that wherever and whenever people engage in an activity they attempt – consciously or unconsciously – to improve their condition. This applies to the objects and relations of their activities, the procedures used to modify those objects and relations, and the instruments used in those procedures.

When we apply this idea to language, we recognize in language uses and language structures both the procedures and the instruments with which we operate on objects and relations in our environment. Our goal is to improve, by linguistic means, our position in this environment, and by doing so consciously and subconsciously modify the linguistic procedures and instruments used, and indeed always attempt to improve them. This holds both for the level of individual innovation and for the level of adoption among individuals and indeed all the way to the point of generalization which we as linguists call language change. Language change is language improvement.

This is a simple thought, but its elaboration into a theory of language change is not a simple task. Three questions are immediately raised by the summary statement that language change is language improvement. *Question 1* can be answered immediately, and I hope to be able to answer *Question 2* in this chapter. *Question 3* opens a new research front and will be the work of future generations of historical linguists:

(1)   *Question 1.* If all language changes are meliorative, then, considering that languages have existed for such a long time, why aren't all languages perfect to a degree that nothing needs to be improved upon any more? Put differently: if everything in language change gets better, why don't languages get better?

Question 2. How do we know in every given case of language change that it is indeed an improvement? How can we distinguish meliorative changes from pejorative ones (assuming that there are any)? How would we recognize a pejoration if we encountered one, this being the only way to invalidate the theory?

Question 3. Since any improvement presupposes a bad prior situation, then, assuming that usually more than one remedial measure will be available in sufficiently complex states of affairs, how do we know which path of melioration will be chosen (consciously or subconsciously) by the speakers?

I said that *Question 1* would be easy to answer, and it is indeed. In any system of sufficient complexity, any meliorative move may have bad consequences. Improvement in such a system can only be improvement on a given parameter of evaluation. This is so in the non-linguistic world, where one person's war profits may mean another person's death on the battlefield. It is so also in the world of languages. Nothing in the universe is good or bad *an sich*; everything is good or bad only relative to a given parameter of evaluation.

The potentially antithetic nature of language changes on different parameters has been well known to linguists for a long time. The best known and most intensively studied of these antitheses is that between sound change and conceptual analogy: both types of change may be meliorative (in my theory they always are). But they are so only within their own domains, sound change improving phonological patterns, analogy improving morphological patterns (more generally: patterns that carry meaning). Outside their own domains, such as in each other's domains, they both may cause great damage: sound change very often impairs the uniformity of linguistic symbolization (the principle of 'one form, one meaning', or Humboldt's Universal), both in the paradigms of lexical items and in the paradigms of categorial markings; and conceptual analogy, both as paradigmatic analogy and as categorial analogy, often introduces into a system phonological complexities which are inherently bad, such as new phonemes, new phonotactic patterns, new prosodies – as a matter of fact, analogy may at a later date re-introduce the same phonological patterns into a language system which had earlier been eliminated by sound change, for example, k and g before the feminine plural suffix -e and in a restricted manner also before the masculine plural ending -i in Italian (amica/amice > amica/amiche, fungo/funghi but still amico/amici). Seen from this angle, Sturtevant's Paradox, 'Sound change is regular but causes irregularity, analogy is irregular but causes regularity', only sounds paradoxical but in reality is not: Both sound change and analogy improve their own domains and may there both be totally regular, while creating irregularity, and thus doing damage, only in each other's domains.

The antithetic character of language changes is evident at other levels as well. For example, morphological iconicity is highly valued by speakers of languages; it is evidently related to the principle of uniform linguistic symbolization. But the iconic construction of words with complex meanings creates many long words, and length is a disadvantage on another parameter, especially for frequently used words. Thus we need not be surprised that the most frequent words of many languages are not iconic but suppletive and are, when lost, often not replaced with iconic constructs but with new suppletive forms. Paradigms of frequent relative adjectives (comparatives, superlatives) and of words meaning 'to be' and 'to go' provide ample evidence for this in many languages.

Antithesis may even be found at a single level, including such seemingly simple domains as that of word phonology. For example, the optimal syllable, viewed in isolation, is one consisting of a single very strong consonant followed by a single very sonorous vowel. The optimal phonological word form, on

the other hand, is one in which the initial syllable, and in addition
any stressed syllable, has a very strong consonant, while all other
syllables have weak consonants and all unstressed syllables have,
furthermore, vowels of reduced sonority. Thus, in isolation, the
syllable [pa], with a forcefully articulated, perhaps tense or
aspirated, [p] and an open, perhaps long, [a] is certainly an
optimal entity of that sort. But as part of a complex phonological
word form such as [ka.pa], especially if the other syllable is
stressed, [ká.pa], the same syllable [pa] does not represent an
optimum at all: a syllable with a weaker consonant and a less
sonorous vowel would be better. Thus we often find strong
syllables weakening in weak word positions, along such paths as
(2).

(2)   [ká.pa] > [ká.ba] > [ká.ßa] > [ká.ua] > [ká.uə]

The extreme development of such syllabic reduction may lead to
the total annihilation of a syllable, namely by denuclearization,
manifested as aphaeresis, syncope, or apocope. Curiously,
improvements of this sort, namely syncope and apocope of
syllables which contain more than just a single vowel, by
necessity cause new deviations from optimality to arise, namely
in the domain of single syllable complexity; this is so because the
debris of the denuclearized syllable must be attached to
neighbouring syllables which thereby contract new segments to
their margins, causing them to deviate, or to deviate further than
before, from the optimal CV pattern, as in (3).

(3.a)   Syncope: CV.CV̱.CV > CV.CCV or > CVC.CV

(3.b)   Apocope: CV.CV̱ > CVC

(3.b')   Example (2): [ká.u̱ə̱] > [kau̯]

It is easy to see, by pursuing this line of exemplification, that it is
impossible to optimize a language in all domains at once. There
cannot be a perfect language but only languages in which certain
parameters are optimized at the expense of others.

While it is true that languages are never perfect, so that
language change will never end, the second formulation of
Question 1 strikes me as non-equivalent to the first, the one I
have discussed so far. I do believe that languages get better, and
that they do so by the very kind of change historical linguists
investigate, though they do not do so in the simple, fragmenting
kind of histories which historical linguists, with their poorly
developed instruments of analysis, presently reconstruct. I
believe that languages get better over long periods of time as part

of the evolution of the human race, periods so long that we cannot with present means observe the overall improvement; and I believe that the individual changes which linguists study and which improve languages only locally are at the same time the vehicles of the global type of change by which languages have slowly evolved and are still evolving, from the meagre communicative systems of early anthropoids through the full-fledged languages of *homo sapiens sapiens* further into ever more supple, ever more effective, ever more beautiful means of communication of a future humankind.

I will now turn to *Question 2*, which is the main topic of this chapter. Evaluating change as meliorative or pejorative presupposes a theory of linguistic quality or, with a term used in Vennemann 1983, a theory of linguistic preferences. If we manage to arrange, in the order of increasing linguistic quality, language systems which differ only on a single parameter or – which amounts to the same – if we can order linguistic properties, for example structural patterns, on scales of linguistic quality from worst to best, then every change on that parameter can as a matter of course be evaluated as meliorative or pejorative, namely as leading from a better state of affairs to a worse one, or from a worse to a better one. The problem to which *Question 2* then boils down is: how can we order language states (or, equivalently, properties of language states) on parameters of linguistic quality?

As for all empirical linguistic questions, the answer will be reached only by an intricate process of exemplification, argumentation, and reference to other, non-linguistic theories. For example, since I am convinced that my theory is correct, I will collect as many instances of language change as I can and arrange the states they start from, and those they lead to, on scales which are to reflect the parameter on which I assume the change to have taken place; and, of course, I make the resulting state or property rank higher on the scale of linguistic quality than the starting state or property.

Now this may look to the uninitiated like a perfect example of a vicious circle: I order language states or properties on scales on the evidence of language change, and then I explain language change by reference to those scales. Needless to say I do not consider this procedure circular. It is not, and for three reasons.

One reason is that one soon discovers that changes on a given parameter always move in one direction, never in the opposite direction. Put more generally, and more exactly: once a scale of increasing linguistic quality has been established on the evidence of changes in a few languages, one soon finds that it is always, in all languages at all times, the worst patterns on that parameter that are eliminated first when that parameter is subject to change. This is, in a slightly different formulation, what I have called the Diachronic Maxim in a recent publication (Vennemann 1988: 2):

(4) *Diachronic Maxim*: Linguistic change on a given parameter does not affect a language structure as long as there exist structures in the language system that are less preferred in terms of the relevant preference law.

The second reason is that the same distribution as the Diachronic Maxim leads us to expect is also found in language systems studied without regard to change. Here we find that languages normally have continuous ranges of structures including the upper end of quality scales, rather than discontinuous ranges, or continuous ranges including merely the lower but not the upper end of quality scales. This is expressed in the Synchronic Maxim (ibid.: 3):

(5) *Synchronic Maxim*: A language system will in general not contain a structure on a given parameter without containing those structures constructible with the means of the system that are more preferred in terms of the relevant preference law.

It says 'in general' in the Synchronic Maxim because discontinuities occasionally do arise on a given parameter, though only as a consequence of changes that are not directed at that particular parameter but only involve it incidentally, such as a borrowing that may be motivated in a totally different sphere, or a change on a different parameter that happens to intersect the given parameter. Borrowing in particular is a kind of change which frequently introduces patterns at the lower end of quality scales, even such patterns as had been eliminated earlier in long histories of change. The Latinate vocabulary introduced into the Romance languages since the Renaissance is a well-known class of examples.

I would like to illustrate with a particularly transparent example the way a quality scale is established on purely comparative grounds and related to both the Synchronic and Diachronic Maxims. I use the scale (6) of increasingly good syllable heads made of two consonants, being able, in this case, to draw on much earlier work on cluster distribution or markedness in different frameworks.

(6) $KP- $KF- $KN- $Kl- $Kr- $KV̯-

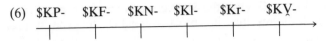

K, P: plosives; F: fricatives; N: nasals; V̯: vowels ('semi-vowels').

Some of the comparative evidence for (6) is the following:

1. Classical Greek had all six sorts of clusters (not quite, because the glides had been absorbed by consonantal monophthongizations). This situation is represented in (7).

(7) $KP- $KF- $KN- $Kl- $Kr- $KV̯-

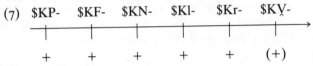

  +   +   +   +   +   (+)

But Contemporary Greek has done away with the worst of them, $KP, i.e. heads of two plosives, namely $pt and $kt, by quasi-nuclearizing the first of the two in each case through frication, $pt > $ft, $kt > $xt or $çt, thus turning it into an appendix (or 'Nebensilbe') of the sort that many languages tolerate, mostly however with sibilant fricatives – clusters which Greek, needless to say, also possesses. Examples are given in (8).

(8) pterò > fterò 'wing', ktízo > çtízo 'I build' (cf. stéfanos 'wreath')

Contemporary Greek now has only the clusters as shown in (9). (This particular way of displaying which patterns of a given quality scale occur in a given language system has been adopted from Murray 1988.)

(9) $KP- $KF- $KN- $Kl- $Kr- $KV̯-

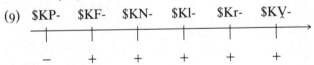

  −   +   +   +   +   +

These are at the same time exactly the types of head clusters that German tolerates in native and firmly established borrowed vocabulary. This shows applications of both the Synchronic and Diachronic Maxims.

2. Old and Middle English had the head cluster types shown in (10).

(10) $KP- $KF- $KN- $Kl- $Kr- $KV̯-

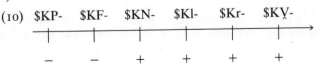

  −   −   +   +   +   +

In Early Modern English the $KN clusters lost their plosives, as in (11), with the resulting inventory of head cluster types in (12).

(11) *knowen > know* [nou̯], *gnawen > gnaw* [nɔ:]

(12) $KP- $KF- $KN- $Kl- $Kr- $KV̯

     −   −   −   +   +   +

3. Scale (12) describes the inventory of head cluster types not only of Contemporary English but also of Classical Latin. Italian, however, has given up the worst of the clusters in (12), $Kl-, sometimes – and quite frequently in dialects – by turning [l] into [r], but mostly by changing [l] into a palatal glide:

(13) Lat. *simulare* > VLat. *sem.lare* > *sem.blare* > Ital. *sem.brare* 'to seem', *sem.bianza* 'semblance'
Lat. *nebula* > VLat. *neb.la* > *neb.bla* > Ital. *neb.bia*, Abruzzese *neb.bra*

Portuguese first changed *$pl-*, *$kl-*, *$fl-* in the Italian way into *$pi̯-*, *$ki̯-*, and *$fi̯-*, clusters which in time all changed into *$ch-*, i.e. [ʃ]:

(14)

	Latin	Portuguese	
(14.a)	planus	chão	'flat'
	plaga	chaga	'wound'
	platus	chato	'flat
	plenus	cheio	'full'
	implere	encher	'to fill'
	plorare	chorar	'deplore'
	plumbum	chumbo	'lead'
	pluvia	chuva	'rain'
	plus	chus	(*nem chus nem bus* 'not a single word')
	poplus	choupo (*via* pop.lo > pop.plo > plop.po > pi̯op.po)	'poplar'
(14.b)	clamare	chamar	'to call'
	clavis	chave	'key'
(14.c)	flamma	chama	'flame'
	flagrare	cheirar	'to smell'

Later on Portuguese changed *$bl-* and *$gl-*, both old and new, as well as newly imported *$pl-*, *$kl-*, *$fl-* in the Abruzzese way, i.e. by turning *l* into *r*; this is best studied by comparing Portuguese examples to their Spanish counterparts, as in (15).

(15)

	Spanish	*Portuguese*	
(15.a)	blanco, -a	branco, -a	'white'
	obligar	obrigar	'obligate'
	oblea	obreia	'Host'
	ablandar	abrandar	'soften'
	noble	nobre	'noble'
(15.b)	regla	regra	'rule'
	iglesia	igreja	'church'
(15.c)	plancha	prancha	'board'
	plato	prato	'plate'
	plaza	praça	'place'
(15.d)	clavo	cravo	'nail'
	clavar	(a)cravar	'to nail (to)'
(15.e)	flaco, -a	fraco, -a	'weak'
	flauta	frauta, flauta	'flute'
	flecha	frecha, flecha	'arrow'
	flota	frota	'fleet'
	flojo, -a	froixo, -a	'slack'
	aflojar	afroixar	'loosen'

After these changes, only the head cluster types described by (16) remained in Italian and Portuguese.

(16)

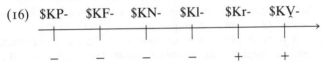

Both Italian and Portuguese have reintroduced $Kl clusters through borrowing in their recent histories, thereby reverting to (12), though, of course, with a totality different kind of motivation; for example, Ital. *blu* 'blue', from Germanic.

4. Finally, Korean and Tahitian exemplify languages with the head cluster type inventories described by (17) and (18), respectively.

(17)

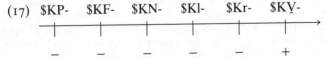

(18) $KP- $KF- $KN- $KL- $Kr- $KY-

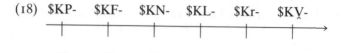

The third reason why my way of establishing linguistic quality scales on purely comparative grounds is not circular is that the scales can, most or all, be explained by theories of neighbouring disciplines, such as sociology, the theory of communication, psychology, the theory of language acquisition, neurology, and phonetics. For example, phoneticians have assured me that the scale (6) of increasingly good head clusters of a plosive and a following speech sound is indeed one of decreasing phonetic complexity or enunciative difficulty. Since I am not a professional phonetician, I have nothing to add to their pronouncement.

Showing in detail for every type of language change that it represents linguistic improvements on a particular parameter would fill several volumes. Even a very superficial sketch of only one group of changes, namely syllable structure changes, for the most part in even less detail than the outline just given for one parameter, has filled a booklet, Vennemann 1988. A survey of nothing but the names of major categories of sound change, arranged by motivation, fills two pages in Vennemann 1985. But I believe that a full demonstration is not needed in this thematic essay. I think I have already reached a major goal of my deliberations by showing that the idea of language change as language improvement is applicable even in a domain where neither fashion nor function plays any role. If in the remainder of this essay I show, by way of reminder, that the idea is *a fortiori* applicable in areas where fashion and function have often been claimed to play an important role, all the work that can be done in a short chapter will have been done. As a matter of fact, I feel I can skip examples of language change by fashion because their meliorative character – namely in relation to the point of view of their inventors or adopters – is too obvious to merit discussion. I can also skip examples of conceptual analogy in morphology because such changes are the most frequently cited by those advocating functional motivation in language change; they are indeed the prototypic examples of melioration, namely of improvements in the relation between meaning and form. And I will certainly omit examples of lexical change, such as the creation or borrowing of new words for new concepts, or the invention of alphabetic formations (letter words and acronyms) for frequently used expressions of excessive length, because their meliorative effect is equally a matter for introductory texts in linguistics (e.g. the detailed description and exemplification in Bartsch and Vennemann 1982: 94–118, 162–77). Rather, I will use the space allotted to me to illustrate the idea with some thoughts about syntax.

Syntactic construction is governed by a number of principles, and since the principles of linguistic construction have been found to be in part antithetical even in the narrowly delimited area of the phonology of words, one expects this to be *a fortiori* true in such a vast area of construction with a great amount of individual freedom of choice as syntax. This expectation is indeed fulfilled.

One principle that one would like to posit on *a priori* grounds is that in the construction of sentences one should first identify that which one would like to say something about and then proceed to saying something about it. This is the principle of placing the topic before the comment, or the theme before the rheme. From the point of view of the conceptual construction of sentences, a theme is in most cases a specifier of its rheme, which is then the specified, or head: The rheme, when a head, identifies the broad conceptual sphere in which a process or situation is located, while the theme, as a specifier, narrows that sphere down. This is illustrated by the Japanese and English sentences in (19); the Japanese examples have been adapted from Kuno 1973.

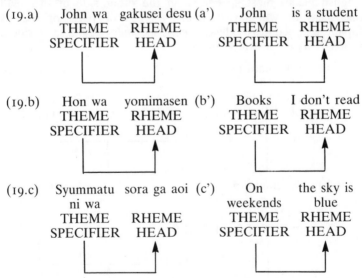

(19.a)   John wa   gakusei desu (a')   John   is a student
         THEME   RHEME   THEME   RHEME
         SPECIFIER   HEAD   SPECIFIER   HEAD

(19.b)   Hon wa   yomimasen (b')   Books   I don't read
         THEME   RHEME   THEME   RHEME
         SPECIFIER   HEAD   SPECIFIER   HEAD

(19.c)   Syummatu sora ga aoi (c')   On   the sky is
         ni wa   weekends   blue
         THEME   RHEME   THEME   RHEME
         SPECIFIER   HEAD   SPECIFIER   HEAD

The situation described in (19.a) is that of being a student; this concept is narrowed down to a situation in which someone in particular, namely John, is a student. The state of affairs described in (19.b) is that of my not reading (anything); this concept is narrowed down to my not reading books. The state of affairs described in (19.c) is that of the sky being blue; this concept is narrowed down to applying to weekends. I would like to stress that this is the conceptual analysis; the pragmatic analysis is, of course, quite different. Specifier-Head structure is a semantic concept based on the categorial construction of complex expressions, whereas theme–rheme structure is a pragmatic concept based on the communicative construction of complex expressions as parts of texts. The two concepts are theoretically independent: both specifiers and heads may become thematic, and both specifiers and heads may become rhematic, namely within the text in which the complex expressions are used. The Specifier-Head structure of a complex expression such as *John is a student* is invariant, but its Theme-Rheme structure is a function of the co- and context in which it occurs. For example, *John* would be rhematic in the expression *John is a student* when used to answer the question 'Do you know any students?', but it would still be specifier of *is a student*. Saying that themes are in most cases specifiers is making an empirical statement.

When sentences get more complex than the examples in (19), English places most specifiers on the other side of the head, regardless of whether they are themes or parts of rhemes. Japanese, by contrast, always keeps specifiers on the same side of heads. This is illustrated in (20).

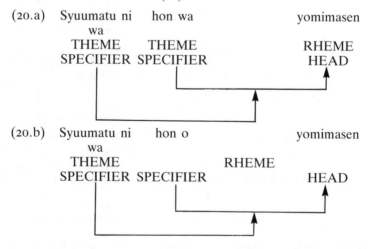

(20.a) Syuumatu ni   hon wa   yomimasen
        wa
        THEME   THEME   RHEME
        SPECIFIER SPECIFIER   HEAD

(20.b) Syuumatu ni   hon o   yomimasen
        wa
        THEME   RHEME
        SPECIFIER SPECIFIER   HEAD

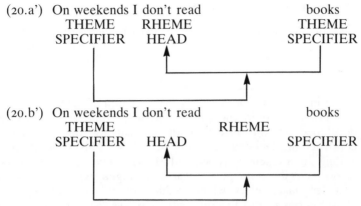

(20.a') On weekends I don't read   books
      THEME   RHEME   THEME
      SPECIFIER   HEAD   SPECIFIER

(20.b') On weekends I don't read   books
      THEME   RHEME
      SPECIFIER   HEAD   SPECIFIER

It is easy to see that Japanese has a simpler word order syntax for dependency relations, i.e. relations between specifiers and heads, than English. As a matter of fact, Japanese has only a single rule, namely, to place specifiers before heads, regardless of whether constitutents carry additional information such as relates them to the theme–rheme structure of the sentence, while English has a host of rules, some of them sensitive to theme–rheme structure, some not. Only languages which are – like Japanese, Korean, and Turkish – consistently prespecifying languages (or XV languages) possess this streamlined simplicity. Needless to say there is value in such simplicity, for example, to the process of language learning; it is therefore easy to understand that so many languages have developed towards complete consistency within this type.

Another principle that one would like to posit on *a priori* grounds is that in the construction of complex syntactic expressions all the way up to the level of sentences, one should first name the conceptual sphere in which the intended concept is to be mentally reconstructed, and then in successive steps narrow down the precise area in which this concept is located. For example, a red barn is first of all a barn and secondarily something red; we locate this concept first in the sphere of barns and only then in the sphere of red objects. A red barn is a barn which happens to be red, rather than something red which happens to be a barn. Similarly, the concept of eating an apple is located in the conceptual sphere of eating processes, rather than in the conceptual sphere of apples. The Italian way of constructing phrases that express those two complex concepts exactly matches the principle: *un granaio rosso, mangiare una mela*. In this manner of constructing phrases the specifier follows the specified or head, see (21).

(21.a) un granaio   rosso   (21.b) mangiare una mela
            HEAD   SPECIFIER   HEAD SPECIFIER

In Latin, as is well known, the construction of such expressions was not defined in the same rigid way. Italian has obviously developed in the direction of intensifying this manner of construction. Quite a few languages have fully generalized it, among them Gaelic, Arabic, and Maori. They are the consistently post-specifying languages (or VX languages). The very fact that languages exist which reduce their numerous syntactic constructions to just this one pattern shows that there is inherent value in such a procedure. This value is easy to identify: the entire word order syntax for the dependency relation is handled by a single rule, the rule of placing the specifier after the head. Part of the history of languages that used to be different but are now of the post-specifying type, whether consistent, such as the three just mentioned, or only approaching consistency, such as Italian, English and Swahili, can thus be interpreted as a process of improving the word order syntax of the dependency relation in those languages.

Both types of consistent languages, the pre- as well as post-specifying ones (XV as well as VX languages), are maximally simple with regard to the number of rules they need (namely one) to serialize their dependency relations. But they both buy this advantage at a cost: pre-specifying languages always place the narrowing concepts first in time, only telling us at the very end of a construction in which conceptual sphere those narrowing concepts are to apply. Post-specifying languages have problems with their theme–rheme structure: some, in order to preserve their consistency, have developed elaborate clefting devices for moving themes to the front; others weaken their consistency by allowing themes to be placed before their rhemes, even if a specifier is thereby placed before its head. The latter disadvantage is apparently the more damaging one, because there are many consistent pre-specifying languages, while most post-specifying languages have exceptions, above all in the serialization of the theme–rheme relation. As a matter of fact, the majority of post-specifying languages systematically exclude a prototypic theme constituent from post-specification, the nominative or absolute (the 'subject', according to some grammatical theories). The preponderance of 'SVO' languages (subject-verb-object languages) over 'VSO' and 'VOS' languages is explained by the meliorative strategy of reserving the initial position for themes, even if all other specifiers gradually move behind their heads.

I would like, by way of example, to return to an account of the development of adverbial sentence negators which I proposed a number of years ago (cf. Vennemann 1974: 366–70) and which has since been incorporated into a much more comprehensive description in Molinelli et al. 1987. I will use examples from my own collection; many further examples, especially from the Romance languages and dialects, and some from non-Indo-European languages, can be found in Molinelli et al. 1987.

The dominant placement of adverbial sentence negators in early Indo-European languages is pre-verbal, which is to be expected in languages derived from an ancestral language with pre-specifying syntax. (I follow Lehmann 1974 in his reconstruction of Proto-Indo-European as essentially a pre-specifying (XV or 'OV') language, though not when he says, 'Earlier the negative particle was post-verbal, as may be expected in an OV language' (ibid.: 125).) The position of negators that is to be expected on typological grounds is a tricky matter. There cannot be a single hard-and-fast rule saying that the position of sentence negators is such-and-such in pre-specifying and the opposite in post-specifying languages. This is so because sentence negators may occur in different categories, with the consequence that they may be either heads or specifiers within their constructions. For example, the Finnish sentence negator is a finite verb, *e-n, e-t, e-i, e-mme, e-tte, e-ivät*, 'I, you, he/she/it, we, you, they do/are not', accompanied by the stem of the 'full verb', i.e. what in Standard Italian appears as the finite verb, see (22).

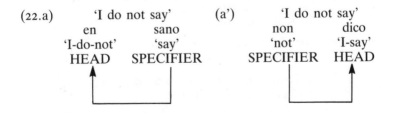

(22.a)   'I do not say'   (a')   'I do not say'
      en   sano   non   dico
   'I-do-not'   'say'   'not'   'I-say'
   HEAD   SPECIFIER   SPECIFIER   HEAD

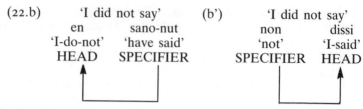

(22.b)   'I did not say'   (b')   'I did not say'
            en   sano-nut   non   dissi
         'I-do-not' 'have said'   'not'   'I-said'
          HEAD   SPECIFIER   SPECIFIER   HEAD

Head and specifier are determined by the criterion of category constancy; it says that that constituent of a dependency relation is the head of the construction which is of the same category as the resultant construction (the case of attribution), or of the same category except for a valency greater by one (the case of complementation). Applying this criterion to the examples in (22), we see that the Finnish sentence negator, being a finite verb, is the head of its construction, while the Italian sentence negator, being an adverb, is the specifier. The Finnish construction of negative sentences as in (22) is thus post-specifying, that of Italian pre-specifying. The Standard Italian pattern therefore is not harmonious with the modern word order type of the language, which is post-specifying; it is a pattern inherited unchanged from Proto-Indo-European where it was harmonious with the pre-specifying word order type.

Whereas Standard Italian has preserved the ancient pattern, English, German, and French (and also some northern Italian dialects, cf. Molinelli in Molinelli et al. 1987: 165–72) have undergone a peculiar development, which I will now illustrate.

Sentence negation was in Old English expressed by placing the negative adverb *ne* immediately before the finite verb. This is, of course, the inherited Indo-European pattern. The examples in (23) are taken from the Old English Orosius (*Ōhthere's Voyage*).

(23.a) *forþǣm hīe* ne *dorston forþ   bi   þǣre ēa   siglan*
       because they not dared   forward past the   river sail
       for   unfriþe
       for-fear-of hostility

(23.b) *Hīe* ne *dorston þǣron cuman.*
       they not dared   on-it come

(23.c) *forþǣm hē hit self   ne geseah*
       because he it himself not saw

(23.d) Ne *bið hē   lengra ðonne syfan elna lang.*
       not is it (the whale) longer than   seven ells long

With certain high frequency verbs beginning with a vowel or a weak consonant (*h, w*), contraction occurred:

(24.a) Hē nysse (= ne wisse) hwæðer.
        he not-knew   which.

(24.b) Næfde (= ne hæfde) hē þēah   mā   ðonne twēntig
        not-had   he though more than twenty
        hrȳðera.
        heads-of-cattle

Old English had multiple negation as a standard feature; it has
survived to the present day in substandard varieties of English
(e.g. *He hasn't got no sorrow, They never executes nobody*). In
Old English, if a negative constituent appeared anywhere in a
sentence, *ne* was added to the finite verb, see (25).

(25.a) Hē cwæð þæt nān man ne būde benorðan him.
        he said that no man not lived north-of him

(25.b) Ne mētte hē ǣr   nān gebūn   land.
        not found he earlier no inhabited land

For emphatic negation, such as is used to reject an explicit or
assumed contradictory assumption, *nealles* (< *ne ealles*) 'not at
all' was added. This gave room in early Middle English to the use
of *not* (< *noht* < *nā wiht* 'no [little] thing') 'not a bit'. As an
emphatic specifier of the verb in a language developing toward
post-specification, this constituent naturally followed the finite
verb in declarative sentences:

(26)   He ne held it noght.
        he not held it not-a-bit

With auxiliaries and modals, *not* stood between the finite part
and the participle or infinitive, because English had the sentence
brace (which is now best preserved in German): *it is not longes
gon* 'it is not long ago ("gone")', *þat þei scholde not drede to don
it* 'that they should not fear to do it'. When the auxiliary *do* came
to be used in negative sentences containing *not* but not containing
another auxiliary or modal, the place of *not* was regularly
between an auxiliary or modal and its complement: Not *Jill, my
wife, rose not here* but, *Jill, my wife, did not rise here.* This is one
of the residues of the verbal brace construction in Contemporary
English. In the spoken language, *not* fuses with the auxiliary or
modal yielding a paradigm of finite negation verbs, similar in
character to the Finnish negator: *don't, doesn't, didn't, isn't,
won't, can't*, etc.

    As can be seen in (26), the negative adverbs *ne . . . not* formed
a brace around the finite verb. This bracing negation soon lost its
emphatic force, and from the middle of the fourteenth century

onward *not* began to be used by itself:

(27) *Gyll, my wyfe, rose* nott *here.*
      Jill   my wife rose not here

Naturally enough, *not* followed the finite verb. (The Middle
English examples have been taken from Mossé 1968.) Schematically, the development in English was that in (28).

(28) *ne* + Verb > *ne* + Verb + *not* > Verb + *not*

The schema shows that what occurred was a development from
pre-specification to post-specification. Clearly, this development
of sentence negation is only a component of the overall
development of English during the period in question.
  German supports this view. In Old High German, sentence
negation involved the use of *ni* immediately before the finite
verb, with multiple negation, contractions, and emphasis by
means of *nalles* 'not at all' very much as in Old English. The
examples in (29) illustrate all of these features (*Muspilli*, vv. 57,
76; *Tatian*, 126.1, 235.1).

(29.a) *Dār* ni *mac denne māk*   *andremo helfan*
        there not can then   one-relative another help
        uora   *demo muspille.*
        against the   muspilli (world's end)

(29.b) *Daz*   *ist allaz sō pald daz imo*   nioman
        that (army) is all   so bold that (to-)it nobody
        kipāgan ni   *mak.*
        resist   not can

(29.c) *Inti* nist (= *ni ist*)*thir*   *suorge fon*   niheinigemo.
        and not-is   to-you worry about nobody

(29.d) Nalles   *thoh uuidaro* ni *forstuontun thie iungoron*
        not-at-all however   not understood the disciples
        thaz iz ther heilant was.
        that it the saviour was

As in English, *nalles* very early gave room, for emphatic
negation, to *niht* (< *niwiht, niowiht* < *ni* [*eo*] *wiht*' 'not [ever] a
[little] thing'), see (30), which is Otfrid 2.5.12, the oldest
recorded instance according to Behaghel 1924: II.70.

(30) Ni *zawēta   imo   es*   niawiht.
      not succeeded to-him of-it not-a-bit
      'He did not succeed in it at all.'

In Middle High German, by the twelfth century, *niht* lost its emphatic force and became obligatory, except in certain special constructions, while *ni* was reduced to a nuclear [ṇ], spelled, *ne*, *en*, or *n*, apparently without a definite spelling pattern, compare *Des newas niht rāt* 'That could not be avoided' to *Des enwas niht nōt* 'There was no need for that'; see (31). (All Middle High German examples are taken from the *Nibelungenlied*, vv. 31.2, 68.2; 151.1, 93.4, 166.3; 151.3, 69.3, 320.2; 113.1, 108.4.)

(31.a) *Daz* en*dunket mich* niht *guot*
        that not-seems me   not good

(31.b) *Ern   kundez* niht *verenden*
        he-not could-it not accomplish

(31.c) *Dine   torsten* niht *versprechen die liudegēres   man.*
        them-not dared not   decline   the Liudegēre's men

Now the reflex of the original negative adverb had become redundant and was lost:

(32.a) *Wir mugen uns* niht *besenden   in sō kurzen tagen*
        we can   us not gather-forces in so short   days

(32.b) *Ir   sult* niht *weinen um den willen mīn*
        you shall not cry   for the sake of-me

(32.c) *Er trouwete* niht *erwerben des   er dā   hete muot*
        he trusted not to-gain   of-which he there had desire

Near-minimal pairs in the same text, such as those in (33), clearly show that the two kinds of construction occurred side by side.

(33.a) *Ine   wil   es   *niht *erwinden*
        I-not want of-it not desist

(33.b) *Nu wil   ich* niht *erwinden*
        now want I   not desist

By the end of the thirteenth century, the old negative adverb had virtually disappeared, leaving *nicht* in sole possession of the field. The development of German sentence negation can be summed up as in (34).

(34) *ni* + Verb > *n* + Verb + *niht* > Verb + *nicht*

While Standard Italian has preserved the Indo-European pattern, French, whose syntactic history has been quite similar to that of Italian in other respects, has developed a bracing construction for sentence negation. There is only one major difference in comparison with the English and German development: since French did not have multiple negation the emphatic element is not itself negative (English nā *wiht*, German ni [*eo*] *wiht*) but is simply a noun corresponding to *wiht* 'small thing': *pas* 'step', *point* 'point', *goutte* 'drop', and others. Their use began in Latin but did not become an essential feature of sentence negation until the thirteenth to fifteenth centuries. It has persisted to the present day, see (35).

(35.a) *Nous* ne *l'*   *appelâmes* pas.
      we   not her called   not

(35.b) *Nous* ne *l'*   *avons* pas *appelée*.
      we   not her have not called

The Latin noun *passus* has become a negative adverb *pas* in this process, and in contemporary colloqial French *ne* is often dropped in the presence of *pas*, se (36).

(36.a) *Je* ne *sais*   pas. OR: *Je sais*   pas.
      I   not know not   I   know not

(36.b) *Nous l'*   *avons* pas *appelée*.
      we   her have not called

We see that French is completing a development that can be summarized as in (37).

(37) *non* + Verb > *ne* + Verb + *pas* > Verb + *pas*

In summary, English, German, and French have developed their sentence negation in strikingly similar patterns, see (38).

(38) ENGLISH: *ne*   + Verb >*ne* + Verb +*not* > Verb +*not*
      GERMAN: *ni*   + Verb >*n* + Verb +*niht* > Verb +*nicht*
      FRENCH: *non* + Verb >*ne* + Verb +*pas* > Verb +*pas*

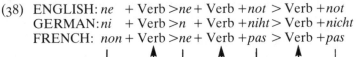
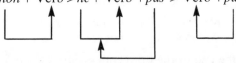

It appears safe to conclude that the transportation of the negative adverb from a position before the finite verb to a position after the finite verb – via the bracing negation – is a typical accompaniment of the development toward consistent post-specification. The intermediate stage, that of the bracing negation, co-occurs with other bracing constructions typical of what I have called (in Vennemann 1974) the 'TVX' type (topic-verb-further specifiers), which appears as an intermediate stage of development between the two consistent word order types. Brace construction is generally disfavoured, as are all processes creating discontinuity. It is never an end in itself but can only result as a temporary by-product of other processes which can always be proven, in the final analysis, to be meliorative moves in other domains.

The great uniformity in the development pattern of sentence negation in several languages has always called for an explanation. To linguists with few explanatory principles at their disposal the answer had to be borrowing (e.g. Lockwood 1968: 208–9), even though the differences in both the substance and the time relations make this appear rather unlikely (cf. Vennemann 1974: 370). Even the authors of Molinelli et al. 1987 are curiously undecided, sometimes pointing out the Sprachbund aspects of the phenomenon (cf. the map on p. 187), sometimes stressing the correlation with other properties of the 'TVX' development (in particular Bernini in Molinelli et al. 1987: 175–6). Even though I think it rather unlikely that such a peculiar construction as the bracing negation will ever be borrowed as such, there may nevertheless be truth in both explanations. The slow drift from pre- to post-specification may, at least in part, be an areal phenomenon. Emphatic strengtheners accompanying negation are used in all languages at all times. In pre-specifying languages they have to occur preverbally. When the language has drifted sufficiently close to the post-specifying type, speakers, without any outside influence, will place their emphatic strengtheners – by the very stage of development the language has reached – post-verbally. This is the stage of development of the conservative varieties of Italian. When two adjacent languages have reached this stage, there is a new basis for areal influence, namely in the substance of the strengtheners: even though speakers experiment quite a lot with strengtheners from various semantic domains (amusing examples are cited by Ramat in Molinelli et al. 1987), it is still striking that only at this early stage, when both French and German were still at the stage of developing negation represented now by Standard Italian, *Tropfen* 'drop' (actually in a reduced form *drof* derived from it) is sporadically used by Otfrid – in Weissenburg, now Wissembourg (Lockwood 1968: 208). But the next step in the development is again one for which I cannot recognize an explanation by borrowing: the loss of the emphatic component of the one-time strengtheners and the resulting grammaticalization of the bracing pattern. Also the final stage, the loss of the preverbal element, seems to me to be purely a consequence of the ongoing drift toward post-specification; mutual borrowing is in my opinion made very unlikely by the simple fact that this step occurred in German, English, and

French with a phase shift of up to six centuries.

This ends my second major example of language change as language improvement. I realize that it is a long way from two examples to the several hundred types of language change on record. But perhaps the two examples are interesting enough to make linguists look at language change in a particular way, namely with a desire to study the motivation for every occurrence of change, and not to desist until they recognize its meliorative character.

But will our work be done when we have developed a complete typology of language change, arranging all changes according to their motivations and characterizing their meliorative impact? I have already given my answer to this question: my answer is *Question 3*. By working on the typology of language change as melioration we open up a new research front, with problems which appear much more formidable than the ones we are working on at present. Needless to say I do not want to belittle the work being done, and still to be done, on the typology of language change as such. I know how difficult this work is, how many mistakes we make, how we rejoice about every bit of progress we accomplish. But the frightening challenge will come when we have completed our typology, or even only significant portions of it. For example, I have, in years of hard work, reached a position where I can say with some confidence that I know and understand the mechanisms by which bad syllable structure is improved, and for one aspect of syllable structure, syllable contact, I believe I have established, partly in co-operation with Robert W. Murray, a complete catalogue of the remedial measures employed in its improvement (cf. Vennemann 1988: 50–5). But I do not even know how to approach the greater problem, which is the question of what motivates speakers of a given language with bad syllable contacts to 'choose' one remedial measure from my catalogue rather than one of the others. And this is still one of the simple parts of the problem, one that remains within the narrowly defined domain of word phonology. The problem is much greater in other divisions of language structure and language use, and greater again by several degrees of magnitude when we compare remedial measures across the boundaries dividing the components of a language. I hasten to add that I am not talking about the actuation problem, the question of when a change will occur in a language in real time, which I consider unanswerable. I am only concerned with the smaller problem of what is the adequate remedy for a bad property of a language, the one which the speakers will apply, given the total context of the structure and use of that particular language. Put differently, the question is: what precisely is it in the overall layout of a language that makes a certain property – one that had been tolerated before, sometimes for thousands of years – so bad that it changes, and what in the overall layout of the language determines by what new property it will be replaced? I believe that approaching this question will provide work for many future generations of linguists.

Acknowledgement

The above chapter was presented as the invited lecture at the Meeting of the Società Italiana di Glottologia in Pavia on 15 September 1988 and published in the proceedings, *Modelli esplicativi della diacronia linguistica*, ed. by Vincenzo Orioles, Pisa: Giardini Editori e Stampatori, 1989 [actually 1990], 11–35. I am grateful to the Società both for the occasion to summarize my thoughts on language change as language improvement and for granting permission to republish the lecture in the present volume.

References

AGOSTINIANI, LUCIANO, et al. (eds) (1985) *Linguistica storica e cambiamento linguistco: Atti del XVI Congresso Internazionale de Studi, Firenze, 7–9 maggio 1982*. Roma: Bulzoni.

ANDERSON, JOHN and JONES, CHARLES (eds) (1974) *Historical linguistics: Proceedings of the First International Congress of Historical Linguistics, Edinburgh, September 1973*, 2 vols. Amsterdam: North Holland.

BARTSCH, RENATE and VENNEMANN, THEO (1982) *Grundzüge der Sprachtheorie: Eine linguistische Einführung*. Tübingen: Max Niemeyer.

BEHAGHEL, OTTO (1923–32) *Deutsche Syntax: Eine geschichtliche Darstellung* (4 vols). Heidelberg: Carl Winter.

DRESSLER, WOLFGANG U. et al. (eds) (1981) *Phonologica 1980: Akten der Vierten Internationalen Phonologie-Tagung, Wien, 29. Juni–2. Juli 1980*. Innsbruck: Institut für Sprachwissenschaft der Universität Innsbruck.

FISIAK, JACEK (ed.) (1985) Papers from the 6th International Conference on Historical Linguistics. *Current Issues in Linguistic Theory*. Vol. 34. Amsterdam: John Benjamins.

GIACALONE RAMAT, ANNA (1985) 'Are there dysfunctional changes?' In Fisiak (1985) pp. 427–39.

KUNO, SUSUMO (1973) *The Structure of the Japanese Language*. Cambridge, MA: MIT Press.

LEHMANN, WINFRED P. (1974) *Proto-Indo-European Syntax*. Austin, TX: University of Texas Press.

LOCKWOOD, W. B. (1968) *Historical German Syntax*. Oxford: Clarendon Press.

MOLINELLI, PIERA, BERNINI, GIULIANO and RAMAT, PAOLO (1987) 'Sentence negation in Germanic and Romance languages.' In Ramat (1987) pp. 165–87.

MOSSÉ, FERNAND (1968) *A Handbook of Middle English*, trans (from the French original) WALKER, J. A. Baltimore, MD: Johns Hopkins Press.

MURRAY, ROBERT W. (1988) *Phonological strength and Early Germanic syllable structure*. (*Studies in Theoretical Linguistics*, Vol. 6). Munich: Wilhelm Fink.

POSTAL, PAUL M. (1968) *Aspects of Phonological Theory*. New York: Harper & Row.

RAMAT, PAOLO (1987) *Linguistic typology*. (*Empirical Approaches to Language Typology*, Vol. 1). Berlin: Mouton de Gruyter.

VACHEK, JOSEF (1981) 'Phonology – non-functional?' In DRESSLER, WOLFGANG U. et al. (1981), pp. 387–90.

VENNEMAN, THEO (1974) 'Topics, subjects, and word order: from SXV to SVX via TVX.' In ANDERSON, JOHN and JONES, CHARLES (1974), Vol. II, pp. 339–76.

VENNEMANN, THEO (1981) 'Phonology as non-functional non-phonetics.' In DRESSLER, WOLFGANG et al. (1981), pp. 391–402.

VENNEMANN, THEO (1983) 'Causality in language change: theories of linguistic preferences as a basis for linguistic explanation.' *Folia Linguistica Historica* **6**: 5–26.

VENNEMANN, THEO (1985) 'Linguistic typologies in historical linguistics.' In AGOSTINIANI, L. et al. (1985), pp. 87–91.

VENNEMANN, THEO (1988) *Preference Laws for Syllable Structure and the Explanation of Sound Change: with Special Reference to German, Germanic, Italian, and Latin*. Berlin: Mouton de Gruyter.

Chapter 12

Bidirectional diffusion in sound change

William S.-Y. Wang and Chinfa Lien

1 Introduction

This chapter deals with aspects of competing tone changes in the Chaozhou dialect, a variety of Southern Min Chinese spoken in coastal parts of eastern Guangdong.[1] A striking aspect of Chaozhou tone behaviour is that the Middle Chinese (MC) Tone III morphemes with voiced initials developed into modern 2b and 3b reflexes in near equal numbers.[2] This intriguing phenomenon led Cheng and Wang (1972) to conduct a computer-assisted investigation trying in vain to correlate tone and segmental developments. Based on the model of lexical diffusion they concluded that the tone change in question is a system-internal development caught in mid-stream.[3]

The tone change in Chaozhou has become a controversial piece of evidence for lexical diffusion. Labov took the Chaozhou case to be a classic example in Chinese dialects in support of lexical diffusion in his 1979 presidential address to the Linguistic Society of America (Labov 1981). However, this account has drawn criticisms from traditional phonologists (Chan 1983; Egerod 1976 and 1982; Pulleyblank 1978 and 1982; Ting 1978). Despite a difference in emphasis in the argument against lexical diffusion they all converge on an implicit assumption of the Neogrammarian regularity doctrine and on the deep-seated belief that dialect mixture is incompatible with lexical diffusion.

In this chapter we will argue against this traditional view by providing evidence to prove that lexical diffusion did occur in sound change induced by dialect mixture in Chaozhou, although it is not as dramatic as it was previously believed to be. There is strong evidence in Chaozhou that after the initial period of mixture, two linguistic systems entered a symbiotic relationship in which they interacted with each other. We coin the term 'bidirectional diffusion' to designate this kind of interaction where sound change is propagated in opposite directions in a lexically gradual manner. Put forward here is a thesis on the basis of a dialectical relation between intra-system and inter-system sound change. Once the interdependence between them is established the alleged antinomy between lexical diffusion and dialect mixture can no longer be maintained. This thesis is independently motivated by evidence from other languages such as in the evolution of the English stress system. Since the controversy between lexical diffusion (henceforth LD) and Neogrammarian hypothesis (henceforth NH) can only be resolved when the basic theoretical assumptions are teased out and clarified, we will dwell at length on some basic ones behind focal points of dispute at the outset in anticipation of the following discussion.

This chapter is organized as follows. Between the introduction (section 1) and the conclusion (section 10) the bulk of discussion proceeds as follows. Section 2 lays the theoretical foundation of sound change by reviewing the basic assumptions intimately associated with the controversy between LD and NH. Section 3 sketches the emergence of tone strata through the agency of segmental constraints from OC to MC. Section 4 presents documentary evidence on the existence of competing tone systems. Section 5 discusses the formation of competing tone systems in Chaozhou, tracing its development in two stages: first, the initial stage of contact, and second, the interaction of colloquial stratum and literary stratum.

Section 6 presents eight possible combinations of colloquial and literary strata in a syllable and thereby points out an insurmountable difficulty facing the regularity hypothesis. Section 7 deals with the ongoing competition between 2b and 3b providing two sets of statistics: the first set shows various degrees of congruity and incongruity of final and tone with respect to the stratal distinction, and the second, the relative strengths of Tone 2b and 3b. An explanation for the eventual merger of these two tones is also offered. In section 8 we propose the thesis of bidirectional diffusion supported by evidence adduced from Chinese dialects such as Chaozhou, Haikang and Wenxi, and the evolution of the English stress system as a telling piece of independent evidence. Finally, in section 9 we resolve the controversy over the Chaozhou case by validating lexical diffusion on the basis of a two-phased account of sound change.

2 The theoretical foundation of sound change

A central theme in this chapter is that there is a dialectical relation between the system-internal sound change and the sound change that is attributable to external factors. A natural language cannot exist beyond time and space. Except for a few rare cases of dialect islands language contact is unavoidable and not infrequently may take place on a grand scale, given the constant encounter and intermingling of different groups of speakers. The effect of language contact is the coexistence of alien and native strata in a linguistic system which accounts for its heterogeneous character. Language change is a constantly integrating process in which a previously external or alien layer is being incorporated into the overall linguistic system to merge with the native layer.

The theory of sound change proposed here that accommodates an interplay between coexisting layers is grounded in the notion of interdependence of components of a linguistic system such as phonology, grammar and lexicon, which we owe to the legacy of Prague school linguistics (Vachek 1966). Based on the view of interrelated linguistic components we will present an extended version of the theory of lexical diffusion to meet the challenges of its critics. The criticism levelled against lexical diffusion is based on the apparent antinomy between lexical diffusion and coexistent systems. We will argue that there is no conflict between them and lexical diffusion is still a viable theory of sound change if a language is viewed as a dynamic entity constantly integrating its diachronically divergent subsystems into an organic whole.

2.1 The controversy between LD and NH

Although the notion of LD has been around since the nineteenth century, many issues of sound change first received a clearly articulated treatment in (Wang 1969). It is partly on the basis of this chapter that many disputes on sound change go on unabated.[4] Wang (1969) spells out four logical possibilities of the mechanism of sound change in the language of a single speaker:

1. phonetically abrupt and lexically abrupt;
2. phonetically abrupt and lexically gradual;
3. phonetically gradual and lexically abrupt;
4. phonetically gradual and lexically gradual.

The first possibility is excluded, since sound change needs time to run its full course. The NH allows for the third possibility: sound change is phonetically gradual but lexically abrupt. That is, phonological categories change without reference to the lexicon.[5]

On the contrary, LD views sound change as being lexically gradual; it is diffusing through morphemes. For the phonetic aspect Wang focuses his attention on arguing the validity of phonetical abruptness (possibility 2) but leaves the question of phonetical gradualness (possibility 4) open (Wang 1979: 359).[6]

Recently the question was taken up again and an attempt is made to validate possibility 4. Working in the framework of LD Fagan (1989) argues that phonetic routes may be both gradual and abrupt and sometimes these modes occur simultaneously. Trudgill (1986: 61) also observes that 'The fudged dialects force a redefinition of lexical diffusion which is usually characterized as being phonetically sudden but lexically gradual. Fudging is both phonetically and lexically gradual.'

LD and NH look at the sound change from different perspectives. LD views sound change as a whole process: inception of sound, variation and the completion of change. There is competition in sound change which accounts for residues or irregularities. Sound changes that developed at different temporal points can be put together and compete with each other. That is, an indigenous sound change follows a path of change which is different from that of an alien sound change. Diachronically motivated change can bring about a synchronical change. LD considers language as a dynamic (rather than static) entity in constant change through time.

The crucial evidence supporting LD comes from the stage of variation. NH looks at sound change as an end result. It claims that sound change is so minute as to be literally imperceptible. It is not surprising that in discussing sound change they turn to the output, which is a logical corollary of their hypothesis.[7]

Critics of LD consider that the strata are unrelated and will not affect each other. NH cannot reconcile the lack of time dimension in their treatment of strata and the fact that sound changes through time. There is constantly an integrating process that remolds the different strata into a new system.

NH and LD do not differ in the regularity of language. They are both for the setting up of constraints on linguistic phenomena. Where they differ is in the way in which the exceptions are treated. For NH the exceptions are attributed to the result of borrowing or analogy, whereas for the earlier version of LD as proposed in (Wang 1969) they are regarded as residues left by incomplete sound change.

Under Schuchardt's close scrutiny the NH dictum that 'the sound laws operate without exception' runs into theoretical problems since both its subject and predicate are not warranted

(Schuchardt 1972). For the subject if the sound laws are taken as natural laws then the NH claim amounts to a tautology since natural laws are by definition exceptionless. Sound laws cannot be natural laws, since language is a social phenomenon which cannot be detached from human activity. Whenever there are human elements, there will inevitably be exceptions and uneven development granting that language is a rule-governed phenomenon.

The predicate does not hold, either, since languge cannot be detached from its temporal and spatial dimensions and yet the predicate does not specify them. If we restrict our attention to a single dialect at a single point of time, it still is not possible to explain the fact that the dialect may vary in spatial distribution. Reduction to the speech of an individual speaker will not salvage the exceptionless claim of the predicate from absurdity. H. Paul (1920), for example, focuses on the idiolect, but idiolect cannot remain aloof from time, space and society. (Weinreich et al. 1968.)

Saussure distinguishes between language (langue) and speech (parole).[8] He regards language as social and speech as individual. On the other hand, language is homogeneous while speech heterogeneous. (Saussure 1959: 14–15) It is the contradiction between the social character of language and its homogeneity that he is unable to solve. As Weinreich et al. (1968) aptly pointed out, this contradiction arises from an assumption that systematicity presupposes linguistic homogeneity. The same assumption led generative linguists to posit a homogeneous speech community as a prerequisite for the systematic study of language (Chomsky 1965: 3–9). Sound law is therefore not a natural law, and it should be put in spatial and temporal dimensions in the context of a heterogeneous linguistic society. Language is a social phenomenon. Even the linguistic system of an individual would not be homogeneous since it may well contain coexisting systems (Fries and Pike 1949; Weinreich 1953).

For an exponent of NH sporadic change is disallowed as a type of sound change (Bloomfield 1933: 353–64). As a diffusionist Schuchardt regarded sporadic change as a kind of sound change (Schuchardt 1972). Sound change may start in a few isolated cases and then spread gradually and finally engulf the whole set of morphemes. He also adduced evidence to show that sound change may be a generalization of conditioned rules to unconditioned rules, that is, obliteration of phonological conditions.[9]

2.2   The interdependence of components of a linguistic system

At the most fundamental level the discrepancy between NH and LD is intimately linked to the theoretical assumptions of each school with respect to what a linguistic system is like and how linguistic components are related.

Nineteenth-century Neogrammarians as well as their twentieth-century congeners Saussure (1959), Bloomfield (1933) and Hockett (1965) advocate autonomous phonology.[10] In contrast, linguists of Prague School (Mathesius, Trnka, Vachek, Jakobson), Wang, Pike and generative phonologists are in favour of the dependence of phonology.[11]

For the Neogrammarians sound change is a purely phonetic process and not affected by semantic factors[12] (Bloomfield 1933: 364). This is a corollary of their implicit assumption of autonomous phonology. Postal (1968) presents argument against autonomous phonology, yet there is still Bloomfieldism in the treatment of meaning of a linguistic sign. That is, generative grammar does not maintain autonomous phonology, yet it still sticks to the principle of autonomous syntax.

If we get to the core question of what constitutes a linguistic sign, the claim of autonomous phonology will become untenable. A defining property of a linguistic sign is its inherent dualism. A linguistic sign is a union of form and meaning. Saussure (1959: 113) observes, 'Language can also be compared with a sheet of paper: thought is the front and the sound the back; one cannot cut the front without cutting the back at the same time.' The dualism of a linguistic sign as an important theoretical assumption of European structural linguistics is also expressly stated in Hjemslev's vivid metaphor: 'The sign was a combination of the concept and the acoustic image into a unit with two halves, like the two sides of a medal or "a two-sided entity, with a Janus-like perspective in two directions"' (Malmberg 1976: 10) (cf. Jakobson (1971b, c)). It is patently clear that a linguistic sign will fall apart if sound is detached from its meaning. Saussure's elucidation of linguistic dualism seems to run counter to his subscription to the Neogrammarian separation of sound change and analogy. This internal conflict is resolved by Prague school of linguistics for which the interdependence of components of a linguistic system is a very important theoretical underpinning.

2.2.1   Interface between phonology and grammar

If the independence of phonology can no longer be maintained, then the possibility is opened up that there is interplay between phonology and other components of language. Let us first consider its interaction with grammar, which is here taken in its traditional sense encompassing morphology and syntax, but not phonology.

Vennemann (1972) argues that the gradual elimination of phonological conditions results in lexicalization of phonological alternation. In other words, phonological alternation has left residues in morphology. Malkiel (1983) discusses the multi-conditioned sound change and the impact of morphology on phonology.

Jakobson (1971b) also shows the interface between phonology and grammar. He criticizes NH for separating the sensible (signans) and intelligible (signatum) and argues for the indissoluble dualism of a linguistic sign. The grammatical processes sometimes may produce a new phoneme. In Byelorussian the contrast between palatal and non-palatal gives rise to a new phoneme, the palatalized /k'/. In line with the patterns of sound change in Jakobson's (1978) seminal paper, first published in 1931, Moulton (1967) turns up a new finding about phonemic change through morphophonemic analogy.

The impact of morphology on sound structure is also found in Southern Min dialects. There are fewer phonological categories in suffixes than roots. Tones are neutralized when a syllable is followed by the suffix -a. There are seven citation tones and six combination tones in Southern Min dialects. (For the discussion of tone sandhi in Southern Min dialects see Wang, 1967.) But there are only two tones when followed by the suffix -a.

combination tones		citation tones
p'au 51-tai 15	'fort'	p'au 21
li 55-kiam 15	'salted plum'	li 51
kɔ 11-tiŋ 55	'paste a lantern'	kɔ 15
kɔ 33-po 15	'great aunt'	kɔ 55
ku 11-kɔŋ 55	'great uncle'	ku 33
tek 5-sun 51	'bamboo shoot'	tek 2
ioʔ 2-tiam 33	'pharmacy'	ioʔ 4

neutralized tones	
p'au 55-a	'firecracker'
li 55-a	'plum'
kɔ 15-a	'paste'
kɔ 15-a	'aunt'
ku 15-a	'uncle'
tek 55-a	'bamboo'
ioʔ 15-a	'medicine'

The -r suffix in Beijing Mandarin also yields a change in the kinds of vowels that are not found in citation forms. Some of the nasal vowels (i.e. the vowel with a nasal coda) are nasalized when followed by the -r suffix: compare /k'ɔŋ/ 'empty' and /k'ɔ̃r/ 'leisure'.

Emeneau (1989) argues convincingly that sound change in some cases is conditioned by grammatical categories. They are not amenable to explanation by invoking analogy or phonetic conditions. Examples he gives are voiced alveolar fricative initial /ð/ in English as well as Indo-Aryan numerals and expressives in Tamil. /ð/ and its unvoiced counterpart /θ/ as a contrastive pair albeit with a low functional load in English are derived from IE *t-. The development of t- to /θ/ is phonetically regular but there is no phonetic condition for /ð/ which only occurs in morphemes of demonstrative and related meanings.

2.2.2   Interface between phonology and lexicon

Phonology not only interacts with grammar but also with lexicon. As shown above, Bloomfield maintains an independent level of phonology: there are shifts of phonological categories which have nothing to do with the words in which they occur. Yet sound change has to do with the frequency of words. A sound category in more frequent words may undergo more rapid change and conversely the same sound that occurs in rarely used words may lag behind. In other words, the speed of change varies with the frequency of words (Phillips 1984). Thus, sound change cannot be dissociated from the lexical component.

The theory of lexical diffusion as expounded above is in essence based on the assumption of dependence of phonology on lexicon and can be viewed in this light as a thesis on diachronic phonology that sound change is lexically conditioned. Recently proposed Lexical Phonology that combines the strengths of traditional and generative phonology distinguishes between lexical and post-lexical levels. The distinction is claimed to accommodate NH and LD: sound change is lexically dependent on the lexical level whereas the post-lexical level tolerates no phonological irregularities (Kiparsky 1982, 1988). Kiparsky (1988; 398–404) devotes a section to motivating a lexically dependent sound change, namely the tensing of /æ/ that is taking place in some varieties of American English especially those spoken in the Mid-Atlantic states, lending support to LD.

2.3 Sound change and analogy

Connected with the Neogrammarian exceptionless hypothesis is the setting of sound change against analogy and borrowing (dialect mixture), and any irregularities are construed as due to analogy or borrowing (Bloomfield 1933: 360–5).[13] This opposition implies that the Neogrammarian exceptionless hypothesis is definitional and cannot be falsified. If it is purely a putative and tautological question, no further empirical research is going to dispute it.[14]

In NH the incompatibility of sound change and analogy is grounded in an antinomy between sound and meaning. This antinomy implies that sound change is physiological and constructive while analogy is psychological and destructive. But Schuchardt (1972) rejected this antinomy and proposed instead on the basis of adduced evidence that sound change may be destructive, that is, destroy paradigm and analogy may undermine a phonetic system. Therefore both may be constructive and destructive.

The situation reminds us of Sturtevant's paradox (1947: 109): 'Phonetic laws are regular but produce irregularities. Analogic creation is irregular but produces regularity.' Sturtevant's paradox arises from the antinomy in each statement that occurs in different components of a linguistic system:[15]

	phonology	grammar
phonetic law	regular	irregular
analogy	irregular	regular

The paradox is resolved in a theory that allows the interdependence of components of a linguistic system. But once the autonomy of phonology on which it crucially hinges is no longer maintained, NH falls apart.

The dependence of phonology can be seen in a quote from Stankiewicz which dwells on the role of analogy in the interrelation of the 'psychological' and 'physiological' aspects of language in the introduction to Baudouin de Courtenay (1972: 22):

> after the appearance of de Saussure's monograph [i.e. Saussure, 1959] it is no longer possible to treat phonetic change apart from morphology or to claim that analogy is an exception to the regularity of phonetic laws. The opposite seemed now rather to be the case, namely that phonetic change disturbs the regular relations of the grammatical forms, while analogical levelling counteracts the 'blind' force of phonetic change.

In discussing sound change Vennemann (1972) distinguishes between phonetic analogy and conceptual analogy. Types of phonetic analogy he discusses include rule generalization and rule reordering. Both types of sound change involve the extension of phonological domain. We can see in (Schuchardt 1972; Vennemann 1972) the thesis that analogy encompasses both conceptually motivated change and phonetically motivated change. It is clear that analogy does not necessarily involve concept and meaning and is not incompatible with sound change.[16]

A distinction between actuation and implementation is made in (Chen and Wang 1975). Actuation deals with why a sound change takes place and what determines its schedule and timing, whereas implementation is concerned with how a sound change implements itself in a lexically gradual manner. With regard to the actuation problem this chapter mainly focuses on the phonetic actuation seeking to explain sound change in terms of system-internal phonetic constraint. Of course, many patterns of sound change are system-internal phenomena, but there are also a range of sound change triggered by language contact. We will propose a theory to explain how a sound change is actuated when two dialects come into contact. When actuation is given this new interpretation, the distinction between actuation and implementation can be used to explain away previous opposition. That is, actuation can be invoked to resolve the antinomy between sound change and borrowing/dialect mixture (see the discussion in 2.4) as well as the conflict between sound change and analogy. Sound change can be accomplished in various ways through lexical diffusion.

One of the ways in the actuation of sound change as cogently argued in (Phillips 1984) has to do with word frequency in which the most frequent words are affected by physiologically motivated factors whereas the least frequent words are affected by conceptually motivated factors. Similar explanation may be made of the phonological development of demonstrative pronouns in Chinese which seems to constitute Neogrammarian 'exceptions' to regular sound change, but as Mei (1986) which draws on (Stimson 1972) suggests, it may be a result of incomplete sound change induced by LD. Frequency may be a factor in the implementation of sound change which may well be responsible for the resistance of demonstrative pronouns to phonological change that applied regularly to their homophones in earlier stages.

The NH exceptionless doctrine of sound change will inevitably disallow sporadic change, whereas for LD sporadic change is a kind of sound change. As one of the precursors of LD Schuchardt (1972) proposes that sporadic change initiated by analogy can gradually spread through words. From the standpoint of LD sound change may start as an irregular change (i.e. in a few words) and then ultimately become regular (i.e. engulf the whole set of morphemes).

Sound and meaning are incompatible in Neogrammarian framework. Sound change is explained solely in physiological terms, and no psychological factors are involved. However, Sturtevant (1917: 84) takes issue with this position as shown in the following quote:

> We have seen, however, that both kinds of sound change are at once physiological and psychological. Indeed, the psychological factor of association is largely responsible for the regularity of many of the phonetic laws; many irregular changes of sound ultimately become regular by the operation of psychological causes. And on the other hand, we have seen that psychological causes may hinder a change from spreading to all words which contain a given sound.

Arguing in Neogrammarian vein Saussure (1959: 162–5) states that 'analogical phenomena are not changes' meaning no replacement takes place. But when a language is viewed as an interconnected system the effects of analogy may bring about a change in phonological structure.

We can conclude, therefore, that there is no conflict between LD and analogy: that is, sound change can diffuse through a lexicon by way of analogy. (See Shen 1987, which also argues for such a position.)

2.4 Sound change and borrowing

Borrowing as well as analogy as shown above is set apart from sound change in NH. The antinomy between sound change and borrowing is a natural consequence of its theoretical assumption. In other words, this ultimately has to do with what a linguistic system is assumed to be. Is it a homogeneous or heterogeneous system? Is it possible to have coexisting systems in a language? The homogeneity hypothesis necessarily implies that there are no coexistent systems. Sound change is operating in a single native homogeneous system, and there is a clear dividing line between the native and alien systems. Besides overall theoretical considerations the evidence that there is an interface between coexistent systems invalidates the posited antinomy between sound change and borrowing.

Chen and Wang (1975) did not try to dismantle the assumed antinomy between borrowing or dialect mixture and sound change. What they did is to try to argue against the existence of dialect mixture. Although they did not express explicitly what a linguistic community is like in their theoretical framework, they seem to assume a homogeneous community, implying that lexical diffusion is exclusively a system-internal phenomenon.[17]

NH and LD as proposed in (Wang 1969) and elaborated on in (Chen and Wang 1975) and (Wang 1979) are not different in regarding sound change as being system-internal. Neither theory considers that borrowing plays a role in sound change. Where they differ is in the way in which 'exceptions' to sound change are interpreted. For NH exceptions could be due to borrowing whereas for LD exceptions are a result of incomplete sound change. A very important argument against the possibility of borrowing put forward by Cheng and Wang (1972: 105) in their discussion of tone change in Chaozhou is based on the constraint that borrowing is not phonetically selective. Any claim of borrowing in Chaozhou would have to deal with this constraint and we will come back to this problem in section 5.

In full cognizance of the theoretical implication of orderly heterogeneity we argue that lexical diffusion can be accomplished within the linguistic system or from the coordination of coexisting systems. In other words, actuation can come from within and without and therefore the NH antinomy between system-internal and system-external change can not be maintained. This theory is founded on the claim that there is an interface between coexisting systems. Coexistent systems do not stand apart from each other. They interact, instead. Diachronically they are from different sources but synchronically they begin to fuse into each other so that the original distinction may become so blurred that the contemporary speakers will be hard put to detect the difference.

Wang (1989a) discusses and endorses two cases of contact-induced change. We are in full agreement with this recent view on the interaction between sound change and borrowing and propose the thesis that there is no conflict between lexical diffusion and borrowing.

2.5 Contact-induced change

An assumption of a linguistically heterogeneous society will in all likelihood eliminate the antinomy between sound change and borrowing/mixture. The NH posited antinomy is connected to an implicit hypothesis that sound change is 'exclusively' a system-internal phenomenon. While granting that many types of sound change certainly occur strictly in a linguistic system, there are also many sound changes resulting from interference from an alien system. In contact-induced change internal change may be triggered by influence from without.

Jakobson has an oft-quoted saying about contact-induced change. It predicts that internal change will be triggered by foreign elements if the structural properties of a native system show affinity and are amenable to a foreign system. In his own words, 'a language accepts foreign structural elements only when they correspond to its developmental tendencies' (Jakobson 1971a: 241; Van Coetsem 1988: 106). There is a body of evidence to be presented below showing that contact-induced change may bring about a change in internal sound structure in a native system.[18]

In the following a set of examples will be provided to support this contention. The first example is the development of fricatives in English as reported in (Vachek 1976: 191). [v] and [z] were allophones of /f/ and /s/ respectively in Old English. But after the domestication of French words in Middle English (henceforth ME) [v] and [z] also occurred in the positions that were occupied by /f/ and /s/ and became phonemicized. In short, as Vachek observed, 'the change of phonemic pattern is promoted by foreign additions to vocabulary, in other words, via the changes affecting the lexical level' (see also Kurath (1956: 439). Trnka (1982a) also observed that [s] and [f] occurring in intervocalic positions were a mark of foreignism in ME, but the words containing these sounds lost their foreign feature and were assimilated into the native system as a result of the phonologization of the voicing of fricatives.

The second example comes from Russian. /f/ was a foreign sound and usually replaced by xv, x or p. But gradually /f/ was integrated into the native system. As a result, the assimilated foreign /f/ and native /v/ became contrastive, so did the palatalized /f'/ and /v'/ (Jakobson 1978: 109).

The third example has to do with a change of the syntagmatic distribution of /dʒ/ that brought about a large-scale adaptation of French words in English. In Old English /dʒ/ never occurred in the word-initial position, but in ME this restriction was lifted because there was a phonological affinity in paradigmatic pattern between French and English (Van Coetsem 1988: 101, 113).

As the fourth example Ho (1986, 1988) turns up an interesting finding in his analysis of Yongxing, a Xiang dialect surrounded by ambient Southwestern Mandarin dialects in Sichuan province. Like a majority of Chinese dialects Southwestern Mandarin has devoiced the MC voiced obstruents yielding aspirated and non-aspirated unvoiced obstruents in level tone and oblique tones, but the voiced element is preserved in Xiang dialects such as Yongxing. When the secondary aspirated unvoiced obstruents of Southwestern Mandarin were introduced to the native system a phonological compromise was formed incorporating the alien aspirated element into the native voiced initials. A contrastive pair of voiced obstruents based on aspiration arises and aspiration thus becomes distinctive in voiced obstruents as well as unvoiced ones. While this four-way opposition occurred in Sanskrit (Trubetzkoy 1969: 86), Yongxing represents an unusual case in the sound systems of modern Chinese dialects. (For a lucid discussion of Ho's finding see Wang 1989a.) Examples attesting to the contact-induced change can be multiplied indefinitely.[19]

Mathesius (1964) of Prague School distinguishes between synchronic and diachronic foreignism. Synchronically, the borrowed system in the former category is still set apart from the domestic one. The borrowed system in the latter category may be thoroughly domesticated and merge with the native one through time. The former is still felt to be foreign whereas the latter is not. For example, he observes that /v/ is being integrated into English in that although it functions as an index of foreignism it has lost its foreign status in short words. [i] in Southern British English is also involved in the problem of domestication (see also Vachek 1976: 162–68). These two types of foreignism correspond to our two-stage development of borrowing.

A phonological distinction in the colloquial layer may be disrupted by the imposition of the literary layer.[20] A phonological rule in the literary layer may also be intersected by a rule in the colloquial layer. That is, rules in different layers may interact (cf. Chen 1992). In some southern Chinese dialects the merger of IIv and IIIv in the colloquial layer is triggered by the tone category resulting from the merger of IIv and IIIv in the literary layer. In Chaozhou tone change, in particular, the merger of IIvo and IIIv when introduced to be coexisting with the native distinction of IIvo and IIIvs has the effect of inducing the merger of IIvo and IIIv. The eventual merger IIvo and IIIv is a simplification of grammar.

We have established that contact-induced change can cause a change in internal sound structure. This undermines the antinomy between sound change and borrowing, which cannot be upheld any longer.

2.6 Interaction between coexistent systems

In the heyday of American structuralism linguists rarely if ever entertained the possibility of coexistent systems in their theoretical framework. Fries and Pike (1949) were a notable exception. They observed that [t] and [d] are phonetic variants of the phoneme /t/ in the native system of Mazateco; the voiced variant occurs after the nasal. However, [t] occurs after [n] in the loan word siento 'one hundred'. In short, there is only one phoneme /t/ in native Mazateco. On the other hand, if the sound of the loan word is included for phonemic analysis, the overall sound system of Mazateco will contain two phonemes /t/ and /d/ since they are contrastive. Here if the loan words constitute a minor part of the sound system and have not been assimilated and integrated into the native system, the exceptions may have to be treated separately. Although the loan words may be too few to have an impact on the native system in Mazateco, they talk about the criteria by which borrowed sounds can be regarded as being completely assimilated into the native system.

Interaction between coexistent systems can be found in lexical borrowing as well as phonetic borrowing. After complete domestication a foreign element will in all likelihood lose its foreign flavour. That is, the dialectal or linguistic distinction becomes a functional distinction. *Sombrero* means 'hat' in Spanish, but when it is introduced into English it narrows down its semantic domain denoting 'hat with a wide brim' and occurs side by side with hat. We can see the interaction between native and loan words. The native word *hat* gets a part of its semantic realm infringed upon by the loan word *sombrero*. The same is true of *wok* which English borrowed from Cantonese. *Wok* means cooking pan in Cantonese but it acquires a specialized sense in English. Jespersen (1982: 62–77) talked about the competition of native and imported forms in English. There is an interaction between these two layers. Sometimes native words crowded out the imported ones and vice versa.

Interaction can even take place on a morphological level. Bloomfield (1933: 454–5) shows that suffixes such as *-able*, *-ible* of foreign origin can be extended and attached to native words. On the other hand, in some German dialects, native words can adopt Latin-French accent patterns.

Coexistent systems in a language do not stand apart from each other. Even the NH proponents have to recognize some cases of contamination but they are still committed to the view of segregation of coexistent systems citing some doublets of literary and colloquial terms to disallow the possible interaction between them. But the examples adduced often represent fairly isolated cases. If the forms in these two layers are abundant and have coexisted for a sufficiently long period of time then it is quite possible that they will interact with each other. The interaction finds ample support from the case of the evolution of the stress system in English and the tonal development in Chaozhou, Haikang and Wenxi dialects (cf. Lien 1993b for a study on the interaction between alien and native layers in Taoist texts). To account for the interaction between coexistent systems we propose the mechanism of bidirectional diffusion which will be substantiated in section 8.

3 The emergence of tone strata

To lay the groundwork for the presentation of our thesis in the following sections, we introduce here the canonical form of a syllable in Chinese, the traditional categorization of systems of initials and finals, and the conditioning factors for the genesis and the subtonal split of four tone categories. A syllable in Chinese is traditionally viewed as consisting of an initial and a final superimposed by tone, a coextensive suprasegmental element. In modern terms the final in its full form is made up of a medial, a nucleus and an ending. The medial is a glide, the nucleus is a vowel and an optional glide, and the ending is a consonant. The only obligatory element of a syllable is the nucleus (Chen 1976: 116–21).

Tone development in Chinese has always been the focus of theoretical dispute. Middle Chinese (MC) definitely has four tone categories as attested in Qieyun.[21] It has long been established that Tone IV in MC is identified by the finals with endings *-p, *-t, and *-k. The existence of stop endings is well attested in modern dialects that preserve Tone IV. For such dialects then, the suprasegmental features of Tone IV are redundant. The other three tones (i.e. Tone I, Tone II and Tone III) are represented by finals without endings and finals with nasal endings. In traditional poetic convention tones are divided into level tone (Tone I) and oblique tones (Tone II, Tone III and Tone IV). One may wonder whether in the early stage of tone genesis Tone II and Tone III as well as Tone IV had some kind of abrupt endings. Indeed, some linguists advanced such a possibility.[22]

If consonantal endings were responsible for the formation of the four tones, then the initials played a decisive role in the subtonal split of each tone category. MC as epitomized in the rhyme book *Qieyun* had a four-way distinction in initials: unvoiced non-aspirated obstruents (un), unvoiced aspirated obstruents (ua), voiced obstruents (vo) and voiced sonorants (vs). The voicing of initials led to the development of each tone into two sub-tones. The four types of initial consonant can be represented by the following tree diagram:

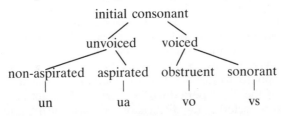

Instrumental studies (Mohr 1971) show that voiced consonants have the effect of lowering the pitch of a syllable. The tone development in Chinese dialects also reflects this universal constraint. The unvoiced (un, ua) initials gave rise to high-pitched subtone a and the voiced (vo, vs) initials yield low-pitched subtone b. The pitch difference between subtone a and subtone b did not become phonemic until the voicing contrast of the initials was lost. Once the pitch difference became phono-logized, the constraint of pitch values by the voicing of initials disappeared. This may result in pitch reshuffling or even flip-flopping.[23] Thus, though tonal reflexes may vary widely in pitch values from dialect to dialect, there is a highly systematic correspondence of tone categories across Chinese dialects. Since we deal only with Tone IIv and Tone IIIv, these two tone categories alone are of immediate concern to our present discussion.[24]

In due course initial obstruents in dialects other than Wu and Old Xiang underwent devoicing, thus obliterating the distinction between u (i.e. un and ua) and v (i.e. vs and vo). However, the distinction between the words bearing these two formerly distinct categories of initials was not lost, since the contrast in the voicing of initials had been rephonologized as a distinction in tone value.

4   Documentary evidence on competing tone systems

Synchronically there are two major groups of Chinese dialects: in one group represented by some variety of Min, Yue, some prototype of Wu and Kejia dialects IIvo and IIIv are still distinct. In another group typified by Mandarin dialects they have merged (Chang 1975). Diachronically there is documentary evidence showing the existence of these two tone systems in the MC period. The tone system in Qieyun, a rhyme book codifying the language of the Nanbeichao period, makes a distinction between

IIvo and IIIv, and the other tone system in which IIvo and IIIv merged is typical of the Tang Chang'an dialect or the Qin speech (Qin being the shorter name of Shaanxi province) or the later Luoyang dialect.

For the dating of the second tone system in the second group many sources of historical document converge to show that the merger of IIvo and IIIv took place no later than the eighth century AD. (Wang 1958: 193–4.) Evidence of poetic rhyming patterns points to the onset of the merger in the early part and heyday of the Tang period (618–907 AD) (Bao 1981). This tone system is reflected in the dialects of such historical figures as Han Yu, Bai Juyi, Huilin and Li Fu, writers from the educated class in various localities.[25] From their biographical background we can infer that Han and Bai might have spoken some form of the Luoyang dialect, while Huilin must have known the Chang'an dialect very well. As Hong (1982: 175–9) observed, Li took the Luoyang dialect as the standard language in his criticism of the Wu element in Qieyun. Thus, the dialects prevalent in Luoyang and Chang'an in northern China share the merger of IIvo and IIIv and can be conveniently subsumed under the pan-northern Chinese dialects.

In sum, the tone system witnessing the merger of IIvo and IIIv in pan-northern tone system is in contrast to the tone system which keeps the distinction of IIv and IIIv in southern dialects. These two contrastive tone systems are attested synchronically in modern dialects and diachronically by historical documents. As will be argued below, they are found to coexist in a synchronic system of some variety of southern dialects such as Chaozhou due to dialect contact induced by population intermingling.[26]

5   The formation of competing tone systems in Chaozhou

This section deals with the formation of competing tone systems in the Chaozhou dialect with reference to the development of MC Tones IIv and IIIv. The development is divided into two stages: initial contact and interaction. External history of the Min dialect group is brought to bear on its chronological strata. The principle that borrowing is not phonetically selected is also discussed.

Buttressed with the full-fledged four-tone system attested in Qieyun, Chinese dialects went through further tone development and fell into two major groups depending on whether or not merger between IIvo and IIIv took place.[27] IIvo and IIvs merged with IIIv and IIu respectively in the literary tone system (Stratum

TABLE 12.1 The literary tone system (Stratum L)

	1	*2*	*3*	*4*
a.	Iu	IIu siau 2a SMALL	IIIu	IVu
	t'iaŋ 1a SKY	IIvs u 2a RAIN	kau 3a ACCUSE	t'ek 4a LIVESTOCK
b.	Iv meŋ 1b BRIGHT	IIvo kiu 2b UNCLE	IIIv su 2b TREE	IVv mok 4b WOOD

L). But IIv including IIvo and IIvs is kept apart from IIIv in the colloquial tone system (Stratum C). Stratum L is a defining feature of Northern Chinese. On the contrary, Stratum C alone or in competition with Stratum L can be found in southern dialects such as Wu, Yue, Kejia and Min. But the distinction is not so simple in such southern dialects as Chaozhou where these two tone systems coexist, which are given in Table 12.1 and Table 12.2. The Roman letters I, II, III and IV denote MC tone categories and u, v, vs, vo, MC initials whereas 1, 2, 3, 4 in combination with a or b refer to modern sub-tonal categories. To reflect the stratal distinction in segment and/or tone we have deliberately chosen doublets for each modern tone category in Chaozhou.[28] For example, 4b is shared by /mok/ in Table 12.1 and /bak/ in Table 12.2.

TABLE 12.2 The colloquial tone system (Stratum C)

	1	*2*	*3*	*4*
a.	Iu t'i 1a SKY	IIu sio 2a SMALL	IIIu ko 3a ACCUSE	IVu t'iok 4a LIVESTOCK
b.	Iv mē 1b BRIGHT	IIvs hou 2b RAIN	IIIv ts'iu 3b TREE	IVv bak 4b WOOD
		IIvo ku 2b UNCLE		

As discussed in detail in section 4, the two-tone strata posited above are well attested in historical documents.[29] Stratum C derived its eight-tone system from the split of the MC four-tone system. Taking the eight-tone system as a basis Stratum L developed its seven-tone system from the merger of IIvo and IIIv. Thus, Stratum L represents a later stage of development, although both evolved from the same source. Diachronically, IIvo and IIIv must have merged in Stratum L before it was implanted into Stratum C. On a synchronic plane one can find both strata competing with each other in a dialect like Chaozhou. Looking at the Chaozhou dialect in itself, we do not know whether the double readings are a result of system-internal development or due to dialect mixture. But when we consider it on a comparative basis, the solution to the problem is immediately at hand.

Language change can take place system-internally, but very often it may be triggered by language contact. The Min dialect boasts of a rich array of dialect strata which accumulated over a long period of large-scale population movement and intermingling. Change in linguistic structure is an index of evolution in social structure. The formation and development of the Min dialect bears witness to the social aspect of language in this regard.

According to Milroys' studies of close-knit networks of language change (Milroy and Margrain 1980; Milroy and Milroy 1985; Milroy 1987) languages are more conservative when social ties are strong but are innovative when social ties are weakened. Throughout its history the Min dialect underwent various stages of linguistic innovation triggered by the weakening of social ties. The weakening occurred when a new influx of population entered to disrupt a close-knit network of a linguistic community. The major event of disruption of social network that occurred at three stages contributed significantly to the multi-layered system in Min dialects including Chaozhou.

In line with (Yuan et al. 1983; Zhan 1981) there are four important waves of population migration from the north in the external history of Min: (1) the first wave that occurred around the Three-Kingdoms period (220–80 AD), (2) the second wave that occurred at the beginning of the Fourth Century toward the end of the Jin period, (3) the third wave that consists of two minor waves occurring in the early seventh century (the early Tang period) and at the beginning of the tenth century (the Five-Dynasties period), and (4) the fourth wave that occurred at the fall of the Northern Song dynasty (the twelfth to thirteenth century AD).

The chronological strata of the Min dialect can be established on the basis of linguistic evidence. Norman (1991) posits that the Min dialect consists of three Chinese strata superimposed on the Yue substratum which is of Austro-asiatic origin (Norman and Mei, 1976). The three strata are the Han dynasty stratum (206 BC–220 AD), the Nanbeichao stratum (420–581 AD) and the Chang'an stratum (the seventh to eighth century).

Norman's account of Min chronological strata jibes well with the migration history of Min as outlined above. The first wave of migration brought the Han stratum, the second wave, the Nanbeichao stratum, and the third wave, the Chang'an stratum. He took a lexical approach to substantiate his stratal assumption. In the case of the Yue substratum he adduced some colloquial Min words which were claimed to be etymologically related to their counterparts in Austro-asiatic languages. As to the Han dynasty stratum he cited the Jiangdong words as recorded in Yang Xiong's (58 BC–18 AD) Fangyan, the earliest extant compilation of Chinese dialects, and Guo Pu's (276–324 AD) commentaries. Although lexical evidence points to the existence of OC traits in Min, Norman (1991) did not provide phonological correlates of dialectal strata. Norman (1979) did give a few doublets or triplets to illustrate the existence of chronological strata in Min, but he did not spell out the phonological system of each stratum, though he touched on some Min phonological traits elsewhere (Norman 1973, 1988: 228–39). Ting (1983) adopted a phonological approach to trace the derivation time of the Min dialects (see also Chang 1984; Chang 1986; Chen and Li 1983; Huang 1982, 1985).

Of course, the symbiotic relation that has developed among chronological strata over the past millennia makes it extremely difficult to unpack them. But thanks to Zhang's (1979a, b, 1982a, b, c) excellent works on Chaozhou there are two coexistent phonological systems that can be set up, that is the Nanbeichao (or Qieyun) system and the Tang Chang'an system. The two systems correspond to the colloquial stratum and the literary stratum. The Han dynasty system is grouped under the colloquial strata along with the Nanbeichao system as opposed to the literary stratum as identified by the Tang Chang'an system, since only these two strata are relevant to the competing tone systems discussed here.

Based on the external history of Min as presented above the formation of chronological strata in the Chaozhou dialect can be sketched in the following scenario. Already in the OC period Proto-Min started its life as a Han Chinese language when it came into contact with the Min-Yue languages in Fujian. Then another ancestral source of Min branched off no later than Qieyun times and therefore escaped the later merger of IIvo and IIIv. The Han expatriates speaking this dialect settled down in the Min area. Later on as a result of waves of more migration from the north this group of Han settlers came into contact with the new arrivals and a new linguistic system (the Tang Chang'an or Luoyang dialect) along with its characteristic tone stratum (i.e. the merger of IIvo and IIIv) was superimposed on the colloquial system. The initial stage of this contact was the coexistence of two competing tone systems, and ultimately they entered into a stage of interaction. The two-staged development is presented below.

Let us first consider the initial stage of contact. If we focus exclusively on the development of IIu, IIv and IIIv, the overlaying of the literary tone system (Stratum L) on the colloquial tone system (Stratum C) yields a mixed tone system in Chaozhou as given in Table 12.3 where the literary (implanted) stratum marked with primes is put above the dotted lines and the colloquial (indigenous) stratum under the dotted lines. At the initial stage of mixture Stratum C and Stratum L coexisted side by side having not started to interact with each other. The tone values of Stratum L and Stratum C in each box were still

TABLE 12.3   The stacking of tone systems

		2		3
a.	IIu' siau 2a' SMALL		IIvs' u 2a' RAIN	
		IIu sio 2a SMALL		
b.	IIvo' kiu 2b' UNCLE			IIIv' su 2b' TREE
	IIvo ku 2b UNCLE		IIvs hou 2b RAIN	IIIv ts'iu 3b TREE

The tones marked with primes represent the literary stratum which came into Chaozhou in later periods different then. For example, 2a′ must have been different from 2a.

Now let us consider the stage when Strata C and L began to interact with each other. At this stage the line of demarcation between Stratum L and Stratum C (represented by the dotted lines in Table 12.3) disappeared. Thus, 2a′ and 2a merged into the modern Tone 2a, whereas 2b′ and 2b coalesced into the modern Tone 2b. From then on, 2b (derived from IIvs) and 2a (derived from IIvs′) became a pair of competing tones, so did 2b (derived from IIIv′) and 3b (derived from IIIv). The Chaozhou tone system as developed at the present stage shows the phenomenon of bidirectional diffusion that occurred in each pair of competing tones exemplified by the competition between 2a and 2b and the competition between 2b and 3b (see section 8 for the deliberation of bidirectional diffusion).

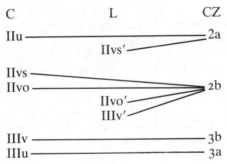

(C = colloquial stratum; L = literary stratum; CZ = Chaozhou)

As shown above, 2b is outstanding among these modern tones in that it is derived from four sources (i.e. IIvs, IIvo, IIvo′ and IIIv′) instead of just one. There are a host of doublets showing variation between 2b forms (derived from IIIv′) and 3b forms (derived from IIIv). The 2b forms are gradually engulfing the 3b forms probably due to the number of words involved: tone 2b includes the reflexes of IIvs, IIvo and IIvo′ as well as those of IIIv′ whereas Tone 3b represents only the reflexes of IIIv.

We have presented above a diachronic scenario of the formation of Chaozhou which came about from superimposing Tone Stratum L onto Tone Stratum C. Let us now present a set of phonological rules to capture these competing tone strata as reflexes of MC Tones IIv and IIIv. The development of Tone IIv stated in the following two rules is discussed first to set the stage for the presentation of the development of Tone IIIv, since both developments are intimately linked.

```
            C   L
IIvs   →   2b  2a
IIvo   →   2b  2b
```

It can be seen above that whereas IIvs developed into two competing tone strata (L = 2a) and (C = 2b), IIvo is tonally realized as one stratum (L or C = 2b), the strata being reflected solely in segmental discrepancy. The development of IIIv (i.e. IIIvo and IIIvs) can be schematized as follows:

```
           C   L
IIIv  →   3b  2b
```

This rule shows the prototypical tone development of IIIv: the IIIv words of the literary stratum are realized as words carrying modern Tone 2b whereas the IIIv words of the colloquial stratum are realized as words carrying modern Tone 3b. In global terms IIvo and IIIv in the literary stratum as well as IIvs in the colloquial stratum have merged to 2b.

As a result of the imposition of the literary system (L) on the colloquial system (C), all the eight modern tone categories each contain both the literary stratum and the colloquial stratum. However, the tone-related stratal distinction is manifested only in the reflexes of IIvs (i.e. 2a (C) versus 2b (L)) and IIIv (i.e. 2b (L) versus 3b (C)). The reflexes of other MC tone categories have lost this characteristic. For example, /t'iaŋ/ is a Iu′ form (L) in Table 12.1 whereas /t'ɨ/ is a Iu form (L) in Table 12.2. But both share the modern tone 1a despite a segmental difference between them (i.e. /iaŋ/ (L) versus /ɨ/ (C)).

In the initial stage of the mixture of two-tone systems the tonal reflexes of Iu′ and Iu must have been different in pitch values before they merged into 1a. Why is it that 2b as a reflex of IIIvs′ and 3b as a reflex of IIIvs have not merged tonally, whereas the reflexes of Iu and Iu′ have been realized as 1a? This is a question that has to do with the important constraint that Cheng and Wang (1972) put foward as a guiding principle to determine whether borrowing takes place or not, namely that borrowing is not phonetically selective. They use this constraint to rule out the possibility of borrowing in Chaozhou tone systems on the grounds that the constraint is violated. Here is their reasoning: Given that there are eight tones in the native system and seven tones in the alien system, there will be fifteen tones in the merged system. However, Chaozhou has only eight tones. Therefore, borrowing could not have taken place on the constraint that borrowing is not phonetically selective. We will argue that the constraint is valid and borrowing did take place. How do we resolve this apparent contradiction? Our argument is presented below.

The answer lies in the fact that in the literary stratum IIIvs' had merged with IIvs' into 2b before borrowing took place, thus preempting further merger with 3b at least for the time being, since some variety of Min dialects such as Xiamen went a step further by collapsing 2b and 3b into a single tone category. However, Iu' did not undergo any merger before it was implanted into the native system. The fact that literary Iu' and colloquial Iu come from the same MC upper tone category accounts for their tone merger while they still remain distinct segmentally. It should be noted that each of the four MC tone categories must have undergone sub-tonal split conditioned by the voicing of initials before the borrowing; otherwise, there will be confusion between Iu and Iv.

6 The literary and colloquial make-up of a syllable

In this section we will present the segmental and suprasegmental makeup of a syllable in terms of two strata (colloquial and literary) to lay the groundwork for our later foray into the difficulty facing the NH. A syllable consists of initial (IN) and final (FN) overlaid with tone (TN). This segmental-cum-suprasegmental construction in interaction with colloquial (C) and literary (L) strata yields a matrix that exhausts the eight possible combinations, as given in Table 12.4. The extraction of strata is worked out on the basis of opposition of phonological values rather than solely on the native speaker's intuition. This principle

TABLE 12.4   Eight possible combinations of colloquial (C) and literary (L) strata in the distribution of segmentals and suprasegmentals

	IN	FN	TN	Examples
1.	L	L	L	su 2b 'to feed', liaŋ 2b 'quantity', nau 2b 'noisy'
2.	C	C	C	ts'i 3b 'to feed', tsua 3b 'oath'
3.	C	L	L	nāu 2b 'noisy'
4.	L	C	C	lou 3b 'dew'
5.	L	C	L	lou 2b 'dew'
6.	C	L	C	tsia 3b 'thank'
7.	C	C	L	niō 2b 'quantity'
8.	L	L	C	si 3b 'oath', sia 3b 'thank'

is followed consistently to avoid the clashes of conflicting strata arrived at independently in terms of the above two different criteria.[30]

The theory of dialect mixture based solely on the NH cannot represent the whole picture in that for eight possibilities it allows for only the first two possibilities, (1) and (2). To make the point even more clear let us conjure a hypothetical situation to illustrate the dilemma of this static model of sound change.[31]

Suppose there is an ancestral form *pi IIIv from which two dialects (C, L) derived their respective present forms. Along with the tone realization of IIIv as 3b later developments generate three phonological changes: (i) the initial *p- turned into a spirant h-, (ii) the final *-i was diphthongized as -ai, and (iii) Tone 3b as a reflex of IIIv merged with Tone 2b as a reflex of IIv into 2b. Now L underwent rules (i) and (iii) whereas C took rule (ii) alone. The application of these three phonological rules and the output are given below:

	C	L
	C	L
ancestral form	*pi IIIv	*pi IIIv
rule (i)	–	hi 3b
rule (ii)	pai 3b	–
rule (iii)	–	hi 2b
output	pai 3b	hi 2b

Suppose that following the application of these three rules L was introduced into C to form a mixed language. Given the NH, one would expect to find in the mixed language only the possibilities (1) and (2) exhibiting the congruity of all three parts (i.e. IN, FN and TN) with respect to the stratal distinction of C and L rather than the other possibilities (i.e. (3), (4), (5), (6), (7) and (8)) which show the incongruity of all three parts, as shown in the following matrix.

	IN	FN	TN	examples
1.	L	L	L	hi 2b
2.	C	C	C	pai 3b
3.	C	L	L	pi 2b
4.	L	C	C	hai 3b
5.	L	C	L	hai 2b
6.	C	L	C	pi 3b
7.	C	C	L	pai 2b
8.	L	L	C	hi 3b

The congruous cases (1 and 2) representing the unchanged

forms and the incongruous cases (3, 4, 5, 6, 7 and 8) representing changed forms exist side by side in this mixed language. The crux of the argument is this. On NH, sound change is phonetically gradual but lexically abrupt. If sound change is implemented in a lexically abrupt manner, then there will be no variation between unchanged formed and changed forms, since we only have access to the end product of the change. This Neogrammarian expectation is either explicitly stated or assumed in the works of students of traditional Chinese phonology Chan (1983), Egerod (1976, 1982), Pulleyblank (1978, 1982), Ting (1978).

In a mixed language like the one shown above if only possibilities (1) and (2) representing the unchanged forms are found, then there is no conflict with the NH. However, since (3), (4), (5), (6), (7) and (8) as well as (1) and (2) occur, it cannot account for them. Thus, it is ruled out as a theory of phonological change. In contrast, this kind of coexistence of changed forms and unchanged forms is exactly what will be expected in the theory of LD where sound change is posited to be phonetically abrupt but lexically gradual. Since sound change is implemented across the lexicon gradually, there will be such kinds of variation.

In this chapter we argue that the NH is unfounded in this regard. Our argument is based on the evidence culled from (Zhang 1979a, b, 1982a, b, c) that all eight possibilities are found in a mixed dialect like Chaozhou. The evidence consists of two sets of distilled data of words with MC IIIv initials: first, the congruity of final and tone including the patterns (LLL, XLL, CCC, XCC, CLL, LCC), and secondly, the incongruity of segment and tone including the patterns (LCL, CLC, CCL, XCL, LLC, XLC) where X stands for the indeterminate status of the initial as to its stratal distinction. In other words, there are twelve patterns altogether consisting of above-mentioned eight patterns (LLL, CCC, CLL, LCC, LCL, CLC, CCL and LLC) and four other patterns (XLL, XCC, XCL and XLC). The final rather than the initial is taken as a primary dimension in interaction with tone since the strata can be more easily distinguished in the former than in the latter. In a sense, difficulty in finding a stratal distinction in the initial in many cases indicates that there is an interaction between these two strata.

As argued above, given NH one would only find congruous patterns CCC and LLL as well as XLL and XCC if the initial is not considered. However, there are eight patterns showing incongruity of segment and final (LLC and CCL), initial and tone (LCC and CLL), final and tone (CLC, LCL, XLC and XCL). All these incongruous cases showing bidirectional diffusion pose an insurmountable difficulty for the NH hypothesis. But this kind of bidirectional diffusion can be adequately explained by the theory of LD. Bidirectional diffusion as used here means that colloquial segment diffuses into literary tone and literary segment into colloquial tone. However, the diffusion proceeds in a lexically gradual manner and does not affect all the items in the class at once. The diffusion may become regular if it runs its full course affecting every word in its domain.

7   The on-going competition between Tone 2b and 3b

In this section we first present the statistics showing various degrees of congruity and incongruity of final and tone respect to stratal distinction and then show the relative strengths of 2b and 3b.[32] First, we know that the synchronic phonology of the Chaozhou dialect consists of the colloquial stratum and the literary stratum. At the beginning when the literary stratum was superimposed on the colloquial stratum there would be a neat correlation among three parts with respect to the stratal distinction. However, after an initial stage of mutually independent coexistence, two strata being in a synchronically symbiotic relation embarked on a sustained period of interaction and intermingling. We can get a cross-sectional profile of ongoing sound change on the basis of the evolution of MC rhyme groups or *she* in traditional Chinese phonology (see Chen 1976). Table 12.5 represents various degrees of the congruity and the incongruity of final and tone with respect to stratal distinction.

In particular, discounting the starred rhyme groups SHEN, JIANG, ZENG and XIAN which have far fewer words, the statistics indicating the percentage of congruity and incongruity are arranged in descending and ascending orders respectively, ranging from GENG/DANG/XIAO through LIU/TONG and ZHI/XIE to ZHEN/GUO/JIA. We can see that the congruity or incongruity between tone and finals as a reflex of MC rhyme groups is not categorial. The gradational distribution in this table shows that the ultimate merger of 2b and 3b which happened in the Xiamen dialect is still in progress in Chaozhou and needs time to run its full course.

Let us now consider the relative strengths of 2b and 3b. We can view the on-going sound change from the perspective of modern tone categories, 2b and 3b. We have established above that 2b as a reflex of IIIv is a literary tone category, since it has the same tone as the reflex of IIvo (see Table 12.1), whereas 3b as a reflex of IIIv is a colloquial tone category which is distinct

TABLE 12.5   Degrees of congruity and incongruity of final and tone with respect to stratal distinction

Rhyme group	Congruity	Incongruity	Total
Geng	13 (100%)	0 (0%)	13
Dang	23 (92%)	2 (8%)	25
Xiao	21 (91%)	2 (9%)	23
Liu	13 (81%)	3 (19%)	16
Tong	12 (80%)	3 (20%)	15
Yu	30 (77%)	9 (23%)	39
Shan	40 (77%)	12 (23%)	52
Zhi	31 (63%)	18 (37%)	49
Xie	28 (61%)	18 (39%)	46
Zhen	9 (47%)	10 (53%)	19
Guo	5 (42%)	7 (58%)	12
Jia	4 (40%)	6 (60%)	10
*Shen	1 (50%)	1 (50%)	2
*Jiang	3 (100%)	0 (0%)	3
*Zeng	5 (100%)	0 (0%)	5
*Xian	4 (57%)	3 (43%)	7

from 2b as a reflex of IIv (see Table 12.2). It is difficult to determine the colloquial and literary status of initials. Therefore, we will focus on the congruity and the incongruity of final and tone alone. Table 12.6 shows the relative strengths of 2b and 3b. The total number of words and the percentage of congruity and incongruity of final and tone are given in left and right columns respectively. A deduction of the percent of incongruity from the percent of congruity for each row turns up such a disparity: row 1 (48), row 2 (62), row 3 (40) and row 4 (22). We can detect from comparing the first two rows and the second two rows a tendency about the relative strengths of the two competing tone categories: 2b, the literary tone (row 1 and row 2) and 3b, the colloquial tone (row 3 and row 4). Intriguingly, whatever the initial (vo or vs), 2b on the whole shows a much lower percentage of deviation from the congruity than 3b. It can be surmised that the force of the literary stratum seems to be a lot stronger than that of the colloquial stratum.

In closing this section we would like to offer an explanation for the merger of IIvo and IIIv that has been completed in Xiamen but is still in progress in Chaozhou. In this chapter we deal only

TABLE 12.6   The relative strengths of 2b and 3b (IN, initial; TN, tone categories; MK, colloquial and literary makeup; NU, number of words)

		Congruity		Incongruity	
IN	TN	MK	NU	MK	NU
vo	2b	LLL	25	CCL	2
		CLL	1	LCL	9
		XLL	37	XCL	11
		total	63		22
		percent	74		26
vs	2b	LLL	48	CCL	1
		CLL	6	LCL	7
		XLL	23	XCL	10
		total	77		18
		percent	81		19
vo	3b	CCC	19	LLC	12
		LCC	11	CLC	9
		XCC	31	XLC	5
		total	61		26
		percent	70		30
vs	3b	CCC	16	LLC	12
		LCC	11	CLC	6
		XCC	13	XLC	8
		total	40		26
		percent	61		39

with the isolation tones in Chaozhou which keep the distinction between 2b and 3b, but according to (Zhang 1979a), a detailed study of tone sandhi in Chaozhou, the two tones have merged in sandhi forms, that is when followed by other full tones. A plausible cause for the merger as suggested in (Chen 1990) in his study of the development of MC IIvo in the Nanhui dialect is the tone confusion that arises from the fact that some IIvo words can only occur in combination form and therefore their isolation tones are lost. This syntagmatic or positional variation results in paradigmatic uniformity through the loss of one variant probably due to the polysyllabication of words. In other words, the merger of the citation tones 2b and 3b is actuated by the analogy with the merger of combination tones and the merger is proceeding from combination tones to isolation tones in a lexically gradual way. When more and more distinctive tones carried by isolation tones make way for the merged tone carried by combination tones, the isolation tones will be affected and ultimately merged.

8 Bidirectional diffusion

In this section we put forward the thesis of bidirectional diffusion. First, we discuss the evidence of bidirectional diffusion in Chaozhou, Haikang and Wenxi dialects. Then independent evidence from the evolution of English stress system is adduced to support this thesis.

Bidirectional diffusion in Chaozhou is manifested in the incongruity of segmentals (i.e. initial and final) and tone as a reflex of MC words with IIIv initials discussed in sections 6 and 7. Let Type A stand for CLC, LLC and XLC, and Type B, LCL, CCL and XCL. Type A and Type B represent two competing forces engaging in a tug of war. In Type A the literary finals infiltrate into the domain of the colloquial tone category. On the other hand, in Type B the colloquial finals encroach on the territory of the literary tone category. Thus, to elaborate on this a little bit, a rhyme group shared by a group of words (Sets M and N) consists of two strata, C and L, represented by Tone 3b and Tone 2b. When the two strata were put together in the first place, the words of Set M and those of Set N adhered strictly to Stratum C and Stratum L respectively. Then in the course of time some words in Set M spilled over onto Stratum L and conversely some words in Set N wedged into Stratum C. This is an on-going sound change for which we coin the term 'bidirectional diffusion' (cf. Lien 1987a: 32). The battle is still going on, but the competition has not ended. Otherwise, two vying tones would have made way for just one, whichever tone category survives the competition, as in Xiamen.[33]

While the battle between 2b and 3b is still waging, the competition between 2a and 2b as a reflex of MC IIvs is at present in favour of the former. There are two pieces of statistical evidence supporting the claim that in the development of IIvs the colloquial Tone 2b is waging a lost battle with the literary Tone 2a. First, on the basis of (Zhang 1979b: 263–4) there are fifteen doublets each of which shows two tones in competition and only six words that occur exclusively in 2b while the majority of IIvs words are realized as 2a forms evidently as a result of former 2b forms being pulled into Tone 2a. Statistics distilled from (Zhang 1982a, b, c) indicate that of a total of 147 MC IIvs words, 2a forms constitute 86 per cent, 2b forms make up only 14 per cent, and there are 15 doublets alternating between 2a and 2b.

Secondly, a look at the agreement of segmental and tone with respect to stratal distinction also reveals that the 2b forms are losing ground to the 2a forms. It can be seen that there are 34 items subsumed under pattern XCL and 7 items under pattern XLC (see section 6 for the definition of the patterns in question). In other words, of the total set of words, the 83 per cent of the items in which the finals belong to the colloquial stratum occur in the literary tone category (2a) whereas only 27 per cent of the items in which the finals are in the literary stratum occur in the colloquial tone category (2b). Thus, in the bidirectional diffusion 2a is winning out on 2b.

Thomason and Kaufman (1988) have added greatly to our understanding of the important role of language contact in sound change. They distinguish two major mechanisms of contact-induced language change: (1) the one involving imperfect learning during pidgin/creole genesis and (2) the other that results from structural borrowing in true bilingualism (ibid.: 35–64). The Chaozhou case doubtless belongs in the second category. The structural borrowing took place at least three times evidenced in its external history as discussed in section 5.

However, they observe that 'in some cases, a language undergoes both types of interference at once' (ibid.: 45). This is true in some aspects of sound change in Chaozhou. For example, the motivating factor for the creation of nasalized vowels may be due to the imperfect learning through language interference. For the presence of nasalized vowels in colloquial stratum in Chaozhou it is quite likely that the native speaker of the Min-Yue languages which supposedly had the syllable without any nasal ending failed to learn the vowels with nasal endings perfectly and nasalized all the vowels. Historically, the nasalization of vowels typified by the colloquial stratum must have been completed before the introduction of nasal vowels of the literary stratum into Chaozhou; otherwise, the two strata would have merged completely. However, unlike phonologists modern native speakers of Chaozhou are not able to appreciate the distinction as manifested in nasalized vowels and non-nasalized vowels as a stratal one. The failure to recognize the stratal distinction may be one of the motivating factors that leads to the bidirectional diffusion of nasal vowels among some rhyme categories of DANG, TONG and ZHEN as discussed above. That is, nasalized vowels as a marker of colloquial stratum that used to occur in the colloquial tone have diffused into the literary tone and vice versa.

Apart from the Chaozhou tone system there is another

southern Min dialect, namely Haikang, lying on the peripheral area reported in (Zhang 1987) which also furnishes evidence of bidirectional diffusion. It is similar to Chaozhou in the preservation of the distinction of words with IIv and IIIv initials in the colloquial stratum:

			C	L	N
1.	IIv	$\rightarrow$	2b	3b	24
2.	IIv	$\rightarrow$	2b		45
3.	IIv	$\rightarrow$		3b	11
4.	IIIv	$\rightarrow$	2b	3b	13
5.	IIIv	$\rightarrow$	1a	3b	23
6.	IIIv	$\rightarrow$		3b	37
7.	IIIv	$\rightarrow$	1a		19
8.	IIIv	$\rightarrow$	2b		37

abbreviations used: II or III coupled with v (i.e. voiced obstruents and sonorants) refer to an MC tone category; 2b, 3b or 1a, a modern tone; C. and L. denote colloquial and literary status of segmentals (i.e. initial and final); N. means the number of words involved.

It is clear that with IIv and IIIv in the literary stratum have merged into 3b, which can be established as a literary tone category. But the situation is more complicated in the colloquial stratum. IIv and IIIv still remain distinct and are realized as 2b and 1a respectively as shown in an opposition between (1), (2) and (5), (7). But IIIv in (4) and (8) have merged with IIv in (1) and (2) into 2b.

2b as a reflex of IIv is carried by words with colloquial segmentals, as in (1) and (2), but as a reflex of IIIv it is mostly carried by words with literary segmentals, as in (4) and (8). Note that nine doublets share literary segmentals. This means that literary segmentals of IIIv have taken on 2b or more exactly migrated into the colloquial tonal stratum. In other words, 2b contains colloquial segments of IIv but literary segmentals of IIIv. In our assumption coexistent tone systems in Haikang as well as Chaozhou are developed out of introducing an alien literary system into the native colloquial system. The above phenomenon shows that the interaction between colloquial and literary stratum must have occurred after the contact and integration of these two systems. The important thing to notice is that words in (5) show the neatest stratal correspondence between tone and segmental.

A note on the relative chronology of the colloquial and literary strata is in order. The tone reflex of IIv in the colloquial stratum must have merged into 1a as a reflex of Iu before the introduction of the literary stratum. Merger of IIv and IIIv must have occurred before the system entered the indigenous system. Otherwise, IIIv of literary stratum could have merged with IIIv of colloquial stratum into a tone category. The same is true of the reflexes of IIv of literary and colloquial stratum.

IVu/vs words are realized as 4a in literary stratum and 3b in colloquial stratum, while IVv words are realized as 4b in literary stratum and 2b in colloquial stratum. The merger of colloquial IV words into non-entering tones such as 3b and 2b is due to the loss of stop endings and should be regarded as system-internal tone change. It is interesting to note that IVu/vs words with colloquial segmentals are realized as 3b which, as shown above, is a literary tone category. Therefore, there is a merger of colloquial segmentals into a literary tone category.

Not only southern dialects like Chaozhou and Haikang, but also northern dialects show the interaction between dialectal layers. Wang (1992) studies the alternative pronunciations of literary and colloquial morphemes and the overlapped sound change in the Wenxi variety of the Shanxi dialect. She distinguished between conditioned and diffusional sound change, on the one hand, and the overlapped sound change that occurs in the dialectal strata, on the other. She argues that the former type of change involves a change in phonemic categories which are restricted by phonological conditions, but not by words and contexts, whereas the latter type of change is a process of lexical competition between dialectal strata. As we argue in this chapter, although literary and colloquial strata belong to different chronological strata, they will interact with each other when the words in the literary stratum are introduced into the colloquial stratum, that is, when they are incorporated in a synchronic system. This hypothesis makes sense since modern native speakers are not sensitive to the chronological strata which only linguists can disentangle. Taking the Wenxi dialect as an example, she shows one type of phonological competition between the old colloquial pronunciation and newly arising literary pronunciation which proceeds in a lexically gradual manner as schematized below:

	t_1	t_2	t_3
col.	strong	equally strong	weak
lit.	weak	equally strong	strong

At time 1 (t1) the morphemes in literary pronunciation take only a tenuous hold of the whole lexicon while the morphemes in colloquial pronunciation still dominate the scene. At t2 both types of morphemes have approximately the equal share of distribution. At t3 the force of literary pronunciation becomes stronger whereas the colloquial pronunciation is on the decline. As she observes, in some cases the change proceeds in the opposite direction: the colloquial elements are crowding out the literary elements. The scenario as presented above is supported by the data he collected of a variety of the Wenxi dialect. The phonological interaction between literary and colloquial strata Wang (1992) independently discovered is exactly the same as we argue for in this chapter. In sum, Chaozhou, Haikang and Wenxi furnish unambiguous cases of bidirectional diffusion in which literary stratum can diffuse into colloquial stratum and vice versa.[34]

Apart from Chinese dialects a most telling piece of independent evidence that lends support to the thesis of bidirectional diffusion comes from the development of stress patterns in English. Halle and Keyser's Chapter 2 ('The evolution of the English stress system') of their 1971 book provides a set of phonoloical rules revised stepwise to characterize the stress patterns at various stages of its development: Old English (Beowulf), Late ME (Chaucer) and Early Modern English (Shakespeare and Levins) (ignoring for our purpose later developments). The study is based on the stress systems as revealed in the metrical verse or rhyming dictionary in each period shown in parentheses. In the Old English period represented by Beowulf, an epic composed 650–750 AD, the stress pattern is characterized by the initial stress rule (i.e. the Germanic stress rule). The metrical works of Chaucer (?1340–1400) contain numerous stress doublets and for each doublet both the Germanic stress rule and the Romance stress rule were at work. The emergence of stress doublets was evidently a result of the influx of a large number of Romance words about three hundred years following the Norman Conquest (1066 AD) (ibid.: 99). However, by the Early Modern English period (the sixteenth and seventeenth centuries) there were few stress doublets left as attested in Shakespeare's verse and Levins' rhyming dictionary.

An important aspect of the stress doublets in Chaucer and other poets of the same period is that 'there is a large number of stress doublets where Germanic forms are stressed in accordance with the Romance Stress Rule and where words clearly of

Romance origin are stressed in accordance with the Initial Stress Rule (ibid.: 102). In the stress doublets of Germanic origin such as hóli/holí or hòlí, and rídinge/ridínge or rìdínge, the first members are stressed according to the Germanic stress rule, and the second members take on the Romance stress rule (ibid.: 102). In the doublets of Romance origin such as comfórt/comfort, discórd/díscord, and rewárd/réward, the first members are assigned the Romance Stress Rule whereas the second members acquire the Germanic Stress Rule (ibid.: 103).

Halle and Keyser explain this incongruity of segment and stress in terms of 'shift of lexical category' which is exactly what we expound in this chapter – 'bidirectional diffusion': words of Romance origin diffuse into the domain of the initial stress rule and words of Germanic origin diffuse into the domain of the Romance stress rule. But there is an important difference that should not be ignored. While they treat cases of incongruity as a system-internal phenomenon on the assumption of a homogeneous linguistic system we take them to be a result of interaction of coexistent systems. The synchronic interaction of these two strata of Late ME is therefore beyond dispute. Furthermore, although Halle and Keyser do not deal with the stress system of Early ME when the English language was brought into contact with the Romance Language, the overall mechanism of transplanting the Romance stratum to the native Germanic stratum and subsequent stratal interaction in Middle English would be quite similar to what we propose for Chaozhou here.

This stratal interaction or rather bidirectional diffusion in English is in effect constrained by the mechanism of variation and selection (Wang 1982). In ME when the language contact occurred on a grand scale there was variation as exhibited by the stress doublets. But after a lapse of several hundred years there was a more uniform stress assignment in the sixteenth century, and it was generally held among the handbooks that 'this uniformity in stress assignment was achieved by subjecting an ever larger proportion of the borrowed vocabulary to the Initial Stress Rule' (ibid.: 110). Jespersen (1982: 96–7) also observes that it took a very long time before the Romance words were stressed according to the German stress pattern. In a sense, the Initial Stress Rule gradually triumphed over the Romance Stress Rule after a long period of competition. Halle and Keyser (1971: 110–11) resort to the Stress Retraction Rule to account for the shift of stress from a later syllable in the word to the initial syllable. (cf. Sherman's (1975) discussion of the evolution of the alternating stress pattern exemplified by some English noun-verb homograph pairs.)

The thesis of bidirectional diffusion is thus motivated by internal evidence adduced from Chinese dialects such as Chaozhou, Haikang and Wenxi, as well as independent evidence provided by the evolution of the English stress system.

9 Resolving the controversy over the Chaozhou case

Among the case studies undertaken in the framework of LD (Cheng and Wang 1972) constitutes one of the early provocative ones (for works done in this paradigm see Wang 1977). It has since become the butt of repeated criticism from phonologists in the traditional camp, as in (Chan 1983; Egerod 1976, 1982; Pulleyblank 1978, 1982; Ting 1978). Egerod and Ting merely contest the advisability of regarding Chaozhou tone change as a case of LD while steering clear of the question of whether LD *per se* is a valid theory of language change. On the other hand, Pulleyblank and Chan are as steadfastly stuck to the Neogrammarian doctrine as they are removed from LD as a legitimate theory of sound change.

General issues regarding the controversy between NH and LD have been addressed in section 2. Here three main points -pertaining to the Chaozhou tone change are singled out for deliberation. Criticisms levelled against LD converge on three issues which are of interest to linguists at large: (1) the nature of a linguistic system, (2) the relation between sound change and non-phonetic information and (3) the role of dialectal mixture in sound change. As the criticism goes, language is a complicated system exhibiting 'socially- and geographically-determined differences' (Pulleyblank 1978: 185). No linguists, including lexical diffusionists, will be so naive as to deny the socio-geographical aspects of language system.

In fact, Wang (1979: 356) supports the sociolinguistic view of speech community exhibiting 'orderly heterogeneity' (Weinreich et al. 1968). And there is no claim that LD is the only explanation for all cases of sound change; rather, it offers an alternative way of looking at sound change. It does not by any means preempt further attempts to deepen our understanding of other aspects of language change.[35] With so vast a body of dialectal material for Chinese we are struck by Pulleyblank's (1978: 185) deterministic attitude, when he predicts, 'As against this omnipresence of dialectal differences, great and small, one will be hard put to find any unambiguous direct evidence for LD at synchronic level.' We have argued in 2.4 that sound change and borrowing are not incompatible. We regard LD as making a theoretical claim which can be subject to empirical verification. As more and more dialect materials appear and our understanding deepens, it is worthwhile putting various theories of sound change including LD to the test, even if this theory may ultimately prove to be wrong.

As to the question of whether or not sound change should make reference to non-phonetic (or rather morphological) information Pulleyblank (1978: 183–4, 1982: 395–7) evokes the orthodox views of Neogrammarians, structural and generative linguists, and reiterates the phonetic autonomy in sound change.[36] We have argued for the interdependence of components of a linguistic system in 2.2, which shows that independence of phonology is untenable.

One familiar topic that Pulleyblank along with many others brings up again and again is the role of dialectal mixture in sound change. In southern dialects bearing witness to waves of migration from the north over the past two millennia language contact and subsequent language intermingling must have left an indelible imprint on the linguistic system as a whole. In tackling questions of sound change such linguistic realities should not, of course, be brushed aside. However, on the one hand, one should be wary of the pitfall of what Chen (1972: 457–98) called the facile and all-embracing use of dialectal mixture as the only explanation. On the other hand, recent theoretical development of LD (Chen and Wang 1975) has led to a careful distinction between actuation and implementation in explaining sound change.

The importance of detaching implementation from actuation can be seen in a quote from (Wang 1979: 362), 'Although it is obviously important to know whether a change is actuated internally or externally, phonetically or conceptually, the implementation by such a process of LD should be the same.' In fact, in a review of (Wang 1977), an anthology of contributions of LD, Hashimoto (1981: 190) expressed the conviction that 'Lexical diffusion can explain not only the internal development of languages, but also developments caused by language contact.' Actuation may be concerned with contact-induced sound change as suggested in 2.3 as well as sound change explainable in physiological and acoustic terms as discussed at length in (Chen and Wang 1975), while implementation deals with how a sound change accomplishes itself – LD being argued as the basic mechanism in the implementation of sound change. In our framework one important addition to the concept of actuation as delimited in (ibid.) is the thesis that sound change can be triggered system-externally by language contact as well as internally by the constraint of physiological, acoustic and conceptual factors. There is no more antinomy between LD and borrowing with dialect mixture assigned to the domain of actuation and LD allocated to the realm of implementation.

As touched on in section 3, a striking tone change in Chaozhou among Chinese dialects which Karlgren (1915–26: 589, 1948: 443–4) was the first to uncover is the realization of MC Tone IIIv as modern Tones 2b and 3b. In particular, the striking aspect of its tone development lies in the partial surfacing of IIIv as 2b. Cheng and Wang's (1972: 104) investigation of the Chaozhou data of Phonetic Dictionary of Chinese dialect (Beijing Daxue 1962) turns up near equal numbers of 2b and 3b lexical items as reflexes of MC IIIv. Furthermore, they made an unsuccessful attempt to correlate tone with the segmentals (i.e. initial or final). They therefore concluded that it is a system-internal development caught in midstream; that is, without any motivated phonetic condition MC IIIv is split in near equal number into 2b and 3b. Because of over-all considerations they were reluctant to hazard a correlation of tone and segmental even though they were well aware of the fact that vowel nasalization only occurs in 3b (Cheng and Wang 1972: 110). In fact, some minor exceptions leak through even this seemingly iron-clad set of rules.

Their view of Chaozhou tone change has raised the eyebrows of many a traditional phonologist. Guided by the Neogrammarian regularity principle they propose instead an account entirely based on the notion of dialectal mixture. But in an earnest attempt to obtain the examples of neat correlation they lose sight of the overall picture of tone change neglecting a rich array of examples violating such a correlation. In section 8 we attribute such a lack of correlation in a portion of the Chaozhou data to the agency of 'bidirectional diffusion'. In other words, talking merely about dialectal strata and brushing aside all the exceptions as due to contamination do not solve the problem at all, especially when contamination is too vague a notion to have any real theoretical import.[37]

To avoid the difficulty of previous studies we unpack the Chaozhou tone change into two stages. First, in keeping with the assumption of dialectal strata there was the overlaying of the literary tone Stratum L onto the colloquial tone Stratum C into a symbiotic diachronic system. Then, with the passage of time, the two strata were thrown into a period of sustained interaction blurring away the distinction between them. In reanalysing the

Chaozhou tone change into two phases – that is, keeping the distinction between actuation and implementation – we hope we have fulfilled the goal of invigorating LD as a valid model for explaining Chaozhou tone change, though in somewhat different perspective, while at the same time benefiting from the traditional wisdom of dialectal strata. This interactive model of sound change accommodating the internal and contact-induced change may apply to similar types of sound change elsewhere. The irregular development of MC IVu tones in Beijing Mandarin is a baffling yet intriguing phenomenon inviting various interpretations. It is viewed as an accretion of dialectal layers through borrowing (Stimson 1962) or residues of incomplete sound change that accumulated through time (Hsieh 1974). Our approach can be explored fruitfully to resolve the conflict between these two theories.

10 Conclusion

We have presented an interactive approach to sound change by providing supportive evidence for the interaction between internal change and contact-induced change. In order to lay the groundwork for this objective we review the basic issues underlying the controversy between NH and LD. Sound change is treated as solely belonging in the domain of phonology independent of lexicon and semantics by NH. In this chapter we have drawn on the insight of previous works to dismantle the opposition of sound change to lexicon and analogy in favour of the theory of LD. The argument is based on a view of a linguistic theory in which each and every component of grammar is interrelated. This view of dependence of linguistic components entails the interaction between phonology and grammar/lexicon. In arguing against the NH assumption of homogeneous linguistic community we propose an extended version of LD in which the conflict between sound change and borrowing can be resolved and there is an interaction between coexisting systems induced by language contact.

As a central theme backed up by the above theoretical underpinnings we propose the thesis of bidirectional diffusion which is built on the evidence adduced by the ongoing tone change in Chinese dialects of Chaozhou, Haikang and Wenxi, as well as the evolution of the stress system in English. The argument is based on an in-depth description and analysis of a body of diachronic and synchronic dialect materials. The case of Chaozhou tone change as thoroughly treated here is a conclusive reply to a series of criticisms levelled against (Cheng and Wang 1972) which is regarded as a faulty case of LD. However, it should be noted that the validity of LD does not rest on Chaozhou only even if our account proves to be wrong. In closing let us consider recent developments of LD and reflect on the prospect for its future advance.

There is a sizeable body of research that has been done in the light of LD along many a line of inquiry – language acquisition (Ferguson and Farwell 1975; Hsieh 1972); linguistic subgrouping (Hsieh 1973; Krishnamurti et al. 1983), language history (Lien 1990a, b; Ogura 1990; Toon 1983), word frequency (Phillips 1984), phonetic experiment (Lin 1990) and mathematical model (Shen 1990), among many others. In a recent personal communication with William Wang, Matthew Chen suggested looking at LD in a broader perspective: (1) LD of lexical (word formation) change, (2) phonological diffusion of lexical change, (3) syntactic diffusion of lexical change, (4) LD of phonological change, (5) phonological diffusion of phonological change, (6) syntactic diffusion of phonological change, (7) LD of syntactic change, (8) phonological diffusion of syntactic change and (9) syntactic diffusion of syntactic change. These are promising areas for future research. To our knowledge there are some linguists currently working on syntactic and morphological change from the viewpoint of LD (see Cheng 1989, 1990; Hsieh 1989, 1990; Riddle 1985; Tottie 1991; among others).[38]

Acknowledgement

Part of the content of this chapter is based on the PhD dissertation of Chinfa Lien, University of California, Berkeley, 1987. Many friends have helped us formulate the ideas here; we would especially like to thank Matthew Chen, Hsin-I Hsieh and Zhongwei Shen for their many useful suggestions.

Notes

1. Min is the abbreviation for Fujian province in southeastern China. The Min dialects spoken in most parts of Fujian province, the eastern part of Guangdong, and Taiwan as well as southeast Asia form one of seven major groups of the Chinese language along with Northern Chinese, Wu, Xiang, Gan, Kejia and Yue (Yuan et al. 1983: 22). The Min dialectal group falls into five sub-groups: Eastern Min, Puxian, Southern Min, Central Min and Northern Min (ibid.: 234). Southern Min dialects include Xiamen, Quanzhou, Zhangzhou, Hainan and Chaozhou. The last two dialects are in Guangdong

province. Unless otherwise noted, the data on the Chaozhou dialect draw on (Zhang 1979 and 1982). Chaozhou is intended as a cover term for a group of the southern Min dialect spoken in the Chaozhou and Santou area (see Li 1979 for the minor phonological distinctions among them). They include such varieties as Chaoyang (Zhang 1979 and 1982), Chaozhou (Beijing Daxue 1962), Jieyang (Dong 1959), etc.

2. Because of the long history of the Chinese language it is convenient to divide its development into several periods. In a section on the periodization of the Chinese language Wang (1958: 32–5) takes Old Chinese (OC) to cover the periods up to the third century AD and MC to be the periods extending from the fourth century to the twelfth century AD. The gap between OC and MC is a transitional period.

The reconstruction of OC is mainly based on the rhyme groups of Shijing, Book of Odes (ca. 1100–600 BC), phonetic compounds, and rhyme categories of verses of Han periods (206 BC–220 AD). MC is codified in Qieyun (601 AD), the earliest comprehensive rhyme book. For the development of Tone IIvo the watershed is around the eighth century AD (see section 5 for detailed discussion). In this chapter colloquial stratum covers the Han and Nanbeichao strata, and the literary stratum, the Chang'an stratum. This distinction in this paper does not correspond neatly with OC and MC in Wang's periodization, since in his scheme the Shijing system belongs to OC and the Qieyun system, MC, yet both systems belong to colloquial strata in our account.

For notational convention we follow (Wang and Cheng 1987). The Roman letters I, II, III and IV stand for MC level tone, rising tone, departing tone and entering tone respectively. The lower case letters un, ua, vo and vs are used to designate types of initials and subtonal distinction. These terms as well as the term 'initial' are explained in section 3. The Arabic numerals together with a or b stand for modern tone classes.

3. The Chaozhou data on which (Cheng and Wang 1972) is based come from (Beijing Daxue 1962).

4. A series of studies on sound change that were inspired by (Wang 1969) were collected in an anthology (Wang 1977) where basic ideas of lexical diffusion were proposed and amply attested by empirical evidence from a variety of languages in the world. The validity of the theory of LD does not stand only on the Chaozhou case. Even if its analysis of Chaozhou tone phenomena proves to be wrong, it does not necessarily follow that its validity should be questioned. Even some critics of (Cheng and Wang 1972) such as Egerod (1982) concede that LD works elsewhere. (See Hagege and Haudricourt 1978) We claim that with some extension LD still works in Chaozhou tone change. As far as language is a rule-governed system LD and NH show no disagreement. It is a serious misunderstanding that LD is a catch-all wastebasket that any irregularities can be thrown into (Pulleyblank 1982).

5. Another important feature of NH connected to phonetic gradualness is that sound change is so minute as to be imperceptible (Hockett 1965). It is output-oriented: the process by definition cannot be observed.
6. Phonetical abruptness is supported by a body of evidence, notably flip-flop of tone and the change that takes place between articulatorily discontinuous sounds like p and k the relationship of which can be accounted for by the acoustic feature Grave in Jakobsonian terms (Wang 1969).
7. The emphasis on the end result of sound change is succinctly expressed in Lass (1984: 329), 'The Neogrammarian Hypothesis might better be called the "Neogrammarian Effect."'
8. In the English version (Saussure 1959) langue is translated as 'language', parole as 'speaking' and langage as 'speech'. The English terms 'language' and 'speech' are adopted from (Weinreich et al. 1968) to avoid the confusion arising from the original renditions 'language' (langue) and 'speech' (langage) which are not in keeping with the common usage in English linguistic literature.
9. Arguing in the framework of NH Hoenigswald (1964) states that there is no cleancut distinction between minor (sporadic) sound change and major (regular) sound change.
10. Among post-Bloomfieldian structural linguists Pike is a notable exception. In his Grammatical prerequisites to phonemic analysis (Pike 1972) provides evidence to show that phonological analysis can not be independent of grammatical information.
11. However, the generative theory should be regarded as a theory that maintains a partial dependence of components of a linguistic system, since syntax is taken as being independent of semantics.
12. The following quotes reflect the spirit of NH about the nature of sound change. 'A phonetic change affects not words but sounds. What is transformed is a phoneme' (Saussure 1959: 143). 'At a given time and in a given area all words having the same phonic features are affected by the same change' (ibid.: 93). The gist of NH is captured in a nutshell in the following well-known dictum: 'phonemes change' (Bloomfield 1933: 354). This dictum presupposes the assumption that phonetic change is independent of lexicon and grammar. But according to (Kiparsky 1988), Bloomfield's sub-phonemic variants (non-distinctive variants) refer to grammatical categories. Therefore, the autonomy of levels cannot be maintained (ibid.: 366–7).
13. The isolation of sound change from analogy is also reflected in Saussure's posthumous work where he observes, 'They (i.e. exceptions) can be explained either by more special phonetic laws or by the interference of facts of another class (analogy, etc.)' (Saussure 1959: 94).
14. 'The occurrence of sound-change, as defined by the neo-grammarians, is not a fact of direct observation, but [an assumption]' (emphasis added) (Bloomfield 1933: 364).
15. According to (Saussure 1959: 153–4) 'consequences of phonetic

evolution are, 1. The breaking of the grammatical bond, 2. the effacement of the structure of words' . . . 'phonetic evolution is a disturbing force . . . analogy counterbalances the effect of phonetic transformation' (ibid.: 161) 'analogy favors regularity and tends to unify structural and inflectional procedures' (ibid.: 162).

16. Trnka (1982b) distinguishes between phonological analogy and morphological analogy. The former may be responsible for the creation of new phonemes, such as /ŋ/ was developed from [ŋ] by analogy of the proportional opposition: t/d/n and k/g/x in Middle English. He also holds that if language is taken as 'a structural system of signs consisting of several subsystems', then the antinomy between sound laws and analogy as set up by NH can no longer be maintained (ibid.: 103).

17. Wang (1969) was not unaware of the social dimension of sound change. However, borrowing is excluded as being irrelevant to or incompatible with lexical diffusion characterized as being solely responsible for system-internal sound change. (Wang 1979: 156) represents a new phase when he explicitly committed himself to the position of orderly heterogeneity put forward by (Weinreich et al. 1968), but he still excludes borrowing or language mixture as a way of explaining sound change.

18. 'language contact has the effect of speeding up the diffusion of change despite its autonomous or language-internal causes. . . . change constitutes a simplification of the linguistic system.' (Silva-Corvalan 1986: 588)

19. Filipović (1989) also talked about filling the empty space in a native system activated by an alien system under the pressure of linguistic borrowing.

20. The distinction of colloquial and literary layers is made in terms of phonological opposition in a linguistic system. It is also a relative concept. If there is a three-way opposition, say A, B, and C, B may be colloquial relative to A, but literary relative to C. It is largely though not entirely isomorphic with native speakers' intuition about the distinction between colloquial and literary speech or informal and formal speech, since many words in the literary layers are active in daily use. For example, the literary pronunciations like *xue* 'to learn' and *se* as in *yanse* 'color' are used in daily speech rather than their colloquial counterparts *xiao* and *shai* in standard Mandarin.

21. The exact nature of Qieyun (601 AD), the earliest comprehensive record of MC, is a topic of perennial interest to Chinese phonologists. There are two schools of thought about it. One believes that it is a mixed or rather eclectic system. Another contends that it is based on a single dialect, be it of Wu, Chang'an or Luoyang origin (Hong 1982: 166–70, 175–9).

A more plausible position, as Hong (ibid.) argues, is that Qieyun is primarily based on the literary tradition of the Luoyang dialect supplemented by that of the Jinling dialect. The tradition comes from the old speech of the Six Dynasties period covering the Three Kingdoms (220–80 AD), Jin (265–420 AD) and Nanbeichao period

(420–589 or 386–581 AD). In a classic paper on the nature of Qieyun and the foundation of its phonological system Zhou (1963) concluded that the phonological system of Qieyun is based on the standard language prevalent among the literati in the sixth century AD, and the codification of fine distinctions of phonological categories is largely in keeping with the literary pronunciation of Southern tradition.

22. Haudricourt (1954) posited a morphological suffix *-s for Tone III. Mei (1970) (cf. Pulleyblank 1973) contended that Tone II had a glottal stop ending citing dialectal evidence to support his claim. If we accept these assumptions, the emergence of tones may have been due to the phonologization of segmental features induced by the loss of the consonant suffix.

23. See (Wang 1967: 102) for the discussion of flip-flops in Chaozhou. From the tone system of Chaozhou in note 28, we can find such flip-flop alternations in Tone I and Tone IV. As discussed in section 3, the pitch height of a syllable is conditioned by the voicing of the initials at the onset of tone formation. The syllable with the MC unvoiced initials is high-pitched whereas the syllable with the voiced initials has a depressed pitch. The subtones of Tone I and Tone IV are called 'flip-flops' because their pitch heights are reversed. See also (Hashimoto 1972).

24. The reconstruction of MC initials as shown in the following table is adopted from (Chou 1986: 79) except that Yun and Yi are represented as *j and *ø. These two reconstructed forms are not claimed to reflect the true values of ancient sounds, since they have multiple sources. The term 'fricated' coined in (Chen 1976: 118) covers affricate and fricative. 'vo' and 'vs' correspond to quanzhuo (full murky) and cizhuo (secondary murky) in traditional Chinese phonology. Another mnemonically more effective way of referring to MC initials is to use the word that has the designated initial. The Chinese words given here are in the spelling of Beijing Mandarin represented by capitalized letters: *b (BING), *m (MING), *d (DING), *DZ (CHONG), *z (XIE), *n (NI), *l (LAI), *ḍ (CHENG), *dẓ (CHONG), *dẕ (CHUAN), *ẕ (CHAN), *ɳ (RI), *g (QUN), *γ (XIA), *ŋ (YI), *j (YUN) and *ø (YI). In the following table which only gives the reconstructed of voiced initials. vo embraces stops and fricated, while vs cover nasals, a lateral and others:

	vo stop	fricated		vs nasal	lateral	other
labial	*b			*m		
dental	*d	*dz	*z	*n	*l	
supradental	*ḍ	*dẓ				
palatal		*dẕ	*ẕ	*ɳ		
velar	*g		*γ	*ŋ		*j
gutturals						*ø

25. The poet Han Yu (768–824 AD) was from Dengxian in southwestern Henan and the comment in his treatise, Hui bian, gave him away as a speaker of the dialect showing the merger of IIvo and IIIv. (Wang 1958: 194). The poet Bai Juyi (772–846 AD) was born in Xinzhen and spent his childhood in Yingyang; both places are in the area adjacent to the east of Luoyang, Henan province. According to Lai's (1982) study of the rhyming practice of Bai's poems the merger of IIvo with IIIv proceeded in a lexically gradual manner. Of the total of sixty-two IIvo morphemes, thirty-three morphemes rhymed with II morphemes only, fifteen morphemes rhymed with III morphemes only, and fourteen morphemes both rhymed with II and III morphemes. In other words, 53 per cent of the total IIvo morphemes remained unchanged in Tone II, 24 per cent of them were in variation between unchanged forms (Tone II) and changed forms (Tone III), and 23 per cent of them had changed into Tone III, that is, merging with III words.

    The Buddhist monk Huilin from Sule in the western part of Xinjiang province knew the Qin dialect, as indicated in the sound glosses he gave in his Yiqie Jing Yinyi (810 AD) (Chou 1948). The Qin dialect refers to the Guanzhong dialect or the dialect prevalent in the heartland of Shaanxi province where the ancient capital Chang'an lay. The onset of the merger of IIvo and III can also be detected from Huilin's Fanqie sound glosses (ibid.). In particular, of 309 IIvo morphemes 239 items stayed in Tone II, nine items occurred in Tone I, and sixty-one items were in variation between Tone II and Tone III showing that the merger had been under way. (The figure is due to Numoto 1982: 1053).

    The scholar-official Li Fu came from the south-eastern part of Gansu province. According to Hong's (1982: 175) editorial comment Li Fu's Kan Wu or corrective note was written in 880 AD. Li criticized Qieyun for lumping some of what he regarded as Tone III morphemes under Tone II. Among many morphemes he cited, Li observed that Qieyun misplaced *giu 'maternal uncle', for example, under Tone II. The alleged misplacement in Qieyun is in fact not a mistake at all. In Qieyun *giu 'maternal uncle' is a Tone II morpheme, whereas *giu 'old' is a Tone III morpheme. In Li Fu's dialect the two items are homophones both segmentally and tonally. This means that in his dialect Tone II morphemes with vo initials had merged with Tone III morphemes with v initials. (For detailed studies of Li Fu's corrective note see (R. Li 1985; Yang 1958.)

26. Traditionally Chaozhou is affiliated with Southern Min along with Xiamen (see note 1). Both dialects share the innovation of nasalization of a set of MC nasal finals in the colloquial stratum, the denasalization of MC initials and the preservation of the MC ending *-m in the literary stratum. However, unlike Xiamen, Chaozhou shares with Jian'ou (Northern Min), Fuzhou (Eastern Min) and Putian (Pu-Xian) in the development of the MC ending *-n to -ŋ. Documentary evidence shows the presence of Han people in

Chaozhou started as early as the third century BC. But it was not until around the seventh to eighth century AD that large-scale migration to Chaozhou became substantial (Yuan et al. 1983: 234–5 and Wang 1969: 127).

27. For a succinct overview of aspects of tone development in Chinese see (Wang and Cheng 1987). (See also Lien 1987b) for a general survey of tone patterns in Chinese dialects.) Recently Wang (1987) proposed a new thesis of tone merger which is a radical departure from the traditional split view. This line of inquiry was further explored in (Pan 1982 and Lien 1986) based on Wang's 1980 manuscript that appeared as Wang (1987). Ting (1989) presents a review of the split and merger theories in historical perspective.

28. The examples given in Table 12.1 and Table 12.2 are gleaned from (Zhang 1982a, b, c), an excellent study of the Chaozhou dialect. Its tone values are given as follows:

	I	II	III	IV
u	mid level	high falling	mid falling	mid
v	high level	falling rising	low level	high

Since IVu and IVv are abrupt tones, they are represented by only a single tone feature. The Chaozhou tone values given here and elsewhere in the chapter are isolation tones rather than sandhi tones.

29. The two-tone strata were arrived at in Chang's (1975) systematic account of the tone-correlated strata in Chinese dialects based on a fairly rich dialectal repertoire.

30. The stratal distinction our discussion is based on basically draws on Zhang's (1979 and 1982). For detailed studies of the development of rhyme categories in Min dialects see (Chang 1984; Chang 1986). See also (Sung 1973), which was, to our knowledge, the first to account for stratal distinction in Min in terms of lexical diffusion.

31. We are indebted to Matthew Chen for the sharpening of the argument presented here.

32. Due to the constraint of length the data from which Table 12.5 and Table 12.6 are gleaned are not given here. But they will be provided in Lien and Wang (1993).

33. The isolation tones of the tone system of Xiamen, a southern Min dialect, are represented in feature specifications as follows:

	I	II	III	IV
u	high level	high falling	low falling	mid falling
v	mid rising		mid level	high

(The tone data is due to Chen and Li 1983: 69.) Unlike Chaozhou which has eight tones, Xiaman in which IIvo and IIIv have merged has only seven tones. However, like Chaozhou Xiamen still manifests a stratal distinction in the tone development of IIvs as shown in the following rule.

$$\text{IIvs} \quad \rightarrow \quad \begin{array}{cc} \text{C} & \text{L} \\ \text{3b} & \text{2a} \end{array}$$

The IIvs morphemes take on Tone 3b in the colloquial stratum and Tone 2a in the literary stratum. Recall that IIvs is realized as 2b in the colloquial stratum in Chaozhou. The 2b in Chaozhou must have been an intermediate stage from which 3b was derived in Xiamen where 2b had merged into 3b bearing the tone value of mid level.

34. Although it is not explicitly stated that lexical items from different strata do not interact with each other, this is exactly what is implied when isolated cases of doublets such as *legal* and *loyal* or *regal* and *royal* are mentioned to illustrate the stratal distinction (Egerod 1982: 170). However, as argued in 2.6, there is clear evidence of interaction between coexistent systems. That is, the lexical items in different chronological strata clearly can influence each other. A close examination of English vocabulary, for example, turns up a host of examples showing the interdiffusion of lexical items of different strata. The interaction on the level of word formation in English is exemplified by such hybrids as *television* (Greek + Latin), *petrify* (Greek + Latin), *automobile* (Greek + Latin), *gentleman* (Latin + Old English), *anteroom* (Latin + Old English), *readable* (Old English + Latin), among many others (cf. Jespersen's (1982: 97–101) discussion of hybrids in English and Berndt's (1989: 48–104) introduction of historical changes in English lexicon).

35. This point is expressly stated in (Wang 1979: 369), 'The Neogrammarian conception of language change will probably continue to be part of the truth. With the benefit of richer data and more powerful methods, our perspective on language change has been enlarged. We see that, given the remarkable complexity of language, which we are always too prone to underestimate, changes occur along other paths as well. Hopefully, this wider perspective will provide a more realistic foundation upon which deeper questions concerning language change and language relations can be raised and explored.'

36. Pulleyblank (1978: 183) states that 'It [i.e. Wang's theory] is, however, contrary not only to the Neogrammarian principle of the autonomy of phonetic factors in sound change, but also to the orthodox view among both structural and generative linguists.' The alleged autonomy of phonology alluded to earlier generative phonology is faulty (see King 1969; Postal 1968). This autonomous view has never been embraced by generative phonologists. Current trends in generative phonology are in favour of the dependence of phonology championed in particular by those working in the framework of lexical phonology (see, for example, Kiparsky 1982 and 1988).

37. In the case of interaction between the two strata (Egerod 1982: 70) refers to it as contamination. In his own words, 'In some cases where the same Ancient Chinese word has two Chaozhou reflexes they may

by contamination both acquire the same tone.'
38. For an introduction to and the state of the art of the theory of LD, see Lien (1993a).

References

BAO, MINGWEI (1981) 'Bai Juyi Yuan Zhen shi de yunxi', *Nanjing Daxue Xuebao* **2**: 36–42.

BAUDOUIN DE COURTENAY, JAN (1972) *A Baudouin de Courtenay Anthology: The Beginnings of Structural Linguistics*. STANKIEWICZ, EDWARD (ed., trans., intro.). Bloomington: Indiana University Press.

BEIJING DAXUE ZHONGGUO YUYAN WENXUE XI and YUYANXUE JIAOYAN SHI (1962) (eds) *Hanyu Fangyin Zihui*. Beijing: Wenzi Gaige Chubanshe.

BERNDT, ROLF (1989) *A History of the English Language*. Leipzig: Verlag Enzykopadie.

BLOOMFIELD, LEONARD (1933) *Language*. New York: Holt, Rinehart and Winston.

CHAN, MARJORIE K. M. (1983) 'Lexical diffusion and two Chinese case studies re-analyzed', *Acta Orientalia* **44**: 117–52.

CHANG, KUANGYU (1986) 'Comparative Min Phonology.' Unpublished Ph.D. Dissertation. Berkeley: University of California.

CHANG, KUN (1975) 'Tonal developments among Chinese dialects', *Bulletin of the Institute of History and Philology, Academia Sinica* **46**: 636–709.

CHANG, KUN (1984) 'Lun bijiao Minyu', *Bulletin of the Institute of History and Philology, Academia Sinica* **55**: 415–58.

CHEN, MATTHEW Y. (1972) 'The time dimension: contribution toward a theory of sound change.' *Foundations of Language* **8**: 457–98.

CHEN, MATTHEW Y. (1976) 'From Middle Chinese to Modern Pekingese', *Journal of Chinese Linguistics* **2/3**: 113–277.

CHEN, MATTHEW Y. (1992) 'Competing sound changes: evidence from Kam-Tai, Miao-Yao and Tibeto-Burman.' *Journal of Chinese Linguistics* **20**; 193–210.

CHEN, MATTHEW Y. and WANG, WILLIAM S-Y. (1975) 'Sound change: actuation and implementation', *Language* **51**: 255–81.

CHEN, ZHANGTAI and LI, RULONG (1983) 'Lun Min Fangyan de yizhixing.' In ZHU, DUXI, ZHOU, ZUMO and WANG, JUN (eds) *Zhongguo Yuyan Xuebao*, Vol. 1. Beijing: Shangwu Yinshuguan, pp. 25–81.

CHEN, ZHONGMIN (1990) 'Shanghai Nanhui fangyan quanzhuo shangsheng de bianyi', *Zhongguo Yuwen* **216**: 187–8.

CHENG, CHIN-CHUAN and WANG, WILLIAM S-Y. (1972) 'Tone change in Chaozhou Chinese: a study of lexical diffusion.' In KACHRU, BRAJ B. et al. (eds) *Papers in Linguistics in Honor of Henry and Renee Kahane*, Urbana, IL: University of Illinois, pp. 99–113.

CHENG, ROBERT L. (1989) 'Competing forces in syntactic changes: the case of aspect and phrase markers in Taiwanese and Mandarin.' Paper presented at the Eighth International Workshop on Chinese Linguistics, POLA. Berkeley, CA: University of California, March 20–21.

CHENG, ROBERT L. (1990) 'Taiwan hua de shitai shitong.' *Proceedings of the First International Symposium on Chinese Languages and Linguistics*, pp. 53–88. Academia Sinica, Taipei: Institute of History and Philology.

CHOMSKY, NOAM (1965) *Aspects of the Theory of Syntax*. Cambridge, MA: MIT Press.

CHOU, FAKAO (1948) 'Xuanying fanqie kao.' *Bulletin of the Institute of History and Philology, Academia Sinica* 20: 359–444.

CHOU, FAKAO (1986) *Papers in Chinese Linguistics and Epigraphy*. Hong Kong: The Chinese University Press.

DONG, TONGHE (1959) 'Si ge Minnan fangyan.' *The Bulletin of the Institute of History and Philology, Academia Sinica* 30: 729–1042.

EGEROD, SØREN (1976) 'Tonal splits in Min', *Journal of Chinese Linguistics* 4: 108–11.

EGEROD, SØREN (1982) 'How not to split tones – The Chaozhou case,' *Fangyan* 3: 169–73.

EMENEAU, M. B. (1989) 'Phonetic laws and grammatical categories.' In HALL, KIRA, MEACHAM, MICHAEL and SHAPIRO, RICHARD (eds) Proceedings of the 15th Annual Meeting of the Berkeley Linguistic Society. General session and parasession on theoretical issues in language reconstruction. Berkeley Linguistics Society, pp. 344–55.

FAGAN, DAVID S. (1989) 'On the phonetic routes of lexical diffusion', *Lingua* 79: 217–28.

FERGUSON, CHARLES A. and FARWELL, CAROL B. (1975) 'Words and sounds in early language acquisition: English initial consonants in the first 50 words', *Language* 51: 419–39.

FILIPOVIĆ, RUDOLF (1989) 'Some contributions to the theory of contact linguistics.' In RADOVANOVIC, MILORAD (ed.), Yugoslav General Linguistics. Amsterdam: John Benjamins.

FRIES, CHARLES C. and PIKE, KENNETH L. (1949) 'Coexistent phonemic systems', *Language* 25: 29–50.

HAGEGE, CLAUDE and HAUDRICOURT, ANDRE (1978) *La Phonologie Panchronique*. Presses Universitaires de France.

HALLE, MORRIS and JAY KEYSER, SAMUEL (1971) *English Stress. Its Form, Its Growth, and Its Roles in Verse*. New York: Harper and Row, Publishers.

HASHIMOTO, MANTAROO J. (1972) 'The linguistic mechanism of flip-flop', *Unicorn*, 1–19. Princeton Chinese Linguistic Project.

HASHIMOTO, MANTAROO J. (1981) 'Review of the lexicon in phonological change', *Language* 37: 183–91.

HAUDRICOURT, ANDRE-G. (1954) 'De l'origine des tons en Vietnamien', *Journal Asiatique* 242: 69–82.

HO, DAH-AN (1986) 'Lun Yongxing fangyan de songqi zhuo shengmu', *The Bulletin of the Institute of History and Philology, Academia Sinica* 57: 585–600.

HO, DAH-AN (1988) 'Guilü yu fangxiang: bianqian zhong de yinyun jiegou.' *Bulletin of the Institute of History and Philology, Academia Sinica*. Special publications No. 90.

HOCKETT, CHARLES F. (1965) 'Sound change', *Language* **41**: 185–204.

HOENIGSWALD, HENRY M. (1964) 'Graduality, sporadicity, and the minor sound change processes', *Phonetica* **11**: 202–15.

HONG, CHENG (1982) (ed.) *Zhongguo Lidai Yuyan Wenzi Xue Wenxuan*. Jiangsu: Jiangsu Renmin Chubanshe.

HSIEH, HSIN-I. (1972) 'Lexical diffusion: evidence from child language acquisition', *Glossa* **6**: 89–104 (reprinted in Wang 1977).

HSIEH, HSIN-I. (1973) 'A new method of dialectal subgrouping', *Journal of Chinese Linguistics* **1**: 64–92 (reprinted in Wang 1977).

HSIEH, HSIN-I. (1974) 'Time as a cause of phonological irregularities', *Lingua* **22**: 253–63.

HSIEH, HSIN-I. (1989) 'History, structure, and competition.' Paper presented at the Eighth International Workshop on Chinese Linguistics, POLA, University of California, 20–21 March.

HSIEH, HSIN-I. (1990) 'In search of a grammatical foundation for dialect subgrouping.' *Proceedings of the First International Symposium on Chinese Languages and Linguistics*, 146–67. Academia Sinica, Taipei: Institute of History and Philology.

HUANG, DIANCHENG (1982) 'Minnan fangyin de shanggu canyu', *Yuyan Yanjiu* **2**: 172–1187.

HUANG, DIANCHENG (1985) 'Minnan fangyan zhong de shanggu danci canyu', *Xiamen Daxue Xuebao* Vol. 4, 134–48.

JAKOBSON, ROMAN (1971a) 'Sur la théorie des affinities phonologiques entre les langues'. In *Selected Writings I: Phonological Studies*. The Hague: Mouton, pp. 234–46.

JAKOBSON, ROMAN (1971b) 'The phonemic and grammatical aspects of language in their interrelations.' In *Selected Writings II: Word and Language*. The Hague: Mouton, pp. 103–14.

JAKOBSON, ROMAN (1971c) 'Retrospect.' In *Selected Writings II: Word and Language*. The Hague: Mouton, pp. 711–22.

JAKOBSON, ROMAN (1978) 'Principles of historical phonology.' KEILER, A. (trans.) In BALDI, PHILIP and WERTH, RONALD N. (eds), *Readings in historical phonology: chapters in the theory of sound change*. University Park, PA and London: The Pennsylvania State University Press, pp. 103–20 (German original 'Prinzipien der historischen Phonologie', *Travaux du Cercle Linguistique de Prague* **4**: 247–67, 1931.)

JESPERSEN, OTTO (1982) *Growth and Structure of the English Language*, 10th edn. Chicago: University of Chicago Press.

KARLGREN, BERNHARD (1915–26) *Etudes sur la Phonologie Chinoise*. Leiden: E. J. Brill. (Trans. into Chinese by Chao Yuenren, Li Fangkuei and Lo Changpei. (1948) *Zhongguo Yinyunxue Yanjiu*. Shanghai: Shangwu).

KING, ROBERT D. (1969) *Historical Linguistics and Generative Grammar*. Englewood Cliffs, NJ: Prentice-Hall.

KIPARSKY, PAUL (1982) 'Lexical phonology and morphology', In Linguistic Society of Korea (ed.) *Linguistics in the Morning Calm*. Seoul: Hansin Publishing Company, pp. 3–91.

KIPARSKY, PAUL (1988) 'Phonological change.' In NEWMEYER, FREDERICK J. (ed.) *Linguistics: The Cambridge Survey*, Vol. I, *Linguistic Theory: Foundations*. Cambridge: Cambridge University Press, pp. 363–415.

KRISHNAMURTI, BH. L. MOSES, and DANFORTH, D. (1983) 'Unchanged cognates as a criterion in linguistic subgrouping', *Language* 59: 541–68.

KURATH, HANS (1956) 'The loss of long consonants and the rise of voiced fricatives in Middle English', *Language* 32: 435–45.

LABOV, WILLIAM (1981) 'Resolving the Neogrammarian controversy', *Language* 57: 267–308.

LAI, JIANGJI, (1982) 'Cong Bai Juyi shi yongyun kan zhuoshang bian qu', *Jinan Xuebao* 4: 97–109.

LASS, ROGER (1984) *Phonology. An Introduction to Basic Concepts*. Cambridge: Cambridge University Press.

LI, RONG (1985) 'Lun Li Fu dui Qieyun de piping ji qi xiangguan wenti', *Zhongguo Yuwen* 184: 1–9.

LI, XINKUI (1979) (ed.) *Putonghua Chaosan Fangyan Changyong Zidian*. Guangdong: Guangdong Renmin Chubanshe.

LIEN, CHINFA (1986) 'Tone merger in the dialects of Northern Chinese', *Journal of Chinese Linguistics* 14: 243–91.

LIEN, CHINFA (1987a) Coexistent Tone Systems in Chinese Dialects. Unpublished Ph.D. Dissertation, University of California, Berkeley.

LIEN, CHINFA (1987b) 'A critical survey of the tone behavior in Chinese dialects.' In BRAMKAMP, AGATHA, SPRENGER, ARNOLD and VENNE, PETER (eds) *Chinese-Western Encounter: Studies in Dissertation–Linguistics and Literature. Festschrift for Franz Giet, SVD, on the Occasion of his 85th Birthday*. Taipei: Chinese Material Center, pp. 61–72.

LIEN, CHINFA (1990a) 'Competing final systems in the Jian'ou dialects', *Tsing Hua Journal of Chinese Studies. New Series* 20: 1–53.

LIEN, CHINFA (1990b) 'Lun Min fangyan de kai he kou.' *Proceedings of the First International Symposium on Chinese Languages and Linguistics*, pp. 223–72. Academia Sinica, Taipei: Institute of History and Philology.

LIEN, CHINFA (1993a) 'Lexical Diffusion.' *Encyclopedia of Language and Linguistics*, Oxford: Pergamon Press and Aberdeen University Press.

LIEN, CHINFA (1993b) 'Language adaptation in Taoist Liturgical Texts.' In JOHNSON, D. (ed.), *Rituals and Scriptures of Chinese Popular Religion*, Berkeley, Publications of Chinese Popular Culture Project.

LIEN, CHINFA and WANG, WILLIAM S-Y (1993) 'Bidirectional diffusion in sound change revisited', *Journal of Chinese Linguistics*, 21.

LIN, TAO (1990) *Yuyin Tansuo Jigao*. Beijing: Beijing Yuyan Xueyuan Chubanshe.

MALKIEL, YAKOV (1983) 'Multi-conditioned sound change and the impact of morphology on phonology. From particular to general linguistics.' *Selected Essays, 1965–1978*. Amsterdam: John Benjamins, pp. 229–50.

MALMBERG, BERTIL (1976) 'Structural linguistics and human communication: an introduction into the mechanism of language and the methodology of linguistics.' Reprint from 2nd revised edn. Berlin: Springer-Verlag.

MATHESIUS, VILEM (1964) 'Zur synchronischen analyse fremden Sprachguts.' In VACHEK, JOSEF (ed.) *A Prague School Reader in Linguistics*. Bloomington, IN: Indiana University Press, pp. 398–412.

MEI, TSULIN (1970) 'Tones and prosody and the origin of the rising tone', *Harvard Journal of Asian Studies* 30: 86–110.

MEI, TSULIN (1986) 'Guanyu jindai hanyu zhidai ci---du Lü zhu jindai hanyu zhidai ci', *Zhonguo Yuwen* 6: 401–12.

MILROY, LESLEY (1987) *Language and Social Networks*, 2nd edn. Oxford: Basil Blackwell.

MILROY, LESLEY and MARGRAIN, SUE (1980) 'Vernacular language loyalty and social network', *Language in Society* 9: 43–70.

MILROY, JAMES and MILROY, LESLEY (1985) 'Linguistic change, social network and speaker innovation', *Journal of Linguistics* 21: 339–84.

MOHR, B. (1971) 'Intrinsic variations in the speech signal', *Phonetica* 23: 65–93.

MOULTON, WILLIAM G. (1967) Types of Phonemic Change. *To Honor Roman Jakobson: Essays on the Occasion of his Seventieth Birthday*. Vol. II. The Hague: Mouton, pp. 1393–407.

NORMAN, JERRY (1973) 'Tonal development', *Min Journal of Chinese Linguistics* 1: 222–38.

NORMAN, JERRY (1979) 'Chronological strata in the Min dialects', *Fangyan* 4: 268–74.

NORMAN, JERRY (1988) *Chinese*. Cambridge: Cambridge University Press.

NORMAN, JERRY (1991) 'The Min dialects in historical perspective.' In WANG, WILLIAM S-Y. (ed.) *Languages and Dialects in China. Journal of Chinese Linguistics, Monograph Series* No. 3, pp. 325–60.

NORMAN, JERRY and TSULIN, MEI (1976) 'The Austroasiatics in ancient South China: some lexical evidence', *Monumenta Serica* 32: 274–301.

NUMOTO, KATSUAKI (1982) *Heian Kamakura jidai ni okeru Nihon Kanjion ni tsuite no kenkyu*. Tokyo: Musashino Shoin.

OGURA, MIEKO (1987) *Historical English Phonology*. Tokyo: Kenkyusha.

OGURA, MIEKO (1990) *Dynamic Dialectology*. Tokyo: Kenkyusha.

PAN, WUYUN (1982) 'Guanyu Hanyu shengdiao fazhan de jige wenti', *Journal of Chinese Linguistics* 10: 361–85.

PAUL, H. (1920) *Prinzipien der Sprachgeschichte*, Halle, Niemeyer.

PHILLIPS, BETTY S. (1984) 'Word frequency and the actuation of sound change', *Language* 60: 320–42.

PIKE, KENNETH L. (1972) 'Grammatical prerequisites to phonemic analysis'. In BREND, RUTH M. (ed.) *Kenneth L. Pike. Selected Writing*. The Hague: Mouton, pp. 32–50.

POSTAL, PAUL M. (1968) *Aspects of Phonological Theory*. New York: Harper & Row.

PULLEYBLANK, E. G. (1973) 'The nature of Middle Chinese tones and their development to Early Mandarin', *Journal of Chinese Linguistics* 6: 183–203.

PULLEYBLANK, E. G. (1978) 'Abruptness and gradualness in phonological change.' In JAZAYERY, AMHAMMAD ALI et al. (eds) *Linguistic and Literary Studies in Honor of Archibald A. Hill*. The Hague: Mouton, pp. 181–91.

PULLEYBLANK, E. G. (1982) 'Review of the lexicon in phonological change', *Journal of Chinese Linguistics* 10: 392–416.

RIDDLE, ELIZABETH M. (1985) 'A historical perspective on the productivity of the suffixes -ness and -ity.' In FISIAK, JACEK (ed.) *Historical Semantics. Historical Word-formation*. Amsterdam: Mouton, pp. 435–91.

SAUSSURE, FERDINAND DE (1959) *A Course in General Linguistics*. BASKIN, WADE (trans.). New York: The Philosophical Library.

SCHUCHARDT, HUGO (1972) 'On sound laws: against the Neogrammarinas.' In VENNEMANN, THEO and WILBUR, T. H. (eds), *Schuchardt, the Neogrammarians, and the Transformational Theory of Change*. Widesbaden: Athenaion, pp. 39–72.

SHEN, ZHONGWEI (1987) 'Cihui kuosan lilun he yuyan bianhua.' In YUAN, XIAOYUAN (ed.) *Wenzi yu wenhua congshu*, Vol. 2, Shanghai: Guangming Ribao Chubanshe, pp. 87–102.

SHEN, ZHONGWEI (1990) 'Lexical diffusion: a population perspective and a mathematical model', *Journal of Chinese Linguistics* 18: 159–201.

SHERMAN, DONALD (1975) 'Noun-verb stress alternation: an example of the lexical diffusion of sound change in English', *Linguistics* 159: 43–71.

SILVA-CORVALAN, CARMEN (1986) 'Bilingualism and language change: the extension of estar in Los Angeles Spanish', *Language* 62: 587–608.

STIMSON, HUGH M. (1962) 'Ancient Chinese -p, -t, -k endings in the Peking dialect', *Language* 38: 376–84.

STIMSON, HUGH M. (1972) 'More on Peking archaisms', *T'oung Pao* 58: 172–89.

STURTEVANT, EDGAR H. (1917) *Linguistic Change: an Introduction to the Historical Study of Language*. Chicago: The University of Chicago Press.

STURTEVANT, EDGAR H. (1947) *An Introduction to Linguistic Science*. New Haven: Yale University Press.

SUNG, MARGARET M. Y. (1973) 'A study of literary and colloquial Amoy Chinese', *Journal of Chinese Linguistics* 1: 414–36.

THOMASON, SARAH G. and KAUFMAN, TERRENCE (1988) *Language Contact: Creolization, and Genetic Linguistics*. Berkeley and Los Angeles: University of California Press.

TING, PANGHSIN (1978) 'A note on tone change in the Ch'ao-chou dialect', *Bulletin of the Institute of History and Philology, Academia Sinica* 50: 257–71.

TING, PANGSIN (1983) 'Derivation time of colloquial Min from Archaic Chinese', *Bulletin of the Institute of History and Philology, Academia Sinica*, 54: 1–13.

TING, PANGHSIN (1989) 'Hanyu shengdiao de yanbian.' Proceedings of the Second International Conference on Sinology. Section on Linguistics and Paleography, pp. 395–408.

TOON, THOMAS E. (1983) *The Politics of Early Old English Sound Change*. New York: Academic Press.

TOTTIE, GUNNEL (1991) 'Lexical diffusion in syntactic change: frequency as a determinant of linguistic conservatism in the development of negation in English.' In KASTOVSKY, D. (ed.) *Historical English Syntax*, Berlin: Mouton de Gruyter, 439–67.

TRNKA, BOHUMIL (1982a) 'On foreign phonological features in present-day English.' In FRIED, VILEM (ed.) *Bohumil Trnka: Selected Papers in Structural Linguistics*. Berlin, New York, Amsterdam: Mouton.

TRNKA, BOHUMIL (1982b) 'On analogy.' In FRIED, VILEM (ed.), *Bohumil Trnka: Selected Papers in Structural Linguistics*. Berlin, New York, Amsterdam: Mouton Publishers, pp. 102–9.

TRUBETZKOY, N. S. (1969) *Principles of Phonology*. (BALTAXE, CHRISTIANE A. M., trans.) Berkeley and Los Angeles, CA: University of California Press.

TRUDGILL, PETER (1986) *Dialects in Contact*. Oxford: Basil Blackwell.

VACHEK, V. (1966) *The Linguistic School of Prague: an Introduction to its Theory and Practice*. Bloomington, IN: Indiana University Press.

VACHEK, V. (1976) *Selected Writings in English and General Linguistics*. The Hague: Mouton.

VAN COETSEM, FRANS (1988) *Loan Phonology and the Two Transfer Types in Language Contact*. Dordrecht: Foris.

VENNEMANN, THEO (1972) 'Phonetic analogy and conceptual phonology.' In VENNEMANN, THEO and WILBUR, T. H. (eds) *Schuchardt, the Neogrammarians, and the Transformational Theory of Change*. Widesbaden: Athenaion, pp. 181–204.

WANG, HONGJUN (1992) 'Liang lei Kuosan.' ms.

WANG, LI (1958) *Hanyu Shigao*, revised edn. Beijing: Kexue Chubanshe.

WANG, WILLIAM S-Y. (1967) 'Phonological Features of Tone.' *International Journal of American Linguistics* 33: 93–105.

WANG, WILLIAM S-Y. (1969) 'Competing sound change as a cause of residue', *Language* 45: 9–25.

WANG, WILLIAM S-Y. (1977) (ed.) *The Lexicon in Phonological Change*. The Hague: Mouton.

WANG, WILLIAM S-Y. (1979) 'Language change --- a lexical perspective', *Annual Review of Anthropology* 8: 353–71.

WANG, WILLIAM S-Y. (1982) 'Variation and selection in language change', *Bulletin of the Institute of History and Philology, Academia Sinica* 53: 495–519.

WANG, WILLIAM S-Y. (1987) 'A note on tone development.' In Chinese Language Society of Hong Kong (ed.) *Wang Li Memorial Volumes. English Volume*. Hong Kong: Joint Publishing, pp. 435–43.

WANG, WILLIAM S-Y. (1989a) 'Theoretical issues in studying Chinese dialects', *Journal of the Chinese Language Teachers Association* 25: 1–34.

WANG, WILLIAM S-Y. (1989b) 'Language in China: a chapter in the history of linguistics', *Journal of Chinese Linguistics* 17: 183–222.

WANG, WILLIAM S-Y. and CHENG, CHIN CHUAN (1987) 'Middle Chinese tones in modern dialects.' In CHANNON, ROBERT and SHOCKEY, LINDA (eds) *In Honor of Ilse Lehiste*. Dordrecht: Foris, pp. 513–23.

WANG, YUDE (1969) 'Fukien no kaihatsu to Fukiengo no seiritsu', *Nippon Chuugoku Gakkaihoo* **21**: 123–41.

WEINREICH, URIEL (1953) *Languages in Contact*. New York: Linguistic Circle of New York.

WEINREICH, URIEL, LABOV, WILLIAM and HERZOG, MARVIN (1968) 'Empirical foundation for a theory of language change'. In LEHMANN, WINFRED P. and MALKIEL, YAKOV (eds) *Directions for Historical Linguistics*. Austin, TX: University of Texas Press, pp. 97–195.

YANG, NAISI (1958) 'Beifang hua zhuoshang bian qu laiyuan shitan', *Xueshu Yuekan* **2**: 72–7.

YUAN, JIAHUA et al. (1983) *Hanyu Fangyan Gaiyao*, 2nd edn. Beijing: Wenzi Gaige Chubanshe.

ZHAN, BOHUI (1981) *Xiandai Hanyu Fangyan*. Hubei: Hubei Renmin Chubanshe.

ZHANG, SHENGYU (1979a) 'Chaoyang fangyan de liandu biandiao', *Fangyan* **2**: 93–121.

ZHANG, SHENGYU (1979b) 'Chaoyang fangyan de wenbai yidu', *Fangyan* **4**: 241–67.

ZHANG, SHENGYU (1982a) 'Chaoyang shengmu yu guangyun shengmu de bijiao 1', *Fangyan* **1**: 52–9.

ZHANG, SHENGYU (1982b) 'Chaoyang shengmu yu guangyun shengmu de bijiao 2', *Fangyan* **2**: 129–45.

ZHANG, SHENGYU (1982c) 'Chaoyang shengmu yu guangyun shengmu de bijiao 3', *Fangyan* **3**: 196–202.

ZHANG, ZHENXING (1987) 'Guangdong Haikang fangyan jilue', *Fangyan* **4**: 264–82.

ZHOU, ZUMOU (1963) 'Qieyun de xingzhi he ta de yinxi jichu.' In Chinese Department, Beijing University (ed.) *Yuyan Xue Luncong*. Beijing: Shangwu Yinshuguan, pp. 39–70.

Index